The African Experience

ROLAND OLIVER

The African Experience

IconEditions
An Imprint of HarperCollins*Publishers*

For Suzanne

CONTENTS

MAPS AND FIGURES

PREFACE

The African Experience is a work of reflection, written for sheer pleasure during the first four years of my retirement from the first Chair of African History ever created in the University of London. It does not attempt to tell a continuous story, but rather to discuss a set of themes, chosen for their significance for the continent as a whole, and arranged in chronological order, from the earliest times until the most recent. While it reflects the teaching and research of forty years, I have deliberately limited most of my references to easily available secondary works published within the last ten years, and I have made particularly extensive use of the two large collaborative histories of the continent – the *Cambridge History of Africa*, of which I was one of the General Editors, and the *General History of Africa* produced under the auspices of UNESCO, of which five volumes had appeared at the time this book went to press. I am aware that my choice of continent-wide themes has resulted in the virtual exclusion of Madagascar and the other surrounding islands, and also in a bias towards sub-Saharan as against Mediterranean Africa. In the interests of the general reader, I have struggled to minimize the number of unfamiliar ethnic and geographical names, but inevitably more remain than can be accommodated easily on the maps. I have therefore attempted to locate them at least roughly in the Index, by indicating the modern countries to which they belong.

Among the friends who have helped and encouraged me by reading and commenting on parts of this book, I have to acknowledge specially my colleagues in the British Institute in Eastern Africa, John Sutton, David Phillipson, Peter Robertshaw and Justin Willis; David William Cohen of the African Studies Program of Northwestern University; and Andras Bereznay who drew the maps.

ACKNOWLEDGEMENT

The publishers are grateful to Cambridge University Press for permission to reproduce Figures 2 (excavation at Olduvai Gorge) and 2a (early tools) from the Cambridge History of Africa, Vol. I, edited by J. Desmond Clark.

The African Experience

CHAPTER 1
EDEN

It seems that we all belong, ultimately, to Africa. Almost certainly, the Garden of Eden, in which our ancestors grew gradually apart from their nearest relatives in the animal kingdom, lay in the highland interior of East Africa, where the equatorial forest belt is broken by mountains and high savanna parklands running south from Ethiopia to the Cape. At the heart of this region lies the Great Rift Valley, its floor strewn with spectacular lakes, its sides rising steeply to high plateaux surmounted by the blue cones of a thousand volcanic peaks. The Rift floor and the plateaux to the east and west grow cereal grasses and have always been the supreme haunt of the tropical African fauna. The plains are grazed by great herds of eland and zebra, buck and gazelle. Elephant and buffalo, baboons and other monkeys address themselves to the lusher vegetation of montane forest and waterside galleries. Giraffe and rhinoceros browse the intermediate bush. Ostriches feed upon the taller grasses. Warthogs scuttle through the undergrowth. The lakes are surveyed by fish-eagles, their margins patrolled by stork and flamingo, their open waters trawled by pelican. And in the midst of all the predators watch and wait – lion, leopard, hyena, jackal, reptiles, man.

Precisely when and how pre-man grew into man will remain forever a matter for discussion. Certainly, it was an immensely gradual process, extending over perhaps a hundred thousand generations, and involving great physical changes in almost every part of the body: such is the reality of creation. The first creatures generally recognized as 'hominids' or human ancestors were the *australopithecines*, whose remains have been found between Ethiopia and the Transvaal in contexts dating from about 4 million to about 1.5 million years ago. The australopithecines were fairly varied. The earliest known examples seem to have been lightly built, but between 3 and 2 million years ago this genus seems to have divided into 'robust' and 'gracile' lineages, the former having a heavy skull, surmounted by a bony crest designed for the suspension of massive jaws. Both lineages stood a little over four feet, and both had brains of about 450 cubic centimetres, or one-third of the modern size. During the course of the same

I

1. THE CRADLE OF HUMANITY: THE HIGH GRASSLANDS OF EASTERN AND CENTRAL AFRICA

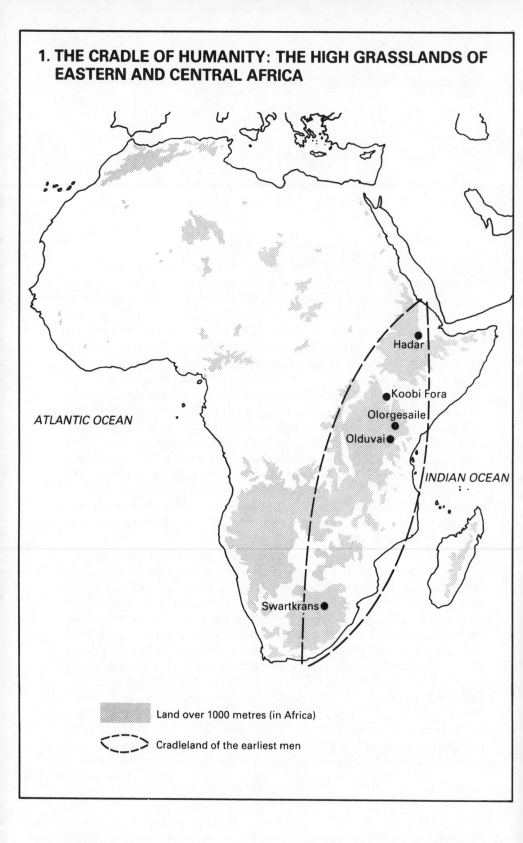

ATLANTIC OCEAN

Hadar

Koobi Fora

Olorgesaile

Olduvai

INDIAN OCEAN

Swartkrans

Land over 1000 metres (in Africa)

Cradleland of the earliest men

million years that saw the emergence of the robust lineages, the gracile lineages seem to have undergone a decisive enlargement of the cranium which, together with some accompanying modifications to teeth and hands, carried them over a threshold into the new genus *Homo*.

It seems likely that both the robust and the gracile australopithecines lived by hunting or scavenging, and also by gathering, although in radically different measure. Contrary to popular belief, a more powerful jaw is needed to masticate a vegetarian diet than a carnivorous one; and it may well be that the robust lineages lived more by gathering than by hunting or scavenging, and so required fewer and simpler tools and a less extensive social organization than the gracile lineages. At all events, it seems to have been the gracile lineages which, some 2.5 million years ago, took a momentous step forward by learning to knap stone in order to produce a variety of sharp-edged tools for cutting and scraping. In doing so, they also started to create an imperishable record of their presence. The concept of 'Man the tool-maker' is based largely on this evidential property of stone as a material. Stone tools quickly lose their sharp edges, and stone cannot be filed or honed. Stone tools therefore need constantly to be replaced. For every maker of stone tools there must be thousands of discarded artefacts and tens of thousands of waste chippings. Although other no less valid definitions of man might be proffered, such as upright posture or a cranial capacity of more than one thousand cubic centimetres, the tool-making criterion is certainly a very convenient one. If we accept it, we can say that our genus is of African origin and that it is approximately 2.5 million years old.

The fossilized bones of australopithecines were first discovered from 1924 onwards in limestone caves in the northern Cape province by the South African palaeontologists Raymond Dart and Robert Broom. It was here that the co-existence of robust and gracile forms was first recognized, and in the course of three decades a great deal of evidence was assembled about the physical characteristics of each. It was realized that here were creatures, bipedal and nearly upright, with nearly human feet, hands and teeth, whose remains were surrounded by those of the animals with which they had shared this part of the South African plateau. However, no stone tools were found in the early discoveries, and it was by no means clear whether the australopithecines had been the hunters or the hunted. Early interest in them was therefore mainly anatomical. They were described as 'men from the neck down', possessing 'every significant human qualification other than man's big brain'.[1] Inevitably, in the scientific journalism of the day they were presented in terms of the 'missing link'. But without any demonstrable sequence of stages linking them backwards to the anthropoid apes or forwards with modern man, the proposition remained quite speculative. In the absence of any system of absolute dating, there was no compelling reason to think that the australopithecine fossils were older than those of other 'half-brained' men from the Solo valley in Java or the Choukoutien cave near Peking. As late as 1950, few specialists believed that mankind had originated in Africa.

It was Olduvai Gorge that made the difference. Olduvai, so called by the local Maasai after the wild sisal bushes that guard its margins, is a little canyon, thirty miles long, half a mile wide and about three hundred feet deep at its lower end, let into the south-eastern corner of the Serengeti plain, in the prime game country of northern Tanzania. From the south and east it is overlooked by the volcanic ranges separating it from the Rift Valley, including Ngorongoro, of which the crater is the most justly famous wildlife park in the world today. The gorge itself marks the line of a little river draining from the nearby mountains to a swamp at its lower end. Four times during the past two million years a new surface layer has been deposited by volcanic action, and the river has patiently carved its way through each, exposing four beds, which are clearly visible to the merest tiro. For the practised eye it is also possible to detect, here and there, chipped stones and fossilized bone fragments protruding from the exposed surfaces of the steep sides of the gorge. At various stages of the erosion process, the river has been trapped in a lake basin, and it was presumably at these stages that the best conditions existed for the fossilization of bone. At all events, it is the occurrence in stratified sequence of concentrations of stone tools and animal bones which gives Olduvai its outstanding importance as an archaeological site.

The first European to discover Olduvai was a German professor, who in 1911 nearly fell headlong down the cliff while chasing the proverbial butterfly. He was aware enough of its possible significance to interest the officials of the geological department in Dar es Salaam, who sent up one of their number, Hans Reck, for a three-month visit. Reck described the geological situation and collected some fossils, but he failed to recognize a single stone tool from any level. Moreover, he came away with an almost complete skeleton of *Homo sapiens*, found in Bed III, which later proved to be a spurious intrusion, which had dropped down a fissure from a Late Stone Age level of about 17,000 years ago.[2] Never mind. It was this skeleton which attracted the attention of a young Cambridge archaeologist, Louis Leakey, who was already engaged in excavating Stone Age sites in the Kenya section of the Rift Valley. In 1925 Leakey visited Reck in retirement in Munich, and in 1931 secured his collaboration in the first large expedition to Olduvai, which he advertized, with all his habitual rash exuberance, as a mission to investigate the provenance of 'the earliest known authentic skeleton of *Home sapiens*'.[3]

The 1930s saw the exploration of Olduvai by Louis and Mary Leakey, and it was not all fun. Though set in a paradise, the gorge itself is an inferno. It is ugly, steep, desolate, stony and hot, and looks altogether like some derelict site of open-cast mining. The tributary gullies included, there are about 100 miles of exposed cliffside, which had to be scrutinized a square yard at a time, while scrambling on loose surfaces amid sharp and thorny vegetation. By 1935, thousands of stone tools and hundreds of fossilized bones had been collected and driven away to Nairobi, where the Coryndon Museum was to become the focal laboratory of the search for human origins. At Olduvai itself, about twenty areas marked by high concentrations of bone and artefacts had been identified as sites which might justify the immense labour of cutting into the cliff.

Not until 1951, however, were the Leakeys able to return to Olduvai, with the funds for sustained excavation now assured by the generosity of Charles Boise, a mining engineer with large interests in tropical Africa. And despite annual expeditions from then on, it was not until 1959 that they achieved their first major scoop. This was the discovery, in a fully stratified context, in the upper level of the lowest of the four geological beds, of the almost complete skull of an extremely robust australopithecine, officially named *Zinjanthropus boisei*, but known more affectionately in the trade as Dear Boy. At once acclaimed as our earliest tool-making ancestor, and assigned on geological estimates an age of some 600,000 years, Dear Boy was soon seen on television, and was the hero of Louis Leakey's first American lecture tour, which brought massive financial support for further excavation, notably from the National Geographic Society of Washington. Meanwhile, the skull itself was sent to Johannesburg, where Dart's successor, Phillip Tobias, now presided over the department of anatomy with the largest experience of australopithecine remains. Soon after its arrival, there was published at the University of California the result of a radiometric dating test, using the new potassium-argon method, of volcanic tuff from Olduvai, which revealed that the real age of the upper level of Bed I was more like 1.8 million years than 600,000. As Tobias himself remarked, 'We badly needed that extra million years'.[4]

As it turned out, Dear Boy was to enjoy little more than a year of unchallenged celebrity, for during the next few seasons there came to light, on the very same living floor, several fragments of a creature so gracile that the Leakeys claimed it as *Homo* rather than *Australopithecus*, and presented it to the world as *Homo habilis*. The new proposition was that *Homo habilis* had been the tool-maker, while *Zinjanthropus* had been merely his client, perhaps even his victim. Some eyebrows were raised at so rapid a change of front, and in *Punch* some light verses by B. A. Young expressed an irreverent scepticism shared by many.

> When the first men were fashioned in the good Lord's forge,
> He sent them, it seems, to the Olduvai Gorge,
> There to be tested and kept an eye on,

With the proto-lizard and the proto-lion.
This hyphen-pithecus and Homo-that,
With the archaeo-elephant and palaeo-cat,
Lived there and died, and were hidden away
Under layer upon layer of African clay,
Till countless millions of years should run
And Leakey discover them one by one . . .[5]

In the event, however, the Prospero and Caliban hypothesis would seem to have been well vindicated by later research. While there is still some lingering controversy among physical anthropologists about whether *Homo habilis* should be described as a gracile australopithecine rather than *Homo*, there is nowadays little doubt that robust and gracile forms existed side by side for at least a million years, and that wherever hominid remains are accompanied by stone tools, the gracile form is present.[6] To label the later manifestations of the gracile species as *Homo* is therefore consistent with the tool-making definition of man.

Stimulated by the hominid discoveries at Olduvai, and also perhaps by growing confidence in the reliability of the potassium-argon dating method, much exploration took place during the later 1960s and 1970s of other localities in the Rift Valley region where sedimentation might have occurred in the context of volcanic rock formations. Starting in 1967, the veteran French palaeontologist, Camille Arambourg, returned with a series of international expeditions to the Omo valley north of Lake Turkana, to re-examine the sediments where he had made an important collection of mammalian fossils thirty years before. He was soon rewarded by the discovery of a hominid mandible, and further skeletal remains found in association with stone tools proved that Olduvai was no isolated phenomenon. The following year Richard Leakey, son of Louis and Mary, found the great fossil-bearing deposits of volcanic tuff around Koobi Fora, to the east of Lake Turkana, which collectively span the period from about 3 million to about 1.3 million years ago. Robust australopithecines occur throughout, but so also, from a date as early as 1.8 million years ago, does a gracile hominid with an even stronger claim than *Homo habilis* of Olduvai to be placed in the genus *Homo*.[7]

Meanwhile, from the northern extremity of the Rift, where the River Awash drops down from the central Ethiopian plateau to the Afar desert, there to disappear by evaporation in the sediments of the Hadar depression, there came to light in 1973 and 1974 plentiful remains of a new variety of australopithecine, lightly built, but more primitive in the face and teeth than any previously known, in sediments dated to about 3 million years ago. The new species was named by its discoverer, Donald Johanson, *A. afarensis*, and its most complete individual specimen received the engaging nickname of Lucy. The new discovery looked as though it

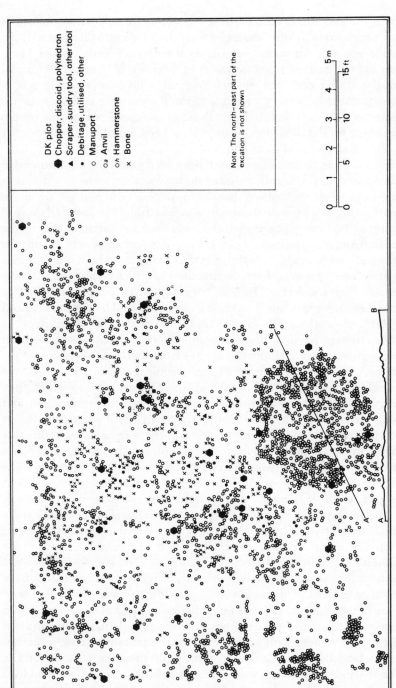

Plan of the occupation surface as exposed by excavation at the site of DK, level 3, Bed I, Olduvai Gorge. The plane shows the pattern of natural stones that seems to represent the footing of a hut or shelter. (After M. D. Leakey 1971.)

might be the ancestor of both the gracile and the robust australopithecines of later times. Soon, further examples were found close to Olduvai itself, in an older volcanic formation known as the Laetoli Beds, where Mary Leakey made the astonishing discovery of three sets of hominid footprints, forming a trail more than 80 feet long, in a layer of volcanic tuff in sediments dated between 3.59 and 3.77 million years ago. Finally, at two localities to the south-west of Lake Turkana, hominid remains as yet too fragmentary for detailed classification have been found in contexts dated between 4 and 5 million years old.

While all these recent discoveries have added greatly to our knowledge of human ancestry, it is still only at Olduvai, and to some extent also at Koobi Fora, that excavation has been pursued in enough detail to reconstruct actual living situations, in which hominid remains and those of the animals hunted or scavenged, the tools used for butchery and all the varied detritus of a hunting and gathering existence can be seen together in meaningful combination. It is thought that altogether about one hundred such situations have so far been documented, of which no less than 81 have come from Beds I and II at Olduvai, covering the period from about 1.8 to about 0.8 million years ago. The basic concept inferred by the Leakeys and their early co-workers like Glynn Isaac was that of a 'living floor', a roughly circular patch of former ground surface, somewhere between twenty and sixty feet in diameter, always sited with easy access to water, where a group of hominids made a base for some considerable time, where presumably they slept and brought up their young, and to which they carried home their prey and their vegetable foods for preparation and shared consumption. The presence of great quantities of waste chippings is proof that tools were normally made on the site, although the raw materials might be carried in from several miles away. The broken bones of animals were left lying around on or near the living floor, and they show that the game hunted or scavenged comprised most of the local fauna, both large and small – elephant and buffalo were consumed at Olduvai, crocodile and hippo at Koobi Fora. It would be natural to suppose that the central feature of a living floor would have been a hearth, and that the need to keep fire alight might indeed have been one of the reasons for a community to maintain a base camp; but there is no conclusive evidence one way or the other, and it is only recently that some archaeologists have begun to entertain the idea that early hominids may have controlled fire.[8] In some of the sites identified as living floors at Olduvai there were found to be semi-circles of unworked stones, enclosing the densest concentration of bones and artefacts, with a completely empty area immediately outside. This was held by Louis Leakey to signify the presence of some kind of shelter or windbreak, which would originally have been surmounted by a hedge of broken branches. Looking at the charts, which show in meticulous detail the position of every bone and stone recovered, it is indeed tempting to picture our untidy ancestors huddled inside the fence, and tossing some, but only some, of their rubbish over the top of it.

Today, alas, it must be said that not many archaeologists still accept that so much can be deduced from the concentrations of worked stone and fossilized bone that occur at Olduvai and other early palaeolithic sites. The arch-iconoclast, Lewis Binford, has propounded the view that early hominids were not really hunters at all, but rather scavengers, who gained their food by clearing up the remains of carcasses abandoned by more powerful predators. Their tools, he thinks, were essentially used for skinning and butchering, and above all for breaking the bones containing marrow, of which there tend to be a disproportionate number in most of the early sites. Binford maintains that no early hominid in his senses would have camped beside water and so exposed himself to the nightly attacks of the major carnivores. Hominids would very likely have nested in trees like other primates, and the so-called living floors must be seen at best as picnic sites, in which bones and artefacts represent the assorted and re-assorted debris of many hunting and scavenging episodes by animals and humans.[9] Very likely, Binford overstated his case, but his impact has been considerable. Glynn Isaac, the excavator of the early palaeolithic site at Olorgesaile in the Rift Valley to the south of Nairobi, and one of the most outstanding archaeologists to follow in Leakey's footsteps, managed before his untimely death to re-examine his own evidence for living floors at Olorgesaile in the light of Binford's assertions (below p. 21). In particular, he studied the bones for the butchery marks and for the tooth-marks of other carnivores. He concluded that a high proportion of the bones, whether obtained by scavenging or deliberate hunting, had been transported to the 'living floors' in the form of jointed limbs still encased in skin, flesh and sinew. In other words, these were not the kill-sites of other predators, but the centres of hominid food-sharing. At the same time, Isaac was humble enough to admit that his own earlier hypotheses about early hominid behaviour had made them seem 'too human'. His reconsidered opinion about the 'living floors' was that they were not so much hunting camps which dominated the surrounding areas as 'places of safety', to which scavengers living in fear of most of their fellow predators had carried away their pickings for communal consumption. The most obvious examples of such places might well have been groves of climbable trees.[10]

Certainly, despite the definition of man as tool-maker, the technical capacity of the early hominids as stone workers was neither exciting, nor, as used to be assumed, was it steadily progressive in quality. The basic chopping-tool was a cobble of a size that could be held comfortably in the hand, from which a few flakes had been removed from one side so as to give it a cutting edge. Some of the larger flakes removed in this way were re-worked into smaller scraping tools which could be held between the thumb and finger. Some of the re-worked flakes were a little longer and more sharply pointed, as if intended for piercing or slicing. All these could be accounted for as tools for skinning, butchering and simple woodworking. The key activity was perhaps the last one, for it must never be forgotten that, behind the stone tools which have survived, there was probably a whole range of wooden tools, which have mostly perished. And these include most of the weapons – poles, staves, spears and clubs. The evidence for deliberate hunting is thus of its very nature more perishable than the evidence for butchery.

It would seem that on the highland plateau of eastern and southern Africa a significant change in the human animal and in its quality of life took place somewhere around 1.5 million years ago. In physical terms this change was about the emergence from all the earlier, imperfectly differentiated species of *Homo* of a form destined to spread rapidly right across the tropical and sub-tropical parts of the Old World as *Homo erectus* – the *Pithecanthropus* of older terminology. The anatomical definitions are hard for the layman, but may perhaps be summed up in the notion that the locomotor structure was now substantially that of modern man in respect of relatively effortless long-distance walking. The changes necessary to produce this were extensive, and included, in the words of one authority, 'an alternating pelvic tilt mechanism, a powerful hip extensor mechanism for erecting or raising the trunk, a pelvic rest mechanism, posterior displacement of the centre of

---

Fig. 2a. Drawings illustrating some of the more important forms of early stone implement and sketches suggesting ways in which they can be used. Archaeologists do not yet know very much about the specific functions of early tools so that the sketches are speculative. Many of the forms illustrated may well have been used in a much wider variety of ways than is shown here. Items 1 to 3 are cores as well as tools and the flakes struck in shaping them would be useful knives, as shown in 8.

1 A *bifacial chopper* shown in front and side view and in use for cutting a branch which could then be made into a digging-stick or spear.

2 A *hand-axe* or *biface* such as characterizes Acheulian industries. One possible use is in skinning and cutting up animal carcasses. They could also be used in cutting bark and wood.

3 A *pick* – here shown in use for hacking off a piece of bark which could be used as a tray container for gathered food.

4 A *spheroid* formed of a battered rounded stone, shown in use for breaking a bone so as to extract marrow.

5 A *scraper* made by the trimming of a concave working edge on a stone flake, here shown in use for sharpening a stick.

6 An *awl* or *borer* formed on a flake by two converging lines of retouch scars that define a stout point such as could be used for piercing hide or for grooving wood.

7 A *scraper* with convex working edges trimmed along two margins of a flake. Here shown in use for scraping hide so as to prepare leather, but equally suitable for whittling and shaping wood.

8 An unretouched *flake* being used as a knife for cutting through the skin of an animal carcass. Flakes such as this are the commonest objects on almost all early archaeological sites. They have usually been treated by archaeologists simply as by-products from the making of core tools, but they make very effective knives and were almost certainly extensively used as such.

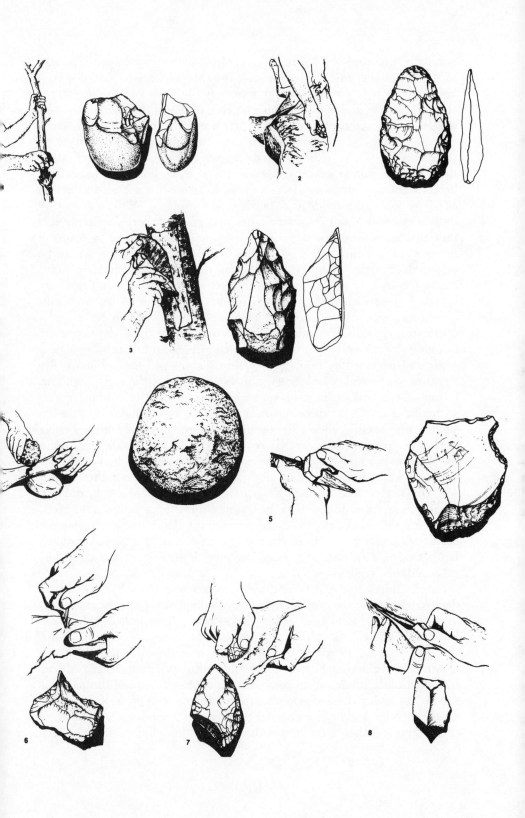

2

3

5

6   7   8

gravity behind the hip joint, transferral of body weight to the pelvis by way of the sacral suspensory mechanism, powerful hip flexion and powerful knee extension'.[11] There were also changes in the limbs and skull which are still imperfectly understood. Above all else, perhaps, the cranial capacity of *Homo erectus* was two-thirds rather than one-third that of modern man.

It was probably, therefore, at this stage that man moved decisively up the scale of predation to become a deliberate and organized hunter rather than an opportunist scavenger. Hunting by early hominids must have been essentially a matter of co-operation, depending for its success on effective vocal communication between the hunters. While stalking by individuals may have been used against very young or very slow game, it is thought that most of the larger prey must have been driven by teams of hunters into swamps or rocky corners where their movements would be impeded, or else simply isolated from the herd and followed until exhausted by lack of food and water. Such operations demand not only speech but also leadership and discipline. A plan has to be made and agreed between those who take part, and there have to be ways of responding in unison to unforeseen contingencies. In recent years the thinking of archaeologists has been much influenced by anthropological studies of present-day hunters, like the Bushmen of the Kalahari, the Pygmies of the equatorial forest, and the Dorobo of the high mountain forests of East Africa. It has been widely recognized that a hunting and gathering way of life can be much more varied and stimulating than the small scale farming which has occupied the majority of human beings during the past 10,000 years. It requires much wider knowledge, more physical fitness and mental alertness. Moreover, it affords much more leisure. Twenty hours is a long working week for a hunter gatherer. Ten will often suffice. And leisure is all spent in company, in communication, in planning the immediate future, in training the young. There is no need, even for civilized people, to regard the hunting life *de haut en bas*. Almost certainly, according to Karl Butzer, the people of this period enjoyed better health, a more balanced diet and more leisure than most agricultural populations do today.[12]

Side by side with the physical development of man himself, there came a decisive change in the product of his tool-making. This was the transition from the earliest industries called Oldowan, to those called Acheulian. Whereas Oldowan is not known to have occurred anywhere outside eastern and southern Africa, and at one or two sites on the northern coast of Africa, Acheulian, which undoubtedly had its origin in eastern Africa, was eventually to spread in some recognizable form to all the parts of Africa not covered by dense equatorial forest, to Asia as far east as southern India, and to Europe as far north as southern England. The most characteristic Acheulian tool was the so-called 'hand-axe', shaped like a rather solid spear-head, flaked on both sides to produce an even shape, and with a sharp edge around most of its outline. In fact, it was presumably a large knife, held in the hollow of the hand and used for skinning and wood-working. For chopping there existed a heavier variant, with one side rounded so as not to injure the user's hand: this is usually called a cleaver. More generally, Acheulian tools show a greater skill in knapping, including the use of a 'soft hammer' made of wood or bone to produce flakes longer and thinner than those obtainable with a stone hammer. They also show a much greater degree of standardization than their Oldowan predecessors. With the Acheulian, it is as if stone-working had become a tradition, with set forms and procedures, rather than an activity dependent on the inspiration of the moment.

It used to be thought that the Acheulian tradition emerged as the result of a slow and steady development from the Oldowan base, passing through an intermediate stage called Developed Oldowan. Today, however, the Acheulian is seen very much as a radical innovation, almost as an intrusion, into the Oldowan scene. The main reason for this is that, just as in the field of physical anthropology the robust australopithecine strain persisted for a million years alongside *Homo*, so in the field of material culture Developed Oldowan has been found to persist for a similar period alongside the early Acheulian. In terms of the stratigraphy of Olduvai, the Acheulian industry makes its appearance in the middle of Bed II, that is approximately 1.4 million years ago. But the Developed Oldowan persists alongside it through the whole of Beds III and IV, that is until around 700,000 years ago. *Homo erectus* appears at Olduvai a little later than the Acheulian industry – at a high level in Bed II. At Koobi Fora the picture is similar. There is a skull clearly attributable to *Homo erectus* at 1.5 million years ago, and there is a so-called Karari industry, transitional towards early Acheulian, from about the same date.

It would seem that there really must be some connection between these important developments in man and in his tool-kit, and that this must be looked for in some striking improvement of the hunting and gathering way of life. We have the essential clue in the fact that *Homo erectus* was to be the first of the hominids to spread beyond the confines of eastern and southern Africa. That would seem to imply that his hunting techniques and capacities had become more extensive, and so adequate to a wider variety of environments. Already in 1967 Loring Brace, writing not just of *Homo erectus* in eastern Africa but of the species as a whole, gave his opinion that the most fundamental advance in this stage of human evolution was the ability of man to cover distance with less exhaustion than any of the animals he hunted – the power to 'walk his quarry into the ground' by keeping it on the move and preventing it from grazing, until from sheer fatigue it could go no further.[13] If this development in the human body resulted in dramatically more efficient hunting, it presumably resulted also in an increase of population, and in pressure to expand the territory occupied. Mankind has always shown a mysterious degree of courage in launching into the unknown. One could suppose, for example, that some bands of *Homo erectus* developed a specialism in hunting the larger riverside fauna, above all the hippopotamus, and so found the confidence to follow the Nile valley northwards across Saharan latitudes. One could equally imagine that others discovered that a good living could be made in proximity to the sea shore, where hunting could be combined with the gathering of shellfish. At Hadar the hominids of the Afar desert were already within walking distance of the Red Sea coast, and a beachcombing existence may have developed very early. If australopithecine remains were ever to be certainly attested in any part of southern Asia, the beachcoming hypothesis would look attractive. In the present state of the evidence, however, *Homo erectus* looks the more likely candidate, with a line of expansion crossing South Asia by the great river valleys of the Indus and the Ganges. While the chronological evidence is still subject to a wide margin of error, recent studies indicate that there were no hominids in East Asia earlier than 1 to 1.2 million years ago.[14] In Europe, and in the temperate latitudes of Asia the chronological gap is much wider.

Writing on the eve of the Second World War, the great Jesuit palaeontologist and mystic, Teilhard de Chardin, had a memorable passage about how silently man had made his entry upon the scene of world history. 'He trod so softly that when his presence was at last betrayed by the indestructible evidence of his stone tools . . . he was already spread across the Ancient World from the Cape of Good Hope to Peking'.[15] That was how it looked before radiometric dating made it possible to compare the chronology of sites in Europe, Asia and Africa. And before excavations around Lake Turkana had shown that, in eastern Africa at least, it is just possible to identify hominid remains that antedate the earliest stone artefacts. Nevertheless, Teilhard's words are worth pondering. The evidence concerning the origins of any genus or species are bound to be extremely tenuous, if only because of the very small populations involved. It is estimated that the hominid communities of Olduvai might have numbered some twenty to thirty individuals. In the eighty-odd 'living' or 'eating' floors so far investigated one might therefore postulate a sample of some 2,000 people. And since the evidence is spread across a period of about a million years or forty thousand generations, the sample may be said to have touched about one individual in every twenty generations. Looking behind the sample to the real population represented, it seems both from standard demographic projections and from the density of surviving hunting and gathering peoples that the total hominid population of eastern and southern Africa at any period up to the

14

emergence of *Homo erectus* is likely to have been of the order of some tens of thousands. Seen in this light, the miracle is that we know as much as we do. For so long as they remained in Eden, our ancestors were still waiting in the wings of history's theatre, flexing their muscles, learning their part.

CHAPTER 2
EDEN OUTGROWN

Until about 1.5 million years ago mankind lived in an Eden comprising mainly the high savannas between Ethiopia and the Cape. From that period onwards Homo erectus began to spread over much of the tropical and sub-tropical parts of the Old World from southern Africa to southern Europe, to southern and south-eastern Asia. One day, when the basic facts are known, the inter-continental outreach of this first great human colonization of the planet will no doubt have pride of place. Meanwhile, it is fair to remember that the earliest and most intensive stages of this expansion took place within Africa itself. Men equipped mostly with Acheulian tools penetrated to every part of Africa saving only the fully forested regions of the Congo basin and the Guinea coastlands. In climatic terms, they learned to inhabit on the one hand areas much hotter and drier than the highlands of eastern and southern Africa, and on the other hand areas that were somewhat moister and covered with a denser vegetation. In terms of the carrying capacity of the land for game animals, it meant spreading out from terrain that could carry between five and twenty thousand kilograms per square kilometre on the highland savannas to that which might carry between one and five thousand kilograms in the lower savanna lands between the desert and the equatorial forest. The carrying capacity of primary forest was much lower still. Five to ten kilograms per square kilometre is normal for the equatorial forest, and this is certainly the reason why these areas were the last to be occupied by man.[1]

In moving outwards from the open highland savannas of eastern Africa, the nearest type of environment in terms both of climate and economic opportunity would have been the somewhat lower, somewhat moister country of which the characteristic vegetation is aptly described as 'orchard bush'. Here various kinds of broad-leaved trees grow to a height of twenty to forty feet, and are spaced at about the same intervals as trees in an apple orchard. The leaves cast a dappled shade for much of the year. Cereal grasses grow more thinly than on the open savanna, and the fauna, though including most of the savanna species, is much sparser. Such country is found over much of Zambia and southern Zaire, and some

3. EDEN OUTGROWN: THE COLONIZATION OF NORTHERN, WESTERN AND WESTERN CENTRAL AFRICA

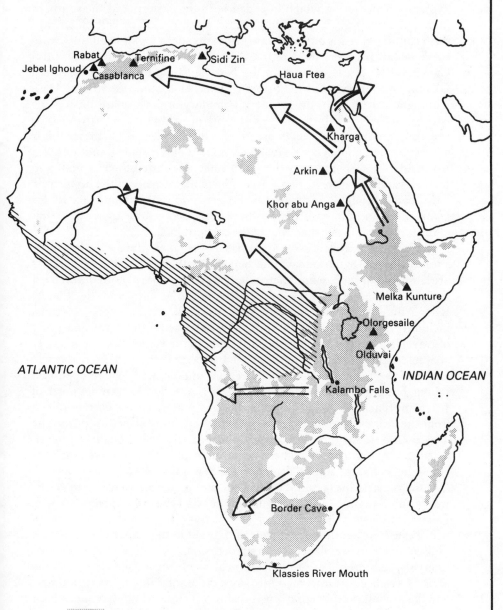

Rabat
Jebel Ighoud
Casablanca
Ternifine
Sidi Zin
Haua Ftea
Kharga
Arkin
Khor abu Anga
Melka Kunture
Olorgesaile
Olduvai
ATLANTIC OCEAN
INDIAN OCEAN
Kalambo Falls
Border Cave
Klassies River Mouth

Land over 1000 metres (in Africa)
Equatorial forest
▲ Acheulian sites
• Middle Stone Age sites

occupation of it by even early hominids must be postulated in order to explain a distribution which included both the eastern and the southern highland savannas. But another, vastly more extensive belt of orchard bush country spreads out westwards from northern Uganda all the way to the Senegal. It covers most of the Central African Republic and central Cameroon. It is the country of the Nigerian 'middle belt', of northern Ghana, of Burkina Faso, northern Ivory Coast and southern Mali. Throughout its length, the southern boundary of the orchard bush is the equatorial forest, with its marked scarcity of wild fauna. Northwards, it thins out into the Sahel, where broad-leaved trees give way to thorn: this is a very different kind of open savanna from that of the eastern and southern highlands – lower, hotter, drier, with unevenly distributed rainfall and much less perennially flowing water. The faunal density of the prehistoric Sahel can be roughly estimated by reference to its carrying capacity for goats, cattle and camels in historic times. It was certainly higher than that of the forest, but lower than that of the orchard bush.

Very little controlled excavation has as yet taken place at palaeolithic sites in the sub-Saharan savanna belt. Nevertheless Acheulian artefacts are known from surface finds across very wide stretches of both the orchard bush and the acacia thorn country between the Atlantic and the Nile. At Khor Abu Anga near Khartoum one large collection of stone artefacts, including many Acheulian hand-axes, was exposed through the quarrying of gravel in an ancient stream-bed tributary to the White Nile. Again, fully characteristic Acheulian hand-axes have been recovered from the tin-mines of the Jos plateau, in the Nigerian 'middle belt', where open-cast mining has followed the courses of ancient rivers. Some 400 miles north of Jos, comprehensive collections of Acheulian material have been obtained from the Adrar Bous in Niger, where the highlands of Air drop into the Tenere desert. All these occurrences have been professionally authenticated, but many more have been reported, especially from riverside sites along the Volta, the upper Niger and the Senegal.[2]

It is a remarkable fact that most of the prehistoric fauna of North Africa was of sub-Saharan African origin. It is not that the present climate of the Sahara is abnormal in interposing an effective barrier to the movement of wild game from south to north, but rather that in the course of the last few million years there have occurred occasional, relatively short, moist intervals, lasting only a few thousand years each, during which parts of the region have been transformed into savanna inhabitable by game animals and the predators which prey upon them. It seems certain that one at least of these favourable intervals preceded the appearance of man, since there are levels in some of the best stratified North African sites which have yielded the faunal remains but not yet those of the human predator. On the other hand, it is likely that at least one such climatic interlude occurred during the period when men living in the sub-Saharan savanna were making Acheulian tools, and so were in the business of following game in and through Saharan latitudes. It could be that one trans-Saharan corridor followed the depression which runs north from the Niger bend and which at times has been the recipient of the upper Niger flood. It could be that, as in more modern times, higher rainfall in the mountain ranges of the central Sahara – the Hoggar and Tibesti massifs – provided another such temporary corridor further to the east. What is certain is that the Nile Valley and the hilly country between the river and the Red Sea provided a third corridor, and one that was more consistently available than the other two.

Evidence for the Nile corridor begins with the Acheulian assemblages from Khor Abu Anga, and continues northwards with the finds of Acheulian artefacts in the Arkin district of lower Nubia, arising from the archaeological rescue operations in the flooded area above the Aswan High Dam. Here, in mid-Saharan latitudes, stone tools and waste flakes were found in concentrated patches suggestive of the 'living floors' of Olduvai and other East African sites, and with arrangements of unworked stones which might have been the bases of fences or windbreaks. Again, Acheulian tools have been recovered from oasis sites just to the west of the Nile valley, at Dakhla and Kharga, where natural depressions dip down below the water table and so provide permanent sources of water in otherwise desert environments. Finally, there is the evidence from the terraces above the present flood plain in middle and lower Egypt, which mark six earlier river levels, of which the three highest contain faunal remains but no artefacts, while the three lowest are said to contain hand-axe industries in various stages of evolution.

The Nile route must surely have been that by which Homo erectus spread to Asia. It is also the most probable route for his expansion into North Africa, even though the earliest evidence at present available comes mainly from Algeria and Morocco. Indeed, the most completely documented sequence has been that established by Biberson on the Atlantic coast of Morocco, where several layers of ancient shoreline deposits are conveniently separated by consolidated sand dunes, so that the stratigraphy is unusually clear. At the Sidi Abderrahman quarry near Casablanca and the Thomas quarry near Rabat fossilized fragments of Homo erectus occur in association with Acheulian artefacts in strata which were underlain by others bearing tools made of chipped pebbles. There is also a site at Ternifine near Oran in western Algeria, where fossil remains of Homo erectus occur in conjunction with Acheulian tools in a spring-fed pool: here again there are also pebble tools which might be considerably older than the Acheulian. At Sidi Zin, a spring-fed pool in Tunisia, what appear to be late Acheulian tools were found in association with a particularly rich collection of fossil fauna, which included elephant, rhinoceros, aurochs, gnu, gazelle and barbary sheep.

The difficulty with all the North African evidence is the absence of any data which might yield an absolute chronology. The estimates presently in favour suggest that the earliest tool-making in the region is unlikely to be more than 1 million years old, while the Acheulian artefacts associated with the fossil remains of Homo erectus might be only half that age. It is thus necessary to postulate an interval of about a million years between the appearance of Homo erectus and Acheulian stone-working techniques in East Africa and their spread to North Africa. This presents no difficulty in relation to Acheulian dates in Europe or western Asia, which are thought to be still later; but clearly it would be difficult to reconcile late dates for Homo erectus in North Africa with much earlier dates for Java and China if these were to be substantiated.[3]

In comparison with northern and western Africa, the eastern and southern side of the continent presents really abundant evidence of the activities of Homo erectus during the period from about 1.5 million to about 200,000 years ago. Partly this is due to the attraction of this region to scientists interested in human origins, who cannot reach the earliest evidence without stumbling on that which is later. Partly also it is due to the possibilities for absolute dating which exist in volcanic areas. But mainly it is due to the fact that eastern Africa was not merely the home of the earliest men but also the cradle-land of their immediate successors. By far the richest single source of evidence about Homo erectus and the development of the Acheulian stone industry is at Olduvai Gorge, where most of Beds II, III and IV belong to this period, and contain some sixty of the eighty 'living floors' so far discovered. These beds have also yielded the fossil remains of ten individuals all classified as Homo erectus. It is essentially from Olduvai, and from the Koobi Fora locality to the east of Lake Turkana, that we know of the first half-million years of this stage of human existence, between about 1.5 and 1 million years ago.

At Melka Kunture some thirty miles to the south of Addis Ababa, where earth movements have from time to time blocked the course of the Awash river and caused the formation of a lake basin, an important set of sites has been excavated by Jean Chavaillon, at which the earliest levels contain Oldowan and Developed Oldowan artefacts which are overlain by a great abundance of Acheulian tools. Some of the 'living floors' may date from around 1 million years ago. The main contribution of this locality to the wider picture is the excellent botanical evidence which has come from the analysis of recovered pollens, showing that the river flowed at this point through grass-covered uplands, no doubt rich in wild game. The actual banks of the river were lined with forest galleries, and it was here that men preferred to camp. Their living

20

floors were sometimes paved with cobbles, suggesting that periods of residence might have been quite prolonged.

At Olorgesailie in the Kenya section of the Rift Valley some 40 miles south-west of Nairobi, huge scatters of Acheulian hand-axes first discovered in the nineteenth century were eventually investigated by Glynn Isaac in the 1960s. He identified an ancient lake basin with sediments radiometrically datable to about 700,000 years ago. The whole of the lakeshore area proved to be studded with artefacts to the extent that a straight traverse across any part of it, scrutinizing a track five to ten metres wide, would reveal a fragment of worked stone every five to thirty metres. In three-dimensional terms this would represent a density of one piece in sixty cubic metres. But in strong contrast to this general order of density, Isaac found some thirty patches where the density of artefacts was 100–200 pieces in every cubic metre. These patches, he wrote, 'attest the organization of hominid movements around spatial foci, some of which were presumably home bases' (cf. Chapter 1, pp. 8–9). Of the tools found at Olorgesailie, which are essentially the same as at any other Acheulian site, Isaac remarked that, taken as a whole, they were no less elaborate than those of some living groups of Australian aborigines, and that by analogy they should have sufficed 'to dismember any carcass; to dress, pierce and cut up hides; to cut down saplings and small trees; and to shape poles, staves, spears, clubs and light wooden vessels'.[4]

On the borders of Tanzania and Zambia, the Kalambo river plunges 700 feet over a cliff's edge into the south-eastern corner of Lake Tanganyika. It is one of the highest waterfalls in the world. Immediately above it, the little river flows through a lake basin with banks rising steeply into a wooded landscape. Here in 1953 Desmond Clark discovered a partially submerged site in which six horizons of Acheulian occupation were overlain by others containing artefacts of the Middle Stone Age, the Late Stone Age and the Early Iron Age. Unfortunately, the site offered little scope for radiometric dating; but even the lowest-lying of the Acheulian tools showed a perfection of finish which suggested a period later than that of Olorgesailie. Moreover, these waterlogged levels contained a mass of wooden items – logs, some of them charred by fire, and other pieces apparently shaped into clubs and digging-sticks. A patch of ash lying on fire-reddened earth offered the first certain evidence from anywhere in Africa that fire was now under human control. A rough semicircle of unworked stones may have been the footing of a windbreak or shelter made of broken branches. The Acheulian tools included not merely hand-axes and cleavers, but heavy picks and choppers perhaps used for the digging of roots and other vegetable foods. The Kalambo Falls site thus offers important evidence of the adaptation of early man to a rather moist woodland environment.

In contrast to the very sparse evidence of tool-making by the earliest hominids of southern Africa (above, p. 3), Acheulian artefacts have been found, at least in surface scatters, in almost every part of the sub-continent from Zambia southwards to the Cape. Of the excavated sites, very few indeed are thought to belong to the earlier part of the Acheulian tradition. More typical is the situation at the so-called Cave of Hearths near Potgietersrust in the northern Transvaal, where Revil Mason identified twelve horizons, of which the first three contained late Acheulian artefacts, together with plentiful evidence of the use of fire. The same pattern occurred at the Montagu Cave near Cape Town, which was excavated by Charles Keller. However, the most interesting of all the late Acheulian sites in southern Africa are those at Kabwe (Broken Hill) in central Zambia and at Elandsfontein (Hopefield) near Saldanha Bay in the south-western Cape province, where Acheulian artefacts occur in association with human fossils of a build more massive than any other hominid yet known. At both sites the associated fauna include many extinct species and so suggest a date of the order of 300,000 to 400,000 years ago. The skulls of 'Broken Hill man' and 'Saldanha man' are so capacious that they have to be classified as Homo sapiens rather than Homo erectus. Yet this earliest variety of sapient man was evidently not very successful. Outside southern Africa it is known only from a single site, tentatively dated to around 100,000 years ago, near Lake Eyasi in central Tanzania. It presumably represents a genetical deviation similar to though earlier than Neanderthal man.[5]

The broad impression created by the million years or so of Acheulian tool-making is that, although man's territorial and climatic range was greatly extended both within Africa and beyond, his way of life and his choice of habitat were still remarkably uniform. He probably lived in social groups that were no larger than those of his earlier hominid predecessors: there were just more groups..In his choice of living sites the availability of game was only the second consideration: the first was proximity to water. Despite all the loudly proclaimed opinions of Lewis Binford (above, p. 9), the fact is that Acheulian camp-sites were almost invariably located beside water, near springs and stream channels, in limestone or dolomite caves, by lakeshores and sea-coasts. And therefore they were very thinly spread. They now covered most of the map, but they did not remotely fill it, even by the necessarily extensive standards of hunting and gathering populations. Life was highly mobile, and groups evidently preferred to divide and separate rather than to compete for crowded hunting grounds. Even so, it took them half a million years to spread from East Africa to North-West Africa, and perhaps just as long to carry the techniques of Acheulian tool-making from East Africa to the Cape.

*

It was the Middle Stone Age that saw a decisive change of tempo. Though difficult of precise definition, this was the period during which most of mankind had reached the stage of sapiency, in the sense that the brain had reached modern dimensions, even if other physical characteristics were still very varied. In terms of tool-making, it was the period which saw the disappearance of the larger items in the Acheulian tool-kit and their replacement by a variety of composite tools, involving the combination of wood and stone and the use of gums and fibres for joining one to the other. By the end of the period most men had reached the modern physical form, known in science as *Homo sapiens sapiens*, but the development of composite tools had still much further to go during the Late Stone Age which followed. The dating of the Middle Stone Age has recently been much revised. Its beginning lies in the limbo between the useful ranges of the potassium-argon and the radiocarbon methods,* and is nowadays thought to lie well before 100,000 and perhaps as far back as 200,000 years ago. The transition to the Late Stone Age is placed around 35,000 years ago.

Culturally, it is clear that the advent of the Middle Stone Age witnessed a process of evolution rather than revolution. The Acheulian uniformity was replaced by regional diversity, but every regional tradition developed from a local Acheulian base. However, regional specialization of the tool-kit was only one aspect of a much denser occupation of the land. Probably aided by a favourable climatic interlude, especially between about 125,000 and 50,000 years ago, hitherto marginal areas were occupied in greater strength, notably in the woodland savanna mosaic adjoining the equatorial forests, but also in the borderlands between savanna and desert. Nevertheless, the greatest increase may well have occurred in the areas which had been longest occupied. As the palaeo-environmentalist Karl Butzer points out, 'there is evidence not only for an increasing number of industries but also of sites. . . . These occur throughout the continent, even in what are now forest settings, as well as in a greater range of microtopographical settings than did Acheulian occurrences'.[6]

By far the most significant of the new regional industries was that known as Sangoan after a type-site at Sango Bay on the north-western shores of Lake Victoria. From its geographical distribution no less than from its character, it is obvious that the Sangoan was essentially a woodland tool-kit, designed for clearing undergrowth and digging roots rather than for hunting in open country. The process of its evolution is most clearly seen at the Kalambo Falls site, where it overlies an Acheulian already showing signs of such specialization (above, p. 21). All across the woodlands of northern Malawi and Zambia, southern Zaire and northern Angola, Acheulian industries were succeeded by Sangoan, and in the woodlands

*This limbo extends from about 500,000 to about 50,000 years ago.

closest to the southern fringes of the equatorial forest these are the earliest tools yet known. Likewise, on the northern borders of the equatorial forest Sangoan artefacts occur above the Acheulian along the Niger and Volta river systems and extend even into the coastal plain of modern Ghana. The Sangoan thus represents both a more intensive occupation of the broad-leaved woodlands and a first penetration of parts of the true forest. It was succeeded by other still more specialized industries – Tshitolian in the forest fringes, Lupemban in the surrounding woodlands.

Again, in North Africa and the Sahara the Acheulian developed during the Middle Stone Age into a pair of rather similar industries called Mousterian and Aterian. The Mousterian, which was common to the whole Mediterranean region, is characterized by the extensive use of flake tools struck from a carefully prepared core. It also tends to be associated with the ruggedly built, though sapient, species called Neanderthal man. In North Africa the Mousterian is known best from Morocco, where its Acheulian origins are attested by the presence of diminutive hand-axes and cleavers in a tool-kit which is clearly designed for lightness and portability. Unlike the Acheulian, it is usually found on the interior plateau and primarily in caves and rockshelters, where it usually forms the lowest occupation layer. The two most important Mousterian sites, at Jebel Ighoud near Marrakech and at Haua Fteah in Cyrenaica, have both yielded Neanderthal human remains alongside that of a typical grassland fauna of gazelle, zebra and wild cattle. The Aterian, which in the Moroccan sites overlies the Mousterian, is a far more widely spread industry, extending right across the Sahara and eastwards to the Nile. Its most significant characteristic is the presence of tanged arrow-heads, which offer the earliest incontrovertible evidence of composite tool-making. It would seem that during most of the period from about 125,000 till about 30,000 years ago, when these industries flourished, the northern third of Africa was experiencing a moister climate than usual. Game animals typical of the dry savanna were thus able to graze over much of the Sahara, and men naturally followed in their wake.

Although the Middle Stone Age expansion is most easily discerned in the regions of near-forest and near-desert which had been till then on the margins of human occupation, it is certain that history did not stand still in the ancient homelands of the east and the south. There is no single comprehensive term corresponding to Sangoan or Aterian, nevertheless the same essential developments were taking place. Acheulian cleavers and hand-axes were disappearing in favour of composite tools with smaller stone components, many of which were flakes struck from a prepared core or 'platform'. The use of fire was universal, and with its help caves, which had hitherto been dark and sinister places, became a favourite habitat and were probably occupied for longish periods at a time. All men were by now sapient, and presumably this implied greatly improved communication within and between hunting bands. At the same time, Middle Stone Age people seem to have been physically very varied, especially in eastern and southern Africa. There was 'Broken Hill man' at one end of the spectrum and Homo sapiens sapiens at the other, with what was probably a wide variety of Neanderthal-like men in between.

In the Rift Valley region of eastern Africa, the upper horizons at Melka Kunture in central Ethiopia (above, p. 20) show the gradual disappearance of Acheulian forms and their replacement by flake tools struck from a prepared core, while a factory site for these new tools at nearby Gadamotta has been dated to around 165,000 years ago. At the Porc Epic cave near Dire Dawa a Neanderthal-like mandible was associated with similar deposits. In Tanzania, the Middle Stone Age tool-kit appears in the Ndutu Beds near Olduvai at a level which may be older than 100,000 years and is thought to correspond with that which produced three skulls of 'Broken Hill man' at the nearby site at Lake Eyasi (above, p. 22). The most arresting evidence of Middle Stone Age developments, however, comes from South Africa, where at Klasies River Mouth in the eastern Cape province a cave site was found to contain 18 metres of post-Acheulian deposit dating from about 120,000 to about 50,000 years ago. Human remains, which occur from near the base of the deposit, are uniformly those of Homo sapiens sapiens. This is the earliest occurrence of fully modern man as yet known from any part of the world, but it is possible that a similar post-Acheulian deposit at Border Cave on the frontier between Natal and Swaziland may go back to as much as 200,000 years ago.[7]

While evidence from human fossils is still as thin as it is both for the Middle Stone Age and the preceding Upper Palaeolithic, any attempt to generalize must be a little hesitant. Yet it does look as though the region where man first reached his modern physical form was the same as that where his remote ancestors first crossed the tool-making threshold to reach the human state. It is therefore difficult to resist the conclusion that throughout all the intervening period of more than two million years Africa, and particularly eastern and southern Africa, had remained at the centre of the stage of world history. It is after all a reasonable proposition that where game was most abundant there the population of hunting predators would be the densest, and there the processes of natural selection would move the fastest. It is likewise only reasonable to suppose that this lead would probably be maintained for as long as hunted game remained the most important item of human diet. Only when it ceased to be so would the centre of gravity be likely to move elsewhere, and the scene be set to shift from the open plains to the alluvial soils of the great river valleys of the Old World. Meanwhile, recent research in molecular biology on a genetic factor known as Mitochondrial DNA appears to confirm that fully sapient man first emerged in Africa, and proposes a date somewhere between 280,000 and 140,000 years ago. It also proffers the stupendous claim that the transformation from earlier forms of man was due, not to a process of parallel evolution taking place in many different parts of the Old World, but rather to a fresh wave of colonization, emanating from an African base and spreading over the whole of the occupied globe, with a minimum of hybridization with earlier strains of man.[8] Should this hypothesis become established, a major revision of the existing literature of prehistory would become necessary, but the resulting modifications of generally received opinion should be less far-reaching for Africa than for other continents.

CHAPTER 3

THE FRUITS OF THE EARTH

Somewhere around 35,000 years ago, human communities throughout the Old World entered upon the final phase of a hunting and gathering existence, which was to end in the very gradual adoption of farming and stock-breeding. In Europe the first part of this period was the heroic age of the last glaciation, when most of Britain and all of Scandinavia disappeared beneath the ice, and when a belt of rich tundra vegetation extended from northern Spain to the Urals. Here, the hardy practitioners of a series of 'Epipalaeolithic' cultures – the Aurignacian, the Gravettian, the Solutrian and the Magdalenian – hunted the reindeer, the mammoth and the horse for their food, and the wolf, the ermine and the arctic fox for their clothing. They left a lively record of their life-style painted on the walls of caves, and they buried their dead clothed and adorned as if in expectation of a life to come. It all makes an inspiring beginning to the career of Homo sapiens sapiens in Europe, save that, with the return of a neothermal climate and the reversion of the tundra to fairly dense forest, the Magdalenian civilization disappeared without further trace. In Africa, the Late Stone Age was more prosaic, but also less ephemeral.

In Africa, as in Europe and Asia, all men now belonged to the single genus Homo sapiens sapiens. The difference is that in Africa some at least of the Middle Stone Age populations had already long reached this stage. In the Cape province of South Africa, we have seen that Homo sapiens sapiens was present well over 100,000 years ago – even before the beginning of the Neanderthal period in Europe. Again, in Africa as in Europe and Asia, Late Stone Age industries were characterized by the number and variety of very small pieces of worked stone, called microliths, most of which were merely the cutting parts of composite tools, such as spears and arrows, knives and chisels, awls and planes. But in Africa such tools had been on the way during much of the Middle Stone Age. The Aterian industry of North Africa and the Sahara had arrow-heads, and right along the southern coast of South Africa an industry of Middle Stone Age cave-dwellers, called after the site at Howieson's Poort, was producing by about 80,000 years ago a whole range of microliths – mostly, it would seem, the points and barbs of small spears, arrows and harpoons – which occur in the midden deposits at a density of as much as 4,000 pieces to the cubic metre, and which would seem to signify a period of very intensive occupation based on the hunting of large and small game, the collection of shellfish, the harpooning of seals and the trapping or shooting of sea-gulls.[1]

In inland South Africa, as also in Zimbabwe and Zambia, industries transitional from the Middle to the Late Stone Age were in existence by about 40,000 years ago. Here, it would seem that the impulse to change may have been given by the advent of a warmer and moister climatic phase, causing savanna to turn into woodland, with a consequent reduction of the larger game animals. In these circumstances human populations had to turn their attention to the smaller creatures of the trees and the undergrowth – hares, squirrels, rats, lizards, snakes and birds – and so to the construction of traps and snares, and to the invention of new weapons like darts and arrows which were armed with tiny blades and barbs. Often the hunting bands of such an environment made their camps in the shelter of caves and overhanging rocks, such as the imposing Kalemba rockshelter in south-eastern Zambia, where David Phillipson in 1971 excavated four and a half metres of deposit, spanning a period of at least 37,000 years.[2] The main message of Kalemba is that there is no need to seek any external cause for the transition from Middle to Late Stone Age industries. On the contrary, there is clear evidence of a purely local progression from flakes to blades, and from unitary tools towards composite ones, with an increasing use of microlithic elements.

By about 20,000 years ago the transition to Late Stone Age industries was virtually complete all over Africa. From this time onwards the dominant stone artefact was a 'backed' bladelet, with one edge sharp and the other quite blunt. Normally, the blunt edge was intended to be inserted in the groove of a wooden shaft or handle, so as to make a knife, razor, chisel or scraper, or else the blade or barb of a spear, dart or arrow. Somewhat later, triangular pieces with two sharp sides were made as the teeth of sickles for clearing undergrowth and reaping wild grasses. Flat, circular stones were bored through the middle to provide weights for digging-sticks. Large stones were hollowed out on one side for grinding roots, seeds and pigments. Both the last operations involved the grinding of stone itself, by rubbing harder stone against softer: this would in due course become the essential technique in the production of 'neolithic' tools, such as axes and hoes for tree clearance and agriculture.

From the stone artefacts alone, it is clear that the Late Stone Age people of Africa, though still hunters and gatherers, were so in a very different sense from their predecessors. Their exploitation of the environment was becoming steadily more varied and more intensive. Growing population, and therefore growing competition, may well have been one reason, but another might have been the growing preference for a fixed base, or at least for bases regularly occupied at certain seasons. While it would be a mistake to imagine that all, or even most, Late Stone Age people were cave-dwellers, the very high incidence of their deposits in caves and rockshelters tells its own story. These places dominate the archaeological evidence because they are so obviously the starting point for scientific exploration. Every African villager knows the whereabouts of the local caves and rockshelters, and particularly of those with painted or engraved rock surfaces. Every archaeologist knows that deposits are likely to occur within what is usually a very confined space between the drip line and the back wall. In comparison, the discovery of open-air sites, even though there must have been many more of them, is usually a matter of almost pure chance. Nevertheless, the very widespread occupancy of caves and rockshelters is an indication of the value now set upon a roof, and the likelihood is that this comfort must have been sought in open-air sites also, by the building of booths and wind-breaks and the excavation of sleeping-hollows. In compensation for such efforts, the builders would have tried to avoid moving on. They would have exploited a wide range of resources in the vicinity of each base.

A great deal of what we know about the Middle and Late Stone Age in North Africa comes from the great Haua Fteah cave, of which the awesome entrance gapes towards the Mediterranean from the northern slopes of the Jebel el-Akhdar, or 'green mountain' of Cyrenaica. The floor of the cave, excavated during the 1950s by Charles McBurney to a depth of 42 feet (though even so not to bedrock) revealed a sequence of occupation extending over more than 65,000 years.[3] It is the North African counterpart of the caves at the Klasies River Mouth in South Africa, and there is no site with a comparable occupation span anywhere in between. We have seen (above, p. 24) that the earliest known inhabitants of the Haua Fteah were men of the Neanderthal type, who practised an early form of blade industry and lived by hunting and by collecting shellfish from the sea shore and land-snails from the neighbouring hillsides. The animal game consisted on the one hand of the typical fauna of the African savanna – gazelle and zebra, buffalo and rhinoceros – and on the other hand of palaearctic species like wild cattle and barbary sheep, which were common to North Africa and western Asia. Homo sapiens sapiens probably made his appearance on this scene from 35,000 to 40,000 years ago, as the manufacturer of punch-struck blade tools comparable with those emerging at the same period in south-western Asia and southern Europe. While larger game was still hunted, the meat diet was increasingly dominated by barbary sheep, and this must raise the question whether, even at this very early date, some form of protection and culling

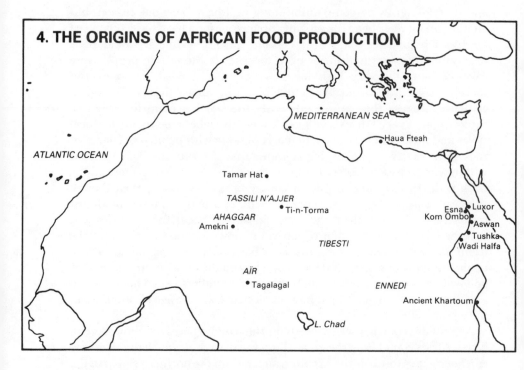

4. THE ORIGINS OF AFRICAN FOOD PRODUCTION

MEDITERRANEAN SEA

Haua Fteah

ATLANTIC OCEAN

Tamar Hat

TASSILI N'AJJER
● Ti-n-Torma

AHAGGAR
Amekni ●

Esna ● Luxor
Kom Ombo ● Aswan
● Tushka
Wadi Halfa

TIBESTI

AÏR
● Tagalagal

ENNEDI

Ancient Khartoum ●

L. Chad

preparatory to domestication was not at work. Certainly such a question cannot be evaded in connection with the Algerian site of Tamar Hat, dated between 21,000 and 17,000 years ago, where barbary sheep constituted over 90% of all identifiable bones.[4] By this time the whole of North Africa, the Haua Fteah included, had adopted a fully microlithic stone industry, dominated by tiny 'backed' blades, which at one stage accounted for 98% of all the worked pieces. As in the rest of Africa, the standardization of microliths was consistent with a very wide range of composite tools and weapons, and with the exploitation of a whole variety of micro-environments. It remained only for a final 'Capsian' phase, starting about 10,000 years ago, to introduce bone tools, grinding stones, shell jewellery and the regular, ceremonial burial of the dead. Of all the varied food resources in North Africa, it was the humble snail which in the end made the greatest archaeological impact. Its discarded shells, mixed with ash, stone fragments and other refuse, built up into substantial mounds, known to French scientists as *escargotières*, which serve as landmarks for the innumerable open-air sites of the Capsian culture of Tunisia, Libya and eastern Algeria.

In the vast middle area between northern and southern Africa, the first part of the Late Stone Age, from about 35,000 until about 20,000 years ago, is as yet little known. In general it was a period of greater than average rainfall, when woodland became forest, when savanna became woodland, and when much of the desert became savanna with access to flowing water. It was therefore a period when men and animals tended to spread out from the moister areas towards those which were drier, but probably without having to make great changes in their way of life. In the Saharan reaches of the Nile valley around Wadi Halfa, for example, a stone industry called Khormusan was practised, which seems to belong much more to the Middle than to the Late Stone Age. In East Africa and the Congo basin, as also in sub-Saharan West Africa, archaeological sequences covering these 15,000 years are still lacking. From about 20,000 years ago, however, the record becomes much richer. The environmental scenario was now one of extreme aridity, during which people and animals moved away from the encroaching desert towards the diminishing woodlands, while even the equatorial forest was deeply penetrated for the first time. The arid phase was evidently stimulating to cultural change. Microlithic industries appeared in the Rift Valley region of Kenya and Tanzania from about 18,000 years ago, and in the Lake Victoria basin from about 15,000 years ago, while at the Iwo Ileru rockshelter, deep in the Nigerian rainforest, a microlithic stone industry was present from about 12,000 years ago. [5] The most significant development of the period, however, took place in the Nile valley, astride the modern frontier between Egypt and the Sudan. At the Wadi Kubbaniya, a few miles north of Aswan, Fred Wendorf identified a series of sites where riverside communities of around 18,000 years ago practised an economy of unprecedented diversity. These people hunted large game, including hippo, hartebeest and wild cattle. They also fished. And they made many grindstones, presumably for the preparation of flour from wild cereal grasses. At the near-by site of Tushka in northern Nubia, dated to around 15,000 years ago, grindstones are accompanied by stone blades bearing a kind of patina known as 'sickle sheen', which indicates their use as reaping tools. Such artefacts become normal at other sites in the neighbourhood from about this time onwards. [6]

Altogether, the discoveries of Wendorf and his colleagues in upper Egypt and lower Nubia have caused a substantial rethinking by archaeologists of the origins of food production, and not only in Africa. The earlier fashion had been to focus interest on the stage at which societies became fully food-producing, and from this angle it had been very tempting to see it, at least in the western half of the Old World, as a process of diffusion, which had its earliest dates in western Asia, and which spread outwards in concentric circles across western Europe, southern Asia and northern Africa, with sub-Saharan Africa following a good way behind. Wendorf's most fundamental contribution has been to indicate the span of time involved in the domestication process. It is nowadays thought that domestication may be said to begin with the use of reaping tools, since the reaper, unlike the beater or hand-stripper, cuts and carries away for storage complete ears of grain, thus creating at least the possibility of selective sowing.[7] If, in round figures, it took ten thousand years for the first uncertain experiments carried out at the very margins of a hunting, fishing and gathering economy, to the point at which farming occupied the centre of the stage, then it follows that domestication must have been going on simultaneously in many different areas. The mistake was to imagine that food production was something positively desired by hunter gatherers, so that, once the principles had been discovered, the practice would follow quickly. In fact, it was a procedure of last resort, begun by a few people living in very special circumstances – in this case, a narrow valley hemmed in by increasingly arid deserts, where hunting had to be supplemented by fishing, and where fishing created the need for a fairly sedentary life style. The gathering effort thus needed to be intensified, and reaping led in due course to sowing, with some small element of selection of the seed sown. But, for several thousand years at least, there was no need for the practice to spread beyond the desert stretches of the Nile.[8]

About 10,000 years ago there occurred another sudden change in the climate of the Saharan and sub-Saharan belts from extreme aridity to quite exceptional humidity. This was by no means the same phenomenon as the return to Neo-thermal conditions in Europe and western Asia following the retreat of the Wurm glaciation, which had occurred some three thousand years earlier and had already set the scene for the development of food production in these regions. In Africa, the so-called 'Holocene West Phase' had its main effect within the first twenty degrees of north latitude and as far west as the Niger bend. Within this region, it encompassed the southern half of the desert, and also the whole of the Sudanic zone to the south of it, which formed the main drainage areas of the middle Niger, the Chari and the upper Nile. Even more remarkable than the spread of savanna conditions into the desert was the enormously enhanced accumulation of water in the Sudanic belt. At the main peak of the wet phase, which occurred between 9,500 and 6,500 years ago, Lake Chad had become a vast inland sea, as large as the Caspian, covering much of the low-lying land between the Tibesti massif and the Chari-Congo watershed, and even at one stage overflowing from the upper Logone to the upper Benue, so as to reach the lower Niger and the Bight of Benin. No less dramatic was the effect on the basin of the upper Nile, where the vast swamplands on either side of the White Nile and the Bahr el-Ghazal were augmented not only by a more powerful flow from the great lakes of Uganda but also by an infusion from the lakes of the Kenya Rift Valley, which overflowed from Lake Turkana into the Pibor and Sobat tributaries of the White Nile. The most impressive effects of all were seen in central Kenya, where Lake Nakuru reached a shore-line more than five hundred feet above the present level, engulfing the neighbouring Lake Elementeita and containing nearly one thousand times as much water as it does today.

For a human population of the Late Stone Age, which had achieved a technology adequate for a way of life based mainly on the rivers and lakeshores, the practical significance of the Holocene Wet Phase was very great. It was not only the fish which multiplied, but hippo and crocodile, waterfowl, rodents and freshwater molluscs. To anyone who has observed the teeming birdlife of the Rift Valley lakes, especially those of southern Ethiopia, where storks and flamingoes, pelicans and fish-eagles hunt side by side in their thousands, the riches of the aquatic biomass needs no emphasis. For men to exploit these riches, a lot of equipment was necessary – rafts, boats, weirs, traps, harpoons, nets, hooks, lines and sinkers – too much to be moved around from one base to another every week or every month. Moreover, in the riparian way of life the food was on the doorstep, and often in quantities sufficient to support communities much larger than the typical hunting band. It was probably the first way of life in human history to permit settlements of a hundred people or more. This in turn favoured the emergence of specialisms, first and foremost that of the potter. With pottery, liquids could not only be stored but also heated. It allowed a culinary revolution described by John Sutton in terms of soup, porridge and fish stew.[9]

The classic excavation for the riparian life-style of the Holocene Wet Phase is that undertaken in 1944–5 by Anthony Arkell in a mound site in central Khartoum. The mound had been left unbuilt on, because it had been used as a cemetery during the siege of the town by the Mahdi's forces in 1885. During the Second World War trenches were dug in it to conceal an anti-aircraft observation post, and it was while manning the trenches as a member of the Sudan's Auxiliary Defence Force that Arkell, who was Commissioner for Archaeology and Anthropology, noticed that the mound was in fact formed of the debris of a Stone Age settlement. A few years later the site was scheduled for building, and Arkell quickly moved in to excavate, using for labour a specially trained squad of prisoners from the local gaol, who achieved great proficiency in the task. The report is a gem.[10] It shows that the Late Stone Age inhabitants were living on a sandbank at the edge of the Blue Nile, which was then flowing about twelve feet higher than the present flood level. From a whole variety of evidence it is clear that the rainfall in the area must have been about three times what it is today. The surrounding countryside was not desert but savanna. The game taken included elephant, buffalo, rhinoceros, croco-dile, hippo, warthog and python, but the most plentiful animal bones are those of antelope, which argues the existence of large expanses of seed-bearing grasses. In their hunting activities the inhabitants of the mound pursued their quarry with bow and arrow, for the barbs and arrow-heads survive in large numbers. Mainly, however, they lived by fishing. Fish bones littered the site, as did the shells of *Ampullaria* snails, which are still used as bait for fish, but never eaten by humans. There were small grooved stones, almost certainly the sinkers for nets and lines. There were small, barbed bone harpoons, probably used for spearing fish rather than hippo. And there was abundant pottery, mostly decorated with a 'wavy line' pattern, made by combing the surface with the middle section of the spine of a catfish, the most common of the fish eaten on the site. The people of early Khartoum stayed long enough in their settlement for some development in pottery styles to be visible. They knew how to build in wattle and daub, using bundles of reeds tied in line and plastered with clay on both sides. And they buried their dead, the skeletal remains showing that they had physical characters very similar to those of the modern Nilotic peoples like the Nuer and the Dinka.

Arkell's excavation was carried out before the invention of radiocarbon dating, but he realized that in three respects at least – the bone harpoons, the 'wavy line' pottery and the negroid character of the skeletal material – early Khartoum had parallels in sites already discovered by French archaeologists in areas of Chad, Niger and Mali now well within the desert belt. He claimed that his findings suggested that there was 'a common fishing and hunting culture spread by negroid people right across Africa at about the latitude of Khartoum at a time when the climate was so different that it was not desert'.[11] Today we know from near-by dated sites that the period is likely to have been between 9,000 and 7,000 years ago, and that the common features extended southwards up the Nile system to Uganda and central Kenya.[12] There is no need to postulate great waves of migration. What is at stake is a limited number of culture traits, which could have been spread by borrowing, as the pre-existing populations of hunters concentrated along the lake shores and river lines to exploit the new resources. The culinary revolution implied in the use of pottery, however, is clearly of great significance. Of the three items proposed by Sutton, soup and fish stew pose no problems, but porridge raises the question of how far the seeds of wild grasses may have figured in the diet of these early fishermen-hunters. It may be that the cooking of gathered cereals was the prime purpose of the earliest pottery, and that this side of the riparian economy deserves more attention than it has yet received. At the very least, it seems likely that the food properties of cereal grasses were already widely appreciated, and that the advent of the cooking-pot may have made their collection seem somewhat more worth the effort.

Our knowledge of what happened in the Egyptian sector of the Nile valley at the time when Africa to the south of the middle Sahara was

34

experiencing the Holocene Wet Phase still leaves much to be desired. At the beginning of the period there flourished on the Kom Ombo plain north of Aswan, and around Esna to the south of Luxor, stone industries with many grindstones and flint blades with the 'sickle sheen' indicative of reaping; but the evidence then fades out until immediately pre-dynastic times. It may be that with better rainfall and higher floods the population of upper Egypt simply reverted to hunting and fishing and dispersed across a much wider terrain.[13] Westwards from upper Egypt, however, in the highlands of the central Sahara beyond the Libyan desert, the riparian life-style developed an all-round vigour and balance which may have made this region the scene of the final transition from gathering to deliberate cultivation. Here, in the great massifs of the Tibesti and the Hoggar, the mountain tops, today bare rock, were covered at this period with forests of oak and walnut, lime, alder and elm. The lower slopes, together with those of the supporting bastions – the Tassili and the Acacus to the north, Ennedi and Air to the south – carried olive, juniper and Aleppo pine. In the valleys perennially flowing rivers teemed with fish and were bordered by seed-bearing grasslands. The outstanding archaeological site is that of Amekni, 25 miles west of Tamanrasset, excavated by Gabriel Camps in the 1960s. Here, on a boulder-strewn ridge of granite with a little river on either side, the first of a series of hunting and fishing communities was established around 8,700 years ago. Pottery was made from the first, and decorated with a variant of the 'wavy line' motif – the same catfish was present to provide the comb. The dead were buried in the crevices between the boulders, and there is no doubt that they were of black African rather than Mediterranean proportions. In levels of the site dated to around 8,000 years ago grindstones began to occur in large numbers, and these, together with the pottery and some plausible evidence from pollen analysis, convinced the excavator that the threshold of deliberate cultivation must have been crossed.[14] Not all the experts agree with this diagnosis, but it can probably be accepted that in the Saharan highlands intensive cereal gathering must have come close to agriculture by this period. And significantly, it is in this central Saharan sector that the earliest dates for 'wavy line' pottery have so far been obtained – at Ti-n-Torha rockshelter in the Libyan Acacus, and at Tagalagal and Temet in the Air highlands, where it occurs at a level of rather more than 9,000 years ago.[15]

In strong contrast to the situation in the central Sahara and areas further south, there is no doubt that when domesticated cereals in the shape of wheat and barley made their appearance in lower Egypt and along the Mediterranean littoral around 7,000 years ago, it was as introductions from south-western Asia. Primarily, no doubt, this was a matter of climate – the vital difference between the tropical pattern of

THE FRUITS OF THE EARTH

equal days and summer rainfall on the one hand, and the temperate regime of unequal days and winter rains on the other. It was also a matter of climatic history, in that the return of Neothermal conditions to western Asia had preceded by about 3,000 years the onset of the Holocene Wet Phase in Sudanic Africa. The centre of western Asian developments was in the Fertile Crescent, and especially in Palestine astride the Jordan valley, where fishermen-hunters practised a stone industry called Natufian. By about 11,000 years ago this was producing as many microliths for reaping tools as for hunting weapons, and the wild grasses so exploited included the direct ancestors of barley, einkorn and emmer wheat. By about 9,000 years ago the Natufians of the Jericho district were living in brick-built settlements that may have housed as many as 2,000 people, and were harvesting cereals that showed signs of deliberate modification towards the domesticated forms. Egypt lay on the southern periphery of this area, and it was only around 7,000 years ago that it received the benefits, which by this time had been extended to include various legumes, such as peas, beans and lentils, and also domesticated species of goats and pigs, sheep and cattle.[16]

Equipped with these domesticates, and aided by the alluvium from the Nile flood, Egypt moved forward to become, by about 6,000 years ago, the first fully food-producing economy in Africa. The rest of the continent had no need to follow suit on any such comprehensive scale. Sudanic Africa was already experimenting with its own food plants, to which the western Asian complex could only be of marginal assistance (below, Chapter 4). It was the animal domesticates that were Asia's great gift to Africa. While there can be no doubt that experiments in herd management and systematic culling had been practised in parts of Africa for many thousands of years, it does not seem that the sheep, the goats, and above all the cattle which came to be herded in Africa in historical times were domesticated within the continent. The domestic sheep of Africa cannot have been descended from the earlier barbary sheep. The domestic cattle of early pastoralism (*Bos africanus*) cannot, despite its name, have been descended from either of the two species of wild cattle previously preyed upon by African hunters. To judge from the archaeological and icono-graphic evidence from the central Sahara, *Bos africanus* appeared relatively suddenly, in a fully domesticated form, and rapidly built up into large herds between 7,000 and 6,000 years ago, just at the time when south-west Asian influences were spreading across Sinai. There are no such early dates for domestic cattle from any other part of Africa to the south of the Sahara. Moreover, the human herders portrayed in the Saharan rock paintings are of a visibly different build from their hunting and fishing predecessors. Though sometimes described as Mediterranean, they resemble more the 'elongated Africans' typical of parts of north-eastern

Africa: they may have come with their herds from the Egyptian deserts or the Red Sea hills. Thanks to the rock paintings, we are able to see that the pastoralists were also enthusiastic hunters, using the bow and arrow and preying upon a wide range of savanna animals – antelope, zebra, buffalo, ostrich, as well as the animal predators which threatened their herds. Scenes involving slaughter or butchery of the domestic stock are distinctly rare, and it may be that, as with so much later African pastoralism, the main motive for herding was to accumulate wealth and prestige.[17] The golden age of Saharan pastoralism lasted from about 6,000 till about 4,500 years ago, corresponding more or less with the second peak of the Holocene Wet Phase. Then, with a climate once more drying up, the herds had to move south. There is every reason to think that the initial spread of pastoralism from the Sahara and the eastern desert of Egypt to the Horn of Africa and the Rift Valley occurred between 5,000 and 3,000 years ago. In very broad terms it may be said that pastoral food production reached the more open parts of the Sudanic belt at about the same time as agricultural food production was becoming normal in the somewhat moister areas to the north of the equatorial forest. In Africa south of the equator, where there had been no Holocene Wet Phase to stimulate change, the 'food-producing revolution' came later still.

CHAPTER 4

THE BRICKS OF BABEL

As a brief and bold generalization, the assertion of *Genesis* that there was a time, before men learned to bake bricks, when all spoke a single language, is on the right lines. The fundamental tenet of comparative linguistics is that languages diverge. Depending on where the line is drawn between a language and a dialect, the total number of African languages may today be somewhere between one and three thousand. Yet the number of distinct languagefamilies represented in Africa is generally agreed to be six, including the Indo-European family introduced by recent colonists from South Asia and Europe, and the Malayo-Polynesian family spoken on Madagascar by the descendants of somewhat earlier colonists from South-East Asia. Until about 1950, a third language family among the six was usually assumed to have intruded into Africa from western Asia. This was the Afroasiatic family, which includes the Semitic languages of south-western Asia and the Ancient Egyptian, Berber, Chadic, Cushitic and Omotic languages of northern and north-eastern Africa. Today, however, it is widely held that this family may just as easily have originated in Africa, to the west of the Red Sea. There remain three other language families of unequivocally African origin. One of them, Nilo-Saharan, generally adjoins the Afroasiatic sphere to the west and the south. Another, Niger-Congo, extends to the west and south of Nilo-Saharan. Last, and during the past three millennia very much in retreat before the southward expansion of Niger-Congo, there is the family called Khoisan, which at one time perhaps occupied most of Africa to the south of the equator.

This does not, of course, mean that the language families of today were each in origin single languages. Rather, they were broad spectra of vocal communication, each of which probably represented a continuous area of interaction and interbreeding by the very small communities of Stone Age times. Right up until the closing stages of the Late Stone Age, hunting bands numbered twenty to thirty individuals, each of which no doubt developed its own dialectical peculiarities. But these communities were probably impermanent and certainly not self-contained. Mating must in

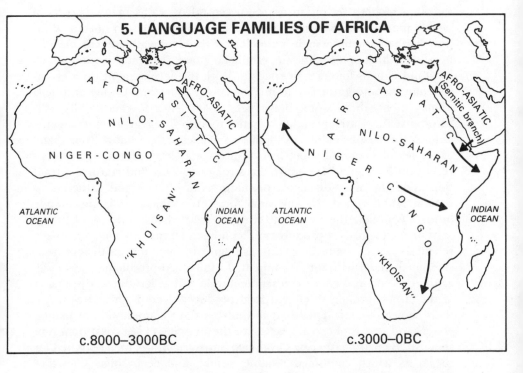

5. LANGUAGE FAMILIES OF AFRICA

c.8000–3000BC

c.3000–0BC

nearly every case have involved the transfer of individuals, and therefore of speech forms and vocabulary, from one small community to another. The linguistic networks so established could have been very extensive. Their boundaries would presumably have been determined by ecological factors, such as the natural tendency of woodland hunters to seek mates among other woodland communities rather than from those living in the open savannas.

How many such networks existed at various periods of man's long progress through the Old and Middle Stone Age, we have no means of knowing. All we can say is that it is likely that by the later part of the Late Stone Age the ancestors of the four surviving African language families existed in parts, at least, of their present spheres, and each loosely associated with an ecological niche relevant to the intensification of plant gathering and herd management characteristic of the approach to food production. What presumably happened during the long prelude to food production was that the size of human communities at last began to grow larger, and therefore genetically more self-sufficient. They also became somewhat more stable in space. In these circumstances the consolidation of dialects into languages could begin, and at the same time the differentiation between language and language. Jean Hiernaux has shown that in a modern setting in northern central Africa as many as 97% of people marry within their own linguistic groups.[1] We do not know for how far back in time such a conclusion could be valid, but it may be helpful to think of a preliterate, ethnic language as the unit within which most individuals found their spouses. With the development from extensive hunting and gathering to intensive food collection, fishing and herd management, there would have been a tendency for genetically self-sufficient and relatively stable societies to form in the areas most favourable to the new economy. And these societies, as we know from many examples of interaction between hunters and food producers in more recent times, would have exerted a strong linguistic and cultural attraction upon the more dispersed populations of hunters and gatherers in their neighbourhood. In any such form of symbiosis it is the mobile hunters who take their wares to the more settled communities of fishermen or incipient food producers. The nomad learns the language of the sedentary, never the reverse. But, as linguistic communities thus grew in size, particularly with the attainment of a fully food-producing way of life, so there would also have been segmentation and geographical dispersion of the largest groups. Incipient food producers were highly selective in their choice of sites. They had to find the right combination of fishing waters and stands of cereal grasses, or the stretches of sea coast richest in shellfish. As plant gathering developed into agriculture, men searched for the areas which combined reliable rainfall and deep soils. Therefore breakaway segments often travelled far from the parent groups – too far for regular contact to be maintained – so that, along with the consolidation of dialects into languages, divergence of languages followed from population growth.[2]

During the second half of the Late Stone Age, then, the most northerly language network was certainly Afroasiatic. It would be a fair hypothesis that it emerged from a series of dialects spoken in the valleys of the Jordan and the Egyptian Nile during the enforced concentration of population beside the rivers during the long dry period between about 18,000 and 8,000 BC when fishing was combined with the intensified collection of winter rainfall cereals like wheat and barley and with the incipient domestication of cattle, sheep and goats at the northern end of its sphere. From such a narrow riverine base, Afroasiatic languages could well have spread out during the Holocene Wet Phase as the languages of fully food-producing people, who carried them both eastwards into the Arabian desert and westwards across North Africa, thus accounting for the Semitic, Ancient Egyptian and Berber sub-divisions. The two deep southward salients of the present Afroasiatic sphere – the one encompassing the Ethiopian highlands and the Horn, and the other driving a wedge through the central Sahara to the plains around Lake Chad – were probably later extensions, made during and after the second peak of the Wet Phase, from the fourth millennium BC onwards, when domestic sheep and cattle were first introduced into Africa south of the Sahara (below, pp. 57–8).

The next most northerly network was Nilo-Saharan, which, even more obviously than Afroasiatic, would seem to have originated among fishing communities, who augmented their diet by intensified collection of cereal grasses, but in this case those indigenous to the sub-Saharan belt, such as millet and sorghum. For most of its known history, the Nubian stretch of the Nile has been occupied by Nilo-Saharan rather than Afroasiatic-speaking people, and it may well be that the communities which produced the early sickles and grindstones of the Wadi Kubbaniya (above, p. 31) at the height of the dry climatic phase were among the Nilo-Saharan ancestors. At all events, during the Wet Phase which followed there emerged a characteristic life-style which combined fishing with intensive cereal gathering and the use of pottery, and which had a distribution corresponding remarkably closely with that of the Nilo-Saharan language family. Since the coincidence was first pointed out by John Sutton,[3] it has received considerable confirmation from recent archaeological discoveries. On the one hand many new sites have come to light beside stream courses in the central Saharan mountains. On the other hand, the western limits of the distribution now seem to have been the area of the Niger bend rather than the Atlantic coast.[4] Given the later intrusion of Afroasiatic languages across the Hoggar and Air, this looks convincing, and is confirmed by the survival of an isolated Nilo-Saharan language, Songhay, to the west of the Afroasiatic salient. Linguistically, Ancient Khartoum should have been squarely within the Eastern Sudanic subdivision of Nilo-Saharan, and the same should be true of the East African Rift Valley sites at the period of high lake levels around the eighth and seventh millennia BC. Here, fishermen speaking Eastern Sudanic languages would thus have preceded pastoralist food producers speaking languages of the Cushitic subdivision of Afroasiatic.

As is well known, some of the worst confusions in African prehistory have arisen from mistaken attempts to identify language with race. These confusions were compounded in the days when race automatically carried intimations of rank in nature. Thus, for example, Charles Gabriel Seligman, one of the best known ethnologists of his day, built a popular text-book around the proposition that the history of Africa was mainly the history of the 'Hamites', a superior 'Caucasian' race, skilled in arms and proud herdsmen of cattle, who had swept through the continent in 'wave upon wave', subjecting and in varying measure civilizing the native races.[5] Seligman's 'Hamites' are today's Afroasiatics, and Joseph Greenberg, the leading modern authority on the classification of the African languages, was one of the first to point out that the Afroasiatic-speakers are by no means the most characteristic and specialized pastoralists in Africa, who are to be found rather among the Nilo-Saharan and even among some of the Niger-Congo-speaking peoples. He concluded that 'the stereotype of the pastoral conquering Hamite must be abandoned'.[6] So it must, and so indeed it has been. That is not, however, to say that Afroasiatic-speakers must not be credited with the introduction of sheep and cattle to Africa south of the Sahara, or that Afroasiatic languages did not increase their geographical sphere as a result of being the languages of the first fully food-producing peoples to enter the region. In fact, the two great southern salients of Afroasiatic are best accounted for in this way (cf. Maps 4 and 5).

In the western salient, the first part of the story must have been enacted in the highlands of the central Sahara, where, during the first part of the Holocene Wet Phase, people resembling those of Black Africa, and presumably speakers of Nilo-Saharan languages, had learned to make pottery and had gone a long way towards developing cereal food production alongside their main occupation of fishing. There, during the late fourth millennium BC, they were joined by pastoralists herding sheep and cattle, who can only have come from the north or the north-east, and must therefore have spoken Afroasiatic languages, possibly of the Berber subdivision, but more probably of that called Chadic. In the easternmost mountain massif, that of the Tibesti, the linguistic encounter went in favour of the Nilo-Saharan speakers, whose languages, Teda and Daza and Zaghawa, survive to this day. In the Hoggar and the Air things went the other way, and a mixed population, which must surely have been more Black African than Mediterranean in physical character, nevertheless became Chadic-speaking. Later still, when the Wet Phase finally came to an end around 2,000 BC, some of the population of Air drifted southwards into the new grasslands created by the retreating margins of the enlarged Lake Chad, where they established an economy that was at first strongly pastoral, but became increasingly agricultural as the population grew denser. In the Hoggar first, and later in Air, further southward drifting of pastoral elements eventually caused a linguistic change from Chadic to Berber.

The eastern salient of Afroasiatic is likewise best envisaged in terms of a southward drift of cattle-owning food producers through the hilly region between the Nile and the Red Sea, starting soon after the introduction of cattle into Egypt in the fifth millennium, gathering momentum during the second peak of the Wet Phase in the fourth millennium, when there was plenty of pasture to be found in Saharan latitudes, and continuing southwards around both sides of the Ethiopian mountain region when arid conditions returned to the Red Sea hills. Cattle pastoralism had reached the Butana plain between the Nile and the Atbara by the late fourth millennium. In Ethiopia and northern Kenya they were present by the mid-third millennium, but in central Kenya not until the late second millennium BC.[7] Evidence that the spread of pastoralism was accompanied by a corresponding spread of the Cushitic branch of Afroasiatic rests essentially on the close coincidence between Cushitic language distribution and typically pastoral terrain. In particular the southernmost surviving cluster of Cushitic languages, in the area where the Rift Valley disappears into the central Tanzanian plain, makes clear sense in relation to a pastoral connection to the north. The origin of the Omotic branch of Afroasiatic is more problematical, but probably one should think in terms of a parallel advance of Cushitic and Omotic, at the expense of Nilo-Saharan languages to the west and Khoisan languages to the east. The archaeological evidence does not at all suggest that the earlier populations were totally displaced. Rather, there was a marked continuity in the various traditions of stone tool-making, with only the addition of certain new features in the specifically pastoral sites, such as stone platters, pestles and mortars, which are widely attested from north-eastern Ethiopia to the Kenya Rift.[8]

Almost certainly, it was the size and complexity of the pastoral communities which provided the cultural attraction to those among whom they settled. The tending of cattle in open country teeming with wild game and predators is not a way of life to be practised by small groups of people. Herds have to be watched and defended by day and night, driven to water, milked, and moved on from one pasture to another. Neither the old nor the very young are capable of the exertion involved: they stay with the women at fixed bases, in tightly stockaded village settlements, close to permanent water and to sources of vegetable foods. There cattle in milk and small stock are grazed, skins dried and tanned, stone knapped, firewood collected, weapons made. There trade is carried on, with the hunters who come down from the high forests with their meat and skins and obsidian flakes, and also with the fisherfolk, who come with pottery and baskets, even if their fish may be despised and tabooed as reptilian by the pastoralists of the open plains and hillsides. Gradually those who come to trade learn the languages of the stockaded settlements. They buy goats and sheep, learn how cereals are gathered, ground and cooked, and perhaps also how seeds are planted. All this and more may be implied in language change, which, for all the difficulty and ambiguity of the evidence, is a subject which no historian of ancient Africa can afford to ignore. And it should be stressed that there is nothing peculiarly potent about pastoralism as a cause of such change. The introduction of agricultural food production by small groups of migrants moving into an area previously occupied only by hunters and gatherers could have exactly the same effect. Indeed, there is an example at the very heart of the Cushitic language area, where the high plateaux of central Ethiopia, with their good rainfall and volcanic soils, provide specially favourable conditions for agriculture. It seems likely that some kinds of agricultural food production, both of cereals and of vegetables, had been practised in the highland areas from the early third or even the fourth millennium. The implantation of Cushitic languages in the western part of the highlands may well have been due more to the development of farming than of stockbreeding. Moreover, the first millennium BC was to see the infiltration of the eastern side of the high plateaux by agricultural settlers from the highlands of the Yemen, who succeeded in establishing their Semitic languages all the way from Eritrea to Harar. A whole variety of Semitic languages was involved, representing a slow infiltration of small groups rather than any massive invasion. Once again, it must have been the relative density of the initial settlements that resulted in the cultural absorption of the earlier inhabitants.

In contrast with the Afroasiatic and Nilo-Saharan language families, the Niger-Congo family clearly belongs mostly to the moist woodland savanna and the equatorial forest. There is a puzzling link, presumably very ancient, between these languages and five small groups of languages spoken in the Nuba hills to the west of the upper Nile.[9] Otherwise, all the Niger-Congo languages are located to the south or the west of the Nilo-Saharan, and there would be much to be said in favour of a cradleland to the west of the Niger bend, around the headwaters of the Niger and the Senegal. Fishing was certainly a major pursuit, and it may well have been the comings and goings of fisherfolk between settlements along the rivers and the sea coast which caused the primary expansion of the language network right across the southern half of West Africa from the Senegal to the Cameroon mountains. Insofar as gathering became more intensive, and developed in the direction of deliberate food production, the wild ancestors of the lighter millets would have been available only along the northern margins of the language sphere. In the west, a more widespread cereal would have been the non-irrigated rice, *oryza glaberrima*, which is still the staple in all the regions west of the Niger bend, while along the forest margin yams and oil-palms were indigenous, and to encourage their reproduction in the neighbourhood of fishing settlements would have been largely a matter of selective clearing and weeding, and therefore of the availability of axes and hoes with ground stone edges.[10]

So far as is known at present, the transition towards food production in the territory of the Niger-Congo languages began considerably later than in either the Nilo-Saharan or the Afroasiatic spheres. It seems clear that the first and most intense period of the Holocene Wet Phase had little effect west of the Niger bend. In the desert areas of northern Mali to the north of Timbuktu it has been established that savanna conditions with their attendant flora and fauna did not occur before about 5,000 BC, some three to four thousand years later than in the highlands of the central Sahara. Around Taodeni, occupation sites with middens containing dense remains of fish, crocodile and hippo have been dated to the middle of the fifth millennium, while fishing settlements along the Atlantic coast of Mauritania date to the same period. In the Tichitt valley of southern Mauritania, excavations by Patrick Munson, and more recently by H. J. Hugot, have revealed a series of settlements that illustrate every stage of the gradual transition from hunting and fishing to the herding of goats and cattle and the cultivation of domesticated millet, all during the course of the second millennium BC.[11] Six or seven hundred miles further south, in the woodland savanna bordering the equatorial forest of modern Ghana, excavations in and around Kintampo by Colin Flight, and more recently by Ann Stahl, have shown that a transition occurred from intensive hunting, gathering and fruit collection to deliberate food production by the herding of goats and the cultivation of oil-palm and other vegetable foods around the middle of the second millennium. In material culture the change to food production was reflected in the appearance of ground stone axes and hoes, which are well known from surface collections right along the edges of the forest from the Atlantic to northern Zaire.[12]

It is a remarkable fact that the equatorial forest of Africa is almost devoid of indigenous food plants. Those that grow there today are nearly all imported from other continents – bananas and coco yams from South East Asia, maize, manioc and sweet potato from Central America. Those that grew there before were imported from the wood-land savanna to the north of the forest, and the price of success was arduous clearance, only possible after the evolution of ground stone tools, and even then intensely laborious.[13] The spread of Niger-Congo speakers into the forest belt must therefore be attributed primarily to the development of fishing settlements along the rivers flowing down from the woodland savanna to the coast. The shell mounds by the lagoons of Ivory Coast and Ghana signal the existence of settlements established during the fourth and third millennia BC, presumably by people who had fished their way down the rivers without planting any crops. Later migrants, equipped with ground stone axes and hoes, would have been able to cultivate plants of the woodland savanna in the alluvial soils by the waterside, with the minimum of forest clearance. It must have been by some such process as this that the Niger-Congo language family developed by far the largest expansion-salient on the

African language map. This is the sub-subdivision of Niger-Congo known as Bantu, which came to include virtually the whole of Africa south of the equator. According to the latest linguistic research, this happened in two concurrent movements rather than a single one. On the one hand the Niger-Congo languages spoken in the woodland savanna spread from west to east along the northern margins of the Congo forest, from central Cameroon to north-eastern Zaire, and on from there into East Africa. On the other hand the Niger-Congo languages spoken in the forest region of south-eastern Nigeria spread south-eastwards into the Congo basin, descending the northern tributaries of the Ubangi and the Congo, and in due course ascending the mainstream of the Congo-Lualaba and its southern tributaries, the Kasai, the Kwango, the Sankuru, the Lubilash, and so eventually reaching the woodland savanna to the south of the forest.[14] In archaeological terms, both movements started as those of Late Stone Age food producers, who lived by fishing and by clearing gardens in the vicinity of their fishing settlements. But the easterly movement along the margin of the woodland savanna and the forest was able to keep a pastoral element in its economy, and at some stage acquired a knowledge of iron-working, whereas the south-easterly movement of forest fishermen with riverside gardens remained with a Late Stone Age tool-kit until iron-working eventually reached it round the eastern margins of the forest. Both movements expanded at the expense of earlier hunter-gatherers, most of whom were gradually absorbed into the language and culture of the food producers, following the principle of the relative density of settlements, already enunciated.

In theory, it should be possible by the use of linguistic evidence to reconstruct, at least in outline, the history of the proliferation of speech communities. The guiding principle is that all languages change over time, and so diverge progessively from their neighbouring relatives. Where neighbouring languages are linguistically close, their separation from a common parent will have been recent. Where they are linguistically distant, the separation will have occurred a correspondingly long time ago. It seems that in most of Africa linguistic distances between neighbouring languages are relatively great, so that their reliable measurement would require many times more primary data than has been, or is ever likely to be, collected. After more than a century of literacy, adequate grammars and dictionaries exist for perhaps one African language in ten. Most of the linguistic classification attempted so far has been based on morphological resemblances and the comparative study of quite short word-lists. While there is today little disagreement about the composition of the main language families, the lower ranks of the linguistic hierarchies, and therefore the story of linguistic diversification

6.

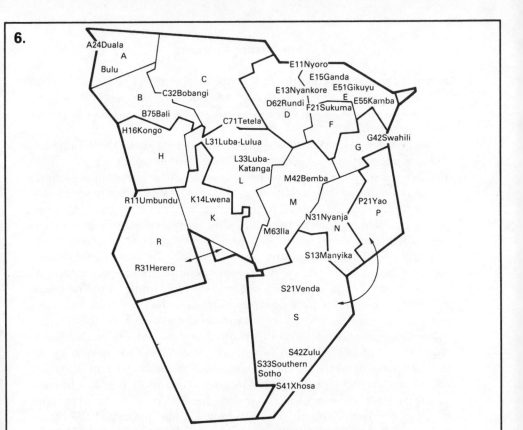

GUTHRIE'S ZONES AND TEST LANGUAGES FOR BANTU

AND

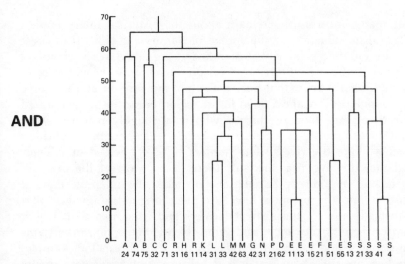

GROUP AVERAGE CLASSIFICATION OF THE TEST LANGUAGES, BASED ON THE COMPARATIVE DISTRIBUTION OF GENERAL ROOTS

through time, are not nearly so firmly established.[15] The basic problem is that in any group of immediately neighbouring languages it is likely that only a small sample will have been recorded in sufficient detail for effective comparison.

Nevertheless, the Bantu languages, numbering some three hundred, are exceptional in being generally no more distant from each other than the Germanic languages of northern Europe. Their internal propinquity can only be due to their relatively recent dispersion, compared with that of most other subdivisions of Niger-Congo or of other language families. There is still the problem that only a minority of Bantu languages has been adequately documented, but Malcolm Guthrie, the last scholar to devote a lifetime to their study, was able to identify some two thousand common word roots with a wide geographical spread, particularly as measured in 28 'test languages' chosen as a fair sample of the region as a whole.[16] Guthrie's rich data provided the basis for an extensive computation of the linguistic distances between each of the 28 languages and the other 27, and this showed beyond any reasonable doubt that the oldest of the Bantu languages were those now spoken in the north-western quarter of the region, and the only part of it which adjoins the territory of the Niger-Congo ascendants of Bantu, while the youngest were those spoken all round the eastern and southern periphery of the Bantu sphere. The computation also permitted the reconstruction of an approximate genealogy of the 28 test languages (Map 6), which, though based entirely on the mathematical calculations of linguistic distance, makes excellent sense when applied to the geographical map[17].

While many uncertainties remain about the historical interpretation of the linguistic evidence for the spread of Bantu, it is difficult to resist the conclusion that primarily it signified the gradual replacement of hunting and gathering cultures by food-producing ones. From archaeological evidence we know that during the first millennium BC the sparse hunting populations of the Congo forest region began to be penetrated by Late Stone Age food producers, who used roughly polished stone axes and hoes to make garden clearings beside what were mainly fishing settlements along the rivers. The hunters were not wiped out. Their descendants, the pygmies, are still there. Two ways of life are still practised side by side by populations of markedly different physical character. Only, the pygmies have lost their original languages, and speak instead those of the nearest farmers and fishermen with whom they barter their surplus meat and skins. This is not because the farmers are stronger and more numerous. In the Ituri forest, for example, the numbers are still about equal. It is because the farming settlements are denser and more permanent than the hunting camps. In any form of contact it is the hunters who approach the farmers, and first learn and then adopt their languages.[18] In relation to the expansion of Bantu beyond the forest into the eastern and southern savannas of Africa below the equator, the evidence is even more overwhelming that what was at stake was the gradual replacement of a hunting and gathering way of life by a food-producing one, and the cultural and linguistic absorption of Khoisan hunters by Bantu farmers. In the eastern and southern savannas the coming of food production was much more dramatic than in the north-western forests, in that it was accompanied from the first by the knowledge of iron-working (below, p. 65). Here, the archaeological record shows no significant period of Stone Age agriculture. It must therefore be presumed that a complete system of Iron Age food production was imported into the region from across its northern frontier. Even so, however, there is massive evidence of the long persistence of the hunting and gathering way of life alongside that of early food production. The story is one of the interpenetration of Late Stone Age hunting bands by small, dense nuclei of Iron Age farmers, who only slowly came to exercise a linguistic and cultural attraction upon their hunting neighbours. In southern Africa at least, there is particularly convincing evidence of the encounter, first in the survival into the eighteenth century AD of a substantial Khoisan population in the areas least suited to agriculture, and secondly in the presence of Khoisan phonetic characteristics in the Bantu languages spoken in the farming areas.

If the view presented in this chapter is correct, that the systems of language affiliation and descent we know today emerged mainly as a result of the larger communities made possible by fishing and intensive food-gathering, then it may be asked how Khoisan came into existence as a family of languages spoken by hunter gatherers using the old, extensive methods and living in the old, small communities which that implied. The answer must be that Khoisan was never a language family in the same sense as Afroasiatic, Nilo-Saharan or Niger-Congo. Khoisan is a category defined only by morphological similarity, notably the various clicking sounds which are the special peculiarity of these languages. For the rest, San is merely an umbrella term for a whole collection of unrelated languages spoken by hunter gatherers formerly living in the southern part of South Africa. Khoi is indeed a language family, consisting of at least three languages which have dispersed from a common parent, but the dispersion would seem to date from the introduction of some kind of pastoral food production not much more than two thousand years ago. The relationship between Khoi and San, or between Khoi and the surviving remnants of East African 'Khoisan' cannot be arranged in any genealogical pattern. The broad impression thus remains that the surviving systems of linguistic relationship date mostly from the early stages of the long transition through fishing towards food production, and that the evidence from basic linguistic classification is most significant in relation to this period.

CHAPTER 5

THE FLESH-POTS OF EGYPT

Only in one tiny corner of Africa did the so-called 'food-producing revolution' live up to its name. This was in the northernmost six hundred miles of the Nile valley, between the cataract region and the delta. Here the temperate pattern of winter rains and long summer days enabled the region to benefit directly from the full range of the south-west Asian food-plants and animal domesticates – wheat and barley, leeks and onions, lettuce and radishes, peas and beans, melons and cucumbers, vines and figs, dates and olives, sheep and goats, pigs and cattle.[1] Still more revolutionary, however, was the fact that in Egypt agriculture could be practised in a uniquely fertile soil and with the very minimum of manual labour. Every year between August and October twelve thousand square miles of the valley and the delta were submerged by the Nile flood, which deposited a fresh layer of silt rich in minerals and volcanic soil carried down in suspension from the Ethiopian mountains by the Blue Nile and its tributaries following the monsoon rains of June and July. Within those twelve thousand square miles, once the land had been cleared, no ploughing, no fallowing, no manuring was necessary. Herodotus describes how, even in the first millennium BC, seed was simply broadcast and animals driven over the land to tread it in. Cereal crops, once harvested, could be stored almost indefinitely in bins dug into the desert sand above the flood level. Until the pressure of human population became too great, conditions for animal husbandry were scarcely less favourable, with the opportunity for regular transhumance between riverside pastures and the seasonal grazing of the eastern desert. Once given the plant and animal domesticates, the possibilities for a rapid increase of human population were almost limitless.

Two other environmental factors were of the utmost importance for the development of population and society in Egypt. First, the surrounding deserts, which inhibited the normal tendency for demographically suc-cessful populations to segment and disperse over a wider territory. Only tent-dwelling pastoralists feeding their flocks along the desert periphery of the settled area, could easily come and go after the fashion of the children of Israel. For the rest, the ecological contrast was too stark for migration to be a serious option. It was always preferable to remain within the valley and accommodate to the problems of growing congestion. That made for economic co-operation within settlements, especially in extending the farmlands by digging and maintaining irrigation channels. It made also for the centralization of society. Here, the river itself played the vital role of a national highway. With winds blowing almost perennially from the north, so that the simplest of craft could sail upstream and drift down again with the current, the Egyptian Nile was exceptionally navigable. And the concentration of population within a mile or two of the riverbank made Egypt the easiest country in the world to govern and police. Food and other resources could be shifted quickly from place to place. Administrative posts, temples and military garrisons could be supplied and relieved. There was hardly a farmstead in the whole country that was not within sight and reach of the waterborne tax-collector with his posse of strong-armed assistants.

There is still some debate about when exactly the Egyptian bandwagon began to roll. The earliest fully food-producing sites so far discovered, which date from the late sixth millennium BC, all lie on the desert fringes of the valley and the delta. It used to be thought that this was because the valley bottom was still uninhabitable at this period, on account of uncleared jungle and undrained swamp. More recently, however, the environmental archaeologist, Karl Butzer, has proved that, on the contrary, throughout most of the period from about 9,000 BC onwards, the valley bottom would have offered unusually favourable conditions for settlement by communities of hunter-fishermen who were also intensive food collectors, and he has hazarded the guess that a population of between 100,000 and 200,000 might have supported itself in this way. If so, it would be very much easier to explain the demographic explosion which undoubtedly followed the introduction of the south-west Asian domesticates, and which is estimated to have resulted in a population of around two million by the end of the fourth millennium.[2] This is a staggering figure, which would imply a density of around 200 people to the square mile in the habitable part of Egypt – higher than that of many modern industrialized countries. Without doubt, it was to the demographic achievement of the pre-dynastic period that Dynastic Egypt owed the basis of its many-faceted progress. It was the density of population in Dynastic Egypt which most sharply distinguished it from the rest of the African continent at the corresponding period.

It was during the second half of the fourth millennium BC that settlement sites along the whole length of the Egyptian Nile began to take on the appearance of permanent towns rather than transitory villages. These are the sites known to archaeologists as Gerzean, and their most significant innovation was in the use of puddled clay, and in some cases of sun-dried bricks, for building. The Gerzean settlements were composed of rectangular houses, with wooden doors and windows. They were mostly built in the flood-plain, so that comparatively few domestic remains have survived the incidence of flood and silt. The overwhelming mass of Gerzean evidence comes from the cemeteries, which were placed a little higher than the settlements, in the desert margins. It is from the sheer size of these cemeteries that the growing density of population can best be estimated. And it is from the immense wealth of grave goods that we know that Gerzean Egypt was already unified economically, if not yet politically. Material culture was largely standardized, and certain features, notably pottery, showed the influence both of mass production by specialists and of regular contact with the parallel civilizations emerging at the same time in south-west Asia. It is from the painted pottery produced by specialists for the funerary market that we know, for example, that boats were being made of a size that required sixty rowers, and that there must have therefore been a striking advance in a whole range of woodworking and constructional skills.

The most important element in the growing technical competence of Gerzean Egypt was the use of metals, above all copper, of which there existed plentiful sources in the eastern desert, the Red Sea hills and Sinai. First used in the form of green malachite as a cosmetic for painting the eye-lids, copper, like gold, was hammered into small pieces of jewellery long before the Gerzean period. By the Gerzeans, however, it was regularly smelted and cast, to make knives and daggers, harpoons and fish-hooks, adzes and saws, axes and spear-heads. It was the advent of copper tools which made possible the development of accurate carpentry and cabinet-making, so that by the very beginning of the Dynastic period, if not before, the wealthier households were furnished with beds and chairs, chests and tables, as well as with a whole variety of vessels in copper, stone and pottery for cooking, storage and decoration. Linen and canvas were woven from flax for clothing and sail-cloth, which was cut with copper scissors and sewn with copper needles. Leather was tanned and dyed for sandals, belts, baggage and cushion covers: the tools employed were once again of copper. When in the early Dynastic period stone came to be cut for monumental building, the huge cross-cut saws were of copper and used with sand as an abrasive.

It is likely that the main cause of political centralization in Egypt arose from the competition between local ruling families to control the sources and distribution of copper and gold. The part of the valley where the decisive phase of this competition was enacted was the stretch of upper Egypt between Hierakonpolis and Abydos, where the river comes closest to the gold and copper deposits of the eastern desert, which are reached by the Wadi Hammamat. One important late Gerzean settlement in the centre of this area was Naqada, which actually means 'the town of gold'. The dynasty which was ultimately successful in extending its rule over the whole of Egypt had its capital nearby at Abydos. It was not just the internal Egyptian market for gold and copper that invited protection and monopoly. The Wadi Hammamat led not only to the mines, but also to the Red Sea, whence came long-robed, bearded strangers, well depicted in contemporary paintings and carvings, who were very different in appearance from the linen-kilted, clean shaven Egyptians, and who used ships with tall, backward-curving prows, quite unlike those which plied on the Nile and the Mediterranean. The strangers were certainly from Mesopotamia, probably from the seaport of Susa on the Persian Gulf. It used to be thought that they came as conquerors – the 'dynastic race' of Flinders Petrie. Had they been unopposed, it is possible that such they might have

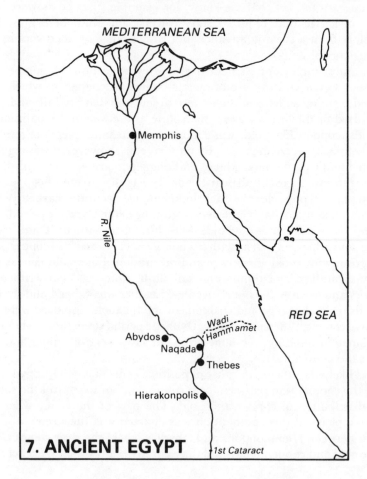

7. ANCIENT EGYPT

become. But it is nowadays thought unlikely that the Mesopotamians who came to Egypt on the eve of the Dynastic period were anything more than merchants, technicians and possibly mercenaries in the pay of one or other of the competing local rulers. Nevertheless, all scholars are agreed that the period of political unification at the end of the Gerzean was also one in which Egypt was penetrated by many influences from south-west Asia. Brick-making was one example, the concept of writing another.[3]

The set of ideas which is least likely to have been imported into Egypt from the outside is that connected with Pharaonic kingship, which has no real parallel in the contemporary systems of south-west Asia. The earliest Pharaohs are depicted holding a crook and a flail, and with an animal's tail hanging down behind the kilt. It may be that these regalia symbolized some ancient north-east African conception of a priestly patriarch, who arbitrated between the rival interests of herders, cereal farmers and huntsmen, such as would have been required during the period when the river valley was being opened up to food production. Local dynasties must certainly have existed by Gerzean times, and Pharaonic practice was no doubt largely built on their experience. It is remarkable, however, that despite all our knowledge of Gerzean cemeteries, there is no example of a royal tomb in any way ancestral to those of the Dynastic period. It is hard, therefore, to fault the argument of Gordon Childe, that the best guide to the growth of the idea of 'divine kingship' lies in the monumental building associated with the early Pharaohs. The earliest tomb of the First Dynasty – that of Narmer at Abydos – is nothing more than a brick-lined pit, measuring 26 feet by 16 feet by 10 feet. From this stage at least, right through to the great Fourth Dynasty pyramid of Khufu at Gizeh, which is nearly 500 feet high and is estimated to have cost the labour of 100,000 people for twenty years, the development is all in Egypt, and it represents the total victory of the Pharaohs over all earlier systems of authority.[4] If there were Gerzean dynasties, they disappeared without trace. The Pharaonic state was bureaucratic, not feudal. Its great title-holders were officials, not hereditary territorial magnates who had been incorporated within a larger unity. The largest triumph of the Pharaohs was the fiscal one. By using to the full the arts of the scribe, the surveyor and the tax-collector, they channelled the surplus production of the flood plain into one set of coffers. Some individuals and some religious corporations were exempt from tax; but only royal officials collected the revenue and mobilized labour for civil and military purposes. Not indeed inevitably, but not by accident either, such a radical growth of the institution produced a corresponding development of its ideological carapace, in the shape of the god-king, paying the highest honour to his god-bearing mother, and practising royal incest with his potentially god-bearing sister to produce the successor god. Meanwhile, the passing generations were marked by the growing line of temple-tombs of the earlier gods, his ancestors – no mere memorials these, but each the centre of an active cult, receiving gifts and dispensing oracles.[5]

The Pharaonic state continued in existence for all but three thousand years, from at least 3100 BC until its final overthrow by the Macedonian Ptolemies in 332BC. Dynasties, traditionally 31 in number, succeeded each other, or occasionally overlapped; but the usurpers had mostly been well trained in the system, and even those who were in origin foreign conquerors appreciated the advantages of maintaining its outward trappings. The priests and the bureaucrats continued in their functions. The language remained the same. The monuments and records of the past were prominent, and fully intelligible to a large literate class. It is no wonder that at the end of the Dynastic period Diodorus Siculus could assert that there was a set time not only for the Pharaoh to hold audience and give judgement, but even for his taking a walk, having a bath or sleeping with his wife.[6] The modern historiography of Ancient Eygpt has been written by outsiders, citizens themselves of nation states, who have been concerned to mark the ups and downs in terms of national unity, international influence and military power. The standard periodization depicts an Old Kingdom spanning most of the third millennium BC (?3100–2180), a Middle Kingdom comprising a little less than half of the second millennium (2080–1640) and a New Kingdom filling most of the remainder (1570–1075). The first millennium BC is almost written off as a period of terminal decline. Yet seen in terms of the size and density of the population, the overall wealth of the country and the astonishing measure of cultural continuity, the accepted periodization has little meaning. The population, which is estimated to have been around two million at the beginning of the third millennium, is thought to have doubled by the end of the second millennium, and to have nearly doubled again by the end of the first millennium. David O'Connor, a specialist on the so-called Late Period, has written that 'Egypt did not need to, and apparently did not, perceive itself as in decline; despite periods of foreign occupation, it remained relatively prosperous for most of the Late Period.'[7] And again, 'Throughout the Late Period, Egypt made a sustained and largely successful effort to maintain an effectively centralized state, which except for the two periods of Persian occupation, was based on earlier indigenous models.'[8] It was only when the Ptolemies established their capital in Alexandria and set about the creation of a Greek-speaking bureaucracy dominated by immigrants, that the long continuity of Egyptian tradition was really broken.

* * *

For virtually all the rest of Africa the three thousand years of Egypt's autonomous prosperity and demographic increase were at best a period of Stone Age food production, when communities seldom numbered more than a few hundred people, and when overall population density would still need to be reckoned in square miles to the person rather than the reverse. It is in fact perfectly possible that throughout all this time Egypt accounted for more than half of the population of the entire continent. In the northern half of Africa the climatic history of the period would have begun during the second peak of the Holocene Wet Phase, which extended from about 3400 till about 2000 BC, and which this time affected the entire Saharan and Sudanic belts, as far as the West Atlantic coast (above p. 32). Within this region, the most prosperous and presumably the most rapidly increasing populations would have been those of the cattle pastoralists, whose impact on the linguistic map of Africa was discussed in the last chapter. In origin at least, the pastoralists were ethnically and linguistically very close to the population of Ancient Egypt. They were the nomads of the adjacent steppes. Unlike the valley dwellers, their destiny was not to concentrate but to disperse. They are best known through the rock-paintings and engravings which they left all over the mountains of the central Sahara, although their real distribution must have been much wider. In the northern foothills of the Hoggar and Tibesti ranges the earliest sites associated with 'bovidian' rock-paintings may go back to the sixth millennium BC, but the most prolific period was the early third millennium, contemporary with the Old Kingdom of Egypt. By this time pastoralism was already spreading in the region immediately to the south of the Sahara – in Air and the Tenere, Ennedi and the Butana. The dates show that this is not to be seen just as a southward drift set in motion by deteriorating climate in the north, but rather as a genuine expansion due to the increase of herds and the general success of the pastoral way of life. The linguistic evidence for the expansion of Afroasiatic at the expense of Nilo-Saharan languages (above, pp. 41–3) suggests that not all of the migrants were four-footed. The Afroasiatics, we know, were spreading through country which had been occupied for four or five thousand years by intensive cereal gatherers who made pots and cooked porridge to eat with their fish stews. The pastoralists moving in among them may have tended to remain rather specialized, inhabiting the drier terrain, and moving to and fro at different seasons, but their presence would nevertheless have added a new dynamism to the early food-producing economy of the region as a whole.

The expansion of cattle pastoralism through Africa was mainly limited by the tsetse fly. This noxious insect which is known to have existed since Miocene times, inhabits the bushy savanna surrounding the equatorial forest, where it preys upon the blood of the larger wild animals, which have acquired an immunity to the parasites disseminated by its bite. To domestic animals especially cattle, horses, mules and donkeys, it transmits trypanosomiasis, which is always fatal. Very much of African history has been affected by the consequent lack of beasts of burden from large areas of the continent. Right across the continent from the Atlantic to the Nile the fly-belt prevents the spread of cattle south of about the tenth degree of northern latitude, and during the Holocene Wet Phase the limit would have been considerably further north. Only in the sector to the east of the Nile did the Ethiopian and East African highlands provide a corridor of fly-free pastureland extending southwards to the equator and beyond. Within the fly-belt, which thus embraced the whole southern part of West Africa and all of the Congo basin, the only evidence of a demographic advance during the last three millennia BC is that signalled by the expansion of the Niger-Congo language family (above, pp. 46–9). Most likely, this amounted to the addition of some intensive river fishing accompanied by a little riparian agriculture to an economy previously limited to the rather meagre opportunities for forest hunting. The result may have been to double or treble a very exiguous level of population. Beyond the forest to the east and the south, Late Stone Age hunting, without benefit of intensive fishing or cereal gathering, remained the rule.

* * *

Towards the end of the second millennium BC the Afroasiatic speakers of northern Africa to the west of Egypt began to be affected by the civilization and commerce of the Mediterranean Bronze Age. Primarily this meant the introduction from the steppelands of western Asia of the horse, and also of a very light kind of two-wheeled chariot, probably equipped with bronze tires to protect the wheels, which enabled the huntsman to chase the larger and swifter game animals, and gave the warrior and the slave raider the means to pursue and terrorize footborne enemies and victims. This development occurred only after the desertification of the Sahara was well under way, and it may be that the charioteers represented an invasion of the central Saharan regions by Libyan Berbers, who were perhaps the ancestors of the modern Tuareg tribes and so replaced earlier Chadic-speaking Afroasiatics who had moved further south in the interests of their cattle. At all events, on the rocks of the central Saharan mountains paintings in the 'bovidian' style now gave way to a new 'equidian' tradition dominated first by scenes of horses and chariots and later by those of horsemen riding. While cattle and sheep continue to occur in the 'equidian' rock art, the overall impression is given that society was now dominated by Bronze Age hunters and slave-raiders working to supply the Mediterranean market.[9]

A similar impression of the situation as it was during the middle of the first millennium BC comes from Herodotus, who describes a series of pastoral Berber tribes, Nasamonians and others, inhabiting the whole of the coastal region from the borders of Egypt right round to eastern Algeria, with a desert tract to the south of them occupied only by wild beasts and those who hunted them. Beyond the hunting-grounds, however, in what must be the Fezzan province of modern Libya, lying just below the northern foothills of the Saharan mountains and receiving their drainage, there lived the most powerful of all the Berber tribes, the Garamantes, who were able to practise cultivation as well as pastoralism, and who were equipped with four-horse chariots which they used for slave-hunting expeditions in the country of the cave-dwelling negroes which lay to the south again. These were presumably the northernmost of the Nilo-Saharan peoples, corresponding to the modern Teda and Daza peoples of the Tibesti massif and its environs. Herodotus was almost ignorant of the world beyond the Sahara. Not completely so, however, for he related the story of a party of rash young Nasamonians who, for a wager, had undertaken to explore the desert, and had at last reached a country to the south of it, inhabited by black people, and with a great river running through it from west to east in which there were many crocodiles. This may well be the first historical account of the Niger, but, if so, it is also a proof of how nearly completely the dessication of the second and early first millennia had cut trans-Saharan communications.[10] Today, we know from archaeological sources that the copper of Air was being mined and hammered in its 'native' form during the second millennium, and that by the mid-first millennium copper was being regularly smelted both in Air and far out to the west in southern Mauritania.[11] All this is presumptive evidence of some occasional contact between the regions north and south of the Sahara during this period, but it certainly does not imply that either copper or gold was being exported across the desert in the tiny chariots used for warfare and hunting, or by any other means. Rather it signifies the very slow beginning of the metal age in West Africa, where the effective use of copper and bronze developed a full two and a half millennia later than in Egypt, only very narrowly preceding the much more complex metallurgical techniques involved in the working of iron. So long as metal tools and weapons were absent, there could hardly be the control over the environment necessary for significant population groupings to emerge.

Even so late as the first millennium BC, there was still only one region of Africa other than Egypt where the demographic base and the internal communications were sufficiently advanced to permit the formation of a large state with an element of city-dwellers and a small literate class.

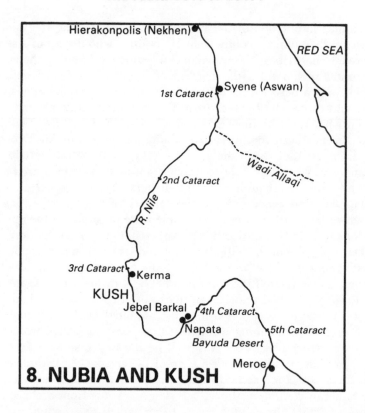

Hierakonpolis (Nekhen)

RED SEA

Syene (Aswan)

1st Cataract

Wadi Allaqi

2nd Cataract

R. Nile

3rd Cataract Kerma

KUSH

Jebel Barkal 4th Cataract

Napata 5th Cataract

Bayuda Desert

Meroe

8. NUBIA AND KUSH

This was in the Nilotic Sudan, and it was partly, though only partly, due to the colonizing activity of Egypt itself. Already during the Old and Middle Kingdoms, between about 3600 and 1700 BC, Egypt had placed garrisons in Lower Nubia between the first and third cataracts, in order to control the copper and gold mines of the Wadi Allaqi district between the Nile and the Red Sea. Beyond this to the south, however, there emerged sometime early in the second millennium an independent Nubian kingdom of Kush, with its capital at Kerma, at the lower end of the Dongola reach, where for a hundred miles or more the Nile flows peacefully through a wide flood-plain, providing the conditions for a comparatively dense agricultural population on the Egyptian model, though on a smaller scale. Although the first excavator of Kerma, George Reisner, interpreted it as yet another Egyptian garrison fortress, there is today no doubt that it represented a distinct Nubian culture, and that it was inhabited by people with a strong negro strain, who spoke a language of the Nilo-Saharan family. This kingdom reached the height of its power during the interval between the Middle and the New Kingdom of Egypt, roughly between 1700 and 1500 BC. During this period eight rulers of Kush were buried in gigantic tumuli, the largest nearly 300 feet in diameter. The grave-goods have been plundered, but the chambers built for them were larger than those in any Egyptian pyramid. Human sacrifices, not practised in Egypt since the First Dynasty, accompanied all the royal burials and may have numbered 400 in the largest tomb.[12]

The signs of wealth exhibited in both the palace fortress and the royal tumuli at Kerma strongly suggest that the Nubian rulers of Kush had used a power base in Upper Nubia to seize control of the gold mines of Lower Nubia during the weakness of Egypt during the intermediate period.[13] During the Egyptian New Kingdom, however, from about 1500 till about 1100 BC, Egypt more than recovered its ancient power, and both Lower and Upper Nubia were quickly conquered and annexed. This was the period of the greatest exploitation of Lower Nubian gold, and Upper Nubia was now subjected to a system of colonial government, under a 'Viceroy of Kush', who was often a member of the Pharaoh's family. Egyptian temples and administrative posts were established at several points along the river, as far south as Jebel Barkal, near the Fourth cataract. Most of the riparian land was taken into state or temple ownership; but some Nubian chiefly families were absorbed into the Egyptian ruling class, their sons being sent to Egypt as student hostages.

It was presumably around some such very highly Egyptianized chiefly family, supported by, and in turn protecting, the Egyptian temple community of Jebel Barkal that a second independent kingdom of Kush was organized when the Egyptian New Kingdom broke down. The home district of the new dynasty was in Napata, just across the river from Jebel Barkal, at the southernmost extremity of the former Egyptian colony. It certainly looks like the age-old story of the marcher lord, encouraged to maintain an army for the defence of the frontier, and therefore in a position to seize authority when there was weakness at the centre.[14] At all events, the Napatans somewhere around 900 BC conquered both Upper and Lower Nubia, including the all-important gold-mines, and by 750 were strong enough to conquer Egypt itself, where their kings ruled for nearly a century as the Twenty-Fifth Dynasty. Driven out of Egypt by the Assyrians in 663, the Napatans retreated to their homeland, but continued to claim the title of Pharaoh, and to carry on the tradition of divine kingship which they had learned at Thebes. Indeed, in some ways the Napatans tried to be more Egyptian than the Egyptians, favouring the artistic forms of the Old Kingdom, building their tombs in pyramidal shape and adorning them with inscriptions carved in Egyptian hieroglyphics. Monumental building remained wholly Egyptian in inspiration. Temples were dedicated to the Theban god, Amun, whose name also figured in the royal titles. Thus, the conceptual framework of the Egyptian state, its bureaucratic structure and its fiscal techniques passed almost complete into the kingdom of Kush just when Egyptian power was on the wane.

However, the economic and demographic base of the new kingdom of Kush was a far cry from that of Egypt. In place of the continuous flood-plain that ran from end to end of Egypt, there was only a patchwork of natural basins which caught the annual deposit of alluvium. The riverside cultivators of Kush must always have been few compared with those of Egypt and most of them concentrated between the Third and Fourth cataracts. Again, in place of the uninterrupted navigation of the Egyptian Nile, the Nubian course of the river was broken by rocks and rapids, and had one long stretch between the Fourth and Fifth cataracts that was not navigable at all, since it was impossible to sail upstream against the prevailing northerly wind. At this point, therefore, the long-distance route to the south had to cross by land from Napata to Meroe and face the hazard of warlike nomads. From Meroe southwards the economy seems to have been more pastoral than agricultural, with transhumant stockraisers moving their herds between the dry season pasture of the riverside and the broader grazing grounds of the Butana plain. On the whole, it would be surprising if the whole huge region from Khartoum to Aswan numbered half a million people in pre-Christian times.

Kush, therefore, was essentially a middleman state, existing on the profits of commerce between Black Africa and the Mediterranean world. This character became more marked towards the end of the first millenium BC, when the Ptolemies were ruling in Egypt. By this time the effective capital had shifted south from Napata to Meroe, where the earliest monumental building dates from the fifth century BC. Great mounds of iron slag are among the more visible remains at Meroe, and much stress used to be laid on its significance as an early centre of iron-working. The archaeologist, Sayce described it in an often quoted phrase as 'the Birmingham of central Africa'. Today, it seems less remarkable that the capital of what was now an Iron Age state, situated where both iron ore and wood fuel were plentiful, should have had a significant iron industry. To William Adams, the author of the most recent major evaluation of Nubian archaeology, it is 'the truly extra-ordinary quantities of foreign-made goods' found in Meroitic sites that gives them a distinctive character, and this holds good not only for the capital but for the peripheries of the state, especially those near the Egyptian frontier. By the end of the first millennium BC, the former Egyptian colony had become a prosperous neighbour of the Hellenistic world.[15] But also, by enduring for so long, the kingdom of Kush was able to preserve the heritage of Ancient Egyptian political and religious ideas until a period when the adjoining parts of Black Africa were reaching a stage when those ideas could at last be usefully borrowed and adapted. In a very real sense Kush was the prototype of the later states of the sub-Saharan savanna.

CHAPTER 6

THE MEN OF IRON

The period from about 700 BC until about AD 700 was one in which the peoples on the eastern and northern side of the Mediterranean basin began to be prominent and to dominate Egypt and the rest of Africa to the north of the Sahara. In the eastern Mediterranean the Greeks, and in the western Mediterranean the Phoenicians, founded seaport colonies, which became the growing-points of economic and cultural transformation, and eventually of political dominance. Egypt and Cyrenaica were conquered in the late fourth century by the Macedonian Greeks, while the Phoenicians of Carthage extended their rule over the coastal plain of Tunisia, Tripolitania and eastern Algeria. Both dominions eventually fell to Rome, which used them with single-minded ruthlessness to feed the capital city of her empire. The system, despite some disturbance from the barbarian invasions, survived the transfer of the capital from Rome to Constantinople and remained basically intact until the Arab conquest of Egypt in 639 AD. Some of the more enduring aspects of Greek and Roman rule in northern Africa will be discussed in the next chapter. The bare outline is recalled here only as the northern backdrop to Saharan and sub-Saharan Africa, for which the same period may be best characterized as the early Iron Age.

In the world scene, the importance of iron as compared with other metals was that it was abundant and therefore cheap. Where copper and bronze could provide precision tools for skilled artisans and weapons of quality for a small military élite, iron was within the reach of all. Everyday weapons for hunting and defence against wild animals, agricultural tools for clearance and tillage, household goods like needles, knives and razors, fishing tackle, tools for working wood and leather, jewellery, musical instruments like the bell and the finger piano, could all be produced by the village blacksmith at reasonable cost – once iron ore could be smelted into a workable form. In most of Africa the impact of iron metallurgy was much greater than in Europe and Asia, in that here there had been no preceding Bronze Age. In Africa south of the sub-Saharan Sahel iron directly replaced stone. And in much of eastern and southern Africa below the equator, where there had previously been no Stone Age food production, Iron Age agriculture directly replaced Late Stone Age hunting and gathering. This made an economic revolution of devastating intensity, and it is hardly surprising that it involved a substantial change of language and population also.

The essential problem in the development of an iron metallurgy lay in smelting. It arose from the fact that pure iron melts only at 1540°C, as against 1100°C for copper. No such temperature could be achieved in any furnace invented before the nineteenth century AD. Prior to this, iron smelting consisted in the reduction of the ore by heating it between layers of charcoal to around 1200°C, until most of the slag melted and drained away, leaving a somewhat contaminated but nevertheless workable 'bloom' – a mixture of solid iron, slag and pieces of unburnt charcoal – which could be broken up and further purified by reheating and hammering in the smith's forge.[1] Even for this limited operation, the pyrotechnic skills required were considerable. For every smelt a furnace had to be built of clay and provided with pottery tuyères – pipes designed to conduct air from eight or ten bellows placed in a circle round the furnace into the combustion chamber. The ore had to be collected from source and carefully loaded into the furnace along with twice the quantity of charcoal made from slow-burning timber. Once lit, the fire had to bellowsed continuously for something like sixteen hours, and even then a successful result was not certain. No wonder that smelting was a mystery carried out by hereditary specialists in out of the way places, and surrounded by a ritual symbolism which compared the act of smelting to sexual intercourse, and the reduction of the ore to the 'cooking' of a child in its mother's womb.[2]

There is no need to postulate a single, unique invention of iron smelting. The carburization of iron ore by charcoal was indeed a discovery of great moment, but it could have occurred many times over, and iron-working has been described by one expert as 'an inevitable technical by-product of copper and lead-smelting, anticipated by the pyrotechnical uses of iron . . . as a flux'.[3] Nevertheless, there was everywhere a considerable time-lag between the working of copper and that of iron, and it is considered very unlikely that iron-working would have been independently invented where the working of copper was unknown. This means that the origins of African iron-working must probably be sought within the northern third of the continent. It does not, however, mean that the ultimate origin of African iron-working was outside Africa. Indeed, it seems that there was a distinctively African way of smelting iron, which was originally common to the whole continent, and which was not practised anywhere else. The African peculiarity was that the tuyères were so placed as to reach, not just to the wall of the furnace, but right into the combustion chamber. This meant that the draught from the multiple bellows was 'pre-heated' before it reached the charcoal, and so a higher temperature was obtained. As a result, the product of African iron smelting was not the 'wrought iron' known in Europe and Asia, but a bloom of high-carbon steel, which was subsequently decarburized in the forge.[4] In some parts of Africa the same effect was produced without the use of bellows, by building furnaces three or four metres high with a shaft narrowing towards the top. Both of these processes can be described as innovations on the part of African metallurgists, and may very well have been developed in Egypt, where the necessary pyrotechnic skills were present at an early date. While it is true that the development of a significant iron industry came later in Egypt than in some neighbouring parts of Asia, this may have been due to the shortage of wood fuel in Egypt.[5]

In searching for the areas where iron-working may first have been practised in Saharan latitudes, one thinks first of the possible role of Meroe, and it is indeed the case that occasional iron objects such as light weapons and household tools have been found in graves which probably date from the seventh century BC. It is therefore likely that at least a small scale iron industry existed in Nubia from the time of the conquest of Egypt by the Twenty-Fifth Dynasty. Bronze, however, remained in more common use than iron until at least the fourth century BC, and there is certainly no reason to think that Meroe had any monopoly of the southward transmission of iron technology.[6] The Ethiopian possibilities look even less promising. Here, a bronze industry was introduced into the northern highlands by about the fifth century BC, occurring at the sites of early stone-built towns like Yeha and Matara. But iron working seems to have been slow in following, since even in the late first century AD the successor state of Aksum was importing iron weapons from the Red Sea trade described in the Alexandrian sailors' guide called the *Periplus of the Erythrean Sea*. Northern Libya, with its pronounced lack of tree cover, would not have been a promising environment for iron working, and a close reading of Herodotus suggests that in the fifth century BC the culture of eastern North Africa was still basically neolithic.[7] But the mountain massifs of the central Sahara – the Tibesti, the Hoggar, the Air – would have offered plentiful supplies both of ore and of fuel, as well as the existence of an early copper metallurgy. A site like that of Sekkiret, near Azelik in the Air highlands, where early iron-smelting furnaces (as yet undated) are found in the immediate vicinity of copper-smelting furnaces of the late second millennium BC, is an example of the kind of evidence which, when firmed up with some more radiocarbon dates, might prove to be of critical importance. The earliest attested date for an iron-working site anywhere to the south of the central Sahara is presently that at Do Dimmi, at the south-western end of the Air Plateau, and probably belongs to the early seventh century BC.[8]

One way of tracing the spread of iron-working is to study the comparative chronology of its appearance in different parts of the continent. In principle, this should be easier in the case of iron-working than of most other innovations because, wherever iron has been smelted, there should be the remains of a furnace, containing a deposit of slag as indestructible and as easily recognizable as a deposit of stone tools. Along with the slag, and preferably sealed beneath it, there should be charcoal, which is the best material for radiocarbon dating. The radiocarbon method, first invented in the 1950s, has been in standard use since the late 1960s, and there are now in existence several thousand dates from the Iron Age sites in Africa. While their interpretation is not a simple matter, since the possibility of several different kinds of errors has to be taken into account in each case, an overall picture is beginning to emerge, which shows most of the earliest dates occurring in North Africa, the Sahara and the sub-Saharan Sahel. The eastern equatorial belt has the next earliest dates, while those from the West African forest region, the Congo basin and the region immediately to the south of it are all more recent. In round figures, the spread of iron-working through the continent seems to have taken a little more than a thousand years, from about the seventh century BC till about the fourth century AD.

It seems most likely that iron-working spread from Saharan to Sahelian latitudes by at least three routes, of which the earliest may well have been one passing through the Air highlands into northern Nigeria. Certainly, one of the Sahelian areas richest in early Iron Age remains is the Jos plateau of north-eastern Nigeria and the lower-lying country immediately to the south of it. This first attracted attention in the 1940s, when open-cast tin-mining, following the lines of ancient stream courses which had been filled in by erosion, began to turn up terra cotta figures of men and animals, executed with great liveliness and panache, in a style which combined naturalness with touches of caricature. These early leads were vigorously pursued by Bernard Fagg, who as Nigeria's first Director of Antiquities successfully enlisted the support of the mining fraternity and collected the finds into a small museum of rare interest on the outskirts of Jos township. One of the finest examples was a broken-off human head obtained from a mining labourer who had been using it as a scarecrow. Thus far, however, the achievement was mainly one of organized treasure trove, for the deposits being worked by the tin-miners were simply the randomly assorted result of hydraulic action. Stone tools were found alongside terracotta, pottery and iron slag, and it was at first assumed that the 'Nok culture', as it came to be called, had straddled the Late Stone and early Iron Ages. Fagg's next concern was to find some undisturbed

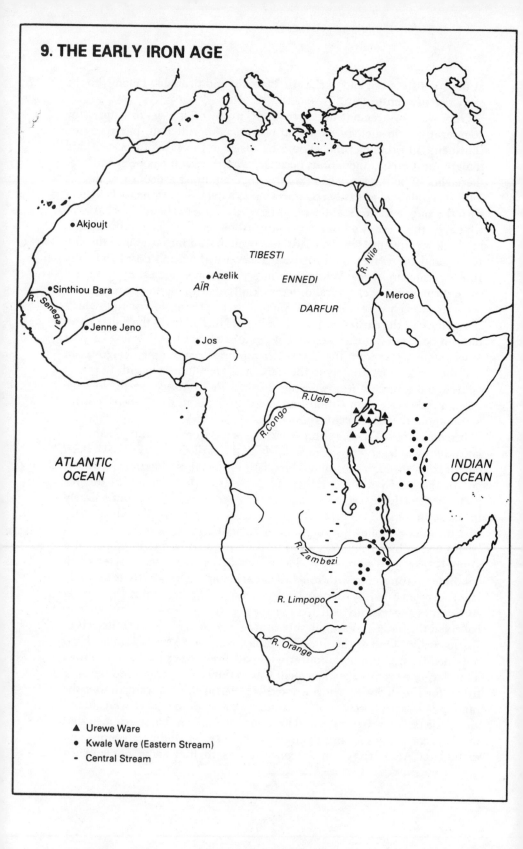

9. THE EARLY IRON AGE

TIBESTI

ENNEDI

AÏR

DARFUR

R. Nile

•Akjoujt

•Azelik

•Meroe

•Sinthiou Bara

R. Senegal

•Jenne Jeno

•Jos

R.Uele

R.Congo

ATLANTIC
OCEAN

INDIAN
OCEAN

R. Zambezi

R. Limpopo

R. Orange

▲ Urewe Ware

● Kwale Ware (Eastern Stream)

- Central Stream

occupation sites, and eventually these came to light in the Taruga valley and some other places below the escarpment, where it gradually became clear that the Nok culture was an exclusively Iron Age phenomenon, dating from about the sixth century BC until about the fourth century AD. Excavations at Taruga revealed some twenty concentrations of iron slag, mostly situated within the remains of smelting furnaces, and surrounded by dense accumulations of domestic pottery, grindstones and plentiful remains of iron tools and weapons, as well as by further examples of the characteristic pottery sculptures. The overall picture is one of a fairly dense agricultural population, which in the course of a millennium cleared enough of the natural woodland of the Jos plateau, whether for fields or for charcoal, to cause rapid alluvial erosion along the banks of streams and rivulets. The artistic tradition expressed in the sculptures was to ramify over much of central and southern Nigeria, where figures were normally made to represent the ancestors in family shrines in the courtyards of private dwellings. The archaeologist Thurstan Shaw has suggested that the Nok sculptures may have been placed in shrines at the edge of cultivation plots and there abandoned when the land went fallow, so that in time they were swept away by the seasonal floods and incorporated in alluvial deposits downstream from the original sites.[9]

A parallel and possibly somewhat later spread of iron-working from Saharan into Sahelian latitudes probably originated from the rich deposits of copper and iron of the Akjoujt region of southern Mauritania, where both metals may have been worked by about the fifth century BC.[10] It was perhaps from this direction that iron-working reached the seasonally inundated area to the west of the Niger bend, which is known as the inland delta of the Niger. Here the crucial evidence has been provided by the surveys and excavations of Roderick and Susan McIntosh near the modern town of Jenne, where the earliest settled occupation occurred around 250 BC. Iron was smelted from the first, despite the fact that ore, and possibly also fuel, had to be carried in from the Benedugu plateau thirty or forty miles to the south. The earliest inhabitants seem to have been fishermen and fowlers, who hunted crocodile and tortoises, as well as the game animals which came to the waterside to drink. By the first century AD, however, they were also farmers, specializing in the dry rice, *oryza glaberrima*, and their permanently sited mud-built villages and towns were beginning to rise on artificial mounds as old structures were replaced by new. These settlements reached their largest size between about AD 300 and about 800. The principal town, Jenne Jeno, covered an area of some 80 acres – somewhat larger than the modern city of Jenne, which has a population of around 10,000. By this time luxury ceramics were being produced, both highly burnished wares and others painted in polychrome, and some at least of the dead were being buried in large pottery urns.

Above all, the presence of many objects made of copper, and some of gold, indicates the importance of long-distance trade in the total economy. It seems likely that, through most of the first millennium AD, as certainly in later times, the inland delta of the Niger was producing dried fish, fish oil and cereals for consumption in the dry savanna and semi-desert areas far to the north. It seems that the Niger waterway was already a major artery of that trade, and therefore that the later trans-Saharan and intercontinental trade-routes developed in Islamic times were made possible by the pre-existence of a very considerable trading system within sub-Saharan West Africa.[11]

A similar conclusion emerges from the excavations by Thilmans and Ravissé of sites on and near the Senegal river, notably that of Sinthiou Bara between Podor and Bakel, where a mound of 67 acres, occupied from about the fifth till about the eleventh century AD, shows the development of a very sophisticated iron-working technology, including *repoussé* work, *cire perdué* casting and wire-drawing. This is coupled with evidence of long-distance trade extending from the Atlantic coast to the Niger bend on one axis and from the Maghrib to the middle Senegal on the other. The inhabitants of Sinthiou Bara made two rather character-istic pottery wares, both of which show a distribution covering about 150 miles of the Senegal valley and suggest that Sinthiou Bara was the metropolis of an economic and political system more or less coterminous with the pottery. Seen in the light of this well documented situation on the middle Senegal, the otherwise rather bare discovery of a 'pre-urban' occupation of the putative site of the capital of ancient Ghana at Koumbi Saleh in southern Mauritania, which is dated to the fifth century AD, acquires a wider significance. The claims reported by later Muslim historians to the effect that the Ghana kingdom originated well before the beginning of the Muslim era begin to look much more plausible than before.[12]

In West Africa south of the savanna zone there are as yet no Iron Age dates earlier than the second half of the first millennium AD. Taken at face value, the evidence presently available would suggest that iron-working spread into the forest region only around the sixth or seventh century AD, when iron technology in the savanna had already reached a sophisticated stage in which welding, wire-drawing and casting were well understood. It could be, of course, that the evidence is biased by the fact that, within the forest zone, so much of the archaeological effort has been concentrated on a few sites like Ife and Benin, selected by reason of their known importance during the early part of the present millennium. All the same, these are large sites, and it seems unlikely that evidence of earlier occupation, had it existed, would have completely escaped atten-tion. It may be, therefore, that the simple hypothesis is valid, that only when an Iron Age agricultural system had thoroughly established itself in the savanna, did its practitioners have the incentive to penetrate the forest, at least in any large numbers. It may be, for example, that after a thousand years of selective deforestation of the slower-burning hardwood trees of the savanna, new sources of fuel had to be exploited. At two pounds of charcoal for every pound of iron ore in the furnace, consumption of wood could have reached levels that changed whole landscapes. It has been calculated that half a million tons of hardwood would have been necessary to create the slag-heaps of Meroe.[13] Again, it is known from pollen analysis that the shores of Lake Victoria were heavily forested until about 500 BC, whereas today there are only a few quite small patches of forest from which pollen could be blown into the lake. Since there has been no significant change of climate within that period, the change may have been caused as much by the need for charcoal as by clearance for farming.[14] Or, it may have been only as iron technology progressed, both in smelting and in forging, that heavier tools such as axes and billhooks became available for the large scale clearance needed for significant penetration of the forest by Iron Age farmers.

At all events, the comparatively late spread of iron-working within the West African forest region needs to be remembered when turning to consider the early Iron Age of Africa below the equator. It has been said (above, pp. 46–9) that the Bantu languages which predominate in this area are of Niger-Congo, that is to say, of West African origin, and that the first part of their spread must have been due to the expansion of Stone Age fishermen-farmers into and round the equatorial forest which covers the northern half of the Congo basin. The knowledge of iron-working reached them, or some of them, at a time when they were already widely dispersed both within the Congo forest and along its northern margins. Barring an independent invention of iron smelting without a previous knowledge of copper metallurgy, it can only have reached them from the north. It could have been, though only indirectly, from the Meroitic kingdom. Or it could have been by some route intermediate between the Chad basin and the upper Nile – perhaps one following the iron-stone plateau of the Ennedi and Darfur highland areas which form the watershed between these two basins. Archaeological evidence from Ennedi and Darfur is still very slight. All we can say is that the first Bantu groups to receive the knowledge of iron-working were those living along both sides of the western Rift Valley, which forms the borderland between modern Uganda on the one side and north-eastern Zaire on the other. This is where the earliest Iron Age dates in Bantu Africa have been found.

The archaeological hall-mark of the early Iron Age in the inter-lacustrine region is a type of pottery with bevelled rims, dimpled bases and a very distinctive range of channelled decoration in festoons and spirals, known after the place of its first discovery as Urewe ware. It has been found in every major segment of the region – around the northern and western shores of Lake Victoria, at the north end of Lake Albert, all down the line of the western Rift to Lake Tanganyika, in Burundi and Rwanda – but always in the moister micro-environments provided by river lines, lakeshores and mountain valleys. Its distribution suggests that it was made by people accustomed to fishing and riparian farming in fairly heavily wooded country. Urewe pottery is invariably associated with the signs of iron-working – slag, charcoal, tuyères and furnaces. In some parts of the region furnaces were built of specially designed wedge-shaped bricks, which could be re-used from one smelting operation to the next. All in all, the idea that the first Iron Age farmers of the interlacustrine region were Bantu-speakers expanding from, say, the upper Uele region of northern Zaire, whose ancestors had there, or thereabouts, made the transition from Stone Age to early Iron Age food production, has much to recommend it.[15] The most serious of the outstanding problems is that of dates. While the overwhelming majority of radiocarbon tests from sites with Urewe pottery have shown results between the first and the seventh centuries AD, there remains a small but obstinate minority of BC dates from north-western Tanzania and Rwanda, which, despite re-testing, refuse to go away. Half a dozen of them are dates in the first half of the first millennium BC. If they are to be accepted, it can only be on the hypothesis of an independent invention of iron smelting in this region. In the opinion of most experts such a hypothesis is too improbable to be adopted without much more controlling evidence from nearby areas. On the other hand, dates going back to the first two or three centuries BC would make good sense.[16]

Whatever the truth about the starting date for the early Iron Age in the interlacustrine region, there is agreement that Urewe ware looks like the parent form of most of the early Iron Age pottery traditions which developed in the rest of Africa to the south of the equator. For some reason the dimpled bases of Urewe ware did not spread beyond the region of origin, and its typical channelled decoration is only found in the region immediately to the south, in southern Zaire and western Zambia. But the vessel shapes, the necks and the everted and bevelled rims occur throughout the subcontinent, always in connection with the earliest practice of iron-working, and with the earliest dates forming a chronological sequence which runs broadly from north to south. The geographical deployment seems on present evidence to have been most rapid directly to the south of the interlacustrine region in southern Zaire and western Zambia. Southern Zaire with its great system of parallel river valleys which descend from the Congo-Zambezi watershed towards the central Congo basin, was a region highly favourable to early Iron Age settlement. The rivers were well stocked with fish. The watershed was rich in copper and iron, and there was plenty of fuel for smelting in the forest galleries which lined the rivers. Flowing water, alluvium and therefore agricultural opportunity was greatest on the northern side of the watershed, but there were extensive grazing lands to the south of it, between the more widely spaced tributaries of the upper Zambezi. It seems almost certain that it was by this route that early Iron Age settlers brought the first sheep and cattle to be introduced into southern Africa. These were not, of course, the great herds built up by the specialized pastoralists of later times, but rather the one or two head of cattle and the half dozen sheep and goats with which early farmers shared their simple homesteads. The middens excavated by Brian Fagan at the mound sites around Kalomo in central Zambia showed that in the lowest layers the bones of domestic stock were greatly outnumbered by those of wild game. Only during the passage of several centuries were the proportions gradually reversed. Nevertheless, the very earliest pottery-bearing sites in Zambia, which occur in the Zambezi valley upstream of the Victoria Falls and which have yielded radiocarbon dates from the third to the first century BC, show the presence of some cattle, and it was most likely from somewhere in this region that cattle and sheep gradually passed into the hands of Khoi hunter-gatherers living in the plains of northern Botswana, where the environment would have been too dry to attract vegetable food-producers to follow them.[17]

Meanwhile, this central stream of early Iron Age culture was being paced by another more easterly one, which spread all down through the region between the Rift Valley and the Indian Ocean coast. Here, the variant of early Iron Age pottery is known as Kwale ware, from a type-site in the Shimba hills behind Mombasa, and its earliest dates are in the first and second centuries AD. So far as can be seen at present, the typical environment for a Kwale ware site would be one situated on the lower slopes of the mountain chain that forms the rim of the East African interior plateau. It would seem that early Iron Age farmers sought out first and foremost the deep, fertile soils below mountain escarpments, and the margins of the forests which formerly covered the upper slopes of the mountain ranges and the great massifs of Kilimanjaro and Mount Kenya. In Kenya and Tanzania the manufacture of Kwale ware pottery did not extend quite to the Indian Ocean coast, where it was perhaps forestalled by another set of ceramic and metallurgical traditions deriving from the Cushitic-speaking region of modern Somalia. Further south, however, in Mozambique, ceramic traditions closely related to Kwale ware certainly did penetrate the coastal plain. Indeed, the very rapid southward spread of early Iron Age settlements through this region, covering more than a thousand miles in less than two hundred years, could be best explained in terms of an initial dispersion of fishermen-farmers down the ocean coast, followed by the inland penetration of southern Malawi and eastern Zimbabwe by ascending the river valleys.[18] In general, the sites associated with this eastern stream of early Iron Age culture do not show any signs of cattle-keeping. Only to the south of the lower Limpopo valley, in Natal and the eastern Transvaal, do sites normally attributed to the eastern stream show the existence of pastoral food production, and this is probably to be explained by contact in these latitudes with sources of cattle derived from the central stream. This fusion of the eastern and central streams probably dated from either the fifth or sixth century AD. Although we still lack early central-stream sites in southern Africa to connect the earliest Iron Age of the upper Zambezi with that of the fifth century Transvaal, the seventh century saw the appearance in eastern Botswana of what must almost be called specialized pastoralism, visible in the 250 sites of the Toutswe tradition, characterized by circular dwellings arranged around cattle enclosures. This would argue a very considerable increase in the original breeding stock introduced into the region about one thousand years before.[19]

The least known segment of southern Africa is that to the south of the lower Congo, comprising the modern territories of Angola, Namibia and the western Cape province. Here, at least as far south as the Kunene, one must trust the evidence of linguistic classification, which shows that the languages spoken in the area belong to the western division of Bantu, with its centre in the Congo forest (above, p. 46). This should mean that there was at least a brief period of Stone Age food production before iron-working spread in from the east. Such a period does in fact seem to be authenticated by the meagre archaeological evidence, which shows the existence of a ceramic Late Stone Age on the lower Congo, dating from about the fourth century BC. By contrast, Iron Age dates in this area seem to be as late as the fourth century AD, and evidence of a connection with the central stream comes from the Urewe-like pottery dug from a mining site at Tshikapa on the lower Kasai.[20] Most of the southern part of the region, however, was too arid ever to attract farming settlement and therefore continued to be occupied by Khoisan, some practising a pastoral way of life with herds of cattle and sheep, while others were hunters and gatherers.

All in all, it may be said that the coming of the Iron Age produced most of the essential characteristics of village life still recognizable in the rural parts of Africa today. Although the overall population of early Iron Age Africa would have been infinitely sparser than any in recent times, the size and appearance of a rural village might not have been very different. There would have been the same round houses, with walls of wattle and daub and conical roofs of thatch. In the savanna belt of sub-Saharan Africa there was already a tendency for some villages to grow into walled towns, which endured for long periods on the same sites. In West Africa this pattern of settlement was carried even into parts of the forest belt, and wherever urban life became established, townsmen would be prepared to meet the needs of shifting agriculture by sending some members of the family to work on quite distant farms, where they would bivouac in temporary shelters for as long as necessary. In eastern Africa, by comparison, all settlements seem to have been quite temporary. The archaeological record suggests that few sites were occupied for longer than a decade. Nevertheless, it would seem that during the early part of the Iron Age villages, though far apart, tended to be larger and more compact than they were to become in later Iron Age times, when the growing importance of stock-raising caused a much more equal spread of homesteads across the landscape.

It becomes steadily more apparent that, even during the early Iron Age, there was a great difference between the parts of Africa to the north and south of the equatorial forest belt, in the extent of local trade in bulk commodities. North of the forest, the steady gradation of climate from moist to dry must have provided a great stimulus to the exchange of foodstuffs between the different zones. These would have included salt from the desert, meat and hides from the Sahel, grains from the savanna, fish from the rivers and the sea coast, yams and palm-oil from the forest margin and kola from the forest itself. But the success of the exchange process depended greatly on the means of transport available, and it was the existence of beasts of burden on the one hand, and on the other hand of some long lines of navigable waterways crossing the various climatic zones, which chiefly differentiated the two parts of the continent. Donkeys had been in use in the Sahel since at least the third millennium BC. Camels spread into the desert latitudes from east to west from about the fifth century BC, reaching southern Tunisia by the second century BC and the Atlantic seaboard not much later.[21] Among easily navigable waterways, the Nile crossed all the climatic zones from the forest to the desert, the Niger flowed from the forest of Guinea to the desert margin at Timbuktu and south again to the forest belt of Nigeria. The Chari and Logone rose in the equatorial forest and flowed to Sahelian latitudes in Lake Chad. In Africa below the equator there were no comparable opportunities except along the Indian Ocean coast. In the interior the prevalence of the tsetse fly prevented the use of beasts of burden, and the rivers flowed in broadly latitudinal directions. Only the southern tributaries of the Congo and the northern tributaries of the Zambezi crossed climatic zones partially corresponding to the forest and savanna belts of northern Africa. In these circumstances only a few items like salt, copper, gold and ivory were valuable enough to justify the costs of head transport. Not until cattle-keeping became a major and comparatively specialized occupation during the later Iron Age was there much scope for the local exchange of foodstuffs which would stimulate the formation of larger and more complex societies.

CHAPTER 7

PEOPLES OF THE BOOK

It seems that for a religion and a religious culture to become widespread, and yet to maintain some cohesion, there must be a written tradition, so that people who will never meet in the flesh may absorb the same fundamental ideas by using as nearly as possible the same words. Translation from one language to another need not be an impediment, provided that it is the translation of written texts. Literacy may be confined to a small minority of those who participate. Oral exposition in unwritten languages may be the means by which the culture is transmitted to the majority of the adherents, provided that almost every local community has its literate élite, capable of handling the written texts and sufficiently mobile to keep touch with their opposite numbers in neighbouring communities and so respond to movements of change and development within the system as a whole. The written word exercises its control not only through space but through time. Inspiration and genius can speak to future generations, and, especially where the literate are few and the means of copying tedious, the archaic text acquires a sanctity which it is difficult for modern minds to appreciate. There are in these circumstances only a few key texts, and people know them almost by heart. Literacy is very close to mnemonics. But until the invention of printing, that is how the great religions were transmitted. What is little realized is that, already between about 500 BC and about AD 1000, nearly half of Africa came under the influence of one or more of three related traditions of this kind.

The earliest of the three to enter the African scene was Judaism, which established itself along the Greek and Carthaginian trade routes to the south of the Mediterranean, as it did to the north. Jewish communities were found in every seaport town, but were by no means confined to the coast. A well-known collection of papyri and pottery shards with Aramaic writing, which were found on Elephantine Island in the Nile near Aswan, show that as early as the fifth century BC a Jewish community in this remote Nubian frontier-post was prosperous enough to support a temple of the same size and design as that of Solomon in Jerusalem.[1] Later, the Ptolemaic regime in Egypt proved especially attractive to Jewish immigrants, who occupied two populous and largely self-governing quarters of Alexandria, but also spread right across the country. Philo, the great Jewish philosopher of Alexandria, whose life straddled the turn of the Christian era, estimated the numbers at a million, more than a tenth of the entire population of Egypt.[2] Clearly, such a scale of adherence was not due to migration alone. Judaism in pre-Christian and pre-Islamic times was a much more outgoing religion than it has since become, making many converts by intermarriage with the local Egyptians and many more by the sheer attraction of its monotheistic faith and moral standards. It was in Egypt during the third century BC that the Hebrew scriptures were translated into Greek as the Septuagint. This in itself shows a faith reaching out to the gentiles and creating not only converts but also a large class of 'God-fearing' fellow travellers of the kind referred to in almost every chapter of the Acts of the Apostles. Again, the distant outreach of pre-Christian Judaism is illustrated by the story of the eunuch treasurer of Candace, the queen-mother of Meroe, who was overtaken by the evangelist Philip as he drove along the Gaza road in his chariot reading the book of Isaiah.[3] It has even been seriously suggested that the Judaic influences so strong in later Ethiopian Christianity may have reached that region in pre-Christian times by the Nile route.[4]

In North Africa to the west of Egypt and Cyrenaica, Jewish communities were established in all the main Carthaginian settlements, where their presence is attested by the remains of synagogues and cemeteries, often with Hebrew inscriptions.[5] As trade with the interior developed in Graeco-Roman times, Jewish merchants spread first into the high plains of central Algeria and Morocco, where the sedentary Berbers of Numidia and Mauritania produced large export crops of corn and olive oil. Later, when the Saharan Berbers took to camel-breeding and developed trade routes across the desert, Jewish traders settled in the oases to the south of the Atlas, where the trans-Saharan caravans had their northern assembly points. Later still, and probably only in Muslim times, a few of them followed the caravans across the desert and established themselves in the towns on its southern side. From each of these numerous nuclei there was doubtless some radiation, through intermarriage, conversion and simple imitation of Jewish beliefs and customs. Just sufficient traces of Judaism were implanted to give rise to a 'lost tribes' literature, first in Arabic, then in Portuguese and latterly in French, suggesting that whole Berber or even Sudanese tribes were of Jewish origin. This literature has been analysed by the Hebrew scholar H. Z. Hirschberg and found to be uniformly worthless.[6] Since the Exodus at least, Jews have not been given to migrating in tribes, and Judaism, unlike Christianity, never undertook missions to the heathen of the kind which could result in the mass conversion of ethnic groups. The fact remains that by early in the Christian era Judaism was widespread in small pockets, not merely along the southern shores of the Mediterranean, but deep into Saharan latitudes, all the way from the Red Sea to the Atlantic. Certainly, it must have acted as a preparation for both of the monotheistic traditions which followed in its footsteps. Wherever Judaism was practised, there at the very least the concept of the 'book' containing revealed truth would become familiar to a wide circle. And, still more perhaps, the idea of a universal community which had conquered distance, and of which the scattered members were always in touch with each other through the written word, and had a constantly remembered place of pilgrimage in Jerusalem, was of lasting significance.

* * *

If Judaism spread through northern Africa as the religion of the trade route and the market place, Christianity was in contrast essentially the religion of the settled, food-producing countryside. Of course, it had its urban bases, and in the absence of any direct evidence about the first two centuries of its existence, it must be assumed that, as in the lands to the north of the Mediterranean, the first Christians were recruited in the Jewish synagogues of the towns by the preaching of the proposition that Jesus was the Messiah foretold in the Jewish scriptures. Always and everywhere that proposition led swiftly to a division of the worshipping community, the 'new way' attracting a minority of the ethnic Jews, but a majority of the gentile fellow travellers, who thereafter tended to be strongly anti-Semitic in their outlook. In fact, the earliest Christian papyri recovered from the sands of Egypt, and dating to the early second century, include a so-called *Letter of Barnabas*, the author of which was probably an early convert from the synagogue of Alexandria and wrote in fanatically anti-Judaic terms. When the curtain next rises upon the Egyptian scene at the end of the same century, it shows first and foremost the catechetical school of Alexandria, directed by Pantaenus and later by Clement, inspiring a strongly missionary church that was aiming its message at the educated Greek-speakers of the city. A century later, however, Christianity was flooding into the countryside and causing, or coinciding with, a massive desertion of the traditional Egyptian religion. The old Egyptian priesthood was foundering for lack of recruits. Hieroglyphic studies were dying out. Mummification was being abandoned along with the offering of grave-goods. A peasantry that was beginning to be largely literate was turning to the Christian church, with its Coptic translation of the Bible, helping to build basilicas in the villages and to endow ecclesiastical foundations.[7] The great persecution of Diocletian, beginning in 303, found the Church supplying martyrs by the hundred, not only in Alexandria, but far away to the south in upper Egypt, where the ecclesiastical historian Eusebius himself witnessed mass executions by beheading, burning and dismemberment, and remarked that, such was the prevailing enthusiasm of the believers, that 'no sooner had the first batch been sentenced, than others from every side would jump onto the platform in front of the judge and proclaim themselves Christians.'[8]

Persecution accentuated one religious tendency, in which Egyptian Christianity led the rest of the world. Since early times in Egypt, it had been a classic response of those who felt oppressed by law-givers or tax-gatherers to retreat into the desert and seek freedom at the price of extreme asceticism. It was hardly a way of life for the family man, but for the mystic, as for the outlaw, it held some attractions. One did not need to walk a great distance from the Nile valley to find solitude, and a community life of a monastic kind could be established in any of the countless ruined villages that littered the desert margin. Moreover, asceticism attracted the veneration of the Egyptian peasantry, so that one could live in the desert, be seen once or twice a year by the riverside, and still exert a real influence on society at large. It was in these circumstances that monasticism developed – the eremitical kind represented by Saint Anthony during the second half of the third century, the coenobitic kind by Saint Pachomius during the early fourth. By the outbreak of Diocletian's persecution, the desert was already well populated with hermits. By the time of Constantine's conversion in 325, Pachomius and others were engaged in founding the first organized monastic communities. Once Christianity had become the established religion of the Roman empire, there was no longer any reason for monasteries to be hidden from the public view, and by the end of the fourth century some had become the proprietors of vast landed estates, extending a highly valued protection to countless peasant families against the rising claims of tax-gatherers and civil landlords. Nevertheless, for many monks the spiritual attraction of the desert persisted, and the monastic proprietors of the river valley were complemented by great numbers of desert hermits and coenobites, who strengthened the opposition of the Coptic-speaking majority of the population to the Greek-speaking élite of the towns.

This opposition had an important theological dimension. For whatever reason, the monks of Egypt (and also of Syria) had from the first espoused a doctrine of Christ which placed the greatest possible emphasis on his divinity, and came near to denying that he had a human nature. In the words of the leading western authority on the Monophysite movement, the monks, 'in perpetual warfare against the demons on the edge of the desert, and haunted by sub-conscious fears of vengeance from the old, dispossessed national gods . . . demanded as their protection the full armour of Christ'. And so, when the orthodox theologians of Rome and Constantinople agreed at the Council of Chalcedon in 451 that Christ was to be worshipped 'in two natures inseparably united', the Monophysite opposition contended, not it would seem unreasonably, that though Christ could be 'out of two natures', he could not be *in* two natures. 'How can Christ incarnate die in two natures?' asked Severus, Bishop of Antioch. 'Which nature was nailed to the Cross?' The depth of feeling involved is perhaps best conveyed in the slogan of the Egyptian bishops at Chalcedon, which said 'Throw out the Nestorians. Christ is God.'[9] Although there was no actual schism for another eighty years, the Church in Egypt and Syria was rent into parties, one representing broadly the Greek-speaking clergy of the cities, who wished above all to keep in line with the orthodoxy of east and west, and the other the Coptic- and Syriac-speaking clergy of the countryside. For a time it remained possible for bishops to be elected from either persuasion. But when in the early sixth century Justin I and then his successor Justinian turned to persecution, driving Monophysite bishops out of their sees, the reaction was swift. All down the eastern frontier of the empire there occurred a mass exodus of Monophysite monks and clergy, who became a missionary force as potent for a time as any the world has seen.[10] The exiles, inevitably, ordained a rival clergy, unrecognized by the Orthodox. There thus came into existence a separate Monophysite (or Jacobite) Church, which infiltrated back across the imperial frontier and eventually made its centre in Egypt under a Coptic Patriarch of Alexandria. It was to this allegiance that the vast majority of the Christians of northeastern Africa henceforward belonged.

Looking beyond the borders of Egypt, the Ethiopian kingdom of Aksum, which had emerged as a vigorously expanding political entity around the first century AD, had its first encounter with Christianity in the fourth century, well before the Monophysite schism. This was a case of a faith spreading from a commercial contact. The material prosperity of Aksum certainly derived from its control of the trade routes leading down from the interior to the Red Sea port of Adulis, the modern Massawa. The sixth century Byzantine historian, Rufinus, tells how, in the early fourth century, an Alexandrian Christian merchant, bound for India, was shipwrecked on the Aksumite coast. His two sons were taken as captives to the king's court and became the Greek-speaking tutors of the royal children. Their local significance was that they spoke the language and practised the religion of the dominant external power. One of them was eventually permitted to travel home to Alexandria, where he was consecrated bishop by the Patriarch Athanasius. He returned to initiate the conversion of the Aksumite court. The real take-off of Ethiopian Christianity, however, occurred two centuries later, with the arrival of the 'nine Saints', a mission composed of Monophysite monks, bearing mainly Syrian names, who brought with them for translation into the local language scriptures and liturgy which were evidently in Syriac rather than Coptic, but who nevertheless established monasteries based on the Egyptian rule of Saint

Pachomius, and who did nothing to alter the ecclesiastical authority of the Alexandrian patriarch.

Thus received, Christianity soon acquired a local momentum and became the religion of the settled farming population of the Ethiopian highlands. It was a religion held together, and transmitted from one generation to another, by monks, most of whom lived in rather inaccessible places, on mountain pinnacles or lacustrine islands, where biblical and liturgical studies could be pursued with the least disturbance from secular events. It is a common fallacy of western Christians to suppose that a religious tradition can only be established and carried on by a clergy operating within a defined parochial system, whereas monasteries exist only for their own members. In the Monophysite world, as in much of eastern Orthodoxy, monasteries were the central institutions of the faith. From them the monks went out to preach and to convert. To them the faithful repaired at great festivals and in times of personal need. Where conditions are really rough, people go to the Church, wherever it is to be found, and leave their first-born there to be trained in its service. It is only in conditions of relative affluence that the parson is expected to call at the house. In medieval Ethiopia, the Church expanded alongside the expansion of the Christian state, sometimes leading the way, sometimes following in the wake of victorious armies. But always its expansion depended on the process of segmentation whereby lively monasteries produced daughter foundations. For a Benedict, a Columba or a Bernard there would have been no problem in comprehending the process.

In Nubia the spread of Christianity up the Nile from Egypt had perhaps begun on a small scale sometime in the fifth century. All this vast area, once the kingdom of Meroe, had been overrun during the fourth century by Nuba peoples from west of the Nile, who had divided it into three comparatively barbarian kingdoms of Nobatia, Makurra and Alwa, which were known and feared for their swift-moving cavalry forces, armed with bows as well as swords, and equipped with the earliest bits, bridles and spurs to be used anywhere in Africa. The subjects of these kingdoms lived by riparian agriculture and fishing, but their rulers got wealth by the slave trade, by slave-worked gold and copper mines, and by raiding the rich cities of upper Egypt. Between the Nile and the Red Sea, the nomadic Beja camel-breeders were the caravan drivers of an overland trade route running straight across the eastern desert from the First to the Fifth Cataract, which provided a direct link between Egypt and the southern-most kingdom of Alwa. Around the middle of the sixth century the evangelization of these Nubian kingdoms took a wholly new direction and impetus as a result of the competition between the emperor Justinian and his Monophysite empress, Theodora. In 542 a Monophysite monk, Julian, persuaded Theodora to send him as a missionary to Silko, king of Nobatia.

Not to be outdone, Justinian despatched an Orthodox mission of his own, which, finding Nobatia pre-empted, moved on to the kingdom of Makurra. Some forty years later, the leader of the Monophysite church in Nobatia by-passed Makurra by using the desert route, to establish a mission in Alwa. The outline of the story comes from the contemporary historian, John of Ephesus. Recent years, however, have seen the excavation of two five-aisled metropolitan cathedrals – that of Nobatia at Faras, and that of Alwa at Soba, twenty miles up the Blue Nile from Khartoum. At Soba only the ground plan can be recovered, as every reusable brick has been robbed. But at Faras scores of splendid frescoes were uncovered, together with several inscriptions and a list of 27 bishops who succeeded each other in the see.[11]

The picture that emerges, at least of the Nobatian church, is of one that, despite its Monophysite theology, followed Byzantine rather than Alexandrian models, the kings in priestly orders and the bishops holding offices of state. The liturgical languages were Greek and Nubian, not Coptic. The practice of pilgrimage to Jerusalem, continued well into Muslim times, helped to keep alive the sense of wider Christian links. And, strangely enough, the coming of Islam to Egypt at first made little difference to Christianity in Nubia, which seems to have reached the height of its material prosperity and its artistic inspiration between the eighth and the twelfth centuries. Here, then, a Christian culture successfully established itself in Saharan and sub-Saharan latitudes, as the religion of rulers and peasants living alongside a navigable waterway. In the end it was overtaken by Islam, which first encircled and finally suffocated it, with a culture that was equally at home among traders and nomads.

In North Africa, the connection between Christianity and the settled life, whether of the towns or of the intensely farmed parts of the countryside, was likewise apparent. Nothing at all is known of it before AD 180, when the spectacular martyrdom of Speratus inspired the pen of the propagandist Tertullian, but presumably it sprang from the synagogues, as it did elsewhere. The Roman connection was regular and strong. The literary language of the faith was Latin, not Greek. The period of widespread evangelization began in the third century, and it quickly extended from the towns to the countryside, to embrace not only the Romano-Punic population of the Tunisian plain, but also the settled Berbers growing corn and olives on the high plateau of Numidia and Mauritania. As in Egypt, an antipathy developed between the rural and the urban Christians, but in this case it had no basis in monasticism or even in theology.[12] The sole issue of principle was disciplinary: it concerned the procedure for re-admitting to communion those who had lapsed during the great persecution of the early fourth century. The latitudinarians were the Latin-speakers of the towns. The rigorists were the Berbers of the countryside, known after the name of their leader as Donatists. These ordained their own clergy, and evolved a pattern of parochial organization in which the typical rural church was built around a martyr's shrine. Throughout the fourth century both systems grew side by side and with almost equal success. The record of a conference held in 411 at Carthage in a vain attempt to end the schism lists 286 Catholic and 284 Donatist bishops who participated, and provides the principal evidence for the geographical distribution of the two persuasions.[13]

Less than twenty years after this event, however, North African Christianity suffered the first of two onslaughts which were to make it impotent to resist the subsequent spread of Islam. In 429 a horde of 80,000 Vandals crossed the Straits of Gibraltar from Spain and ravaged their way eastwards to Carthage, where they established a principality that lasted just over a century. The Vandals were Arian Christians, and this gave them the excuse to burn the churches and seize the wealth of Catholic and Donatist alike. The Catholics of the cities suffered worst, and many of the leaders emigrated to Italy. The remainder lived under constant harrassment. But the gravest consequence of the Vandal irruption was the breakdown of the southern frontier of Roman North Africa. The nomadic Berbers, particularly the camel-riding Lewata from the desert margin, broke in upon the olive orchards and the barley fields where the Donatist population was densest. The nomads helped to overthrow the Vandals and to prepare the way for a brief Byzantine reconquest of the coastlands during the sixth century. But the spread of Christian culture into the interior had been irrevocably halted. The future lay with the religion that could command the allegiance of the warrior and the nomad.[14]

* * *

In a very simple form, probably known best as *din Allah*, 'the religion of God', Islam was present in Africa from 639, when the Arab armies invaded Egypt and defeated the Byzantine garrison. However, this was at least a century before the development of a literary tradition in Arabic, and nearly two centuries before the earliest written codifications of the *Shari'a*, the law of Islam, and the Koran, the book of God, which contains the truths revealed to the Prophet Muhammad. The *din Allah*, then, was purely an oral tradition, not yet defined and guarded by any class of learned specialists, something to be seen almost as an aspect of the military discipline imparted by the commanders to their Arab soldiers, the *muhajirun*, and to the local levies, the *mawali*, recruited among the conquered peoples. Certainly, no picture could be more false than that which long prevailed in western Christendom of a creed imposed upon the subjected at the point of the sword. Early Islam in Egypt and North Africa was the religious practice of the military camp, in which allies, concubines, wives and children were included as a privilege consequent upon their association with the ruling race. When Islam eventually became a religion of the book, other 'people of the book', Christians and Jews, were specifically excluded from the operations of the holy war, *jihad*, which was practised more to get slaves than to gain converts. Jihad was the perpetual state of hostility which must always exist at the barbarian frontiers of Islam, which was the realm of submission and therefore of peace.

The development of Islam as a potentially universal religion, capable of absorbing non-Arabs in large numbers, followed only after the emergence of Arabic as a literary language during the first half of the eighth century. It happened only after the centre of Arab military and political power had shifted away from Arabia, first to Syria and then to Iraq. Few of the first men of Arabic letters were themselves Arabs by birth. Most were descended from the educated Greeks or Persians enslaved in the wars of conquest, who were recruited as bureaucrats by the Umayyad and Abbasid caliphs for their knowledge of earlier systems of law and administration. It is increasingly widely recognized by modern Islamicists that the way these men went to work was by codifying the law and custom of their own times and then authenticating their findings by attributing them to the oral tradition handed down from the Prophet and his contemporaries. The literary culture of Islam was thus a much more sophisticated and broad-based system than could ever have emerged from the seventh century Hijaz, and it was only after it had reached this form that men of learning began to migrate to Egypt and Tunisia to establish schools of theology and law capable of attracting an educated Christian population into the Islamic fold. The crucial figure for Egypt was the jurist al-Shafi'i, who settled in the garrison town of Fustat, the modern Cairo, in 814. The Shafi'ite school grew into one of the four orthodox (Sunni) systems for the study of Islamic law. Another system, the Malikite, established its main African base in Kairouan, the garrison town of Ifriqiya, comprising Tunisia, Tripolitania and eastern Algeria. Between them, these two schools produced most of the learned men, or *ulama*ʿ, on whom the unity of orthodox Islam came to depend. Pupils came to them from all sides, and eventually returned to their home areas as judges and schoolmasters who spread Islamic culture throughout northern and western Africa.[15]

Meanwhile, during the eighth and ninth centuries proselytization spread gradually from the garrisons to the slave soldiers, from the Arab governors to the locally recruited clerks and officials, from the masters to the servants, and from originally nomadic Arab pastoral migrants (*beduin*) to their Christian farming neighbours. In Egypt, Coptic Christianity survived mostly in the towns. In the rest of North Africa, known henceforward as the Maghrib, the Arab west, it scarcely survived the conquest. The Catholics of the coast continued to emigrate to Europe. The

Donatists of the interior plateau became Muslims like their nomadic neighbours. The great practical superiority of Islam over Christianity in the African context was in its power to appeal beyond the farmer and the townsman to the merchant and the nomad. Here, orthodoxy in the early stages counted for little. Precisely because of its inaccessibility, the Maghrib became a refuge for every kind of Muslim dissenter, or Kharijite, most of whom claimed kinship with those who had been thrust aside in the Umayyad seizure of the caliphate in AD 659. Such, in particular, were the Ibadis, who came from southern Iraq and established a series of settlements in the northern fringes of the Sahara from Tripoli westwards to the Atlantic, of which the political centre was the little mountain state of Tahert in the eastern Atlas. With their eastern connections, the Ibadis were well set to develop the new east-west trade routes which sprang up in the wake of the Arab conquests. From their vantage-points at the termini of the desert caravan routes, they were also well placed to feed into these routes the commodities of the trans-Saharan trade, above all the trade in slaves. The Ibadis made their converts among the nomadic Berbers whose camels supplied the transport for the caravans. And before long they accompanied them on their journeys to the south. The first Muslim communities to be established in, or to the south of the desert during the ninth century were those of the Ibadi traders. Such were the origins of West African Islam.[16]

The trans-Saharan slave trade was, in fact, the key to the politics of medieval North Africa. Slaves were required first and foremost as soldiers. Locally recruited slave soldiers enabled small groups of immigrants, like the Ibadis, to create small states, some of which later grew larger. They also enabled the imperial governors of the Muslim caliphate to make themselves independent of the authority which had appointed them. From the early ninth century a family of Abbasid governors, the Aghlabids, made themselves virtually independent as sultans of Ifriqiya. They did this by building up an army of bought slaves, of which the early recruits were mostly Berbers from the Aures and Kabyle mountains, but the later ones mostly blacks from across the Sahara. In Egypt it was the same story. In 868 Ahmad b. Tulun came as one of a long series of Abbasid governors, but succeeded in establishing a nearly independent principality by building up an army of black slaves from the Nilotic Sudan and white ones from Greece and Turkey. But the outstanding example of political power based on bought slaves was that of the Fatimids. Beginning as an obscure family of refugee Shi'ites in the caravan town of Sijilmasa in southern Morocco, the Fatimids built up enough military power, first to displace the Aghlabids in Ifriqiya, and then to conquer Egypt, where they established a dynasty which brought that country to the very pinnacle of its medieval prosperity and splendour. This was important for all of Muslim Africa, because Egypt was the nodal point not only of the east-west trade routes, but also of the pilgrim traffic passing through to Mecca and Medina. The Fatimids were Shi'ite heretics, but for Africa that scarcely signified. What the pilgrims remembered, apart from the sheer expense of staying in Cairo, was the resplendent image of a theocratic monarchy established in a palace city – a model for every aspiring potentate or courtier from either north or south of the Sahara.

The trans-Saharan slave trade was only one symptom of a growing circulation of people and ideas which by about the eleventh century had come to affect nearly every part of Africa north of the moist savannas and the Nile swamps – everywhere, in fact, where beasts of burden could penetrate. It was this circulation which spread the appetite for a religion and culture comprehending a much wider world than that of the local speech group, a religion which prepared people for the experience of travel and enabled them to find friends and brothers even when they were far from home. Such was the special appeal of Islam to the nomad and the trader. And with its acceptance there came the further stimulus to travel for pilgrimage, education and general self-improvement. Pilgrimage provided Muslims from the remoter parts of the Islamic world with the opportunity to keep in touch with developments at the centre. This was of particular importance in the transformation of the earlier, orally transmitted varieties of Kharijite Islam by the orthodoxy of the four great literary traditions of the Sunni. The classic example is that which gave rise to the Almoravid movement. In 1035/6 the chief of a small tribe of nomadic, camel-owning Berbers from the south-western corner of the Sahara went on a pilgrimage to Mecca. On his return journey he stayed for a while in Kairouan, where he consulted a leading jurist of the Malikite school about how best to reform the lax and corrupt observance of Islam by his own people. The jurist referred him to a former pupil, Wagag, who had established a kind of militant religious community called a *ribat* in the Sus region to the south of the High Atlas. Wagag produced a disciple, Abd Allah bin Yasin, who accompanied the returning chief and was duly shocked by the state of religion among his subjects, most of whom did not pray or know anything of Islam beyond the bare declaration of faith, that there is no God but God, and Muhammad is his Prophet. Abd Allah 'began to teach them religion, to explain the law and the Sunna, to command them to do good and forbid them to do evil'.[7] From this initiative among an obscure desert tribe there emerged a movement of religious reform and political regroupment among the Sanhaja Berbers of the western Sahara powerful enough to supply a conquering dynasty to Morocco and southern Spain on the one side of the desert, and to invade and disrupt the negro kingdom of Ghana to the south of it. But behind the immediate military and political consequences of these events lay the

87

deeper religious and cultural process whereby the rigorous, literate Islam of the Malikite school of Kairouan transformed the vaguer, preliterate Islam of the Ibadis and the other Kharijites, first among the peoples of the Sahara, and later among those of Morocco and Ghana. The core population of Ghana were the Soninke, who were the northernmost of the large family of Mande-speaking peoples. According to the account of the Arab geographer al-Bakri of Cordoba, written shortly before the Almoravid invasion, Islam was the religion of a minority important enough to be accorded a special quarter of the capital town containing twelve mosques. Already, it would seem, there must have been plenty of Soninke Muslims, including most of the king's ministers. Following the Almoravid invasion, however, the evidence begins to show Muslim Soninke traders dispersing in a broad arc to the south and west, throughout the Mande-speaking country and even beyond it, taking their religion with them and imparting it to their clients and colleagues as a mark of cosmopolitan status.

Patterns of Islamic expansion, not identical but essentially similar, can be discerned throughout most of the Sudanic belt of open savanna country that extends for five or six hundred miles to the south of the Sahara. In all these areas there existed a class of merchants and long-distance traders – people who bought and sold in quantity, people who organized caravans and employed armed men to protect them, people who established depots and store-houses where goods could be accumulated in between the passage of caravans. Such people tended, from about the tenth and eleventh centuries onwards, to be Muslims. In towns they tended to live together, so as to be near the mosque and the Koranic school. Having more complex legal affairs than ordinary people, they would take them to Muslim *qadis* to be judged according to the *shari'a* law. They were the cosmopolitan, outward-looking element in a whole series of African societies, and they tended to acquire prestige and power because they travelled and corresponded, and so knew what was happening elsewhere. Until the fourteenth century at least, the literate Christianity of the Nubian kingdoms and Ethiopia interposed a barrier between the expansion of Islam in western and eastern Africa, but beyond it to the east Afar and Somali Muslims penetrated the southern borderlands of Christian Ethiopia, while down the eastern coast of Africa the connection of Islam with commerce showed that it had a maritime aspect. Whereas the Atlantic coast was by reason of winds and currents extremely difficult of navigation, the Indian Ocean with its regular monsoon winds was exceedingly easy. Long before the days of Islam, ships from southern Arabia had traded there, and Indonesian adventurers had even crossed it in their outrigger canoes in sufficient numbers to populate the island of Madagascar, which no African population had reached. The early centuries of Islam, however, brought Muslim contacts both from the Red

Sea and the Persian Gulf. The first to come were probably Ibadi Kharijites from the Gulf, and their main destination was the archipelago of offshore islands which straddles the modern frontier of Kenya and Somalia. So much, at least, is suggested both by the earlier layers of oral tradition recorded in the coastal towns, and also by the earliest Islamic architecture so far excavated on the islands of Manda and Pate.[18] The islands provide good anchorage after passing the rather desolate shoreline of Somalia. Lying within the equatorial rainbelt, they are lined with mangrove forests, providing valuable cargoes of roofing timber for treeless Arabia, as well as some larger trees suited for ship-building. Again, the islands and the adjacent mainland are the home of Kiswahili, originally the north-easternmost of the Bantu languages, which was to become the lingua franca of all the maritime settlements as far south as the Zambezi. The early Muslim traders were probably few in number, and content to live like their Swahili hosts in houses of mud and thatch. The Swahili, already adapted to a maritime environment, probably soon learned to build bigger boats with better rigging than they had been accustomed to use for local fishing, and so they equipped themselves to organize a coasting trade with the lands further to the south. It now seems likely that the earliest trading settlements on Pemba and Zanzibar, Mafia, Kilwa and the Comoros, were established by lightly Islamized Swahili during the ninth and tenth centuries. Intercontinental trade grew greatly during the period of Fatimid rule in Egypt in the late tenth and eleventh centuries, and this corresponded with an intensification of Islamic influence, probably now of a literate, Sunni kind, and with the building of mosques and palaces in cut coral in the more prosperous settlements. The main difference between the subsequent spread of Islam here and in West Africa lay in the relative absence of any large trading network in the East African interior. This was tsetse-infected country, in which all trade depended on human porterage and was therefore confined to the most valuable items only. Generally, there was much less mobility in eastern Bantu Africa than in the Sudanic belt, and there would have been no possibility for any community of Muslims in the East African interior to keep open sufficient contact with the heartlands of Islam for the faith to survive. The conditions for the spread of a universal religion did not yet exist, save at the calling places of Indian Ocean shipping. It is no wonder that East African Islam was long thought to have been an affair of foreign immigrants.

CHAPTER 8

CITIES OF THE PLAIN

To many observers Africa appears as predominantly a rural continent, in which towns spell the influence of foreigners as rulers, traders, industrialists and miners. For about half of Africa such a notion has some historical validity. When the Portuguese began to travel in Ethiopia in the early sixteenth century, they noticed a dense rural population, but none of the tightly packed, walled cities to which they were accustomed at home.[1] And, in fact, from the Ethiopian highlands and the Nile swamps southwards to the Cape and Natal, the characteristic pattern of settlement, at least during the later Iron Age, was one of maximum dispersion. Population might be dense or light according to ecological circumstances, but either way homesteads tended to be spread more or less evenly across the countryside, so that even villages were rare. In general, only the courts of chiefs and kings attracted quasi-urban concentrations, housing officials and men-at-arms, specialist artisans, and the numerous wives and servants of the great. And as a rule these agglomerations were highly transitory, built of impermanent materials and relocated at frequent intervals, as fire or sanitary conditions or the erosion of woodwork by termites might dictate. The granite kopjes of Zimbabwe and the Transvaal enabled stone walls to be built in place of fences and palisades, and so provided a motive for some greater stability of place. Otherwise, the only permanent towns of eastern Africa were those on the Indian Ocean coast, where coral provided a durable material for mosques and palaces and encircling walls, and where natural advantages such as offshore islands and sheltered anchorages made it worthwhile to remain permanently on the same sites. In the absence of such special incentives, it would seem that people mostly preferred to live as far away from each other as possible.

In western Africa, on the other hand, there was an indigenous tradition of urban settlement, which went back, in some places at least, to the very beginnings of the Iron Age, and perhaps a little further. In part, this may have been due to the ease and the relative permanence of mud building in the dry climate of the sub-Saharan savanna. There, certainly, the building process was almost incredibly simple. If a house or a room was to be built, a hole was dug in what was to be the middle of the floor, and filled with water, in which the spoil from the hole was puddled into a sticky clay paste and then laid to form one course of the surrounding wall. When this had dried out, another course was added, and so on. In really dry climates flat mud roofing could be laid on timber joists, with a result that was nearly fire-proof. Provided that gutters protruded far enough to carry rainwater away from the wall surfaces, such structures could last for many decades. And when at last they fell in, the materials could be recycled on the spot – to the utter despair of later archaeologists.[2] There was thus every advantage in keeping to the same site. Moreover, defensive walling to enclose any agglomeration of buildings from a hamlet to a city was a relatively simple operation, involving a good deal of communal labour but no great outlay on materials: a thick mud wall well laced with rubble was highly effective. Once built, the defensive wall was another factor making for stability of place. The pattern of town building was so successful that it was carried south from the savanna into the forest, where, even though roofing had to be made of thatch, defensive walls of mud were still common.[3]

The earliest example of urban building in the West African region is that of the 'fortified villages' of the mid-first millennium BC, surveyed and partially excavated by Patrick Munson in the Tichitt valley of southern Mauritania (above, p. 45).[4] These were built of stone, which lay ready to hand in the cliffs overhanging the valley. Besides being perched upon the cliffs, all the villages had defensive walls, some of them enclosing as much as a square kilometre, which would suggest that the larger ones were inhabited by several thousand people. Such density is probably to be explained by the concentration of a population, which had formerly occupied a large area of the south-western Sahara, around the lakes of the Tichitt valley during the final stages of the desiccation which followed the Holocene Wet Phase. These people were herding livestock, but also, and increasingly, cultivating pennisetum millet with neolithic tools. Certainly, they were negroes and belonged to the Soninke, or northern Mande-speaking group of peoples, who formed the central population of the later kingdom of Ghana. Their style of building resembled that of the historical Soninke. Clearly, one of the most interesting problems of the Tichitt sites is presented by the defensive walling. To Munson this suggested the proximity of external enemies, for which role he postulated the existence of horse-borne Berber raiders from northern Mauritania, perhaps equipped with iron spears, such as those depicted on rock engravings in the area. To judge from the purpose of defensive walling among later Mande-speaking peoples, however, no external enemy need have been in question. The walls could just as well have been built to protect one town against its immediate neighbours, practising an almost institutionalized kind of warfare among themselves for cattle and human captives.[5]

Another early example of urban development, once again from what must have been Mande-speaking country, though in this case from the homeland of the southern Mande, is that investigated by Roderick and Susan McIntosh at the southern edge of the Inland Delta of the Niger (above, pp. 69–70). Here Jenne Jeno, encompassing an area of 30–40 hectares, may have had a population of between 5,000 and 10,000 people, but it was still only the largest of some forty mud-built towns and villages to emerge within a radius of some 25 kilometres during the last centuries BC, and to develop side by side during the first millennium AD. It may be that the whole complex formed part of a single political and economic hierarchy, but at least six of the town sites are large enough to have been the centres of parallel hierarchies, sharing a common culture. Certainly, however, it was an urban culture, created by people who lived on closely built, permanent sites, from which fishing and hunting, agriculture and stock-raising were all practised by town dwellers. No doubt, the larger units included some specialist artisans, metal and wood-workers, potters, tanners and others who did not normally work in the fields. No doubt, there was an exportable surplus, at least of fish and rice, and a class of specialist traders who organized its transport up and down the Niger waterway, but especially to the more arid region around the great bend of the Niger, where it could be exchanged for minerals and salt. Nevertheless, it is clear that for the great majority of the inhabitants of the flood-plain of the Inland Delta an urban pattern of life had been established, which was functioning at full strength by the middle of the first millennium AD.[6]

A third area where urban life seems to have emerged at an early date was in the neighbourhood of Lake Chad, in particular beside the banks of its two great southern affluents, the Chari and Logone. Here, a whole congeries of peoples speaking languages of the Chadic sub-family (above, p. 42), and known to their northern neighbours as Sao, lived in densely built settlements on every natural bluff and eminence rising from the broad flood-plain of the two rivers. Here, as by the Inland Delta of the Niger, fishing could be combined with intensive agriculture and stock-raising, and the surplus shipped away northwards across the lake to Borno and Kanem, and southwards up the rivers to the equatorial forest. The Sao peoples of this period were certainly not included in any great political hierarchy, but they had in common a rich material culture. Their potters were active as artists in terracotta, and their metal-workers, using imported copper and tin, cast bronze sculptures using the lost-wax technique. Despite many years work by Jean-Paul and Annie Lebeuf, the stratigraphical evidence is not all that could be desired, but it seems likely that some at least of some six hundred identified sites of small mud-built towns in the area date from the very beginning of the Christian era.[7] The earliest settlements are said to have been undefended by surrounding walls, and a decisive moment seems to have occurred in urban history, perhaps during the second half of the first millennium, when the early sites were abandoned except at sacred groves, and the population regrouped itself in larger settlements, each enclosed within a defensive wall.[8]

The main lesson of the early, archaeologically attested, urban situations is that towns did not grow up as isolated exceptions out of a generally rural scene, but rather that in certain circumstances whole populations would convert to an urban life-style, organized for the most part in very small units, but practising a common culture. Describing the southern Mande, who in late medieval times formed the nuclear population of the Mali empire, Yves Person concluded that their basic settlement unit, known as a *kafu*, consisted of a walled town with its surrounding farmland, fallow bush and forest, of which the inhabitants might number anything between 1,000 and 15,000. Not every citizen lived all the time in the town, but each had a residential stake in it, and in particular the right to take refuge there in times of danger. For *kafus*, even when they formed parts of larger political groupings, retained enough sovereignty to raid neighbouring *kafus*, and even to conduct siege warfare against their towns. Hence, each town included within its walls plenty of unbuilt land which could be used for intensive cultivation in case of need.[9] At the same time, although potentially hostile within well understood limits, neighbouring *kafus* depended greatly on each other. They were connected by paths, and traders and other specialists could normally travel freely from one to another. Women were exchanged between *kafus*, whether as wives or war captives, and this helped to maintain a basic unity of language.

The most essential transformation effected by an urban pattern of settlement was that people of different lineages had to devise the political means to live together at close quarters. Dispersed settlement was invariably based on lineage, and the minimal government required was that of the family patriarch and his senior relatives. Compact settlement, particularly on permanent sites, involved the establishment of states and dynasties, on however small a scale. Among the southern Mande the ruler of a *kafu* was known as a *mansa*, and his functions were very limited. Within a town most people lived in family compounds governed by lineage heads, who settled all matters which affected only their own kin. The *mansa* dealt with inter-lineage disputes, with the allocation of land for farming and fallow, with the co-ordination of seed-time and harvest, with relations with traders and other strangers, with matters of peace and war, of booty and captives. The greatest scope for a *mansa* to increase his power lay in the acquisition and employment of captives, who formed an element independent of the local lineages. They therefore made ideal policemen and soldiers, and could also be recruited into occupational castes such as smiths and armourers. Person remarks, however, that the periodic

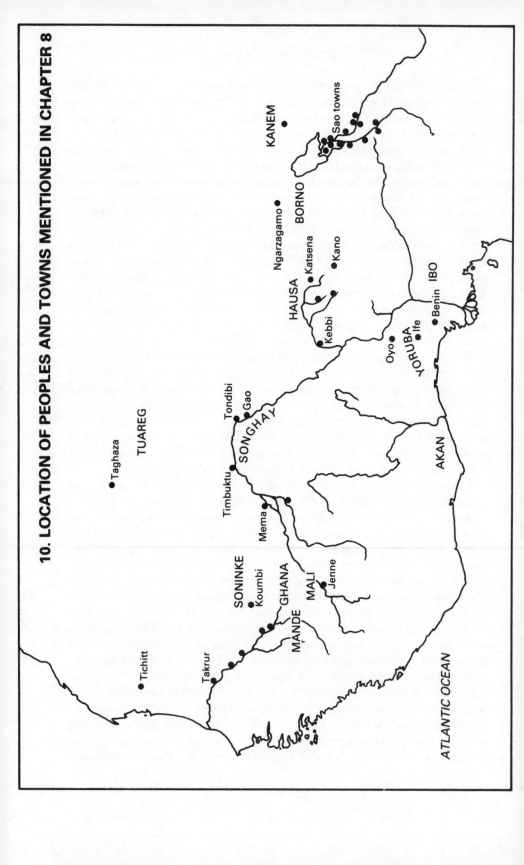

10. LOCATION OF PEOPLES AND TOWNS MENTIONED IN CHAPTER 8

KANEM

Sao towns

BORNO

Ngarzagamo

HAUSA

Katsena

Kano

Kebbi

IBO

Benin

YORUBA

Ife

Oyo

Taghaza

TUAREG

Tondibi

Gao

SONGHAY

AKAN

Timbuktu

Mema

SONINKE

Koumbi

GHANA

MALI

Jenne

MANDE

Tichitt

Takrur

ATLANTIC OCEAN

outbursts of militarism which resulted in the creation of larger political units were usually not initiated by the traditional *mansas*, but by ambitious military commanders, who took the *mansa* title and applied it at a higher superstructural level. As a rule, the traditional *mansas* continued to function within the traditional *kafus*, supervised to some small extent by imperial officials, but retaining enough of their sovereignty to resume full independence whenever the central authority broke down. Seen in this light, the emergence of great states in the western Sudan becomes relatively intelligible. The building-blocks of empire were already in position, and the aims of the empire-builders were limited. They wanted tribute from the traditional *kafus* and customs duties from the trade carried on by foreigners. In the great spaces of West Africa this was most easily done by a system of indirect rule in which nearly everyone carried on as before. The existence of the *kafus*, and the corresponding small-town states to be found in most neighbouring ethnic areas, made such a system possible.[10]

Person's picture of the small towns of southern Mandeland is probably near the mark for many other peoples living in the same latitudes. For example the Akan, living to the south-east of the Mande, in modern Ghana and Ivory Coast, seem to have been organized in comparable urban communities since the earliest times at which we can identify them in the historical and archaeological record, which is around the fourteenth century. The Akan, it would seem, developed their food-producing economy along the northern fringes of the equatorial forest, based upon the yam and the oil-palm, both of which were originally savanna species. The earliest known settlements were already small towns rather than villages. As population grew, it became necessary to expand into the forest, where the work of clearing was so heavy as to require the combined efforts of a town-sized labour force. Ivor Wilks has calculated that 'to create from virgin forest a single farm capable of supporting a family of between five and ten people, and utilizing a system of land rotation such as to sustain the long-term fertility of the soil, would involve the removal of the order of 7,500 tons of vegetation'.[11] With the Akan, the process was perhaps hastened by the discovery of gold at bedrock level in many of the forest valleys. This necessitated the employment of captive labour, which increased the size of the settlements. Helped on by the international interest in the gold-trade, political hierarchies began to develop among the urban settlements by the seventeenth century and culminated in the emergence of the great state of Asante in the eighteenth. But the small-town states of earlier times were the indispensable foundation.

Another region where small-town states grew up in the moist savanna and spread at an early date from there into the forest is that to the south and west of the lower Niger, inhabited by the Yoruba and Edo-speaking peoples. Such a scenario remained for long disguised by the beguiling, but utterly misleading legends of origin handed down in the great city states which eventually emerged. These traditions looked back to a common founder, Oduduwa, said to have reigned at Ile Ife, whence he had despatched numerous sons and grandsons to rule in other places. The stories of Ife's primacy were not one-sided. They were believed in most of the larger city-states of Yorubaland, and also in Benin, where it was also said that the art of lost-wax bronze-casting had been learned from a specialist metal-worker sent from Ife. In Oyo and Benin genealogies leading back to Oduduwa were recorded in apparently convincing detail, which showed that some twenty-three generations of rulers had succeeded each other in each place by the early twentieth century. This suggested a period of origin around the thirteenth or fourteenth century, and this likewise appeared to be the message of the early excavations undertaken by Graham Connah in the palace quarter of Benin City. One way and another, the case for a common process of state foundation in late medieval times began to look as though it was being authenticated by valid research.

As this research progressed, however, the conquest theory began to fall apart. Ongoing excavation at Ife produced earlier and earlier dates, ranging from the twelfth to fifteenth centuries for the widely scattered domestic sites with the potsherd pavements associated with sculpture in bronze and terracotta, with traces of earlier occupation going back to the eighth and ninth centuries. Ongoing research at Benin, notably by Patrick Darling, showed that the city walls were but the kernel of a vast system of walled occupation sites with an estimated total of more than 10,000 miles of defensive walling, some of it much earlier than the great wall of the inner city.[12] In a recent, very persuasive survey of the evidence, Ade Obayemi has argued the case for a 'pre-dynastic' period of Yoruba and Edo history, which would have consisted of autonomous small-town settlements, extending over the length and breadth of Yoruba, Edo, Idoma, Ebira, Nupe and Borgu country. The strongest part of the argument rests on the detailed evidence of small-town 'mini-states' which have survived into modern times in the peripheral areas between the grander state systems. Next, by a detailed topographical analysis of the place-names mentioned in the Oduduwa legends, he shows that the founding fathers would in fact have been the heads of hamlets situated within a few miles of Ife. His suggestion is that 'dynastic' Ife emerged from the amalgamation of a few closely neighbouring settlements, which probably took place around the ninth century. The resulting larger town became famous, not for its military might, but for its metal and glass industries, and especially for the blue *segi* beads with which the royal crowns of all the main Yoruba cities were decorated. The marvellous tradition of naturalistic sculpture in terracotta and cast brass, which was eventually to bring Ife to worldwide fame, was merely the foremost among a family of local traditions extending across Yorubaland, Nupe, Igala, Benin and northern Iboland. Its emergence demanded a background of some material prosperity, for copper, tin and lead had all to be imported from a distance, but it did not demand the existence of a large and powerful state.[13] It is indeed questionable how far any large state ever grew up around Ife itself. The centres of far-flung political power developed, rather, at the north-western and south-eastern poles of the region, at Old Oyo and Benin, and neither of these reached any great size before the fifteenth century. It was the pattern of small urban settlements which was fundamental to Yoruba civilization, and to that of neighbouring peoples to the west of the lower Niger.

It is in the belt of West Africa lying next to the Sahara that the problem of urban origins is most confusing, because it is here that the claims of outside influence shout loudest in the historical sources and have to be accorded at least some recognition. According to an earlier historiography which lacked the archaeological evidence available today, the Berbers, once equipped with the camel, opened the trans-Saharan routes, and caused the black peoples to the south of the desert to reorganize themselves so as to take the best advantage of the long-distance trade. Hence the emergence of states in Ghana, Gao and Kanem, of which the first handled the trade with Morocco, the second that with Algeria and Tunisia, and the third that with Tripolitania and Egypt. The reorganization involved the enlargement of territory in order to protect trade routes, and the creation of entrepôt towns where camel-loads could be redistributed onto donkeys or into canoes, with a corresponding change in the ethnic character of the carriers.[14] Today we see that the urban pattern of settlement long antedated the development of the trans-Saharan trade. On the one hand there were the oasis settlements, where the remnants of the old negro population of the southern Sahara had congregated. These, as we have seen from the example of Tichitt, were essentially urban phenomena, and it is most likely that the capital of the Soninke kingdom of Ghana at Koumbe Saleh should be seen in this light. On the other hand, there were the urban settlements, equally those of black people, along the river lines which created special conditions suited for intensive agriculture in the otherwise arid Sahelian belt. Such were Takrur, Silla and Ghiyaru on the Senegal; Mema, on the western shores of the Inland Delta of the Niger; Kukiya, on the eastern arm of the Niger bend, where there was an alluvial flood plain similar to that of the Inland Delta; Gungu, the ancient town of Kebbi, on the Sokoto tributary of the Niger; Pauwa and Santolo beside the small rivers of the Hausaland plateau; Kangoma, Kamuku and Gurmana in the gold-bearing valleys of the Kaduna river system. All these settlements would appear to have been founded by speakers of Niger-

Congo languages, whose basic occupations were fishing and farming, who needed to defend themselves against the pastoralists of the surrounding savanna, but otherwise had little incentive to enlarge their little self-sufficient states.[15] And beyond them to the east were the Chadic-speaking Sao, with their urban settlements along the water-lines of the Chad basin.

In between these two types of urban settlement – those of the oases and those of the rivers and lakes – there circulated populations of more or less transhumant pastoralists, with their camels and cattle, horses, sheep and goats. These people were not Niger-Congo speakers. They were in origin Saharan peoples – Sanhaja Berbers in the west, Tuareg Berbers in the centre with western Chadic-speakers ancestral to the Hausa to the south of them, and Nilo-Saharan-speakers in the east. Basically, the economies of pastoralists and cultivators were complementary: they exploited different though neighbouring environments and had every motive to exchange their surpluses. The effect of the trans-Saharan trade was in some measure to reduce this harmony. By turning some of the pastoralists into caravaneers, it put the accent on military accomplishments. By creating a demand for slaves for export, it militarized many more. Given that, for purely geographical reasons, the pastoralists of the Sahara had to receive Islam before it could reach the cultivators of the Sahel, the slave hunter was provided with an ideology of jihad, which encouraged aggression against naked animists wherever these were to be found. Moreover, the pastoralists had horses, and even though they had to be ridden bareback and with bitless bridles, the small horses long indigenous in the Sahara and Sahel were an effective aid in slave-catching. When supplemented by the big Barbary horses of North Africa, complete with saddles and stirrups, with proper harness and padded horse-armour, and with suits of chain-mail for the riders, cavalry became the decisive, unstoppable weapon against all who were not similarly armed.[16]

At the eastern end of West Africa, the Nilo-Saharan pastoralists steadily infiltrated the country of the Sao peoples, gradually building a large state in Kanem to the north-east of Lake Chad, and later transferring its active centre to Borno on the western side of the lake. Although the rulers became Muslims in the eleventh century, Kanem was seemingly a rather barren hegemony, deriving its momentum almost entirely from the annual slaving campaigns undertaken by the royal armies against group after group of the little urban settlements of the Sao. Nevertheless, some political integration took place at the centre of the system, which over four or five centuries turned Kanem-Borno into a land of settled townships, all looking towards a vast, brick-built capital at Ngarzagamo, while the taxes paid by the citizenry gradually overtook in importance the profits of the slave trade.[17] Westwards from Borno, it was the Hausa pastoralists drifting south from Air who showed that, when nomads entered settled

98

country, they could best do so by creating townships larger and better defended than those that were there before. Thus, Kano grew up beside Santolo and ultimately destroyed it, while Katsina did the same to Pauwa. Muslim merchants from Mali, seeking gold and slaves, established themselves in the new Hausa towns, and put them in the way of modernizing their cavalry, so that from the fourteenth century onwards there was a growing polarization between Muslim towns and animist countryside, in which animists were enslaved in annual razzias, those not exported being resettled in slave plantations around the growing cities. Such acts of deportation became a standard feature of urban growth in large areas of West Africa. When sophisticated cavalry warfare spread southwards from Hausaland to Nupe and Yorubaland in the fifteenth century, Oyo, situated on the northernmost edge of Yoruba country, became the first beneficiary, and a large proportion of the captives taken in its wars of expansion were settled around the capital city, in what had previously been a lightly populated region. Some of the huge concentration of suburban settlements around Benin city is surely to be explained in the same way.

The largest increases in political scale, all to some extent due to the stimulus of long-distance trade across the desert, had their centre in Mande-speaking country. Of these, the earliest and the least considerable was the Soninke kingdom of Ghana. Though it is generally held to have comprised most of the territory between the Upper Niger and the upper Senegal, the position of the capital in an unpromising oasis on the very edge of the desert,[18] suggests that its authority outside its own immediate locality was mainly that of a military overlord, policing one desert trail leading northwards to Awdaghust and Sijilmasa, and a series of trade routes fanning out through scarcely populated country to other Soninke *kafus* based in more favourable surroundings to the south-east, the south and the south-west. With these the relationship would have been mostly tributary, the sons of their rulers being collected as hostages at the oasis capital. The trading caravans would likewise have contributed their tolls, especially those travelling to the main market of the Bambuk goldfields at Ghiyaru on the upper Senegal. The best contemporary written source, al-Bakri of Cordoba, whose information was probably gathered at the Moroccan terminus of the trade route, at Sijilmasa, in the middle of the eleventh century, credits the king of Ghana with an army of 200,000, including 40,000 archers, but this is clearly a tenfold, or even twenty-fold exaggeration.[19] If Koumbe Saleh was indeed the capital, its utmost population has been reckoned at 20,000, and with barren country all round it, Ghana can have been little more than an average-sized *kafu* which had made the best of its geographical position to dominate its nearest neighbours and engross the trade of a region. The fact that its hegemony lasted longer than that of either of its successors may indeed be due precisely to this limit of scale. Ghana ruled only those who spoke Soninke.

Mali is another story. Mali sprang not from an oasis but from a stretch of fertile riverside. It controlled the access to gold-fields as rich as those of Bambuk, and once it had dominated the rest of the Upper Niger waterway, it possessed a trade route running from the forest in the south to the desert in the north, and one far better able to handle bulk cargoes than the donkey trails of Ghana. Mali could settle its war captives on plantations by the shores of the Inland Delta, and carry the produce away to feed Timbuktu and Gao and the oasis towns of the southern Sahara. Above all, Mali's dynasty was converted early to Islam, and not merely tolerant of it like the kings of Ghana. During the period of its great expansion in the thirteenth and fourteenth centuries, most of its kings made the pilgrimage, and saw with their own eyes how governments and armies were organized in the Muslim heartlands. Their wealth enabled them to buy the Barbary horses and the coats of mail long before their pastoral Tuareg neighbours to the northward. With Mali it is clear that most of the prerequisites existed for the emergence of a state greatly transcending the parts out of which it had been built. And, far beyond its political borders, its long-distance traders, nearly all of them Muslims, developed the trade in kola nuts from the forest region to the south, and in doing so discovered and promoted the exploitation of the gold-producing regions of the Lobi country by the White Volta, and of the Akan forests. Eastwards, they reached Air and Hausaland, where they introduced the rulers of Kano to the Islamic faith. And yet Mali's mastery of the western Sudan lasted a bare two centuries. Long before its northern territories had been conquered by the successor state of Songhay, the empire had simply fallen apart. The Tuareg seized control of Timbuktu. The Soninke *kafus* to the west of the Niger bend resumed their independence. The Fulbe states of the upper Senegal ceased to pay their tribute. The central dynasty retreated to its native woodlands high up the upper Niger, and there continued to enjoy a primacy of respect more than of real obedience from the *mansas* of the other Malinke-speaking *kafus*. Although a stronger power was building up on its eastern side, Mali had not been conquered. The urban ideal had simply triumphed over the imperial one.

The third attempt to build a great state in the western Sudan was initiated in Songhay, which had its homeland along the eastern arm of the Niger bend. It was from here that the conquest was undertaken. Within a generation, however, the lead had passed into Soninke hands, and there was a close alliance between the new Askia dynasty and the Tuareg of the central desert. The effective capital was at Timbuktu. This was a cavalry empire, stretching from Hausaland in the east to the Atlantic coast in the west, and reaching out across the desert to include the inexhaustible salt-mines of the Taghaza depression. It controlled the whole arc of the Niger bend, but stopped short of the forest. It inherited the slave plantations of Mali on the Inland Delta, and added to them copiously. Its armies being almost perpetually in action against dissidents at one or other frontier of its vast territory, there was no shortage of captives, but the most regular source of supply was from the stateless peoples within the Niger bend, and from the little cavalry-based slave-raiding states of the Mossi, Mamprussi and Dagomba in the same region. The Askia dynasty, indeed, made serious efforts to overcome its ethnic problems by the use of slaves as soldiers and officials, artisans and labourers for public works. It had a better supply than Mali of educated Muslim clerics and lawyers. Scholars of international repute taught at the university mosque of Sankore at Timbuktu; and important cases were judged according to the Shariʿa law. But, once again, the attempt proved short-lived. After sixty years of reconquest and firm government by two outstanding soldier statesmen, Songhay began to falter at the edges, and in 1590–91 it only took a little plotting between the Moroccans and the desert Tuareg to bring a daring expedition of 3,000 Moroccan mercenaries, equipped with fire-arms and some small pieces of artillery, across the desert road to Timbuktu and Gao. On 12 April 1591 twelve thousand Songhay cavalry and fifteen thousand infantry went out to meet them on the field of Tondibi, and were decisively defeated. The Moroccans established a garrison at Timbuktu, which exercised some lasting authority around the arc of the Niger bend. Elsewhere, the urban ideal became once more the norm.

CHAPTER 9

PASTURES GREEN

There can be little doubt that the dispersed pattern of settlement characteristic of most of eastern and southern Africa during the later Iron Age was due mainly to the relative importance of animal husbandry in this part of the continent. Just as the highland savanna of the central plateau had once been the supreme grazing ground of the wild ungulates of prehistoric times, so under increasing human pressure they were gradually transformed into the prime pasture land of domestic herds of cattle, sheep and goats. The earliest pastoralists, we have seen (above, Chapter 4), were relatively specialized in this branch of food production, and they were concentrated in the central highland areas between the Red Sea hills and the eastern Rift. Later on, during the early Iron Age, agricultural food production became established in the moister country to the west, the south and the east of the early pastoralists. During the later Iron Age the two systems progressively fused. On the one hand cultivators living in terrain that was not suited to large herds nevertheless perceived the advantage of keeping some cattle for manure. On the other hand pastoralists took to practising some agriculture. They were also driven by the increase of their herds to spread out from their early highland savanna strongholds to seek out the pockets of grassland existing in the primarily agricultural areas. This brought them into much closer relationship with the cultivators. There remained, of course, some large areas where the potential for stock-raising was negligible, notably in the Congo basin and in the belt of fairly thick, tsetse-infected woodland that extended from the Congo-Zambezi watershed eastwards to the Mozambique coast. Here, some larger village settlements more characteristic of the early Iron Age continued to be found, particularly in the alluvial land beside rivers and lakes. Otherwise, even where overall population was dense, dispersed settlement had become the rule.

So far as we know, the earliest pastoralism was also the most specialized. Though spread over a wide area of north-eastern Africa from the Sudan to northern Tanzania, most of the relevant research has so far been carried out in the Rift Valley and the western highlands of Kenya, where a pastoral way of life became established about 1000 BC and continued with singularly little change for some 1,500 years. The settlements of these neo-lithic pastoralists resembled the stockaded enclosures of the Maasai, who today occupy much of the same countryside. Their sharp tools, however, were made not of iron but of the black, volcanic glass known as obsidian, which occurs fairly widely in the Rift. The commonest obsidian artefacts are arrow-heads, and it must be assumed that their main use was in defending the herds from animal predators. Though the land must have been thick with game, it would seem that the pastoralists were not keen hunters, for their middens contain only a small proportion of bones deriving from wild fauna. More than half the bones are those of sheep and goats, which were usually slaughtered when quite young. Cattle were also eaten, but often in old age, which suggests that they were kept primarily for milking. The larger obsidian tools are mostly blades, presumably used for butchering, tanning and woodworking. Pottery was used for containers, and stone platters for some kinds of food. These were evidently of ritual importance, for they were buried with the dead, as were small stone pestles and mortars, evidently used for some kind of grinding. Wild grain was almost certainly gathered, but of domesticated cereals there is as yet no convincing evidence.[1]

The significance of neolithic pastoralism in central and western Kenya is that it bestrode the fairly narrow corridor of savanna grassland connecting the parts of Africa north and south of the equatorial forest zone. The Lake Victoria basin remained heavily forested until the late first millennium BC. Only as the early Iron Age cultivators cleared the forest for agriculture and charcoal, was a new pastoral corridor opened, running north and south through western Uganda between Lake Victoria and the western Rift towards the grasslands of eastern Rwanda and Burundi and north-western Tanzania. Although it is likely that the early Iron Age Bantu who effected this clearance brought some cattle with them from the region to the north of the Congo forest, it is only sensible to assume that most of the cattle to reach the early Bantu settlers of eastern Africa came from the homeland of neolithic pastoralism and were transmitted by trading and raiding between the Southern Cushitic pastoralists of the eastern Rift and their Bantu neighbours to the west, the east and the south. It may even be that, before the Bantu closed in to the south, there was some direct contact between the Southern Cushites and the most northerly of the ancient Khoisan peoples, through which the earliest domestic animals were able to reach southern Africa in the hands of people who were not yet cultivators. More likely, however, they passed through the hands of early Bantu intermediaries, reaching the Khoi of northern Botswana and western Zimbabwe by about the first century BC. Cattle were at all events present in the hands of early Iron Age farmers in Zimbabwe by the fourth century AD, and in the Transvaal at least by the fifth.[2]

It is thus clear that a very wide distribution of cattle, sheep and goats, and therefore of potential breeding stocks, had been achieved in eastern and southern Africa by the middle of the first millennium AD. From this stage onwards there is no absolute need to postulate further introductions from the north to explain the growth of herds in this or that part of the subcontinent. Where conditions for pastoralism were favourable, as they undoubtedly were in parts of southern Africa, local breeding stocks could create their own ripple effects and even flow back over the original lines of introduction. Nevertheless, some further important developments do seem to have spread from the northern part of the region: first and foremost, that which is usually held to mark the transition from the early to the later Iron Age in northern East Africa. In the Rift Valley and the western highlands of Kenya, this involved the absorption of most of the Southern Cushitic-speaking, neolithic pastoralists by Iron Age farmers speaking Nilotic languages and practising a pattern of food production in which pastoralism and agriculture were mixed in nearly equal proportions. In the Lake Victoria basin and westwards to the Congo forest, the same movement resulted in the penetration of the Bantu settlements of the early Iron Age by fresh groups of mixed farmers, who were capable of utilizing the drier as well as the moister environments, and so of filling up the gaps in the pattern of food production hitherto occupied only by the remnants of the hunter-gatherers of Late Stone Age times. The archaeological indicator of this transition is the disappearance of the distinctive Urewe pottery made by the early Iron Age people and its replacement by a range of coarser roulette-decorated wares with a broad affinity to those produced in the central and southern Sudan in post-Meroitic times. This ceramic change has so far been convincingly dated only in Rwanda, where it occurred between the seventh and eighth centuries AD, but it looks like a sensible date for Uganda and western Kenya also.[3]

It seems very likely that much of the momentum for a new economic strategy combining agriculture and pastoralism came from the Nilotic-speaking peoples living in the south-western foothills of the Ethiopian mountains, to the east of the Nile swamps. The northern part of this country contains the main sources of Ethiopian gold, and a Greek inscription of the sixth century AD from the Red Sea port of Adulis tells how this gold was traded for great herds of cattle driven southwards on the hoof in huge biennial caravans.[4] This may afford a contemporary glimpse of how Eastern Nilotic peoples, already practising cereal agriculture, may have been adding a pastoral dimension to their economy which ultimately caused some of them to seek a wider territory. All theories of long-distance migration are today rightly suspect. The reality is more likely to have been a population drift extending over centuries than any swift series of military campaigns. There would have been intermarriage between newcomers and older residents, bilingualism, cultural compromise and adaptation to new environments at every stage. Nevertheless, where the drift was one of Iron Age people with a complex economy into the country of neolithic pastoralists, linguistic absorption could go in favour of the newcomers, and so it seems to have been in western Kenya, for which the main evidence lies in the Southern Cushitic loan-words abounding in the Southern Nilotic, Kalenjin languages still spoken in the western highlands.[5] Where, as in Uganda, the impact was upon Iron Age populations with a broader, food-producing economy, the newcomers would lose their languages, while still effecting important changes in the life style of their hosts.

The most essential feature of the later Iron Age pottery of the Lake Victoria basin is that, unlike the earlier Urewe ware, it occurs in every type of environment, moist or dry, lakeshore, grassland, orchard bush or mountain valley. Clearly, its advent heralded a marked increase of population and a much more diversified economy. The food-producing occupation of the grasslands must have involved a strengthening of pastoralism, while that of the orchard bush probably depended on the introduction of a dry country cereal such as eleusine, already long domesticated in the Sudan and Ethiopia. We do not know when bananas were introduced to the mountain valleys of Masaba and Ruwenzori and to the well-watered lands west of Lake Victoria, but it is most unlikely that a South-East Asian cultigen reached East Africa with the early Iron Age Bantu coming from the west. A later Iron Age introduction is more likely, and certainly traditions from the west of Lake Victoria hold that there were not many bananas until people learned how to pack manure around the young shoots. Fruitful groves required the presence of some cattle. While the great herds kept in the grasslands by specialized pastoralists might look conspicuous, the beasts maintained in twos and threes in the households of cultivators to the east and west of the grassland corridor may have been in the aggregate even more important.

It is to a stage of development of something like this order of complexity that the earliest layers of oral tradition surviving in the Lake Victoria basin seem to refer. Essentially, these are traditions about the formation of large numbers of minuscule states, which in size of population and territory were probably very similar to the *kafus* and other small states of West Africa. The difference was in the absence of any urban nuclei other than the somewhat extended family compounds of the ruling dynasts. But their territories are still mostly recognizable in the names of small districts which later became included within one or other of the larger political units of more recent times. As with the small urban states of West Africa, the crucial act in their emergence consisted in the decision of local lineage heads to recognize one of their number as sovereign. The chosen dynast

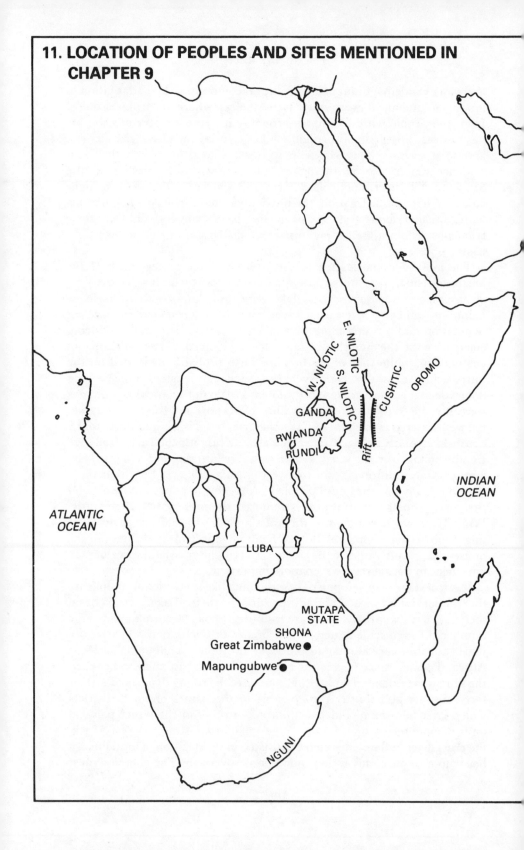

11. LOCATION OF PEOPLES AND SITES MENTIONED IN CHAPTER 9

W. NILOTIC

E. NILOTIC

S. NILOTIC

CUSHITIC

OROMO

GANDA

RWANDA

RUNDI

Rift

ATLANTIC OCEAN

INDIAN OCEAN

LUBA

MUTAPA STATE

SHONA

Great Zimbabwe ●

Mapungubwe ●

NGUNI

normally institutionalized his position by taking a wife from each of the participating lineages and by allotting ceremonial offices to each of the lineage heads, so that one would run his household, another supervise his war captives, while a third would supply him with pottery or bark-cloths, and a fourth would herd his cattle, and so on. The fact that whole sets of small states remember the founding dynasts by identical titles, such as Kintu ('the wonder'), or Mukama ('the milker'), or Ruhinda ('the thunderer'), suggests that, as in West Africa, state formation was often a collective process which swept across a whole area at about the same time. Sometimes it may have been occasioned by the need to accommodate migrants, as is strongly suggested by the early layers of tradition preserved in Buganda and Busoga. Sometimes, however, it may have been due simply to the jostling for land caused by the natural increase of people or their herds. Certainly, as in West Africa, state formation must have had a military dimension. In eastern Africa there were few city walls, but the stockaded enclosures of the early dynasts would have been the rallying points for warriors assembling from their flocks or their farms at the sound of the dynast's big drum, either to conduct a cattle raid against the small state fifteen miles away or else to repel a similar intrusion from outside. It is no accident that the primary articles of chiefly insignia consisted of spears and drums.

The economic and political strategies developed around the Lake Victoria basin towards the beginning of the later Iron Age were potentially relevant to wide regions stretching away to the south and south-west. They were not, however, the only ones to emerge at this time. A rather different pattern occurred where specialized pastoralism was penetrated by agricultural practices, as seems to have happened on both sides of the eastern Rift from central Ethiopia in the north to central Tanzania in the south. Here the essential feature of the transition seems to have consisted in integrating the food-producing activities appropriate at different altitudes. The grassland suited to the pasturing of large herds was to be found mainly along the valley floor, at altitudes between 3,500 and 5,500 feet. On the other hand, the best of the rainfall was enjoyed by the mountain ranges on either side of the Rift which, once cleared of primary forest, were habitable up to 8000 feet or more. The occupation of the higher levels by cultivators depended on a long, slow process of forest clearance, as a result of which the farms moved further and further from the pastures. Nevertheless, some animals were kept to manure the fields of the high farmlands, even if sometimes they had to be kept penned and stall-fed. Equally, where streams ran down the escarpments, upland agriculture could be practised with the aid of terraces and irrigation channels, right down to the valley floor. It is a mistake to imagine the existence of separate economies at different levels. Rather, the Rift Valley and its adjacent highlands seem, during the later Iron Age, to have been occupied by a whole series of societies whose economic strategies embraced both mountain agriculture and valley herding, with a constant interaction between one and the other. In the Ethiopian sector of the Rift, it is clear that the ancestors of the Oromo people occupied both the valley floor and the Bali highlands to the east of it, keeping their cattle in the valley and cultivating barley and other crops on the hills above.[6] In the Kenya sector of the Rift it is equally clear that, before the advent of the Maasai, both the valley floor and the highlands to the west of it were occupied by the Kalenjin, who grew eleusine and sorghum, and planted bananas, on the high plateau, while sending out their young men and boys to pasture the herds in the valley below.[7] The characteristic remains left by the Kalenjin herdsmen were the stone-lined hillside hollows known as 'Sirikwa holes', used for penning livestock, which are scattered in hundreds across the pasture lands of the Rift and the adjacent highlands to the west. They are likely to have been a local development, since wherever excavated they have yielded dates three or four centuries later than the earliest pastoral sites of the later Iron Age.

Although archaeological evidence from central and southern Tanzania is still very thin, there seems to be a *prima facie* case for supposing that the later Iron Age economic pattern of the Lake Victoria basin spread southwards through western Tanzania, while that of the Rift Valley spread around the rim of the East African plateau to reach the Iringa highlands and the Livingstone mountains overlooking Lake Malawi.[8] South of Lake Tanganyika, however, the later Iron Age of Zambia, Malawi and Zimbabwe seems to belong, at least in part, to a different story, of which the centre lies in southern Zaire, where, in the Upemba depression, the Lualaba traverses a lakeland region of quite exceptional opportunity for human settlement, though of minimal significance for animal husbandry. The potential of the Upemba depression lay in the opportunity to combine intensive fishing and agriculture, with easy access to the mineral riches of the Copperbelt and to forest timber for charcoal and smelting. Ethnically, the depression lay at the heartland of the Luba people, who had presumably occupied it since the earliest part of the Iron Age. Economic diversification began to burgeon around the ninth and tenth centuries with the development of elaborate metallurgical and ceramic traditions which progressively affected the surrounding regions. It was from this direction, around the eleventh century, that eastern and central Zambia, Malawi and eastern Zimbabwe acquired a new ceramic tradition and a more advanced metal-working industry, both probably spread by travelling specialists from the Copperbelt area. At about the same time, however, there took place a dispersal from the earlier Iron Age pattern of dense village settlements to a more even spread of homesteads, suggestive of an increasing concern with stock-keeping as an element in mixed farming.[9] This element was certainly not derived from the upper Lualaba, but it could easily have arisen from the natural increase of the early Iron Age breeding stock, perhaps assisted by some continuing southward migration of specialized pastoralists from the interlacustrine region in later Iron Age times. At all events, a new economic system emerged, similar in essentials to the interlacustrine one, and probably carrying the same political corollary of many hundreds of very small states, each comprising a few hundred square miles and a few thousand inhabitants.

In western Zambia, western Zimbabwe, eastern Botswana and the Transvaal the transition from early to later Iron Age food-producing strategies may have followed a rather different pattern. Most of this area was open grassland corresponding, in the southern hemisphere, to the Rift Valley grasslands of the north-east. Here, it does seem very likely that some kind of Stone Age pastoralism had been developed by Khoi people before the appearance of iron-using Bantu cultivators (above, p. 73). There seems to be no other way of accounting for the fact that in all the Bantu languages spoken to the south of the Limpopo the words for 'cow', 'milk' and 'sheep', together with a variety of other pastoral terms, are of Khoi rather than Bantu origin.[10] Here, then, sheep and cattle may have been present in considerable numbers during the early Iron Age, and it has at least to be considered whether the renewed emphasis on pastoralism characteristic of the later Iron Age could have been the result simply of efficient management of the existing herds. In the Transvaal at least, there is no decisive break in the ceramic tradition, and the advent of the later Iron Age can be seen more in terms of the scale of mining and metallurgy, in copper and gold as well as iron, in the development of ivory-working and cotton-spinning, and in the evidence of imports of glass beads, textiles and porcelain, all showing the growing influence of the Indian Ocean trade. It is indeed a strange fact that southern Africa's earliest links with the outside world should have been based on the Limpopo valley and not on that of the Zambezi or any more northerly river. In view of all this, it is not surprising that some enthusiasts should have come forward to claim that the whole later Iron Age phenomenon of southern Africa had its origins in the Transvaal and spread west and north from there.[11] However, viewed from the upper end of the Limpopo valley, the later Iron Age transition has too much in common with the nearly simultaneous developments to the north to be written off as a completely separate process. At the Nthabazinga (Leopard's Kopje) sites near Bulawayo, at Mapela on the Shashi tributary of the Limpopo, and at Bambandyanalo and Mapungubwe on the upper Limpopo itself, all dated to the eleventh or twelfth centuries, are signs of a vigorous pastoral expansion which was not simply a development from the preceding early Iron Age. The new pastoral phase had ideological manifestations in the numerous figurines of humped, long-horned cattle, and in the ritual burials of cattle and cattle-horns. Typical settlements had cattle enclosures at the centre, and the human dead were buried in the accumulated dung of the kraals. There was also a total break in the ceramic tradition. At the same time, the new pastoralism was by no means exclusive. Despite the generally arid environment, great attention was given to agriculture, even to the point of building dry stone terraces on steep hillsides to prevent erosion. The seeds of sorghum, eleusine, cow-peas and ground-beans have been widely recovered.[12] The picture is essentially similar to that of the transition to the later Iron Age in regions further north – that is to say, a preoccupation with cattle, but coupled with a new efficiency in the agriculture suited to dry environments, which permitted much more land to be brought under some kind of food production and so put an end to the remnants of the ancient hunting and gathering economies which had managed to survive in pockets through the early Iron Age.

What was unique in south-western Zimbabwe and the northern Transvaal was the speed with which the minuscule states characteristic of the first phase of the later Iron Age grew into distinctly larger and more permanent formations. The evidence for this is to be found primarily in the siting and lay-out of what must have been capital settlements, many of them occupied continuously through three or four centuries, from the eleventh or twelfth until the fourteenth or fifteenth, and many of them built with house platforms and terraces of stone and with the principal houses built of *daga*, a kind of cement made from pounded ant-hill which gave a more lasting result than the more usual mud and wattle. These sites suggest the existence of rulers powerful enough to organize labour for building, mining, elephant-hunting and trade.[13] Without doubt, the mineral wealth of the region was a factor of great importance. Both the Limpopo valley and that of its southern tributary, the Oliphants, are rich in copper, the mining of which goes back at least to the eighth century. As in many other parts of Africa, copper rather than gold was the metal preferred for adornment by the local populations. Pastoralists in particular admired the wearing by women of twenty or thirty pounds of copper on the legs and ankles, since it forced them to move with the slow dignity of the cattle. The copper of the Limpopo was thus, first and foremost, the means of obtaining for export the gold of south-western Zimbabwe and the ivory of a much wider region on both sides of the river valley.[14] In exchange for gold and ivory, the Indian Ocean trade brought in large quantities of glass beads, mostly from western India; unknown quantities of textiles, but enough to cause the local peoples to grow cotton and to use spindle-whorls, which are found in the sites; and very small quantities of high status luxuries like the porcelain bowls of southern China. An unanswered question, but one of great interest, is whether cattle from northern East Africa figured among the imports by sea. What is certain, both from the architecture of the settlements and the contents of the middens, is the association of cattle ownership with high social status in these communities.

The ruined city known today as Great Zimbabwe was in origin merely one among many capital settlements of small, later Iron Age states formed about the eleventh century on the southern slopes of the watershed plateau separating the Limpopo from the Zambezi. For the first two centuries of its existence, it was not a place of any special pre-eminence, nor did it apparently enjoy any great natural advantages over its rivals. It was well to the south of the gold belt, which followed the line of the watershed. It was well to the north of the Limpopo valley, with its resources of copper and ivory. It did, however, have its own little copper mine, and cast its own rather insignificant H-shaped copper ingots. It did not command any obvious trade route to the Indian Ocean, though the little river which rose near the site led conveniently enough to the valley of the Sabi, and thence to the coast within easy distance of the port of Sofala. But although not in prime, all year round grazing country, it was, as Peter Garlake has shown, well situated to develop a system of transhumance in which the herds moved uphill and down, from lower levels in the dry season to higher levels in the wet.[15] It may well have been the successful organization of such a system by a cattle-owning dynasty, infiltrating from the Leopard's Kopje area to the south-west, that the Zimbabwe state began to grow in size and prosperity. Large herds needed protection. Herd-boys of the warrior age-group could be formed into a standing army that was almost self-supporting.

There is no means of measuring the territorial expansion of the Zimbabwe state. However, it is clear from the archaeological record that from about 1250 till about 1450 the capital town was growing into a metropolis, with a much larger population, more and better stone-built constructions, and much more evidence of luxury imports, than any of the other capital sites in the region. The population of the town at this period has been estimated at between ten and twenty thousand. All the houses were still circular, with thatched roofs and only the best of them were of *daga*. Most of the dry stone walls were simply doing the work of fences, enclosing compounds or marking the divisions within them. But the platforms and terraces of the hill-top settlement, weaving in and out of the giant granite boulders placed there by nature, have a collective grandeur which has survived five centuries of decline and final abandonment, while the palace enclosure in the valley beneath, with its great perimeter wall more than thirty feet high and with its main gateway facing the hill-top complex towering some 600 feet above, creates a sense of magnificence unique in Africa. Of course, even the fully developed Great Zimbabwe of the early fifteenth century had little indeed of the sophistication of contemporary Jenne or Timbuktu, or Kano or Ife or Benin. It would not have contained a mosque or a book, or a horse or a sculpture or a glass foundry. Nevertheless, Great Zimbabwe represents a concentration of wealth and power unrivalled in the interior of eastern Africa, and its period of prosperity coincides so closely with the peak period of the gold and ivory trade passing through the coastal ports of Sofala and Kilwa, that it seems certain that its rulers must have found some means of engrossing the export production of a wide region. Most probably, this was achieved by conquering and placing under tribute the two main Shona kingdoms of the coastal plain of central Mozambique, Uteve and Madanda, and so monopolizing the coastal markets. When, sometime around 1450, the hegemony of Great Zimbabwe was overtaken by that of the Mwenemutapa dynasty, based some 250 miles to the north on the edge of the Zambezi escarpment, it was the conquest of Uteve and Madanda that signalled the essential transfer of economic control.

The Mutapa state was not, as it used to be thought, the simple result of a northward migration by the rulers of Great Zimbabwe. Rather, as David Beach has shown, it grew from a process of competition among fifty or sixty very small states previously existing among the northern Shona, all striving to control the copper and ivory trade of the Zambezi valley in the same way as Great Zimbabwe controlled that of the Limpopo. Since it matured later in time, we know much more about it, both from Portuguese writings of the sixteenth and seventeenth centuries and from the oral traditions of the region collected in modern times. On the one hand these sources show that the ideology and rituals of Shona kingship belong to a general pattern fairly widespread in Bantu Africa from the interlacustrine region southwards, in which rulers lived secluded in their palace enclosures and followed a pastoral routine, except at lunar festivals when they emerged to distribute sacred fire to their vassals and to consult the spirits of their ancestors through the persons of ecstatic mediums. On the other hand, they show that the political history of the region was not all about the control of the intercontinental trade and its profits, but much more about the possession and increase of large herds of cattle in the hands of the rulers. The word 'pastoralism' has acquired pacific associations, but these pastoralists were not characteristically men of peace. The herdsmen were also soldiers. The chief herdsmen were the military commanders. All stranger herds were up for grabs. The herdsmen were also the colonists, seeking out new pastures on the fringes of the area and occupying them. Every cultivator had to accommodate to the needs of the ruler's cattle. By their very way of life, the herdsmen were compelled to live in separate settlements to the cultivators, and often these were far from home. It was all too easy for them to develop the apartheid practices of a ruling caste.[16]

* * *

In West Africa later Iron Age pastoralism, in the sense of the managed transhumance of cattle in and through areas mainly occupied by cultivators, was outstandingly the affair of a single ethnic group. The Fulbe, or Fulani, developed their pastoral system in the Senegal basin, where their language is closely related to that of the surrounding sedentary peoples. From here, and much more because of their economic utility than their fighting qualities, they spread out across the Sahel as far east as Lake Chad. They operated on the margin of the desert and the sown, moving their herds northwards in the wet season when crops were growing in the south, and bringing them southwards in the dry season to eat the stubble and manure the fields of their hosts. Like other pastoralists, the Fulbe tended to be lean, hard men, well capable of defending themselves in any scuffles with the sedentary farmers. From time to time they erupted in larger acts of insurrection and conquest, but when they did so, it was usually at the instigation of their urbanized relatives, who were almost as widely dispersed as preachers and teachers of Islam. Fulbe jihads were led from the towns. They did not bring many pastoralists into the position of rulers of the local sedentaries. This was after all the land of the armoured knight, to whom the pastoral nomad, even if mounted, was not usually a military menace. Moreover, most of the bases of sedentary civilization were established further south than cattle could safely go. There was no real possibility for a pastoralist ethos to become dominant.

In much of eastern and southern Africa the bias ran the other way. Not only were cattle actually of more importance than in West Africa, but people tended to behave as if cattle were even more important than they really were. The main message of Evans-Pritchard's classic study of the Nuer of the southern Sudan is that, although one would never suspect it from their conversation or their rituals, these people were in practice just as much cultivators as pastoralists.[17] The same was true of the Western Nilotic Lwo who expanded from the southern Sudan into northern Uganda and western Kenya from about the fifteenth century onwards. All this was much more agricultural than pastoral country, yet the rulers lived in their cattle enclosures and referred to their subjects as 'the herd'. Western Uganda, north-western Tanzania, Rwanda, Burundi and Kivu all evolved during the later Iron Age under dynasties which subscribed to the pastoralist ideal. It did not mean that the rulers were the descendants of conquerors from afar, who were superior in civilization to the local cultivators. It meant that cattle, besides being considered beautiful, constituted storeable, self-multiplying wealth, and that rulers did their best to monopolize it. As the more successful dynasties gradually expanded their herds and their territory at the expense of weaker neighbours, so the organization and management of the royal cattle grazing in different parts of a kingdom became an increasingly important aspect of centralized government. In Rwanda and Burundi, by the eighteenth and nineteenth centuries, the defence of frontier districts was confided to the herdsmen of 'bovine armies', while nearer the capital there emerged a class of rich cattle-owning families, whose members filled the great offices of state.[18]

The main lesson of recent research on the oral history of the interlacustrine region has been to show how gradual was the growth of the larger states. Bunyoro emerged in the fifteenth century, and was raiding as far afield as northern Rwanda by the sixteenth, but only institutionalized its expansion in the seventeenth and eighteenth centuries. Buganda, the central nucleus of which had become recognizable by the fifteenth century, did not become a large state until the middle of the eighteenth century, and expanded much further during the nineteenth. Rwanda was insignificant until the seventeenth century, Burundi until the eighteenth, and, like Buganda, both achieved their largest gains only during the nineteenth century.[19] It would be quite erroneous to suppose that the existence of large and elaborate pastoral states in the interlacustrine region gave rise to the same phenomenon in Zimbabwe – or vice versa. In both areas large states grew out of pre-existing smaller states in their own neighbourhoods. The connection between pastoralism in different regions occurred much earlier, through the dissemination of ideas about cattle keeping and herd management towards the beginning of the later Iron Age. It may be that we can best understand what was involved in the process by looking to the situation at the very end of the chain, among the Nguni peoples of Natal and the eastern Cape. Here, until the late eighteenth century, there was still room for expansion of population and herds. Consequently chiefdoms remained small, dividing whenever population exceeded an optimum size of a few thousands. About the preoccupation of society with cattle ownership there could be no doubt. People lived in patrilineal families, each around its cattle byre. Cattle were the indispensable sacrifices at puberty and marriage, during sickness and at death. As Monica Wilson pointed out, the effect of polygyny in such societies was to permit the rapid increase of those lineages which controlled large herds at the expense of those which did not.[20] It was probably in this way that the early Iron Age populations were absorbed into a new social framework. Wilson's concluding observations to her description of Nguni society merit verbatim quotation:

The Nguni show marked similarities in economy, local grouping, law, ritual and symbolism with the cattle people of the Sudan, Uganda and Kenya borderlands. The identification of a man with a particular ox in his herd, the poetry in praise of cattle, the shaping of cattle horns, the association of the shades with river pools, the forms of divination and prophecy are alike. So, too, is the dispersion of homesteads, each occupied by a cattle-owner with his wives and sons and grandchildren, and the forms of marriage whereby cattle may even be given on behalf of a dead son so that seed may be raised in his name. Each item, taken alone, has little significance, but when there are many, one begins to speculate on what ancient movements of people linked the Sudan with the Transkei, for it is unlikely that the whole pattern has been twice invented.[21]

However much a modern view of African historiography might wish to minimize 'movements of people' over such vast distances, it would seem that room still has to be made for a wide diffusion of new food-producing techniques involving the combination of pastoralism with dry land agriculture around the beginning of the present millennium, the general direction of which must have been from north to south.

CHAPTER 10

MASTERS AND SLAVES

It is a fair assumption that for so long as men have fought with each other, they have also taken captives. Hunting bands doubtless fought over territory, and besides those killed or driven off, there must also have been captives, if only women and children. After the coming of food production labour assumed a new importance, and neighbouring communities probably began to raid each other for booty, including both human captives and domestic livestock. Early farming communities, experiencing no shortage of land, had everything to gain by increasing their numbers, and women and children could be easily absorbed into polygynous households. But not always willingly, nor yet as equals. There would more normally be a hierarchy of labour, in which menial tasks like the search for firewood and the carrying of water were allotted to recent captives. And there would be the tasks like mining, quarrying and porterage, so arduous, boring or dangerous that they would be performed only under duress.[1]

At an early stage of pre-dynastic Egyptian history, when communities were still of village size, the painted pottery of Amrat shows groups of captives, their arms pinioned behind their backs.[2] This raises at once the crucial distinction between captivity and slavery. Especially where societies were small, freshly taken captives were sure to be close enough to home to escape, unless physically restrained by confinement or bonds. And yet a tied captive was also a useless one. Only when transported to a distance where escape was unthinkable, only when conditioned by isolation and intimidation, deracination and degradation, could a captive be freed from his bonds and become once again, even though as a slave, a useful member of society. Slavery could only be achieved by a wide dispersion of captives. It was therefore very seldom the simple result of military action followed by resettlement in the predator community. Only exceptionally large states, like Dynastic Egypt, Meroe and Aksumite Ethiopia, could locate their own war captives sufficiently far away from the point of capture to prevent escape. And even here, many of the captives acquired by great states came to them in the form of tribute paid by their weaker neighbours, who had raided them from further afield. Almost always, therefore, the captives taken in warfare or raiding would pass through many hands before reaching the destinations where they would finally be acquired and absorbed as slaves. It is scarcely too much to say that effective slavery required the existence of a slave trade.[3]

The trade in captives was probably an important factor in the development of inter-regional caravan networks throughout the continent. Of these, the earliest would certainly have been those which used the Nile valley and those which fed into it from the surrounding deserts and savannas. From Ancient Egypt we have records from the early third millennium of raids against the neighbouring pastoralists which yielded tens of thousands of cattle and thousands of human captives. From this time onwards, slaves were regularly bought and sold in Egypt. From the early second millennium the presence of hundreds of sacrificial burials in the royal tumuli of Kerma, the capital of the Nubian kingdom immediately to the south of Egypt, offers nearly certain evidence of large-scale slave-owning in Nubia (above, p. 61).[4] The sacrifice of slaves in dynastic burials was to have a long history over wide stretches of Africa to the south of the Sahara. All authorities agree that the scale of slavery in Egypt increased greatly with the conquests of the New Kingdom. From this period at least, slaves were taken regularly as tribute, and the Pharaoh Rameses II claimed to have provided the temples with more than 100,000 slaves during the course of his reign.[5] In the mid-first millennium BC Herodotus reported what was probably an already long established slave-catching industry in the mountains of the central Sahara (above, p. 59). The appearance of defended villages in southern Mauritania and around the Inland Delta of the Niger at about the same period, makes it likely that slaving and slave-trading were in progress likewise throughout the sub-Saharan savanna, as they certainly were by this time in the Nilotic Sudan and Ethiopia. In the forest region and the lands to the south of it, slavery may have emerged somewhat later, if only because food production and the formation of larger communities were slower to develop there. Nevertheless, the plastic art of medieval Ife depicts captives trussed and gagged for sacrifice. And the Portuguese voyagers of the late fifteenth century encountered an already existing slave trade in regions as far apart as Senegambia, the Gold Coast, Benin, the Niger delta and the Congo.

There can be no doubt that throughout the whole northern half of Africa slavery and the slave trade received a great impetus from the rise and spread of Islam. The Prophet Muhammad had, after all, lived his life in a slave-raiding, slave-owning and polygynous society, in which it was customary for the men of the defeated group to be put to the sword and for the women and children to be taken as slaves by the victors.[6] The Arab armies, as they spread out across the Middle East and North Africa, quickly learned to reward themselves with the wives and children of the conquered, and as the Caliphate developed its palace cities at Damascus and Baghdad, and its great garrison towns from which the provinces were governed, so a huge international market grew up for slaves of all races and colours. In North Africa large numbers of captives were at first taken from the Berber tribes which, unlike the Egyptians, had resisted the Arab advance. Many of these were enrolled in separate regiments of *mawali* clients, which were used above all to garrison Egypt. But by the ninth century the Berbers, including the camel pastoralists of the Sahara, were converting to Islam, and the main fresh sources of supply were found among the black peoples to the south of the desert, who extended an already existing system of raiding and trading in slaves so as to sell into the trans-Saharan market. It would appear that the majority of those who actually crossed the desert as captives were women and children. Nevertheless, from these and from their progeny there came not only concubines and domestic servants but also the tens of thousands of black slaves employed in the armies of local sultanates all the way from Morocco to Egypt.[7]

The development of the trans-Saharan trade in Islamic times certainly had an effect on the ways in which slaves were taken in the Sudanic belt. In place of the kidnapping of individuals and the semi-institutional raiding between neighbouring towns, there developed specialized cavalry operations, using imported Barbary horses and horse-trappings, and padded armour to withstand the arrows of hostile archers, which would set off for two or three months at a time to scour the peripheral, hilly, 'middle belt' regions inhabited by the least sophisticated, stateless peoples. The ultimate description of such activities is that of the explorer Heinrich Barth, who accompanied an expedition from Borno to the Mandara mountains some 300 miles to the south. He recorded that, at the village of Kakala on 27 December 1851,

a large number of slaves had been caught this day, and in the course of the evening, after some skirmishing in which three Borno horsemen were killed, a great many more were brought in; altogether they were said to have taken one thousand, and there were certainly not less than 500. To our utmost horror, not less than 170 full-grown men were mercilessly slaughtered in cold blood, the greater part of them being allowed to bleed to death, a limb having been severed from the body.

The expedition returned to Borno after two months of such proceedings with somewhere between 3,000 and 10,000 captives, the great majority of them being either women or children under eight years of age, nearly all the grown men having been killed at the scene of capture.[8]

Barth's experience of slave-catching in Borno was large in scale and late in time, but it may stand as an example of the predation practised by the well-equipped horse-owning societies of the Sahel and the Sudan upon their weaker, mostly southerly, neighbours from about the thirteenth century onwards. It may also serve to emphasize the fact that enslavement, whether by simple kidnapping or in organized warfare, was an utterly traumatic process, in which individuals were snatched from their homes and their kindred amid scenes of horror and violence, and carried away into the unknown, where further hardships awaited all but the most fortunate. 'Slaves must work in the house,' says the Darfur folk-song. 'If they are unwilling to work, they must be beaten with the whip or the stick. Then they begin to cry and to be willing to work.'9 'Slaves were generally ill-treated', writes the historian of the Chewa people of central Malawi and eastern Zambia.

They were forced to do onerous work with blunt instruments such as worn-out hoes, to eat their food from the floor like dogs and to drink their beer from broken or dirty gourds. Female slaves usually received better treatment than their male counterparts. It was feared that they had the capacity to poison their masters, since they were the ones who fetched water, ground the flour and prepared the food. The slave's character or behaviour would determine his immunity from being sold to foreigners. Every lineage needed hard-working and meek slaves to supplement its manpower.10

Evidence from one end of the continent to the other agrees that the captured or bought slave, male or female, juvenile or adult, was a person entirely without rights, who could be put to any kind of work, punished at will, killed as a sacrificial victim or sold as a chattel either inside or outside the community.11 Where one part of Africa seems to have differed from another was in the presence or absence of manumission, and in the degree to which the descendants of captured or bought slaves could gradually free themselves from the total servility of their parents. Formal manumission seems to have been confined to the world of Islam, where it was praised by the Koran and practised above all in the case of slave soldiers, at the conclusion of their training. Manumission, however, does not seem to have been customary anywhere to the south of the Sahara, even among Muslims. Here, the general rule was that children took the status of their mothers. Most slaves were married to slaves. The children of the slave wives of free men were normally slaves, and in most societies male slaves were absolutely forbidden to marry free women. Only in some matrilineal societies in which free children were customarily brought up outside the parental home were the children of slave wives normally accepted as free.12 Elsewhere, the stigma of slavery persisted indefinitely. Out of consideration for personal feelings, it might seldom be mentioned. But everyone knew it, and at the crucial moments of marriage and inheritance it could not be avoided. It is significant that, even after the end of the colonial period, eighty years or more after the legal abolition of slavery, the consciousness of slave status remained a very real thing in many parts of Africa.[13]

Legal considerations and questions of esteem apart, the practical conditions of servitude in Africa were almost infinitely variable. Among bought and captured slaves, the most fortunate were perhaps those who passed into the service of ruling houses, where many hands made light work, and where loyalty combined with detachment from local kinship ties could lead to promotion and privilege – Joseph the son of Jacob, who was sold into slavery in Egypt and became the favourite of the Pharaoh, is but the best known of countless examples. Another highly privileged kind of slavery was the military type, since it involved the encouragement of qualities of courage and initiative which were precisely those most apt to be suppressed in the training of other kinds of slaves. In the Muslim states to the north of the Sahara military slaves were normally manumitted, and even to the south of the desert slave soldiers could expect to share in military booty and even aspire to owning slaves of their own. Noble captives often became slave soldiers, but most military slaves were recruited from those born in slavery in the households of the rulers.[14] Next in good fortune, there were the slaves who ended up as one of two or three in an ordinary peasant household. These would call the head of the family 'father', and would work alongside his sons and daughters in the fields and in the family compound, often enjoying a material standard of life scarcely distinguishable from that of the master. Less fortunate as a rule were those who were settled as plantation slaves in special villages in the neighbourhood of some town or royal residence. These people worked in gangs under overseers, and the best they could hope for was to be allocated a family plot on marriage, which they could work for their own profit on perhaps two days a week. Slave plantations of this kind seem to have existed at least as early as the great days of the Mali empire in the thirteenth and fourteenth centuries, when they were used for supplying the commercial towns of the Sahel and the Sahara. A chronicle of the successor empire of Songhay (above, p. 100) refers to slave communities taken over from the rulers of Mali, and even to the periodic culling of the children of plantation slaves for sale on the trans-Saharan market.[15]

With this single recorded exception, it seems to have been the general rule that slaves born in captivity could not be sold, and that in the case of extreme ill-treatment they could even attach themselves to other masters. This meant that they were free from the severest sanction hanging over the heads of all first generation captives, and that in consequence they could usually escape the harshest forms of servile labour, such as mining and porterage. Moreover, with the passage of the generations, people of slave stock would gradually acquire in practice most of the privileges of the free. They would be trusted to come and go, to carry on trades and accumulate property. Though much unpaid labour might still be required of them, it was often no more than was expected of children by their parents. Even the right of partial inheritance might in practice be allowed by a generous master to a trusted slave. Only the ban on marriage with free women, and the denial of any right to participate in judicial and political matters might ultimately distinguish the slave from the free. And, even here, some societies were less rigorous than others.[16]

It was this steady practical, if not juridical, absorption of slaves into the ranks of the free which made it necessary for slave-owning societies to replenish their stock of captured or bought slaves in every generation. Only so could the very hardest tasks continue to be done. This in turn continued to increase the proportion of slaves in the population as a whole, and more so in those societies which were rigorous about the maintenance of slave status than in those which were lax. It would seem that this proportion was largest among the Tuareg of the southern Sahara, where by the nineteenth century 70–90 per cent of the population are thought to have been slaves. It was not that the Tuareg actually required any more slaves than other people, but rather that among them the consciousness of slave status was almost ineradicable. The next highest proportions were those from the Sahel and the savanna immediately to the south of it. Here, the general consensus among the European observers who travelled there during the nineteenth century was that approximately half of the population were slaves. These were, of course, the Islamic and cotton-growing latitudes, in which towns were inhabited by large numbers of artisans – weavers, dyers and leather-workers – many of whom were slaves, and most of whom were fed from the produce of slave plantations scattered around their walls. Here again the consciousness of slave status tended to be very persistent. It would seem that in the forest belt the proportion of slaves was much lower, in places as low as 10–20 per cent. This was not because fewer wars were fought or captives taken, but because those born in slavery were more easily absorbed into free society.[17] The lowest proportions of all, however, at least in Africa north of the equator, were among the stateless peoples of the 'middle belt' between the forest and the savanna. These peoples were more raided than raiding. They, too, recognized the status of slavery. There were even cases where they permitted the plantation slaves of others to farm in their midst. But, overall, these were the societies which lost population through the slave-catching activities of others. It has been estimated that one such population living near the upper Volta lost at least 17 per cent of its numbers into slavery during the second half of the nineteenth century alone.[18]

Slavery in eastern and southern Africa has been less comprehensively studied than in northern and western Africa, but so far as the evidence goes, it would seem to be consistent enough. The main theatre of slaving warfare from late antiquity onwards was that which encircled the expanding frontiers of the Christian kingdom of Ethiopia, which pursued a relentless policy of conquest and cultural assimilation, while rival Muslim war-lords operated in the borderlands to the east and the south. The Christians practised wholesale enslavement and deportation of the conquered populations within their growing dominions, while the Muslims concentrated more upon the export trade of the Red Sea, which became the main source of African slaves reaching Arabia and the lands surrounding the Persian Gulf.[19] All down the Indian Ocean coast of Africa there grew up, from the eighth century onwards, a series of maritime city states, of which the well-to-do Swahili citizens owned both domestic and plantation slaves, captured or bought from the peoples of the interior. Though some slaves were exported by sea to the Persian Gulf, the numbers do not seem to have been large compared with those from the Ethiopian region.[20] Demographic evidence from Madagascar suggests that the western half of the island was extensively populated by Africans, of whom most were probably transported there as slaves during late medieval and early modern times.[21] In western Bantu Africa the Kongo kingdom and its neighbours certainly knew the status of slavery before the earliest European contact. Kongo in particular was in origin a conquest state, established by Kongo-speaking settlers from north of the lower Congo river over a sub-stratum of Mbundu people, many of whom were enslaved during the wars of conquest. Sixteenth-century observers were of the opinion that in parts of Kongo slaves outnumbered the free and performed most of the menial and manual work. It has been written of the early sixteenth-century Kongo king, Alfonso I, that his correspondence shows that he was convinced that one man might be the property of another by reason of birth, poverty, punishment or the laws of war, and that he never doubted that a slave, like any other property, might be passed on by sale, trade, gift or inheritance.[22] For the deep interior of Bantu Africa we have for the most part only modern ethnographic evidence, but it tells essentially the same story. The early twentieth-century missionary, John Roscoe, provides an egregious example when he writes that 'The status of slavery was not so dreadful in Uganda as in many other countries. In many cases the worst that could be said against it was that a slave was deprived of his freedom, that neither his wife nor his children were his own, and that his life was at his master's disposal.'[23] If not the worst, it would seem enough. A colleague of Roscoe's commented that it was difficult to account for the ratio of 3.5 to 1 between women and men in central Buganda otherwise than by the constant influx of women into the country as prisoners of war. It was these slave women who mainly cultivated the banana plantations of the Ganda chiefs and officials and carried provisions and tribute from the provinces to the capital, while male slaves worked on the roads, carried for the armies on campaign, and collected building materials for the houses and compounds of the élite.[24]

It is against some such background of slavery and slave trading within Africa that the development of an intercontinental trade in African slaves has to be considered. The oldest directions of such a trade were those which crossed the Mediterranean, the Isthmus of Suez and the Red Sea from classical times onwards. The Muslim era saw a great increase in the trade from north-eastern Africa into south-western Asia, and in later medieval times the African entrepots of this trade proliferated southwards down the Indian Ocean coast, while its points of delivery extended eastwards to western India, Bengal and South-East Asia. But the most dramatic increase in the intercontinental trade came with the opening of the Atlantic coast of Africa by European seafarers, starting in the middle of the fifteenth century. The Portuguese were the first to arrive, and they maintained a near monopoly for a century and a half before they were joined by the British and the French, the Dutch and the Danes. During the period of the Portuguese monopoly the scale of the trade remained quite small, rising from less than 1,000 slaves a year at the beginning to 5,000–6,000 a year at the end. Only about 1600 did the scale of the Atlantic trade draw level with that crossing the Sahara. By the end of the seventeenth century, however, stimulated by the growth of plantation agriculture in Brazil and the West Indies, Atlantic shipments had increased to about 30,000 a year, and by the end of the eighteenth century they were nearly 80,000. It is thought that during the same period the trans-Saharan trade may have risen from about 5,500 to about 7,000 slaves a year, of whom the great majority went no further afield than North Africa and Egypt. The Red Sea and Indian Ocean trade may have risen from about 3,000 to about 4,000 slaves a year during these two centuries.[25] It is thus clear beyond any doubt that, in terms of world history, the forced migration of some eleven to twelve million Africans to the New World was of far more significance than their introduction into parts of western Asia and southern Europe. The more difficult question is how far the Atlantic trade caused additional numbers to be enslaved, and how far it merely provided new destinations for those who would have been enslaved in any case.[26]

In one sense, the Atlantic coast of Africa was all virgin territory. Before the Portuguese, no one else from any part of the outside world had established more than passing contact. But this did not mean that the coastal peoples had been isolated from each other, or from their vast hinterland. At most of their regular ports of call the Portuguese found a commercial infrastructure already in existence which was capable of supplying them with viable cargoes of slaves, and of distributing the European goods – mainly textiles, metals and hardware – which they brought in exchange. In the Senegambia they traded with the same Dyula merchants who supplied the caravans of the western Sahara. At

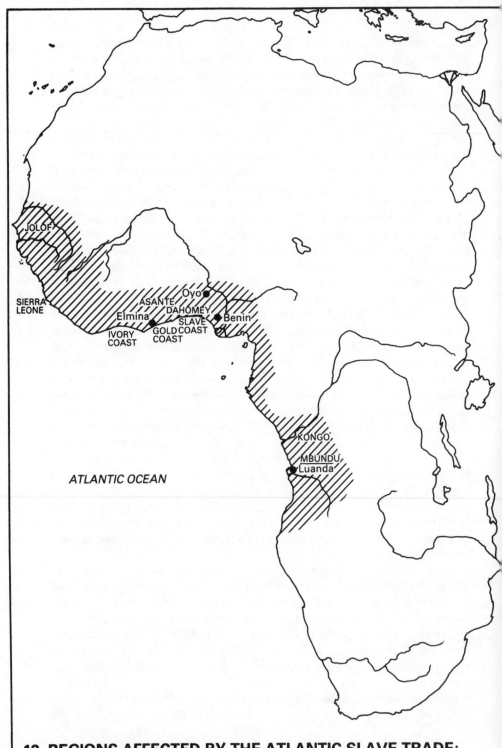

JOLOF

SIERRA
LEONE

ASANTE   Oyo
Elmina   DAHOMEY
           SLAVE   Benin
IVORY   GOLD COAST
COAST   COAST

ATLANTIC OCEAN

KONGO

MBUNDU
Luanda

**12. REGIONS AFFECTED BY THE ATLANTIC SLAVE TRADE:
16–18TH CENTURIES**

Elmina on the Gold Coast they found members of the same great trading confraternity in control of one route leading northwards to the Niger bend and another following the coast eastwards to Benin. In this instance the Portuguese gained their entry by competing with the local foot-porters and canoe-men in carrying slaves and cloth from Benin to Elmina, in exchange for the gold of the Akan forest. Both in Benin and in the Niger delta beyond there was an established system for the marketing of slaves brought down the rivers from the interior. In the Kongo kingdom state trading seems to have been the rule. Nevertheless, slaves were offered for sale to the earliest Portuguese navigators to reach the Congo estuary, so presumably there existed a distribution network which brought captives from the frontier wars of the interior down to the coastal provinces. It may even be that there was an existing canoe traffic between the Congo estuary and the Bight of Biafra.[27]

Even at the Atlantic coast, therefore, the slave trade was no novelty. The problem is rather how it grew to reach its seventeenth- and eight-eenth-century dimensions. The short answer is that it did so through warfare between Africans. Even at the height of the Atlantic trade, most slaves originated as war captives, and it is striking how seldom it seems to have been the Europeans who called the tune. Here and there, the circumstances which provoked the warfare can be attributed to their presence. More often it would seem that the causes of warfare were essentially local, and that the wars would have occurred even had there been no ocean trade to carry away the captives. In general the Europeans had to conduct their business according to the opportunities offered by a complex and highly changeable pattern of inter-ethnic relations, and to shift their bases to and fro as local events might dictate. In northern Senegambia, for example, there existed at the time of the first Portuguese contact a large, loose confederation of Wolof and Serer kingdoms known as the Jolof empire. During the late fifteenth century it started to disintegrate partly, but only partly, because the Portuguese were selling arms and war horses to its coastal provinces, which were thereby enabled to defy the central dynasty inland. The resulting warfare brought in many slaves, who were among the first to be shipped to the Spanish colonies in America.[28] When the Jolof wars subsided, northern Senegam-bia ceased to be a prime source of slaves, and Portuguese attention shifted to southern Senegambia and Upper Guinea, where Mande migrants from the interior were carving out little kingdoms among the previously stateless 'West Atlantic' peoples of the coastal forest region. During the second half of the sixteenth century one such Mande group, the Mane, entered the Sierra Leone hinterland and fought its way to the coast, taking hundreds of thousands of war captives, whom they sold to the Portuguese. By the beginning of the seventeenth century the Mane

had achieved their ends and settled down in the territory of the van-
quished, with the result that the slave trade there virtually ceased to exist
until it was revived in the second quarter of the eighteenth century by
the Fulani conquest of Futa Jallon.[29] Similarly, Benin when the Portuguese first came there, was in the final stages of a great territorial expansion. So long as its armies were campaigning actively at the frontiers,
Benin was a prime source of slaves. But when, around the middle of the
sixteenth century, Benin reached the natural limits of its power to control distant provinces, the flow of slaves dried up, and the European
traders had to look elsewhere for their supplies.[30] They found them,
first and foremost, in the war captives taken by the rising state of Oyo,
which was using newly acquired cavalry forces to conquer the little
states of northern and western Yorubaland. During most of the seventeenth and eighteenth centuries Oyo was exporting large numbers of
slaves both northwards to Hausaland and southwards to the Atlantic
coast west of Lagos. Oyo's most significant tributary was Dahomey,
which engaged in a parallel process of conquest and political consolidation among the Aja people living to the west of the Yoruba in a region
where the open savanna dips right down to the coast, allowing the use
of the new cavalry weapon. The contribution of Oyo and Dahomey to
the Atlantic slave trade reached its apogee between about 1680 and
1730, when some 20,000 captives a year were sold on the beaches
between Badagry and Whydah, which thus acquired the sinister name
of the Slave Coast. By the mid-eighteenth century both states had
reached their ethnic and territorial limits. The exports of the Slave Coast
had fallen to fewer than 5,000 slaves a year, and the European traders
were turning their attention to the developing markets to the east of the
Niger delta. By no stretch of the imagination, however, could it be said
that the Europeans provoked the expansion of Oyo and Dahomey,
which was a direct consequence of the southward spread of cavalry
warfare from the northern to the southern savanna and would doubtless
have occurred irrespective of whether or not there had been a southerly
outlet for the captives taken.[31]

Meanwhile, in the hinterland of the Gold Coast a parallel process of
political consolidation had been taking place, which culminated in the
late seventeenth century in the emergence of the great state of Asante.
At least three earlier attempts at regional domination had been made
earlier in the same century, and the resulting warfare had converted the
area into a major exporter of slaves, which were sold at one or other of
the forty or so picturesque castles built by the rival European trading
companies at intervals of only a few miles along the surf-beaten, sunlit
coast. However, the Akan did not merely fight each other. Their contending states also engaged in huge slave-raiding expeditions, above all

in the hilly country inhabited by the Ewe people to the east of the lower Volta. And the captives taken were by no means all for export. Here, as also in Oyo, the conquering dynasts were concerned to increase the number of their own subjects, so that they could the better dominate their neighbours. Slaves were used to staff the royal households, to build up standing armies, to carry trade goods, to perform specialized crafts, in mining operations and agricultural clearance. Among the last group were many who could be called deportees rather than slaves. They were forced migrants, who had been brought from a distance and settled in the neighbourhood of the growing towns. Probably they owed their virtual freedom to the fact that there were simply too many of them to be controlled in a servile condition. Had there been no Atlantic slave trade, there would perhaps have been even more of them, for to the Akan state builders war captives had a political as well as an economic significance. As the Ghanaian historian Kwame Daaku concluded, 'Even without the slave trade, it would have been necessary for the rulers to pursue policies of territorial expansion, especially in the auriferous regions, so as to encompass the gold mines within their territories.'[32] By the mid-eighteenth century Asante, secure in its dominion over the central forest region, had reached the limit of the territory which it could rule directly. More distant peoples conquered by its armies were placed under tribute, including especially the cavalry-owning state of Dagomba in the open country to the north-east of the forest. Dagomba's tribute was paid in slaves, mostly taken from among the stateless peoples living still further to the north, and these tribute slaves sufficed to buy the essential imports, such as fire-arms and smelted iron and copper, which Asante still required from the Atlantic trade. When a nineteenth-century Asantehene boasted that neither he nor his ancestors ever waged wars 'to catch slaves in the bush like a thief', he meant that captives were incidental to warfare, which was waged for political domination. When the dominion was sufficiently extensive, slave-catching could be left to underlings.

Fully one-third of the eleven to twelve million slaves who crossed the Atlantic between the fifteenth century and the nineteenth came from Africa south of the equator, between the Cameroon estuary and the Kunene. During the first seventy years of European contact these consisted overwhelmingly of the captives taken on the frontiers of the still expanding Kongo kingdom. By about 1560, however, the lines of communication of the Kongo armies were becoming overstretched, and neighbouring peoples, such as the Mbundu to the south and the Yaka to the east, began to counter-attack, taking slaves from Kongo, which they exported down the Kwanza valley to Luanda, where Portuguese traders were already settled at the nucleus of what was to become the colony of

Angola. Here in western Central Africa, the Portuguese came closer than any other Europeans of the slave-trading period to direct involvement in the process of enslavement. From Luanda they built a line of forts up the Kwanza valley, of which the garrisons became the military overlords of local Mbundu chiefs from whom they levied annual tribute of so many slaves. From their coastal bases the Portuguese also regularly sent African trading agents (*pombeiros*) to buy slaves at the interior markets – such direct participation in the overland trade would never have been tolerated in West Africa north of the equator. However, the great impulse to slave-taking warfare in this part of the continent came from the deep interior of what is today southern Zaire, where a process of political consolidation was taking place among the Luba and Lunda peoples, which had repercussions all the way from there to the coast. The first overspill from these disturbances to reach Angola were formations of highly militarized refugees from the borders of Lunda country, who went under the name of Imbangala. Before settling down as a ruling class among the Mbundu, they proved the perfect partners for the Portuguese garrisons along the Kwanza. They operated a war economy, 'cultivating with the spear', living on the crops of their Mbundu victims, of whom they incorporated some and sold others. Ultimately they built states, notably one called Kasanje, which became the main broking centre for the trade between Angola and the expanding Lunda empire.[33]

In terms of African history, then, the Atlantic slave trade is to be seen mainly as a reflection of the intensification, within a limited part of the continent, of an aspect of warfare which had long been familiar to most African peoples. Only one characteristic of the Atlantic trade differentiated it sharply from the rest of the slave trade within Africa, which is that two-thirds of those transported were male. This was evidently how the plantation owners of the New World saw their advantage, and their preference was reflected in the prices paid for men and women, boys and girls.[34] For Africa, the first consequence was that not so many men were killed at the scene of enslavement as occurred elsewhere. Next, however, it meant that a high proportion of female captives remained in Africa, even though not in their own societies. Since all African peoples were polygynous, it may be assumed that virtually all female slaves became mothers and probably had as many children as they would have done at home. Doubtless, there was population loss in the southern part of the savanna, where most of the slaves actually originated, but the Guinea forest and the coastal belt of both West and western Central Africa must have experienced considerable population increase as a result of the Atlantic trade, of which the emergence of larger and more centralized political groupings was one of the signs. In due course slavery would be replaced by wage labour, but for that it was necessary to await the creation of still larger and more complex societies in which governments could take over many of the functions previously performed by kindred groups.

CHAPTER 11

THE SWELLING CARAVANS

If the build-up of slavery in Africa gives some impression of the capacity for violence existing in the relations of large numbers of small societies, the development of regional and interregional trade from one end of the continent to the other shows how often and how effectively violence could be avoided where mutual interest required it. Trade routes could indeed be closed by war, but especially where states were small, there was usually another way round. More often, however, the threat of violence could be avoided by travelling in some strength and by being prepared to pay handsomely for protection at ethnic frontiers and while trading at the main markets. Typically, therefore, all longer distance trade was conducted in caravans, each representing a temporary combination of merchants and carriers, with or without beasts of burden, with armed men for defence and to guard consignments of slaves, and ordinary travellers, usually pilgrims or students, who joined for reasons of safety. For the duration of the expedition, the caravan became a political society as well as a commercial one, recognizing a leader who could enforce discipline and represent all the members in transactions with local authorities along the route. In Muslim regions the caravan leader was installed with religious ceremony, and travelling clerics and pilgrims saw to it that the daily prayers were performed as regularly as possible.[1] In much of Africa there was state trading, conducted by officially appointed caravan leaders, and one common pattern, practised for example by the Luba, Lunda and Bisa peoples of southern Zaire and northern Zambia, was for the caravan leader to be invested with the royal title, while the commanders of the various contingents of soldiers and carriers would each take the title of one of the provincial chiefs.[2] Thus, a caravan was organized as a kingdom on the move.

The most spectacular caravans of Africa were those which began to criss-cross the Saharan belt following the introduction of the camel from western Asia. As Richard Bulliet has brilliantly shown, this remarkable animal, which could carry twice the burden of an ox and at more than twice the speed, and which could move freely across terrain impassable by any wheeled vehicle, had during the first millennium BC virtually superseded the ox-drawn cart throughout the Near and Middle East.[3] In Africa its first significant victory was over the long distance river traffic of the Nubian Nile by the establishment of a direct route across the eastern desert from Aswan to Meroe, which by-passed the whole of the cataract region with its long portages and consequent exposure to raiders.[4] From Egypt and Nubia the camel spread westwards to the Atlantic and southwards through the lowlands of the Horn of Africa, where its presence as a purely pastoral animal among the Somali, Borana and Rendille is a reminder of the purpose for which it was originally domesticated by the nomads of Arabia.[5] The literary references to the camel in African trade and warfare, coming as they do from Romans, Byzantine Greeks, Arabs and Western Europeans, are apt to ignore the continuing and necessary pastoral basis of the camel's spread and reproduction, and to leave one with the impression that the main initiative for the Saharan caravans came from North African merchants operating from the northern fringes of the desert at oasis towns like Sijilmasa, Wargla and Ghadames. One has to look very hard at the texts to discern the nomads who actually lived in the desert and bred the camels and acted as guides and security guards, without whom there would have been no trans-Saharan trade to speak of.

What chiefly distinguished the camel caravans from others was their capacity to carry goods in bulk. A baggage camel could carry between 450 and 550 pounds, or nearly a quarter of a ton. By late medieval times there must have been hundreds of thousands of camels engaged in carrying on the Saharan routes. Idrisi, writing in the mid-twelfth century, described the rich merchants of Aghmat in southern Morocco, each of whom would despatch 170 or 180 camels annually to the western Sudan, 'bearing immense sums in red and coloured copper and garments and woollen cloth and turbans and waist-wrappers and different kinds of beads of glass and mother-of-pearl and precious stones and various kinds of spices and perfumes and tools of worked iron'.[6] By joining up with others, such contingents would make the desert crossing in caravans of between one and two thousand camels, and therefore with a freight approximating to that of an early steam-driven goods train. Some caravans were much larger. The Moroccan invasion of Songhay in 1590–1 was accompanied by a baggage train of 8,000 camels.[7] By the mid-nineteenth century, the annual salt caravan from Bilma in the middle of the central Sahara to the Hausa cities of eastern Niger and northern Nigeria numbered 10,000 camels. By the early twentieth century it had risen to 20,000.[8] At the same period the salt caravans plying between Timbuktu and Taodeni employed between them 25,000 camels and carried 5,000 tons of salt.[9]

In medieval as in modern times, salt was the principal bulk commodity of the camel caravans. The best salt came from the natural depressions of the Sahara, where the drainage systems of the Holocene and earlier periods of wet climate had terminated in inland lakes, which had slowly dried up, leaving deep saline deposits to be exploited by open-cast mining. The first large deposit to be worked was that near the Atlantic coast at Awlil in southern Mauritania. In Idrisi's time most of the product was being carried by canoe to the mouth of the Senegal, and thence to a string of upriver markets in Tekrur, Ghana and Mali.[10] By the thirteenth century Awlil had been superseded by Taghaza, some 600 miles to the east and roughly half way across the desert route from southern Morocco to the Niger bend. From the sixteenth century on Taghaza was replaced by the nearby deposit at Taodeni. All these places were situated in territory controlled by the nomads; the actual mining was carried out by their slaves; and from the two last salt could be moved and food supplies for the miners brought in, only by camels bred and operated by them. Northern merchants participated in some of these caravans, bringing to the western Sudan the manufactures and hardware of Egypt and North Africa, and taking out in exchange gold, copper, ivory and slaves. For the outside world this northern trade had a special glamour, in that the rather small quantities of gold involved nevertheless constituted, from the eleventh till the seventeenth century, something like two-thirds of annual world production.[11] But the bulk of the Saharan trade was that between the desert nomads and the Sudanese sedentaries, compared with which the trade that was strictly speaking trans-Saharan was but the gilt on the gingerbread. It was the same in the central Sahara, where the literary sources highlight an important trans-Saharan trade in Sudanese slaves, which was in existence from the earliest Islamic times, but give comparatively little attention to a far more significant bulk trade, which consisted in the exchange of Bilma salt for Borno grain and Hausa textiles, all carried on camels bred and operated by the Tuareg nomads of Air, the hilly region on the southern edge of the central desert.[12] The carrying capacity of the camel caravan is perhaps best illustrated by the fact that in the mid-nineteenth century the citizens of Timbuktu were mostly dressed in cotton garments woven in Kano, which reached them, not by the Niger waterway, but by an immense double traverse of the desert via the oases of Ghat and Tuat, and sometimes even via Ghadames on the Tunisian/Tripolitanian border. Of the weavers of Kano the explorer Barth remarked, 'There is really something grand in this kind of industry, which spreads to the north as far as Murzuk, Ghat and even Tripoli; to the west, not only to Timbuktu, but in some degree even as far as the Atlantic, the very inhabitants of Arguin dressing in the cloth woven and dyed in Kano.'[13] But the grandeur could not have been achieved without the Saharan camel and its Tuareg proprietors.

If there were many camel caravans which operated entirely within the southern sector of the Sahara, between the salt-mines and the Sudan, there were many others which were engaged only in the east-west traffic along the desert's northern edge. Here, at least from the eleventh century on, most of the camel-owning nomads were Arabs or arabized Berbers, whose main pastoral activity was with sheep which were grazed on the slopes of the Atlas ranges. However, camels were also bred and used for transport, which developed steadily throughout Islamic times and carried at least as great a bulk of goods as the coastal shipping of the southern Mediterranean. The main commodities carried in each direction were textiles – on the one hand the woollen cloth of North Africa, on the other hand the cottons and linens of Egypt and the luxury silks and muslins of the eastern trade. But, above all, these caravans were accompanied by many more people on foot than those of the southern Sahara, of whom most were pilgrims coming and going from the Holy Places and students travelling to the great schools of Cairo and Kairouan, which by the eleventh century had become the main centres of Arabic learning.[14] It is significant that the trunk routes kept well within the desert, passing the oases of Ghadames and the Fezzan, Awjila and Siwa, and so avoiding the cities and farmlands of the coastal plain. The desert was free from tolls, and even poor pilgrims could afford to have their modest luggage and daily provisions carried for them on a merchant's camel. The desert terrain was also that which best suited the all-important beast of burden.

From Egypt the caravan routes continued eastwards, during the first three centuries of Islam, across the Sinai peninsula, south to the Holy Places, and thence across the Arabian desert to Basra and Baghdad. Trade between Muslim Egypt and Christian Nubia was at first almost confined to the one-way transfer of Sudanic slaves paid as tribute. But from the Fatimid conquest of Egypt in 969 AD until the Portuguese incursion into the Indian Ocean, the Red Sea became the main route for trade between Asia and Europe, and for most of this period the terminal port on the Red Sea coast was Aidhab in northern Nubia. From here goods and passengers travelled for two or three weeks by camel caravan to Aswan, and thence by boat down the Nile. This crossing of the eastern desert must have been one of the busiest caravan routes anywhere, and from the twelfth till the fourteenth century the European crusaders, by threatening the security of the pilgrim route through Sinai, made it more so. During this period pilgrims from North Africa and the western Sudan made for Aidhab and thence took ship for Jedda. Most pilgrims walked. Some rode atop the baggage. For the very wealthy there were covered litters slung between two camels, which gave a smooth enough ride for the occupants to amuse themselves by reading or playing chess.[15] The camels employed on this route were those of the Beja nomads of the Red Sea hills, whose northern lineages were being increasingly penetrated and islamized by Arab

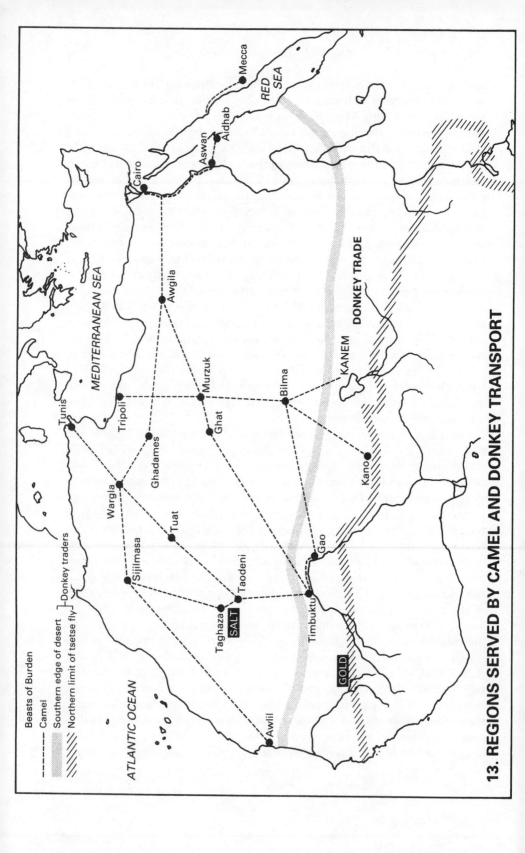

13. REGIONS SERVED BY CAMEL AND DONKEY TRANSPORT

Beasts of Burden
- — — — Camel
- ▨ Southern edge of desert
- ▨▨ Northern limit of tsetse fly] Donkey traders

ATLANTIC OCEAN

MEDITERRANEAN SEA

RED SEA

Mecca

Aidhab

Aswan

Cairo

Awgila

Tunis

Tripoli

Murzuk

Ghat

Bilma

KANEM

DONKEY TRADE

Kano

Ghadames

Wargla

Tuat

Gao

Sijilmasa

Taodeni

Taghaza
SALT

Timbuktu

GOLD

Awlil

bedouin pressing southwards through the deserts of upper Egypt. Meanwhile the southern Beja, and their Saho, Afar and northern Somali neighbours were establishing themselves as the commercial intermediaries between the maritime traders of the Red Sea and the settled farmers of the Ethiopian highlands. The luxury commodities of this region included gold, ivory, civet musk and the most highly esteemed young male and female slaves in all Africa; but the bulk exchange which formed the basis of all the rest was that of desert salt for highland grain. Here, as in the Sahara, the nomads were early converts to Islam, and their significance is demonstrated by the fact that, even in the Christian highlands, the caravan trade was always monopolized by Muslims.

The deserts of the Horn extend unusually far to the south, almost reaching the equator in northern Kenya, where camels still graze on the dry plains between Lake Turkana and the Indian Ocean. Elsewhere, it is at about Latitude 15 North, roughly from the mouth of the Senegal to the confluence of the Blue and White Niles, that camel caravans must turn round, and their loads must be redistributed onto the backs of donkeys and pack oxen, which can safely go for about another five degrees to the south. Broadly, the southern limit of the camel coincided with the northern limit of cereal agriculture, so it was not merely the beast of burden that changed, but the whole system of regional distributive trade. The grand trunk routes of the desert broke up into a network of trade paths connecting all the main markets of the Sudanic belt. In these latitudes caravans were smaller and more specialized. A few numbered a thousand people and the same number of pack animals. Most were smaller. They camped for a night or two outside the gates of market towns, repairing and re-using the rough booths occupied by the last comers. Their movements were carefully co-ordinated with the local agricultural cycle, so as to pick up the export produce of each region. The explorer Nachtigal caught the picture for late nineteenth-century Borno and Kanem in a way that probably holds good for much of this climatic zone. Here, at the first hint of rain in March or April the fields were weeded and the crops sown – cereals, ground-nuts, beans, sesamum, cotton and indigo. All hands were needed in the fields until harvest, after which the produce was processed – women and children pressing the sesamum for oil and cleaning and spinning the cotton, while the men wove and sewed, and boys and slaves herded.

As soon as the fields and meadows have again dried up . . . the time for travel comes, and larger and smaller merchants traverse the country in every direction. Supplies of grain, cotton, indigo, oil-seeds, domestic animals and local manufactures like woven strips of cotton, ready-made garments, dyed cloth, carved wooden bowls, baskets and mats are directed to the markets of Kuka and the larger villages, and from these chief market places European and native trade goods are distributed all over the country. Great caravans of oxen, donkeys and pack-horses carry the natron of the Chad shores . . . to the Niger countries, and thence and from the Hausa states bring back cotton cloth, leather goods and kola nuts. Others carry desert salt, tobacco, clothing, dyed goat leather, horses and European goods to the south . . . . Martial enterprises, which are directed almost every year against the pagans in the south and west of the empire, are also usually postponed until this time of year, and anyone who has no opportunity to make trading journeys is glad to attach himself to a razzia in order to bring home some modest spoils without expense.[16]

This remarkable passage puts the trans-Saharan trade into perspective. There were some European goods, including at this time cottons from Manchester and scissors from Sheffield. There were horses from North Africa. There were the great blocks of salt from the mid-Sahara. Again, there were the kola nuts preserved with infinite care on their long journey from the Akan forest, and the slave captives from the Mandara mountains and the Jos plateau. But all these more or less distant commodities were but the extensions of an active and varied regional trade of the West African savanna belt, without the existence of which the longer distance elements could scarcely have entered the commercial scene.

The donkey traders of nineteenth-century Borno were partly local and partly Hausa. On the other side of Lake Chad, in Kanem, they were partly Kanembu and partly Jellaba, that is to say, small-scale but long-distance merchants from the valley of the upper Nile. These people, like their Hausa counterparts, were invariably Muslims. They would set out from their homes with a few loads of cheap Egyptian cottons, amber and glass beads, which they would exchange for camels in Wadai, selling the camels in Kanem and Borno for natron, which they would carry to Nupe and Ilorin on the southern edges of the savanna, returning northwards again with kola nuts from the Yoruba forest, and picking up cotton and leather goods as they passed through the Hausa states. Passing eastwards through Wadai and Darfur, they would exchange these manufactures for ostrich feathers and slaves, and so return to the homes from which they might have been absent for as long as ten years.[17] The Jellaba trade, however, was of relatively modern origin. It could not have antedated the fall of the Christian kingdoms of Nubia, and it probably built up slowly through the seventeenth and eighteenth centuries. It was not merely that the region between Nile and Chad was remote and inaccessible, but that its home industries were feeble and lacked any traditions of excellence.[18] It was one of the last regions of Africa to be opened up.

The donkey traders with the deepest historical roots were undoubtedly those of the Mande-speaking peoples, generally known as Dyula. These had almost certainly emerged during the first millennium AD as the caravan traders of ancient Ghana, engaged above all in the exchange of desert salt and savanna grain, but encouraged to spread their activities more widely by the profits to be made from the trade in gold with the mining areas on the edges of the forest around the headwaters of the Senegal and the Niger. At the northern end of their sphere, the Dyula bought and sold with the merchants of the camel caravans. Intimate relations were cultivated, involving hospitality, trust and credit, and as Islam spread among the desert traders, the Dyula were the first of the savanna peoples to acquire it, and to use it as a kind of freemasonry distinguishing the few who travelled from the many who did not. As time went on, the religious identity became more important than the ethnic one. Anyone could become a Dyula whose occupation was trade and whose religion was Islam.

The largest extension of the Dyula trading network took place as a result of their active development of the trade in kola nuts. Grown deep in the Guinea and Akan forests, and apparently little appreciated by the forest dwellers themselves, kola became, from early medieval times on, the great addictive stimulant and aphrodisiac of the whole sub-Saharan Sudanic belt. Its intensely bitter taste relieved the thirst felt in high temperatures. It was enjoyed in private, offered to guests, and consumed in the sealing of marriage and business contracts. To have it to offer was a sign of prosperity and social status. The Prophet never having experienced its delights, it was uncondemned by Islam, and equally acceptable to Muslims and non-Muslims. Its marketing was big business, which gave employment to tens of thousands. To obtain it, the Dyula had to establish a permanent presence as close as possible to the points of production, and beyond the safe range of the donkey with its liability to trypanosomiasis. As in the gold trade, the Dyula were never allowed direct contact with the primary producers, but they settled in groups around the northern margins of the production areas, doing their business with local middle-men, who acted as their hosts and guarantors, and with whose daughters they intermarried to cement the business relationship. Often these settlements grew into market towns, Muslim in religion, and specializing in the commerce of a particular language or dialect area, maintaining good relations with the local political authorities and advising them in their external affairs. The big commercial fortunes tended to be made by the leading Dyula of these settlements. They knew the locals and could speak to them in their own languages. They had the warehouses in which imperishable goods like salt and iron could be stored until the price was right. And if kola were needed in a hurry, they could organize a party of local women to go and collect it from the producers. But there still remained the all-important task of getting the fruit to the customers several hundred miles away, in perfect condition. It was a delicate and highly perishable crop. It had to be packed in damp leaves of a certain kind, and undone and repacked every five days. Any delay in transit risked total loss. The market was intensely sensitive to size, freshness and quality. In these circumstances the best transport was on the shoulders of an individual entrepreneur, who bought his own load at one end and sold it direct to the consumer at the other. But for safety he had to travel in company with others of his kind. In addition, there were some bigger men in the transport business, who could afford to buy donkeys to carry salt and iron southwards, and slaves to carry the kola northwards. Slaves were exchanged both ways, the forest people buying the war captives of the savanna, and selling those from their own neighbourhood in order to reduce the risk of escape.[19]

The Hausa trading network, which came to extend over the whole of Nigeria and large parts of Cameroon, Dahomey, Togo and modern Ghana, has never been so comprehensively described as that of the Mande Dyula. Its origins were certainly later, and probably owed something to early contact with the Dyula system. The arrival of Mande merchants is recorded in the traditional history of Kano as a major event of the fifteenth century, and the origins of the kola trade in Hausaland are attributed to the same period in the traditions of the neighbouring state of Zamfara. The kola in this case is likely to have been that of the Akan forest, the trade in which was perhaps initiated by the Dyula merchants who helped early Akan rulers to develop the gold resources of the forest.[20] Many of the kola groves appear to have been controlled by Akan kings, who sent the produce northwards with caravans of porters to the savanna belt, where it was bought by donkey merchants at market towns in Dagomba and Mamprussi. The largest market was at Salaga in Dagomba, and by the eighteenth century at least it was a Hausa preserve. The explorer Clapperton, writing in 1829, described Hausa caravans of up to one thousand men and women, with the same number of baggage animals, travelling the 600 miles from Salaga to Kano through Borgu and Nupe: 'They carry their goods on bullocks, mules, asses, and a number of female slaves are loaded . . . . Some of the merchants have no more property than what they can load on their own heads.'[21] By the nineteenth century, if not earlier, the Hausa trading network had extended itself southwards to the ocean coast, every major Yoruba city having a Hausa quarter, where resident traders could live and practise their religion as well as their commerce. It may be that in the part of Yorubaland north of the forest these relations go back to the sixteenth century, when the kingdom of Oyo grew powerful by the importation of horses from Hausaland. Again, it may have been the late-developing kola trade of the Yoruba forest which took the Hausa traders still further south. As with the Mande Dyula, the secret of Hausa success seems to have been their preparedness to settle far from home, to intermarry with local people and learn their languages, and so build up a clientele of loyal sponsors.[22]

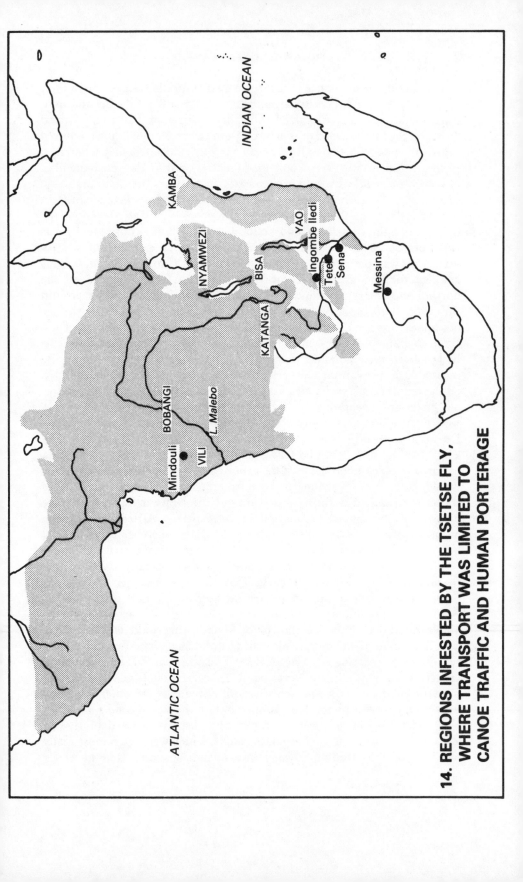

14. REGIONS INFESTED BY THE TSETSE FLY, WHERE TRANSPORT WAS LIMITED TO CANOE TRAFFIC AND HUMAN PORTERAGE

In general, the incidence of the tsetse fly dictates that the southern limit of the beast of burden occurs around Latitude 7 or 8 North. Beyond that, until the advent of mechanized transport, everything had to be carried either on the human head or else by dug-out canoe. Both methods required much physical effort, but Robert Harms has calculated that whereas a porter would usually carry a 60lb load for 10–15 miles a day, each member of a crew of paddlers would move nearly three times that amount 40–50 miles a day downstream and 25–35 miles a day against the current.[23] In other words, given the waterway, the canoe was nearly as efficient as the camel. Like the camel, it could be used to carry bulk produce as well as luxuries. South of the Sahara, the most obvious example of a busy waterway was the stretch of the Niger between Gao and Bamako. This enabled the two great cities of Timbuktu and Gao, and also all the northbound desert caravans, to be provisioned with cereals grown around the inland delta of the Niger. Within the forest belt of West Africa, the use of canoes was most conspicuously developed around the shores of the Bight of Benin, where a considerable population of fishermen and salt-boilers lived on sandbanks rising from saline lagoons, which were quite incapable of cultivation. The very existence of the coastal people depended on the regular bulk exchange of salt and dried fish for the yams and palm-oil, goats and sheep of the Ibo interior. Fleets of large dug-out canoes were maintained, each with a crew of up to sixty paddlers, for this purpose. During the period of the Atlantic slave trade, the canoes belonging to a single fishing town could be sent upriver and return six days later with a cargo of 1,500 to 2,000 slaves. The 'canoe boys', themselves mostly slaves, would often outnumber the free-born fishermen of the settlements.[24] This shows the scale of trading in and around the Niger delta; but in some measure every coastal population in sub-Saharan Africa lived by the exchange of cereal foodstuffs for salt and fish, and wherever a river flowed into the sea, the coastal fishermen would use their canoes partly for trade.

The use of inland waterways as trade routes was usually, once again, a by-product of the fishing industry. This has been a subject very much neglected in research, but the pioneering study by Robert Harms on the Bobangi, who dominated a stretch of some 400 miles of the middle Congo above the Malebo Pool, has shown how river fishing could in itself involve a mobility akin to that of transhumant pastoralism. Virtually all rivers are subject to alternating seasons of flood and low water. The permanent villages of river fishermen had to be placed on the bluffs which were safe from the flood; but the best catches were often made at low water, when the fishermen left their homes and camped out on the islands and sandbanks near which the fish were feeding. Again, river fishermen, particularly in a forest environment, needed vegetable foods, which were often most easily obtained by long trading voyages into savanna country. The quest for ivory, metals, slaves and other luxuries led to the construction of larger canoes, to the recruitment of slave paddlers, and to the assembly of fleets capable of self-defence when navigating among strangers. Above all, the network of human contacts was extended by blood-brotherhood and inter-ethnic marriages, so that there would be allies and sponsors available at distant ports of call.[25]

The Vili people of the Loango coast in modern Gabon were, like the Bobangi, great specialists in long-distance canoe trading. Originally coastal fishermen, they took to mining and distributing the great copper resources of Mindouli, some 300 miles in the interior, which they carried by porterage where necessary, but wherever possible by canoe. Some of their earliest trading voyages were up and down the Atlantic coast, but here they were displaced by the Portuguese, who from the early seventeenth century sent sailing ships from Luanda to capture the coasting trade in rapphia cloth, copper and other items. The Vili responded by extending their commercial links with the interior, developing land and water routes via the Ogowe and the Alima to the middle Congo, and thence ascending the Kwango and the Kasai in order to compete with the Portuguese and their Angolan allies for the slave trade of the Lunda empire. Phyllis Martin has shown that the key to successful long-distance river trade consisted in the organization of food supplies along the route. The Vili did it in much the same way as the Dyula, by planting colonies among the indigenous peoples through whose lands they travelled, making local marriages and establishing agricultural estates to feed their porters, their boat-crews and their slaves in transit to the coast.[26] While the canoe trade of the Bobangi and the amphibious activities of the Vili are the only ones in the Congo river system which are known to us from anything like direct evidence, the existence of a much wider network of water communications can safely be inferred. For example, the caravan traders, often of mixed race, organized by the Portuguese in Kongo and Angola to bring slaves and other exports from the interior to the Atlantic ports were known as *pombeiros*, because their most frequent inland destination was the district of Pumbe on the southern shores of Lake Malebo, where regular markets were held. Malebo being the reservoir where all the Congo waters are collected before they plunge into the long series of falls and rapids which descend to the estuary, the markets of Pumbe can only have been the entrepôts between a large network of river transport covering most of the Congo basin and a corresponding series of short, parallel porterage routes by-passing the rapids of the lower river.

The existence of long-distance river traffic on both the Limpopo and the Zambezi, the origins of which go back to pre-Portuguese times, can similarly be inferred from indirect evidence. The coastal fisher folk of southern Mozambique were the Tsonga, and those of them living around the Limpopo mouth were already in the time of Vasco de Gama the established middlemen for the copper of the interior, which they obtained in exchange for imported textiles.[27] The largest deposits of copper were those at Messina in the Limpopo valley, just within the limits of wet season navigation. The rich hill-top site at Mapungubwe, dating to the eleventh century (above pp. 109–10), could well have been chosen for its command of the junction of river and land routes. With the Zambezi the situation is clearer. The sixteenth-century Portuguese approached the Mwenemuta-pa's capital by way of the river valley, and they soon found it necessary to take control of existing riverside markets at Sena and Tete, about 150 and 300 miles upstream respectively. Above Tete, the Cabora Bassa gorges necessitated a portage, but above them the river continued to be navigable to Ingombe Iledi in the country of the Tonga, where a rich trading settlement, handling gold and copper, ivory and cotton textiles, had existed since at least the early fifteenth century.[28] The Portuguese did not venture on this section of the route until the eighteenth century, when they established a trading settlement at Zumbo, at the confluence of the Zambezi and the Luangwa, but its earlier existence is certain from the archaeological evidence from Ingombe Iledi.

While the contribution of water communications was greater than has usually been recognized, there remained a vast area, stretching diagonally across most of eastern and central Africa from the Somali desert to the Kalahari, where the only means of transport was by human porterage. Naturally, in these circumstances the volume of long-distance trade was much smaller, and the value of commodities carried was correspondingly higher. In this region as others, the priority of shorter distance trade was to remedy local deficiencies of salt and iron. In longer distance exchanges the key commodity may well have been copper which, as we have seen (above p. 110), was more highly valued within Africa than outside. What is of great interest is that until the late eighteenth century long-distance caravans did not originate from the coast but in the interior. This suggests that lines of communication developed independently of any great external stimulus. The earliest coastal imports into the East African interior seem to have been sea-shells, and the coral grinding-stones used in their preparation are a common feature of early coastal sites.[29] The glass beads of the Indian Ocean trade, which occur in large numbers in nearly every later Iron Age site to the south of the Zambezi, are distinctly rare to the north of it. Imported textiles seem likewise to have been unknown in the East African interior until the late eighteenth century.

Typically, head porterage in eastern Africa was the speciality of certain ethnic groups, often those whose homelands had the fewest natural resources. Such were the Kamba, who occupied the north-eastern rim of the great central plateau between the Rift Valley and the Swahili coast.[30]

Such were the Nyamwezi, living to the east of Lake Tanganyika, and the Yao, whose homeland was in the mountains south-east of Lake Malawi. Such, above all, were the Bisa of the inhospitable Luangwa valley in north-eastern Zambia. Lacking good agricultural land, these peoples maintained into the later Iron Age a large interest in hunting. Hunters were essentially mobile, and, needing good weapons, encouraged the arts of the smith. They knew how to defend themselves when on the move. As peaceful caravaneers, they would use hoe-blades to buy their food. Their stock in trade consisted at first of dried meat, salt and skins, but when they learned of its value in the outside world, they became hunters and traders of ivory. The Yao were the first into this trade. When the Portuguese placed their custom houses at the Zambezi mouth, the Yao pioneered an overland route connecting the country north of the lower Zambezi with Kilwa. Later, they became the intermediaries between the Chewa people to the south-west of Lake Malawi and the east coast. Their caravans were concerned above all with ivory.[31] The Bisa began by carrying the ivory of Lubaland to the Portuguese on the Zambezi, but by the early nineteenth century they had found better markets on the Zanzibar coast.[32] But it was the Nyamwezi who developed the widest trading network. The explorer Richard Burton, who travelled through their country in the late 1850's, found that porterage on the long and toilsome journey of some 600 miles to the east coast was regarded by them as a test of manliness. 'The children imbibe the idea with their milk and at six or seven years they carry a little tusk on their shoulders.'[33]

'The Nyamwezi,' wrote Burton, 'make up large parties of men, some carrying their own goods, others hired by petty proprietors . . . . The average number of these parties that annually visit the coast is far greater than those commanded by stranger merchants. In the Nyamwezi caravan there is no desertion, no discontent and little delay . . . . They walk half or wholly naked . . . . They ignore tent or covering and sleep on the ground. Their only supplies are their own country's produce, a few worn-down hoes, intended at times to purchase a little grain or to be given as blackmail for sultans, and small herds of bullocks or heifers that serve for similar purposes.'[34]

The Nyamwezi caravans were by no means confined to the paths connecting their own country with the east coast. Westwards, they travelled even greater distances to trade in the copper of Katanga, the ivory of the Ituri forest and that of the interlacustrine kingdoms of Karagwe, Buganda and Bunyoro. Like other trading nations, they planted colonies abroad, where resident merchants purchased and stored copper and ivory and organized food supplies for passing caravans. In particular, the route to Katanga was studded with Nyamwezi settlements, of which the most significant was that placed in the heart of the Copperbelt by a group of northern Nyamwezi known locally as the Yeke. Originating around 1820 as a purely commercial base, its leaders became so wealthy that they were able to train a local army in the use of imported fire-arms, and so to seize political power from the local Lamba and Sanga chiefs and to defy their nominal overlord, the Lunda king Kazembe. By the 1870s the Yeke state in Katanga was sending its own caravans to the Nyamwezi homeland on one side and to the South Atlantic coast at Benguela on the other.[35]

Among the late-comers to the business of overland caravaneering were the Swahili people of the East African coast and its offshore islands. Since the very early days of Islam, the Swahili had specialized in the maritime trade of the ocean coast, using sailing canoes with outriggers to collect the dried fish, the cereals and the mangrove poles from their own settlements in the coastal plain, and the ivory, slaves and rare skins brought to them by traders from the interior. It was only during the late eighteenth century, spurred on by the growing demand for slaves for the French sugar plantations in the Mascarene islands and by rising prices for ivory on the world market, that the Swahili started to go inland themselves, using their slaves as porters and defending their caravans with imported fire-arms. As time went on, their enterprise was increasingly fortified by outside finance, mostly provided by Indian merchants who concentrated their activities in Zanzibar, where they were protected by the Omani Arab dynasty permanently established there since 1840. Due to their preferential access to Indian finance, a few members of the Arab élite of Zanzibar became leading figures in the Swahili caravan trade, and so gave their ethnic stereotype to the whole enterprise. In reality, the coast-based trade of the late eighteenth and nineteenth century was a Swahili rather than an Arab affair and, even so, it was of less importance than the caravan trade conducted by the Nyamwezi and other peoples of the East African interior. Its specifically Arab aspect was of more significance in politics than in commerce, and was mainly felt during the decade or two preceding the European partition of the continent.

CHAPTER 12

POMP AND POWER

Not all of the Africans tried to found states. The hunters and gatherers did not do so, for their communities were too small and too thinly spread to require it. Again, transhumant pastoralists did not normally form states, although they sometimes took over by conquest the states of others. Among cultivators, the inhabitants of mountainous areas, living on ridges and divided from each other by steep valleys, often felt no need for communities wider than those of kinship. Sometimes, as in Morocco, such areas were actually enclosed within the frontiers of a large state, but no attempt was made to conquer and govern them. But there were also some areas of relatively flat and accessible country, particularly in the West African 'middle belt' and in corresponding latitudes to the east of Lake Chad, where quite large populations of cultivators apparently preferred to live in kinship groups, even though this left them defenceless against the regular attacks of more centrally organized neighbours. The persistence of such communities through centuries of harrassment is one of the unsolved problems of African history.

Most Africans, however, lived, apparently from quite early in the Iron Age, in states, and these states were invariably in some sense hereditary monarchies. Primogeniture, though not unknown, was rare. Usually systems of succession provided a choice of candidates from among a limited group of 'royals'. Sometimes the choice could be peacefully stage-managed by a group of inner councillors, but very often it would be decided by warlike means. The Ganda word for a 'reign' is *mirembe*, which means the period of peace following a succession struggle expected to last for years rather than for weeks or months. Apart from the need to defeat rival claimants, there seems to have been the idea that a new king should prove himself to be the man of destiny by a display of military force among his own people. Often there was a parallel assertion of authority over the animal kingdom, expressed by means of a ceremonial hunt in which the new king was expected to kill a lion or a leopard. From such beginnings the divinity which hedged an African king developed. Africans excelled at the theatre of royalty – special regalia, special greetings, special premises, special food, special fire, special artefacts of all sorts, all with special names. Islamic influence, wherever it was present, added some of the gorgeous paraphernalia of oriental despotism, notably the state umbrella, which spread widely through West Africa and down the East African coast. People approached the royal presence with eyes averted, one or both shoulders bared, prostrating themselves to the ground, throwing dust on their heads. Kings held the power of life and death, and were expected to exercise it with due drama. In the absence of prisons, death and mutilation were the common punishments.

But if the courts of African kings were awesome places, they also had charismatic and unifying functions. For example, the largest feature of any royal compound was the harem, and the significance of royal polygyny in Africa is hard to exaggerate. Ordinary men might have several wives if they could afford to, but kings consciously tried to take wives from most of the lineages of their subjects, and they were expected to engender a number of children consonant with their rank. In large states like that of the Mwenemutapas, royal wives might number two or three thousand, and even if many of them never actually met their lords and masters face to face, the royal household was none the less a unique nursery of future citizens who would grow up to have a national rather than a merely local and kinship-oriented outlook. Far too little serious research has been devoted to royal polygyny, but its potentialities have been demonstrated by David Cohen in a grass-roots study of one hill-top in Busoga, Uganda, where he found that more than half the population of some 1,500 was descended from a single petty dynast who had settled there less than a century previously.[1] We need to know what connection existed between the children of the royal harems and the boys usually described as 'pages', who were brought up at the courts of kings and were destined for leading positions in the military and civilian service of the state. Many sources suggest that some of these were hostages for the loyalty of their parents, who might be tributary rulers or provincial chiefs. Many more were probably slaves, whose very kinlessness was their main qualification for positions of trust. But the children of minor royal wives were very likely the largest element, and one very relevant to the formation of indigenous élites. The daughters of minor wives no doubt found much of their employment in the kitchens and plantations so necessary for the exercise of royal hospitality.

Another unifying function of the royal court arose from its reception and redistribution of tribute. Since this was mostly paid in kind, in the shape of livestock, grain and beer, much tribute had to be consumed on the spot or else passed on quite quickly to others. The court had to feed its own population of wives, slaves, soldiers and servants, but it was also a place where a poor man might come and beg for a cow to pay the bride-price for a wife, and while he waited his turn for an audience he would be fed. Aidan Southall has recorded the traditions of quite small kingdoms among the Alur of north-western Uganda and north-eastern Zaire, which tell how neighbouring groups of stateless people would request incorporation and agree to pay tribute because of the advantages they saw in the redistributive functions of Alur chiefs.[2] By the same token, the court was also a place where mightier subjects might expect to be rewarded for their loyalty with the prestige goods that came from international contacts and state trading. These, trickling down through the hierarchy, would reinforce the bonds of political allegiance.

As everywhere else in the world, African statecraft was much involved with religion and magic. In Muslim states sultans would process under their state umbrellas to the Friday prayer, and the *shari'a* law would be enforced at least in the higher courts. In Christian Ethiopia the kings frequently led lives of intense piety, patronizing the Church and using it to create a sense of religious nationalism which could help with the absorption of conquered peoples. But they could not afford to ignore the demands of African royal polygyny, without which the necessary alliances with external dynasties and internal magnates could not have been properly sealed. In pagan Africa the courts of kings were nearly always seen as the centres of the most potent magic in the state. This took many forms, but the most widespread were cults of spirit possession, associated with the tombs or temples of past kings, where spirit mediums would live and devote themselves to be the vehicles through which the dead addressed the living with words of warning, comfort and advice. Not exclusively but typically, it was a kingly cult, involving the royal dead and living royals. The sixteenth-century Portuguese missionary, Joao dos Santos, described how, once a year, a tributary of the Mwenemutapa called the Kiteve would go on pilgrimage to the royal tombs, where he would remain secluded for a whole week, while drums beat incessantly. On the eighth day he would emerge in public procession before the assembled company, in converse with a spirit medium who acted the part of his late father, even imitating the dead man's voice and gestures.[3]

On the whole, it would seem that, until the outside world broke in upon them with the power of modern weapons, the Africans were not lacking in political structures and supporting ideologies appropriate to the circumstances in which they lived. The monarchical idea, in particular, is one which seems to have occurred naturally to the human mind the world over. In essence it consisted merely in the elevation of one family over others, on the basis of prior settlement or later conquest, and the subsequent buttressing of that pre-eminence by sociological and ceremonial means. Basic kingship did not require a numerous constituency. It could function admirably in a community of five or ten thousand people, in which the monarch could know almost all his subjects by sight. In these circumstances the court, consisting of wives, children, young men-at-arms and clan elders acting as councillors and courtiers, might number between one and two hundred people, who would grow most of their own food and who did not need to be too much of a burden to the community at large. And it is certain that, even at the very end of the precolonial period, the vast majority of African states, encompassing between them perhaps half the total population of the continent, were still of this order of magnitude. It was normal for such states to form in clusters of twenty or thirty, each cluster representing a common language and culture. These common features probably indicated the long residence of a nuclear population within a common environment, together with a significant degree of intermarriage between the neighbouring units in a cluster. European observers later tended to describe such clusters as 'tribes', meaning something more than a collection of intermarrying clans, but also something less than a nation, particularly in the lack of any overarching political institutions. Indeed, the states forming a cluster were more accustomed to fight among themselves than to combine against a common danger. An intruder from outside would usually find plenty of allies, all seeking to involve him on their side in the local struggles.

As time went on, various influences operated to cause the emergence of some larger states among the clusters of very small ones. In the interlacustrine region of East Africa, for example, it is possible to trace in some detail the gradual emergence of six states which by the mid-nineteenth century had come to dominate the region now comprised within southern Uganda, north-western Tanzania, Rwanda, Burundi and the Kivu province of Zaire. At the beginning of the period for which oral tradition is of some use, five or six hundred years ago, the region was probably organized in some two hundred minuscule states, forming three main clusters of linguistic and customary relationship. By the mid-nineteenth century, the total number of states had been reduced to about one hundred, through the absorption of the remainder into one or other of six much larger kingdoms which had established a momentum of territorial growth and political centralization. The six had control of the most productive areas, and four of them had probably achieved populations of around one million apiece. The hundred or so remaining small states occupied the peripheries of the region and perhaps accounted for another million people between them. By the end of the period the six had gone a long way towards creating centralized institutions. The royal capitals had expanded to include ministers as well as courtiers. The provinces, which often coincided with the areas of conquered statelets, were usually administered by royal nominees rather than by the ancient ruling families. Provincial and district chiefs were supported by the

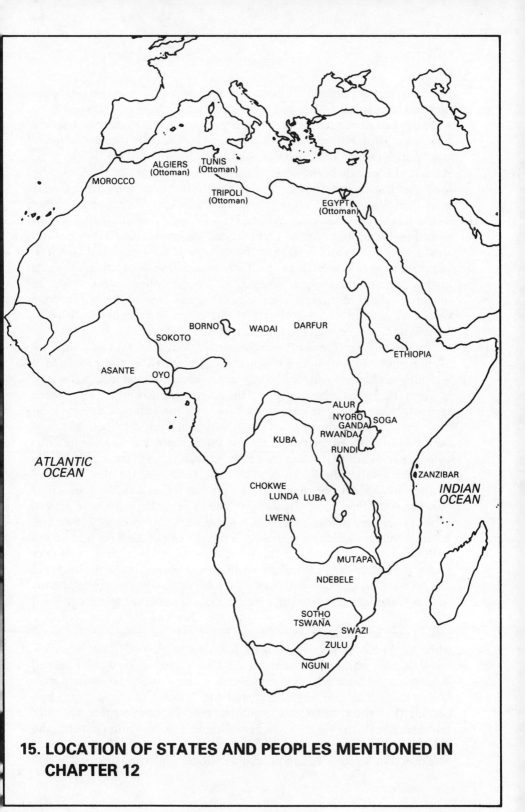

15. LOCATION OF STATES AND PEOPLES MENTIONED IN CHAPTER 12

revenues from designated estates and were expected to maintain establishments at the capital as well as in their counties. Tribute and corvée labour was supplied at regular intervals and used mainly for roads and public buildings. Military leadership was organized separately from the administrative structure by professionals, who held official lands for the purpose. Rank and file soldiers, however, were still mostly short-term levies, who fought with spears and bows and with a minimum of military discipline. It is an interesting question how much further this process of consolidation might have gone, had East Africa been left to develop on its own for sometime longer than in the event it was. Probably, the six large states would have grown still further at the expense of the peripheral statelets, but there is no reason to think that there would have been amalgamations among the six themselves. Indeed, as their frontiers came closer to touching, their mutual relations, never good, would probably have deteriorated. And divided, they had not much more capacity to resist outside interference than the smaller states in their midst.[4]

Usually, the trend towards enlargement of political scale was a regional phenomenon, in which the leading states apparently competed, as if watching each other and borrowing each other's political ideas. There is, however, the remarkable instance of the Kuba state in central Zaire, which seems to have emerged quite on its own, as the result of a very local migration by the Bushong people from the north bank to the south bank of the Sankuru river. In their new territory the Bushong had to come to terms with a pre-existing population of Kete people, and the result of the encounter was gradually to establish the Bushong, together with the northernmost Kete among whom they first settled, as a ruling aristocracy over the rest of the Kete population. The rulers occupied a core area of about 110 square miles – just enough to accommodate a capital town and the slave villages which grew its food, while the rest of the Kete population was forced to pay tribute, with a tax collector from the capital residing in each Kete village. The central government was carried on by the king and about 120 titled officials, each of whom had his own praise-name and his special insignia made from the feathers of the different species of local birds, while the most important officers also had their own peculiar installation and funeral ceremonies. The total population of the state, when its traditions were studied by Jan Vansina in the 1950s, was only about 70,000, but, as he described it, 'The system allowed the Kuba to become so intoxicated with organization, and above all with public honours, insignia and pageantry, that the "mirage of the feather" had become the central value in the political culture.'[5] Seeing that no other centralized state developed anywhere within a hundred miles of them, the political inventiveness of the Kuba is astonishing.

More often, a course of conquest and political expansion pursued by one state against its immediate neighbours would have repercussions a little further away, in which the part played by refugees was frequently of crucial importance. For example, some time around the mid-sixteenth century, the westernmost of a series of small Luba kingdoms between the upper Lualaba and the upper Kasai conquered its western neighbour, an even smaller state, belonging to the Lunda language area. The resulting Luba/Lunda state grew in the course of the following century into one of the largest political systems in Africa south of the equator. The core area of the state was lightly populated, and the ruling élite devoted its main efforts to warfare and hunting, mutilating their war captives so as to make them identifiable, and setting them to work on agricultural estates around the capital. For the rest, they turned their conquests into tribute obligations, placing an official collector at the headquarters of each tributary chief, and sending ferocious punitive expeditions against defaulters. One consequence of their harsh methods was that many of the Lunda-speaking populations preferred to emigrate before they were attacked. But this carried the condition that they themselves had to conquer others in order to find new places to settle, and so a ripple effect was created, which spread westwards to the Atlantic coast and southwards to the upper Zambezi. Peoples like the Lwena, the Chokwe and the Imbangala underwent a political transformation as an indirect result of the initial Luba/Lunda disturbance. Raiding bands of Imbangala were encountered by Portuguese coastal traders in the neighbourhood of Benguela in 1600, and were encouraged by them to settle as allies of the Portuguese in the Kwanza valley (above, pp. 127–8). Meanwhile, the main Lunda kingdom to the east of the Kasai was being expanded and consolidated, and its kings, known by the title of Mwata Yamvo, were the most powerful in central Africa.[6] From the mid-seventeenth century their westbound caravans sold slaves to the Portuguese in Angola. By the eighteenth century they were sending ivory eastwards through the territory of a great vassal, the Mwata Kazembe, to the Portuguese on the Zambezi. Like the Mwenemutapas and other sacred kings, the Mwata Yamvos practised royal incest, kept royal fire, ate and drank in secret, and maintained an elaborate cult of royal ancestors through spirit mediums. But, situated at the very centre of the continent, they could not keep pace with the acquisition of fire-arms by those to the east and west of them, and their empire was eventually extinguished not by any European intruder, but by the well-armed ivory hunters of the Chokwe, whose ancestors had been among those who retreated westwards from the original Lunda conquests.

Of the Mwenemutapa's kingdom (above, pp. 112–13) there remained by the eighteenth century only a remnant, entirely confined to the lower Zambezi valley. On the Zimbabwe plateau power had fallen by insurrection and conquest to a new dynasty, that of the Rozvi Mambos, which ruled with militaristic efficiency from a series of stone-walled capitals situated around the south-western edges of the plateau. The Rozvi placed tribute collectors in every district and forced the output of the gold mines to pass through state-trading channels. Their military strength consisted of the warlike Rozvi cattle herders who tended the royal herds dispersed over all the best pasturelands.[7] But the Rozvi state was smashed early in the nineteenth century by a new and far more professional military system, which had emerged among the Nguni peoples living to the south of the Limpopo, in Swaziland and Natal. Here, as in the rest of South Africa, growing populations had usually been able to be accommodated by deforestation and the opening up of new land for agriculture and pastoralism. In political terms, this meant the segmentation and prolifera-tion of minuscule states. Those of the Sotho-Tswana on the interior plateau were based around concentrated settlements, whereas the Nguni in the coastal lowlands favoured a more dispersed settlement pattern, but the principle of segmentation was the same. When a political community came to number more than about ten thousand people, it would divide, and some would stay put, while others sought new land on which to build a new state. By the late eighteenth century, however, this process was reaching saturation point, and the crisis came to a head in northern Nguni country, where two sets of rulers endeavoured more or less simultaneously to solve it by policies of militarization and conquest. The essential innovation in both cases consisted in the conversion of temporary groupings for the initiation of youths to adult manhood into long-serving regiments of disciplined soldiery, who lived for anything up to fifteen years in special military encampments before they were given permission to marry and settle down in the traditional way. Such standing forces could be used not only for fighting but also for occupying conquered territory. Their productive work as farmers and herdsmen enhanced the wealth of the rulers, whose control of the age of marriage was also an important means of relating population to resources.[8]

From their beginnings as minuscule states in the late eighteenth century, the nuclei of the Swazi and Zulu hegemonies swelled rapidly, so that by the second decade of the nineteenth century each had achieved a population of between 100,000 and 200,000. Had it been possible for other southern Bantu peoples, particularly the prosperous Sotho-Tswana societies of the interior plateau, to achieve a comparable consolidation, it is conceivable that the Dutch frontiersmen of the Cape Colony might have been deterred from their Great Trek into the interior during the 1830s. But the refugees from the Swazi and Zulu wars of conquest put any such development out of the question. As with the Luba/Lunda expansion, the fundamental fact about the refugees is that they were not just the poor, starving, homeless victims of conquest. They included whole communities which fled before the tide of conquest reached them, and whose quest for a new homeland could only be achieved by conquering others. They included also breakaway groups of Zulu and Swazi warriors trained in the new methods of hand to hand fighting invented by the Zulu king, Shaka. Their objective was actually to find new subjects to dominate by terror tactics, massacring many and incorporating the rest. The most serious disturbances on the plateau occurred between 1822 and 1824, during the course of which most of the little states of the Sotho were utterly destroyed, their stone-walled capital sites abandoned, their cattle seized, their populations dispersed. Of the original formations, there survived only the Pedi and Venda at the northern edge of the plateau and the westernmost Tswana chiefdoms along the fringes of the Kalahari. In the southern mountains, the great self-made leader Moshweshwe gradually built up the nucleus of the modern Lesotho by attracting many small groups of refugees to join him in his rugged fastness. But the heartland of the former Sotho cluster of states in the central and southern Transvaal was occupied by a Zulu warlord, Mzilikazi, who established there the first Ndebele kingdom, in which a nucleus of some 300 Nguni warriors gradually incorporated a much larger number of Sotho survivors in their military system. There was nothing in all this scene that could resist the penetration of some 15,000 Boer trekkers with their cattle, their covered wagons and their fire-arms, who were not initially concerned to conquer but only to fill the gaps which had been cleared for them. The Ndebele co-existed with the Boers for fifteen years on the Transvaal highveld before deciding, on the basis of two brief encounters, to move away northwards and build a new state in the territory of the Rozvi empire.[9]

Meanwhile, several other breakaway movements from the two main Nguni systems were busily 'cultivating with the spear' between the lower Limpopo and the Zambezi, and in all the high mountain country surrounding Lake Malawi. Some raiding bands encircled Lake Tanganyika and even reached the shores of Lake Victoria. The further the ripples spread, the more insignificant the proportion of those of Nguni descent. It was the spread of a system of military organization and warfare rather than a conquering race, but it caused the most extensive disturbance in the known history of Africa. On the whole, one must conclude that it exposed the political weakness of southern Africa rather than its strength. The subcontinent was moving towards the emergence of larger political systems, and a few examples did appear, but with repercussions that were overwhelmingly destructive. In interlacustrine Africa the more gradual growth of larger states seems to have been a beneficial and not a very violent process. In southern Africa the 'Zulu aftermath' was mostly a disaster.[10] And certainly it did more to help than to hinder the outside intrusions into the region that were soon to follow.

Not surprisingly in view of the earlier history of the region, the more stable of the larger states still existing on the eve of the modern period were to be found in Africa north of the equator. For the most part, however, these were no longer the important states of medieval times. Egypt, Tripoli and Tunis, along with the new state of Algiers, had all fallen during the seventeenth century under the suzerainty of Ottoman Turkey, and were governed by juntas of immigrant soldiery, who lived on the taxes extorted from the local farmers and pastoralists and on the profits of systematic piracy practised all over the southern Mediterranean. Until the nineteenth century, when Egypt developed a strong military and political momentum of its own under the leadership of the Albanian Mamluk, Muhammad 'Ali, the strength and stability of these states was in large measure due to the Ottoman connection, loose though it might be in practice. Morocco, by realigning its trade towards western Europe and so gaining access to a regular supply of modern fire-arms, had managed to preserve its independence from the Turks, and at the same time to keep its European trading partners at arm's length. But its own attempts to monopolize the trade of the western Sahara had not been quite so successful. It had conquered Songhay, but had failed to hold it together, to the extent that its garrisons around the Niger bend had become a self-perpetuating military caste rather like the Turkish garrisons in North Africa. On either side of the Moroccan colony, dynasties of Fula origin had taken the place of Songhay provincial government. Further south, the Mande-speaking population had reverted to small, autonomous units. Within the savanna belt, only Borno and the city states of Hausaland had developed without a break from their medieval beginnings. East of Lake Chad, new Islamic states had emerged in Wadai, Darfur and on the upper Nile, but were scarcely dynamic entities, except in the business of slave-raiding and slave-trading practised by small elites of horsemen and cameleers. To the east again, Christian Ethiopia survived, but from the early eighteenth century in a state of decline in which the Solomonic dynasty became of less and less account. It would be rescued during the nineteenth century mainly through the striking initiative of one of its provinces, the little kingdom of Shoa, which by its resolute pursuit of the ivory trade made itself into the best armed state of sub-Saharan Africa. Thanks to Shoa, Ethiopia became the only African country except Morocco which was able to maintain its independence into the twentieth century.

During the eighteenth century especially, all these states suffered from a general economic stagnation that affected the whole of the Muslim Middle East. The maritime nations of Europe had taken over most of the trade of the Indian Ocean and had diverted it to the Cape route. The Red Sea was no longer the essential corridor, and all the feeder routes leading to it from the African interior suffered a corresponding decline. Economically, the up-and-coming parts of Africa north of the equator were those which traded with the Europeans on the beaches and river estuaries between the Senegal and the Congo. The best situated of all were those which could trade both northwards across the desert and southwards to the sea. Asante and Oyo were the most obvious examples. Asante had the advantage of being able to supply both gold and slaves, and here if anywhere there seemed to exist the possibility of an African state large enough and strong enough to hold its own against all comers, to learn what it did not already know by contact with outsiders, and from there on to keep pace with developments in the world at large.

Asante had been founded in the 1680s by a highly sophisticated nucleus of political adventurers and refugees from earlier Akan states, and the paramount ruler, the Asantehene, was every inch an African king – a greatly magnified version of what every Akan-speaker already knew at the local level. The Asantehene was of royal birth. He had his golden stool of office, allegedly conjured down from the sky by the first high priest of the realm. He had his gorgeous silk *kente* cloths and a mass of golden insignia. He had his processional litter attended by beautiful maidens wielding fly-whisks, his royal drums and his huge state umbrellas, each providing nearly as much shade as a full grown tree. He had his 'linguists', through whom he gave judgement and conversed with strangers. Above all, he had his annual 'yam ceremony', when every subordinate chief attended with his retinue, swelling the population of Kumasi from its normal 15,000 to as much as 100,000. By a policy of conquest, enslavement, deportation and incorporation, mostly achieved between 1700 and 1750, a metropolitan region of about 10,000 square miles had been created, with a dense population of some 750,000, which was directly administered from Kumasi. Of these a large proportion were in some sense unfree, and provided manpower for the army, the mines and the agriculture necessary to feed the capital. By the mid-eighteenth century the standing army had been provided with fire-arms, which made it superior to the cavalry armies of the savanna states to the north; and a new phase of expansion added a long series of tributary provinces, some situated in the southern part of Akan-speaking country between Asante and the coast, others in non-Akan country north of the forest. It is thought that the population of the southern provinces roughly equalled that of the metropolitan region. The northern provinces were probably even more populous.[11]

By the early nineteenth century, therefore, Asante was ruling an area comparable to that of modern Ghana, with a standing army dispersed around the country under military chiefs, and with a central bureaucracy of some 250 major administrative chiefs who lived and worked in Kumasi and controlled a network of resident commissioners in each of the tributary provinces. A system of cleared roads and provisioned staging posts enabled messages to be transmitted throughout the metropolitan region within about five days, and to the most distant of the tributary provinces within about 16 days. Besides the oral messages, there was written correspondence in Dutch, English and Arabic, carried on by a staff of foreign clerks. The Asantehene, said a nineteenth-century witness, was one of the busiest people one could imagine. 'He must attend to all the petty affairs of his kingdom, and also to war, to religion, to commerce, to agriculture, to weights and measures, to prices and tariffs, and finally to the exercise of justice, which is not the least of his responsibilities.'[12]

The economic basis of Asante's power rested on the production of gold in the metropolitan region, and on tribute from the provinces, which was paid mostly in gold by the southerners and mostly in slaves by those to the north. Till the early nineteenth century, a proportion of the slaves were exported overseas, along with gold-dust, and so helped to pay for imports of textiles, hardware and fire-arms. Of accumulated gold the Great Chest of Asante is thought to have contained 400,000 ounces – the equivalent of two billion dollars in modern money. The accumulation of wealth by individuals likewise reached astonishing levels. One high official who died in 1814 left 45,000 ounces of gold. Three years later, another left 27,000 ounces.[13] Clearly the abolition of the Atlantic slave trade gave a jolt to the system, in that it left Asante without the means to pay for all of the European imports to which it had become accustomed. But already in 1817 the governor of the Dutch trading forts at the coast was pointing the Asantehene towards a new economic policy, to make his kingdom rich again by the cultivation of tropical produce, such as cotton, sugar, coffee and indigo. The export of such produce in bulk would necessitate the improvement of the roads so that wheeled vehicles could be used, even if they had to be pushed by men. But the new agriculture would enable the king 'to conquer all his enemies and extend his boundaries as far as he shall please, through the improvement of the arts of war, which his generals will obtain by intercourse with the Whites'.[14] No doubt, the governor was to some extent guilty of playing the part of Satan in the temptations of Christ, but he had his finger on the essential problems. If African states were to survive through the nineteenth century, let alone through the twentieth, there would have to be more, and more varied, contact with the outside world. There would have to be agricultural production for export. And there would have to be mechanical transport of some kind to get the local produce to the coast and the imported manufactures to the interior. The great weakness of Asante, as of nearly all the largest states of Africa, was that military hegemony failed to develop into cohesive nationhood. The tributary states, which made up two-thirds of Asante, felt no loyalty to the central institutions. The northern tributaries only paid under threat of military reprisals. And even the southerners, who were culturally related to the Asante, knew well that if they failed to pay their tribute in gold, the next demand would be upon their manpower, in the shape of slaves or military recruits or mining labour.[15] They also knew that, between the British, the Dutch and the Danes, there existed alternative protectors whose demands might be less exacting than those of Asante. At the end of the day, therefore, it would be the metropolitan region which would have to face the challenges of a hostile world, in which its former tributaries were aligned with the enemy. Asante, one feels, did just have the possibility of creating a nation by uniting the Akan-speaking peoples. But its apparent unity was insufficiently consolidated to cope with a changing international scene.

If even Asante failed to adapt to the nineteenth century, it is easy to understand why others did the same. Oyo was another military hegemony, based on cavalry power rather than on fire-arms. It had a natural constituency in the Yoruba-speaking peoples, of whom it conquered during the seventeenth and eighteenth centuries the half who lived to the north of the forest. Its non-Yoruba subjects were the Fon-speaking peoples of Dahomey, who inhabited an anomalous region where the savanna, and therefore the theatre of cavalry warfare, extended southwards to the sea. The Fon were certainly never anything but unwilling tributaries. The southern Yoruba stood firmly independent behind their forest defences. Even among the northern Yoruba, there were those who preferred the hegemony of Benin to that of Oyo. Robin Law, the historian of Oyo, is bleakly realistic in concluding that the two basic ingredients of its power were the employment of slaves in agricultural production and the levying of tribute from subject communities.[16] An early misconception about the fall of Oyo is that it was a victim of conquest by the Fulani 'empire' of Sokoto. As Law points out, the jihad in Oyo was not in any sense an invasion, but an insurrection by local elements – Fulani pastoralists, Hausa slaves and Yoruba Muslims. The process of disintegration had started a full fifty years before.[17]

As for the caliphate or empire of Sokoto, it became during the first half of the nineteenth century the largest system of theoretical political allegiance in Africa, except for the Turkish dominions in the north. It stretched from the east of the Niger bend far to the south-east of Lake Chad, a four-month journey from west to east, and from Air to Ilorin, a two-month journey from north to south. But it never functioned as an empire. It represented a connected series of coups d'état by Muslim and Fulani elements, undertaken in a number of pre-existing states at the invitation of those who led the original jihad in the Hausa state of Gobir in 1804–5. The leaders of these coups received flags from Sokoto, and were known as emirs. But, as Murray Last has put it, 'They were ruling communities with enough momentum to continue without aid, as without aid they had started.'[18]

The Fulani emirs were essentially old-fashioned rulers, seeking to re-establish pristine standards of Islamic observance. In economic matters they sought to tax, but otherwise to leave well alone. In matters of defence they had all the cavalryman's typical contempt for innovation. As in the Turkish dominions, muskets were considered suitable for slaves.

It is increasingly recognized that the first generation of professional historians of Africa tended to look at the few big states of the continent through rose-coloured spectacles. These were the areas of hope, which pointed the way to what the Africans, left to themselves, might have achieved. These were the examples which could most easily be compared with the political institutions of other continents. Here at least were some relatively tidy and intelligible islands in the sea of minute and scarcely memorable societies. Their existence helped to focus the attention of beginners in the subject, and at the level of research it was here that there tended to be a readily recognizable corpus of oral tradition which could be recorded and studied for its historical content. From the vantage-point of present knowledge, however, it becomes ever plainer that the largest states of precolonial Africa tended to have the fragility of card-houses: one unexpected challenge, and they would disintegrate into their component particles. By contrast, the minuscule states of ten or fifteen thousand people seem often to have had greater cohesion and durability. They could be annexed into larger formations and yet retain their individuality. Only they were far too numerous to be studied by historians in any comprehensive fashion.

CHAPTER 13

STRANGERS AT THE GATES

In a sense, there had always been strangers at the gates. Long before the nineteenth century, Egypt and North Africa had suffered conquest and colonization by Assyrians, Phoenicians, Persians, Greeks, Romans, Vizigoths, Byzantines, Arabs, Portuguese and Spaniards. Eastern Africa had experienced the colonization of its offshore islands by settlers from maritime South-East Asia, India, Persia and Arabia, as well as from Portugal and France. From the fifteenth century onwards western Africa had likewise seen the colonization of its offshore islands and the establishment of fortified trading posts on parts of the sea coast between the Senegal and the Cape of Good Hope by Portuguese and Spaniards, British, Danish, Dutch, French and Swedes. Inland, however, the story in Africa south of the Sahara had been quite different. For some two hundred years there had been a Portuguese presence of missionaries and traders at the capital of the Kongo kingdom. Otherwise, the only European or Asian establishments anywhere in the African interior by the late eighteenth century were some French riverside trading forts on the Senegal, some Portuguese trading stations on the Kwanza and the Zambezi, and some pastoral farmlands in the hinterland of the Dutch revictualling station at Cape Town. Foreign goods of some description had indeed penetrated to almost every part of Africa, just as African exports, both of people and of precious commodities like gold and ivory, had made their impact on the outside world. But whether from the Sahara southwards or from the Atlantic and Indian Ocean seaboards, the caravan trade had been organized by the Africans themselves, and it had not fundamentally upset the political structures of the continent. Imports, including imported weapons, had mostly found their way into the hands of the traditional rulers, who had used them to strengthen their political authority by enlargements of scale and increased centralization of administrative systems.

The nineteenth century, however, saw a radical change in the tempo of the intercontinental trade, which led to a large increase in the penetration of Africa by coast-based caravans, some of them under non-African leadership. Expeditions now increasingly made their way into the interior using main force when necessary, and having arrived at their destinations, created alternative systems of authority to those of the traditional kings and chiefs, surrounding themselves with well-armed local followers not merely for protection but also in order to seize what otherwise would have to be paid for. The key commodity in this new system of rapine and barter was ivory, always of importance in the intercontinental trade between Africa and Asia, but now subject to surging demand from the growing middle class of Europe and North America, which required knife handles, piano keys, billiard balls and a hundred other luxury items best made from the soft, easily carved tusks of the African elephant.[1] The vital commodity passing in the opposite direction was the trade musket – essentially the same muzzle-loaded, flint-lock hand-gun, firing a single ball, which had been entering the African market since the mid-seventeenth century, but in numbers which had risen dramatically since the conversion of European smelting furnaces from charcoal to coal in the later eighteenth century. Production had further increased during the Napoleonic wars, at the conclusion of which there proved to be a large surplus available for sale on the world market. Muskets were the favourite import of Africa. They were used not only, or even mainly, for warfare, but also for hunting, and for the protection of herds and crops from the depredations of birds and wild animals. Unlike the precision weapons which were to follow in the second quarter of the nineteenth century, muskets could usually be repaired by African blacksmiths and fired with locally manufactured powder and shot. However, their effective use in warfare depended on training and tactics, and it was here that the armed guards of a coast-based caravan were usually superior even to the élite troops of an African ruler, who could make enough noise to frighten their less sophisticated neighbours or even the horses of a mounted enemy, but who were apt to fire without even putting their guns to their shoulders and taking proper aim. One such marksman, when asked how much powder he used when loading, replied that it depended on how angry he was feeling.[2]

From early in the nineteenth century, the difference in weaponry between the coast-based intruders and those who lived in the interior began to be increased by the gradual spread of the rifle. Vastly more accurate than the musket and effective at much longer range, the rifle was beyond the capacity of most African blacksmiths to repair, and suitable ammunition could not be locally improvised. By the second half of the century a few of the wealthiest African rulers were accumulating small stocks of rifles and ammunition, but only Ethiopia was in a position to deploy any significant numbers in skilled hands on the battlefield. It was the same with breech-loaders, which greatly increased the speed of firing, and which began to reach Africa after the Franco-Prussian war. And the difference was to reach its climax with the introduction of the Maxim machine-gun, which began to be available to stranger armies just in time for the wars of conquest. Thus, all through the century the disparity in weapons between insiders and outsiders was growing, and only this factor can explain how a continent which had hitherto managed to keep strangers at arm's length could by the end of the century find itself unable to resist the forcible occupation of its territory.[3]

Meanwhile, conquest and occupation were preceded and facilitated by a proccess of political destabilization, which developed almost contemporaneously throughout the continent, but took rather different forms in different regions. One particularly clear pattern was that which unfolded in Egypt and its hinterland following the opening of the country to western influences through its conquest and brief occupation by Napoleon between 1798 and 1801. Napoleon was accompanied by a retinue of scholars and publicists whose work aroused the lasting interest of western Europe. Traders and entrepreneurs of every kind flocked to Egypt, and the Ottoman Sultan Selim III, determined to have done with Mamluk rule, introduced an Albanian contingent into the garrison and appointed an Albanian viceroy. From 1805 till 1848 the office was held by Muhammad 'Ali, a soldier of outstanding qualities, who recruited a new army trained by French instructors and established a civil administration organized in departments with a ministerial system similar to those of western Europe. As a generalissimo, he was so successful that he was able to reconquer the Hijaz for the Ottoman Sultan, and, in 1821, to annex the northern Sudan to Egypt by invading and conquering the Funj kingdom of Sennar, which had ruled most of Nubia since the sixteenth century. Thus a typical cavalry-armed, slave-raiding Muslim state of the sub-Saharan savanna was overthrown by a coastal neighbour with access to modern weapons and military training.[4]

However, Muhammad 'Ali's Sudanese empire did not stop at the frontiers of the Funj state. Convinced that the deep interior of central Africa was rich in gold, he spurred on his governors, based at the new colonial capital of Khartoum, to open up the animist regions higher up the White Nile. As soon as sailing vessels could be built, armed expeditions were despatched to try to find navigable channels through the great papyrus-filled swamps of the Sudd, where Shilluk, Nuer and Dinka pastoralists carried on a self-contained, transhumant existence, clustering on the ridges at flood-time and spreading out across the rich pastures when the waters receded. There was no point of contact with these people, who had no desire for trade and nothing of commercial value to offer. But at last in 1839 an unusually persistent convoy broke right through the Sudd into the southern savanna in the neighbourhood of modern Juba. Here the Egyptians found the Bari people both willing to trade and at the same time

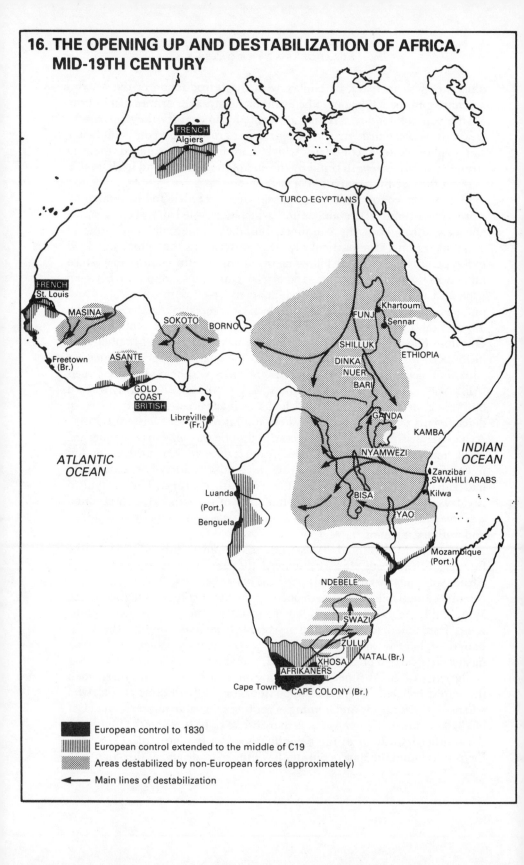

16. THE OPENING UP AND DESTABILIZATION OF AFRICA, MID-19TH CENTURY

FRENCH
Algiers

TURCO-EGYPTIANS

FRENCH
St. Louis

MASINA

SOKOTO   BORNO

Freetown
(Br.)   ASANTE

GOLD
COAST
BRITISH

Libreville
(Fr.)

Khartoum
FUNJ
Sennar

SHILLUK

DINKA
NUER
BARI

ETHIOPIA

GANDA

KAMBA

NYAMWEZI

ATLANTIC
OCEAN

INDIAN
OCEAN

Zanzibar
SWAHILI ARABS

BISA

Kilwa

Luanda
(Port.)

YAO

Benguela

Mozambique
(Port.)

NDEBELE

SWAZI

ZULU

XHOSA   NATAL (Br.)

AFRIKANERS

Cape Town   CAPE COLONY (Br.)

■ European control to 1830

▥ European control extended to the middle of C19

▨ Areas destabilized by non-European forces (approximately)

◀— Main lines of destabilization

ignorant of the value of ivory, so that many fine bargains were struck, in which the accumulated tusks of elephants hitherto hunted only for their meat were exchanged for trivial quantities of glass beads.

It did not continue that way. On the one hand, the news of such an El Dorado spread rapidly among the cosmopolitan trading community of Khartoum, who began to build their own boats and to hire and arm their own strong men. On the other hand, the Bari, and their neighbours to the east and west, soon exhausted their accumulated ivory and their enthusiasm for trade beads. A new pattern of relationships developed, which was soon to characterize the whole region from the Ethiopian borders to the shores of Lake Chad, whereby the so-called 'traders' became in practice the captains of private armies, based in stockaded encampments right across the savanna country, from which they raided the local villages for slaves and cattle. The slaves mostly went to reward the soldiery, who kept some as wives and porters and sold the rest into the trade. The cattle, which were the most prized possession of every society in the region, were traded back to the survivors in exchange for ivory. Worst of all for political stability, was the fact that these conflicts were not simple ones between insiders and outsiders, for the usual entry tactic of the traders was to help one side or the other in local disputes. Moreover, the camp followers, and sometimes even the ordinary soldiery of the private armies, were local people recruited by capture into the ranks of the oppressors.[5]

Egypt, meanwhile, was itself coming more and more under foreign influence. During the 1860s especially, westerners came in their tens of thousands to build railways and the Suez canal, and to participate as irrigationists, processors and merchants in the cotton boom caused by the cutting off of trans-Atlantic supplies by the American Civil War. And to support all these activities European bankers lent money, and debts accumulated to the point where European governments, at first singly and later in concert, brought pressure to protect the interests of their nationals. It was against such a background that Muhammad 'Ali's grandson Ismail (1863–79) embarked on plans still further to extend Egypt's colonial empire, employing first Samuel Baker and then Charles Gordon to carry the boundaries of the Sudan southwards to include the Bantu kingdoms around the sources of the Nile, recently publicized by the travels of Speke and Grant. Both Baker and Gordon managed to lead armed expeditions through parts of northern Uganda without actual disaster, but with no lasting result. Both men came to realize that, just to keep troops alive and mobile among societies which produced nothing of commercial value, it was necessary to use the same methods as the 'traders' from Khartoum. Their efforts merely extended the area of destabilization.[6]

In eastern Africa, as in the Nilotic Sudan, the nineteenth century witnessed a process of political destabilization, partly as a result of the general diffusion of trade muskets, and partly through the penetration of the interior by coastmen armed with superior weapons. The coastal polity in this case consisted of the African empire of the Arab rulers of Oman, who had driven the Portuguese from all of their coastal footholds north of Cape Delgado at the end of the seventeenth century, and who by the mid-eighteenth century were beginning to establish a local metropolis for their dominion on the offshore island of Zanzibar.[7] The Omani state had nothing like the population or the economic potential of Egypt, but the Swahili-speaking people of the East African coastal towns had an economic and cultural cohesion which long antedated the Omani supremacy (above, pp 88–9). Since the very early days of Islam they had been a part of the Indian Ocean trading system, in which the ivory of the interior, as well as the gold of the Zimbabwe plateau, had been important components. Yet all the indications are that, until late in the eighteenth century, the trade between coast and hinterland had been organized by the inland peoples, especially the Yao, the Bisa, the Nyamwezi and the Kamba (above, pp. 142–4). The Swahili had remained coastbound, managing the coastal traffic and acting as middle-men between the inland carriers and the oceanic traders from India and the Gulf.

The galvanizing event, which affected the whole region, was the French occupation in 1735 of the hitherto uninhabited Mascarene Islands (today Mauritius and Réunion) and their development as slave-worked plantation colonies on the West Indian pattern. The slaves were at first imported from Madagascar, where the military expansion of the Merina kingdom was yielding great numbers of war captives. From 1770 onwards the emphasis switched to the East African mainland, where Kilwa became the main port of shipment. It was from the French slave-traders that muskets began to spread among the Swahili and their inland partners. It seems that by about 1780 coast-based caravans were reaching the shores of Lake Malawi in search of slaves and ivory.[8] Likewise, it was from the Mascarene example that the idea of slave-worked plantations began to be applied to the growing of cloves on Zanzibar and Pemba.[9] The clove industry confirmed the ascendancy of Zanzibar as the entrepot between coastal and oceanic shipping, and greatly increased the interest of the islanders in the mainland trade. Indian merchants and money-lenders settled there to buy ivory and to supply the caravans with trade goods. By 1820, at least one Indian merchant had joined a community of coastmen who established a regular trading settlement at Unyanyembe, some 400 miles inland in the heart of the Nyamwezi country. During the second quarter of the nineteenth century the great Omani ruler Sayyid Said (1806–56) turned his attention increasingly to his African dominions, and in 1840 actually transferred his own headquarters from Muscat to Zanzibar. All the coastal towns from Cape Delgado to southern Somalia were now firmly under his control, and since his revenue was derived mainly from customs duties on the inland trade, a great impulse was given to the extension of ivory-hunting in the virgin areas of the far interior. Soon Unyanyembe was but a stepping-stone. Coastal caravans were crossing Lake Tanganyika by the 1840s and Lake Victoria a decade later, and although the coastmen paid due deference to the powerful rulers of the interlacustrine kingdoms, their activities in the eastern half of the Congo basin closely resembled those of the traders on the upper Nile. All through the Ituri forest and the savanna to the south of it, long-term settlements were established, where the Swahili/Arab magnates lived in greater style than any local chief, while their private armies ranged in all directions, hunting elephant themselves, and forcing the local people to do the same by terror tactics and the taking of hostages. Even where rulers were stronger, the power of the coastmen would be felt in every succession struggle.[10]

In considering the impact of the Swahili/Arab penetration, however, not all the emphasis should be placed on the destructive effects. The intruders had their followers as well as their victims, and in the course of a generation or two nearly every foreign trading settlement became in effect a new state, offering an alternative system of government to the traditional systems found in the neighbourhood. For example, at Nkota Nkota on the western shores of Lake Malawi an enterprising Swahili caravan leader settled in the early years of the nineteenth century to the business of running a ferry across the lake and supplying provisions to the caravans which used it. He acquired many slaves and developed big plantations. Thriving villages grew up on his domain, and he performed the functions of a chief among his subjects, of whom an increasing number learned to speak the Swahili language and to identify with the religion of Islam. When, in 1889, British envoys came to make treaties in the area, they met the grandson of the founder still ruling the district, and they treated him as a chief in his own right.[11] It was the same with the Swahili Arab settlements in eastern Zaire. To the west of Lake Tanganyika there emerged a new, quasi-ethnic term, *Manyema*, which was applied to all the local subjects and followers of the coastmen. Its implications were by no means derogatory, for it signified those individuals from all the western Bantu societies who had become detribalized – those who could speak Kiswahili and comprehend the affairs of a wider world. By the end of the century the Manyema had developed a sense of community which would express itself in the first organized resistance to the encroachment of King Leopold's rule. They had become an élite which felt its position threatened by a new overlord.[12]

It is a striking thought that, had the Swahili Arab penetration persisted without challenge for another decade or two, the whole of central Africa from the southern Sudan to the Zambezi might have become a predominantly Muslim region. In the event, however, other strangers from the outside world soon followed in their footsteps. The third quarter of the nineteenth century saw the passage of caravans led by the Europeans who would be known in their own countries as the 'explorers' of central Africa – Livingstone, the missionary, trekking up from the south to spend twenty years criss-crossing the region between the Zambezi, Lake Malawi and the upper Congo; Burton and Speke following the Swahili Arab highway to Lakes Tanganyika and Victoria; Speke and Grant visiting the interlacustrine kingdoms and returning down the Nile; Cameron following the trade routes across the southern savanna from Lake Tanganyika to Luanda; Stanley descending the Congo through the great forest to emerge at last on the estuary. To the Africans through whose lands they passed there can have been little difference between the white men's caravans and those of their Swahili/Arab contemporaries. Both traded cloth and beads, and occasionally fire-arms, in exchange for protection, food supplies and ivory. The difference lay in the words which the explorers wrote in their journals as they sat by their tents in the evening – words which, when published, would be eagerly read by hundreds of thousands in Europe and America, of whom a few would be stirred by them to significant action. It was the habitual use of written communication that distinguished the Christian penetration from the Muslim, and it was in the shape of Christian propaganda that the first results fed back into Africa. Within a few years of Livingstone's death four different Protestant missionary societies were despatching agents to the lands around Lake Malawi, with a series of river steamers to connect them with the Indian Ocean coast. Within three years of Stanley's coast-to-coast journey, British Anglicans and French Roman Catholics were competing for the attention of the Buganda court. Not much direct evangelization took place during the early years of a mission. There were languages to be learnt and a new environment to be mastered. But most missionaries, like their Swahili Arab counterparts, would acquire land and establish plantations to support not only themselves but the growing communities of refugees and ransomed slaves who would become in effect their subjects, forming little states alternative to the traditional ones. Even in a powerful kingdom like Buganda, their technical skills and knowledge of the outside world would bring them secular influence much wider than any strictly religious following, to the extent that within a decade of their arrival political divisions would be expressed in terms of the three kinds of foreigners – Swahili, French and British – to whom the Ganda élite turned for advice.[13]

The destabilization of southern African societies had in a sense begun in the late seventeenth century, when small groups of whites from the Dutch colony at the Cape, equipped with guns, horses and ox-wagons, began to trade and fight for cattle with the Khoi pastoralists of the immediate hinterland. As a result of these contacts, some Khoi lost their herds and became absorbed into colonial society as servants and labourers. Others retreated inland and reorganized themselves for a new way of life as hunters and cattle-traders operating on the fringes of the slowly expanding territory of the colony. Until well into the nineteenth century these Khoi bands of the northern frontier, soon equipped themselves with guns, horses and wagons, were nearly the equals in power of the white frontiersmen whose means of livelihood were so similar to their own. As late as 1800, the white population numbered only 16,000, of whom the great majority still lived in Cape Town and made their living from the seaborne trade between Europe and Asia. British annexation of the Cape Colony in 1815 soon doubled the number of whites, but the Khoi frontier in the north remained intact until the eve of the Great Trek in 1836.[14]

More significant in the long run than the Khoi were the Bantu-speakers living to the east of the Cape Colony. These were the Xhosa, the southernmost of the Nguni peoples, and they were present in numbers which greatly exceeded those of the colonists. Unlike the northern Nguni, they were still in the early nineteenth century organized in minuscule states, which tended to subdivide in every generation. That did not stop them from developing trade with the whites, and long before their frontiers touched, Xhosa caravans brought cattle, karosses and ivory to Hermanus Kraal on the Fish River, where traders from Cape Town came with their wagons to meet them.[15] Thus, the Xhosa chiefs acquired horses and guns, while their subjects bought metal hoes and steel tips for their assegais. As the areas of white and Xhosa settlement began to intersect, there was episodic fighting, but also regular interaction. The settlers needed labour and absorbed as tenants and share-croppers the strangers, known as Mfengu, many of them refugees from the Shakan wars in Natal, who formed the underclass of Xhosa society. These were among the earliest Bantu-speakers to become Christianized, and in the frontier wars they fought alongside their white masters against the Xhosa.[16] By the 1820s, missionaries were settling inside Xhosa territory, and every early mission station became a little state composed of people who had largely renounced their allegiance to the traditional chiefs in order to lead a new kind of semi-westernized life, farming intensively for the white market, transport-riding, practising new artisanal skills as smiths and carpenters, and later assisting as migrant workers in the mining of gold and diamonds. Seen in this light, the piecemeal extensions of the eastern Cape Colony to the Kei in 1847, to the Mbashe in 1858, to the Mthatha in 1878, and to the Mzimkhulu in 1894, merely set the seal on a process of economic and social change that was already far advanced.[17]

In southern Africa the first clear demonstration of the crushing power of modern weapons used by skilled hands came with the Great Trek, when some 5,000 Afrikaners, accompanied by a similar number of Black and Coloured servants, crossed the northern frontier of the Cape Colony into the country of the Sotho peoples, recently devastated by the invading hordes of Ndebele and other refugees from the Shakan wars (above, pp. 152–3). The Voortrekkers could not even keep together. If only to feed their herds, they had to spread out. Their small parties included a large majority of women and children. Of the men only a handful had received any formal military training. Most were frontier farmers, well practised in the use of rifles against wild game and human stock thieves. They were good horsemen, accustomed to fire from the saddle, but their most lethal technique was the defensive one of lashing their wagons in a tight circle, or *laager*, from which they could beat back spear-armed attackers in numbers far larger than their own. The decisive victories were won, not against the dispersed and demoralized Sotho, but against the trained and concentrated regiments, first of the Ndebele of the Transvaal and then of the Zulu of Natal. In January 1837 a commando of 107 Afrikaners was able to sack the Ndebele capital of Mosega, killing 400 of the defendants. Ten months later, another encounter on a similar scale was sufficient to drive the Ndebele northwards across the Limpopo. Within weeks of this victory, most of the Voortrekkers, anxious to secure an access to the sea coast, had descended the Drakensberg passes into the Zulu homeland in Natal. In February and March of 1838 the Zulu scored some early successes against them, killing more than 350 Voortrekkers in surprise attacks. But in November a Voortrekker commando of just 500 men, with 57 wagons, inflicted a decisive defeat on the main Zulu army, which lost 3,000 killed without causing a single fatal casualty in return. Next year, the Zulu nation started to break up, when an unsuccessful candidate for the throne led 17,000 of his people to make peace with the Afrikaners and to settle under their rule. In January 1840 the legitimate ruler, Dingane, was defeated, and he himself killed.[18] A long sequence of piecemeal conquests of Zulu, Swazi, Pedi and others remained to be enacted over the next forty years. Some of it involved larger scale fighting than that between the Trekboers and the northern Nguni, for between 1840 and 1880 the Pedi in particular engaged regularly in migrant labour and brought back home first muskets and later rifles with their earnings.[19] But inevitably during a period when the efficiency of armaments was developing rapidly, the whites had more up-to-date weapons than the blacks, and there could be no doubt of the ultimate outcome. In 1879, in an attempt to win the approval of the Afrikaners of the Transvaal, the British picked a quarrel with the Zulu kingdom of Dingane's nephew Cetshwayo, and through the incompetence of their general, Lord Chelmsford, suffered an initial grave defeat at the battle of Isandhlwana, losing 1,600 men out of its total force of 8,000. But it proved only a temporary setback, for less than six months later a reinforced British expedition burnt the Zulu capital at Ulundi, captured Cetshwayo and set in train the final disintegration of the Zulu kingdom.

On the surface at least, West Africa during most of the nineteenth century showed fewer signs of impending destabilization than any other part of the continent. Here, the dominant theme seemed, on the contrary, to be the triumphant enlargement and consolidation of Islamic states under indigenous dynasties. There was the reform of the Hausa and other neighbouring states, and their incorporation within a single caliphate of Sokoto, which followed from the Fulani jihad launched in 1804 in Gobir by `Shaykh Usuman dan Fodio (above, pp. 157–8). There was the corresponding reform and revitalization of the ancient state of Borno by Shaykh Muhammad al-Kanemi, a religious leader from east of Lake Chad, called in by the legitimate ruler of Borno to defend him from the Fulani of Sokoto. And there was another huge consolidation of Islamic political ascendancy in the region to the west of the Niger bend, which began with the jihad declared around 1818 by Ahmad bin Muhammad in the Fulani state of Masina, which developed into a rival caliphate to that of Sokoto, with its capital at Hamdallahi, midway between Timbuktu and Jenne. In 1862 it was incorporated within the still larger empire of another reforming jihadist, al-Hajj 'Umar, which extended over the whole area between the upper Niger and the upper Senegal.[20] Thus, both in eastern and western West Africa political power passed into the hands of devout Muslim rulers, who were served by literate bureaucrats and by judges learned enough to apply the Shari'a law of Islam in all the higher courts. Beyond the frontiers of the two caliphates, Islam was spreading in a more superficial way across the middle belt and into the southern part of West Africa, so that by mid-century there were numerous converts among the Yoruba, the Mossi and the southern Mande-speakers. Though inspired by the pilgrimage experiences of the religious élite, and helped by the expansion of brotherhoods which spanned the Muslim world, these jihadic reforms were entirely indigenous in leadership and execution. In any cool assessment of the nineteenth century history of West Africa, the reform and expansion of Islam must take pride of place.[21]

And yet, even in West Africa, the rising influence of strangers was not far to seek. All around the coastal fringes were the places where gold and slaves had been exchanged with European sea-borne traders since the fifteenth century. Around each of these places there had grown up a client population of middleman traders, market gardeners, boatmen and porters, whose primary loyalties lay with the strangers rather than with the traditional authorities. With the gradual suppression of the sea-borne slave trade during the first half of the nineteenth century, these client populations took on a new significance. Henceforward, the commercial interests of the Europeans were in agricultural produce – in the western sector, ground-nuts, in the eastern sector, palm-oil – which required the development of contact with the ordinary farming population of the coastal hinterland. The client populations of the European forts and mooring-places, with their local family connections spreading into the hinterland, supplied the army of petty traders indispensable to such an economic revolution.[22] Another group of great significance were the 'recaptive' slaves freed through the action of the anti-slave-trade squadrons during the first half of the century. Most recaptives were initially landed at the special settlements established by the British at Freetown, Sierra Leone, and by the French at Libreville in modern Gabon, where they were exposed to Christian missionary influences and their children to some degree of western education. Before long, however, many recaptive families sought ways of repatriating themselves, not necessarily to their actual homes, but at least to somewhere within their own linguistic and cultural communities. Thus the Yoruba returnees tended to settle in the coastal towns of Lagos and Badagry, the Akan at Cape Coast, and the Wolof in the charming Franco-African town of St Louis on its island in the Senegal estuary. The returnees tended to be those who had done well in the recaptive settlements. Nearly all were traders. Many were Christian. They knew the value of mission education. They formed the nucleus of an aspiring, westernizing bourgeoisie, who assumed that western influences were destined to grow stronger in West Africa, and who saw themselves as the mediators in that process.[23]

Foreign rule during the first half of the nineteenth century was an affair of tiny enclaves, designed to enable handfuls of European traders to regulate their relations with their employees and their middlemen clients. It did not always involve the direct participation of white officials or armed forces. Committees of merchants, judging disputes with their African counterparts and enforcing decisions by economic sanctions, was one formula employed by Dutch and Danes as well as British over much of the West African coastline. Consular supervision was sometimes added, together with some naval back-up, but ships' guns were only useful against waterside targets. Before 1875, only about half a dozen isolated enclaves enjoyed full colonial status, with official governors exercising civil and military power, raising revenue and conducting diplomatic relations with neighbouring African states. There were two potential flashpoints, where a colonial enclave bordered on the sphere of a major African power. One was on the Senegal, where the French colony felt threatened by the westward expansion of the empire of al-Hajj 'Umar. During the governorship of Louis Faidherbe from 1854 till 1865 the area of French rule was extended some 300 miles up the river valley in anticipation of this threat. The other flashpoint was on the Gold Coast, where, by 1800 or soon after, the kingdom of Asante claimed to have extended its suzerainty to the coast. The Dutch, with their bases in the western Gold Coast, admitted the Asante claims, trading directly with Asante caravans and supplying them with the most modern weapons as trade goods. The British and the Danes, with their bases further to the east, had their dealings with Fante and Ga, who had been subjected to Asante raids, but did not seem to have accepted their suzerainty. In 1824 a British governor of the coastal settlements tried to organize the Fante states in an act of combined resistance, but was defeated and killed by Asante forces. During the next fifty years the controversy simmered. The British bought out the Danes in 1850 and took over the Dutch forts in 1872. The following year the Asante entered Fante territory in force, and the British responded with a major military expedition, involving 2,500 British troops, together with Fante auxiliaries. Kumasi was reached and sacked in February 1874. But it was a punitive expedition, not an act of conquest. The day after their arrival, the British forces started to withdraw. The only territory annexed as a result of the 'Ashanti War' was that of the Ga and Fante, which amounted to little more than a consolidation of the coastal plain in which the European trading forts had been situated in close proximity to one another for so long. Nevertheless, the strongest power in West Africa had been defeated and humiliated, and the tributary states of Asante all read the message and began to distance themselves from their overlord.[24]

Oddly enough, it was North Africa which saw the stranger arrive in greater military force than anywhere else on the continent during the first half of the nineteenth century. The French conquest of Algeria, which started in 1830, was a totally anomalous event. It was not caused by any need to colonize, nor by any well considered strategic objective. It was designed as a *coup de théâtre*, to persuade the French people that Bourbon rule was great and glorious; but although it quite failed to do so, no successor regime until the Fifth Republic dared to face the ignominy of retreat. It was correctly calculated that 35,000 French troops would be ample to subdue the Turkish garrisons of the coastal towns, which numbered about 15,000. It was not foreseen that the real resistance would come not from the Turkish military caste, but from the Arabs and Berbers of the countryside and that it would be religiously inspired by the Muslim horror of being ruled by Christians. Soon, 100,000 troops were needed to defend about the same number of settlers, of whom the majority were not even French. It had been hoped to confine the colony to the narrow and fertile coastal plain, but the nature of the resistance made it necessary to patrol the Aures mountains and the foothills of the eastern Atlas, and to dream of a future that would encompass the northern Sahara and the oases from which the caravan routes led south to West Africa.[25]

To the east of Algeria, in Tunis and Tripoli, the stranger presence felt most insistently through the first sixty years of the nineteenth century was that of Britain, which rightly regarded the Gulf of Sirte as the northern shore of West Africa. It was reckoned that through most of this period some 10,000 slaves a year crossed the Sahara, of whom half were sold in Tripoli for destinations in Turkey, Syria, the Balkans, or Egypt. The British campaign against the trade was waged in the Mediterranean no less than in the Atlantic. Recaptives taken at sea were landed in Malta. The Greek War of Independence was seen as part of the struggle, and the Crimean War ultimately put Turkey in a position where, in 1857, the abolition of slavery in the Ottoman empire could no longer be refused. Closer to Africa, however, the strong consular presence, which was made stronger by the British refusal to recognize the French action in Algeria, enabled pressure to be put on Tunis and Tripoli to take corresponding action. Inland a whole generation of travellers, from Denham and Clapperton in the 1820s to Richardson and Barth in the 1840s and 1850s, took the long road south from Tripoli to Borno and Hausaland, carrying the message that the exchange of produce must soon supersede the trade in slaves. During the last twenty years of this period trading vice-consuls were even appointed in the desert oases of Murzuk and Ghadames in an attempt to prove that 'legitimate' commerce could be profitable on the Saharan routes. These efforts petered out in the 1860s, as it was gradually realized that with the advent of the river steamer the trade of the central Sudan would find its most economical exit by the Niger river system. It was thus the opening of communications in southern West Africa which finally undermined the desert routes.[26]

To the west of Algeria, Morocco tried to pursue a policy of trading with the Europeans while confining their consuls and merchants strictly to the ports of Tangier and Mogador. Inevitably, however, it was drawn into the Algerian conflict. Abd el-Kader, who led the religious jihad against the French, had his bases along the Moroccan frontier, and the Moroccans aided him with arms and places of refuge. In 1845 a Moroccan army was badly mauled by the French, and following this defeat, Spain, with its ancient enclaves at Ceuta and Melilla, began to jostle for more. In 1860 a Spanish force occupied Tetuan, allegedly to counter Moroccan raids, and withdrew only on payment of an indemnity so large as to put Moroccan revenues in hock to foreign financiers.[27] While Moroccan independence was to outlast the nineteenth century, the growing weakness of the central government was observed and exploited by the perennial forces of unrest in the peripheral and mountainous areas, so that constant military action was necessary to keep the peace. Here, as elsewhere, the stranger was knocking at the gate. It was only a question of how and when he would effect an entry.

CHAPTER 14

THE DRAWING OF THE MAP

The growing disparity in weapons and military organization between the traditional states of Africa and those of the outside world during the first three-quarters of the nineteenth century made it certain that the degree of foreign interference would increase as the century drew to a close. Nevertheless, it was by no means inevitable that this interference would take the form of a partition of the continent into some forty colonial territories, which would broadly demarcate the independent states of modern Africa. By 1875 it was clear that, in Algeria on the one hand and in southern Africa on the other, colonies of European settlement had been established, each with a settler population in excess of 250,000, which had developed an economic and demographic momentum sufficient to ensure that the metropolitan countries would be politically bound to support them in their competition with the indigenous peoples into whose midst they had moved. In Algeria the French, after 45 years of nearly continuous warfare, were still engaged in subjugating the Kabyle tribes who lived in the eastern half of the mountainous hinterland. In southern Africa the decade from 1876 till 1886 was that which saw the conquest of most of the African peoples – Xhosa, Thembu, Mpondomise, Sotho and Zulu – and their incorporation into one or other of the colonial states of the region. It also saw an unsuccessful attempt by the British to annex the Afrikaner state in the Transvaal.[1] Yet all these actions, in southern Africa as in Algeria, were internally motivated acts of colonial consolidation. They carried no implications for Africa between the tropics of Cancer and Capricorn.

Down the western side of tropical Africa there prevailed in 1875 a very different kind of situation, in which Britain, France and Portugal had each developed loose spheres of commercial and missionary interest, based upon small coastal enclaves governed and activated by Europeans who were only temporary migrants from their home countries. These spheres did not touch, and there were wide stretches of coastline where the trading stations of European and American companies competed freely side by side. Yet, on the Senegal at least, the French had already developed one enclave which looked towards the deep interior of the western Sudan. Their way was blocked by the Tokolor empire of al-Hajj 'Umar and his son Ahmadu (above, p. 169), and further south by the rising state of Samory Ture on the right bank of the upper Niger; but from 1876 they were actively building up the force of about 4,000 Senegalese troops, commanded by French officers and NCOs, which would reach the Niger in 1881, occupy Bamako in 1883 and there launch river gunboats which could patrol downstream to Timbuktu and beyond.[2] The British had no such dynamic, well thought out policy as the French, but it was clear that their interests were centred in the coastal regions rather than the far interior. They had consolidated the coastal enclaves along about 300 miles of the Gold Coast and sent a costly punitive expedition against the Asante (above, p. 171) to assert the independence of the coastal people from Asante rule. And the Gold Coast colony was flanked by the long established settlements on the Sierra Leone peninsula and the Gambia estuary to the west, and by Lagos island and a long stretch of actively patrolled coastline between the Niger delta and the Cameroon mountain to the east. The whole of this deltaic region was regularly visited by British merchant shipping engaged in the palm-oil trade, and from 1879 onwards many of the individual companies became amalgamated into the National African Company, which aimed to establish a monopoly of the river trade on the lower Niger and Benue.[3] By the early 1880s it was becoming increasingly likely that the situation in the western bulge of Africa was pointing towards an ultimate rationalization of French and British spheres, whereby the British would withdraw from the Gambia and the French from their little-used trading stations on the Ivory Coast between Sierra Leone and the Gold Coast and at Whydah between the Gold Coast and Lagos. Such a scheme had in fact been discussed in a desultory way by the British and French foreign offices from 1875 onwards, though without any sense of urgency on either side.[4]

Around the rest of the African coastline, from the Cameroon estuary to the Red Sea and the Mediterranean, the situation during the later 1870s was far less predictable. From the Cameroon to the Congo lay a thousand miles of coast unpunctuated by any colonial enclave save the French settlement for freed slaves at Libreville on the Gabon. Between the Congo mouth and that of the Cunene, and on the eastern side of the subcontinent from the Limpopo mouth to that of the Rovuma, were the ancient spheres of Portuguese influence deriving from the sixteenth-century colonies of Angola and Mozambique. The Portuguese settlements, like those of the British and the French, were nothing more than enclaves. The only way of getting from one to another was by sea, for they were separated by independent and frequently hostile African societies. Most were inhabited only by a handful of *mestizo* soldiers and a few small traders dealing in local produce. In Angola the inland 'fairs' of the seventeenth and eighteenth centuries had been abandoned in the nineteenth. In Mozambique, the agricultural estates of the lower Zambezi valley were Portuguese only in name.[5] Nevertheless, there was a presence, which could at any rate be compared with that of the Omanis higher up the east coast, where the Sultan of Zanzibar maintained a governor and a customs official, supported by a handful of Baluchi mercenaries, in perhaps fifteen to twenty Swahili or Somali coastal towns where there was an inland caravan trade worth taxing. The British and French, poised in the Mascarene islands, on Mauritius and Réunion respectively, were well aware how fragile was the hold of these ancient hegemonies; yet until the early 1880s neither wished to step into their places. Instead, they hoped that both would prove strong enough to deter other European claimants, while providing some political protection for their own trading interests. Until 1881 they applied the same doctrine to Tripoli, Tunis and other North African territories of the Ottoman empire.

It was the sudden appearance of competition from European states which had not previously shown any interest in African adventures that turned what had hitherto been only a slowly developing tendency into an active scramble for African colonies. The catalytic influence was that of King Leopold II of the Belgians, who had spent twenty years in the search for a tropical colony when at last he found in the Congo basis, as revealed by the explorations of H.M. Stanley, a goal worthy of his desires. Knowing that Belgium did not share his expansionist dreams, he made his approach under cover of an international organization, which turned itself gradually into the Congo Independent State, in which form it existed from 1885 until 1908, when Belgium finally assumed responsibility. Already by about 1878 Leopold's preparatory moves were beginning to attract the attention of would-be imitators. Colonial pressure groups were founded in both France and Germany, and expeditions were despatched to obtain treaties with African rulers in areas considered suitable for future colonies. Meanwhile, in 1881, France declared a protectorate over Tunis, and in 1882 army officers in Egypt organized a coup d'état against the Khedive's government, as a protest against the economies imposed by the country's European creditors. Britain and France agreed to act together to quell the revolt by a temporary military occupation. At the last minute the French withdrew from the projected expedition for reasons of internal politics, so that Britain occupied Egypt alone, thereby greatly stimulating the acquisitive fever developing in the rest of Europe. It was in these circumstances that the German Chancellor Bismarck called a conference of the European powers, which met in Berlin from December 1884 until April 1885, to discuss the future of western Africa. Ostensibly, the purpose was to restrain expansionism rather than to encourage it. Freedom of

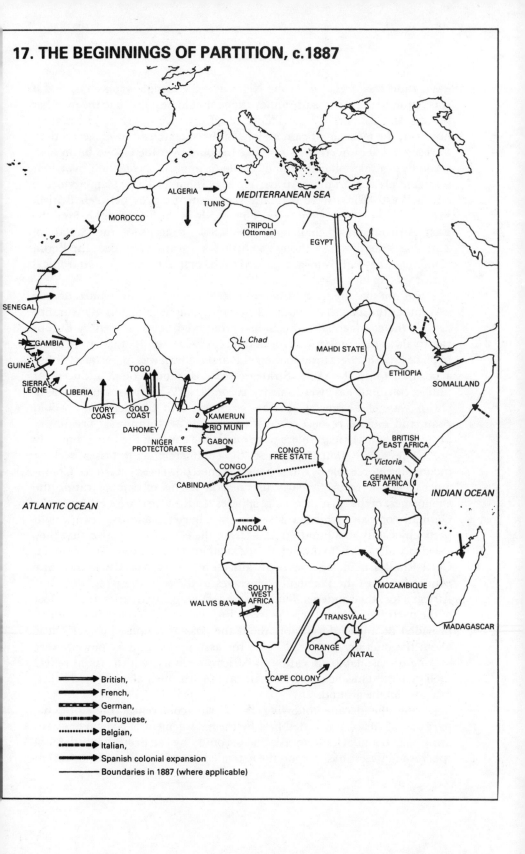

17. THE BEGINNINGS OF PARTITION, c.1887

MEDITERRANEAN SEA

ALGERIA
TUNIS
MOROCCO
TRIPOLI
(Ottoman)
EGYPT

SENEGAL
GAMBIA
GUINEA
SIERRA
LEONE
LIBERIA
IVORY
COAST
GOLD
COAST
TOGO
DAHOMEY
NIGER
PROTECTORATES
KAMERUN
RIO MUNI
GABON
CONGO
CABINDA

L. Chad

MAHDI STATE

ETHIOPIA

SOMALILAND

CONGO
FREE STATE

BRITISH
EAST AFRICA
L. Victoria
GERMAN
EAST AFRICA

INDIAN OCEAN

ATLANTIC OCEAN

ANGOLA

MOZAMBIQUE

MADAGASCAR

WALVIS BAY
SOUTH
WEST
AFRICA

TRANSVAAL

ORANGE
NATAL

CAPE COLONY

British,
French,
German,
Portuguese,
Belgian,
Italian,
Spanish colonial expansion
Boundaries in 1887 (where applicable)

navigation was declared on the Niger and the Congo waterways, and it was required that any future annexations should be notified to the member powers and supported by evidence of effective occupation. In practice, however, the most significant actions of the assembled powers were, first, to recognize the sovereignty of King Leopold over the Congo basin and, secondly, to take official note of German imperial protection over four scattered areas of tropical Africa. Three of them, in Togo, Cameroon and South West Africa, were carefully placed in the gaps between British, French and Portuguese enclaves. The fourth, in the hinterland behind the East African coast, challenged the whole concept of the Sultan of Zanzibar's dominion. Although so little was formally decided, the Berlin Conference has rightly been regarded as the first public signal that tropical Africa was up for grabs.[6]

It was not that great profits were expected from African colonization. It was rather the idea that colonial sovereignty offered a means of insurance against the commercial protectionism that might be practised by European rivals as the competition for markets grew fiercer. If others were likely to place tariff barriers around their colonial trade, it was important to be in a position to do the same. Strategic reasons, though often adduced for public consumption, were mostly secondary. What was sought was a cheap way of acquiring African empires, with frontiers that would command mutual respect, even if occupation was minimal. Treaties of protection with African rulers were one of the cards in the game, but only one. They were much favoured by commercial enterprises seeking monopoly enforceable by quasi-governmental powers as Chartered Companies. They were particularly useful as a means of demonstrating the shallowness of the existing coastal spheres. In East Africa, for example, the German company which was seeking a Charter made its treaties with petty chiefs fifty to a hundred miles from the coast, who denied that they owed any allegiance to the Sultan of Zanzibar. In Zimbabwe and Zambia, Cecil Rhodes made treaties with kings and chiefs who disclaimed any connection with the Portuguese enclaves to the east and west. But most Africans lost their independence without signing any treaties at all. Most of the partition of Africa took place in Europe, on the basis of maps which provided detailed information about the coastal regions, but very little about the interior. It took place on the assumption that all powers were seeking a reasonable allocation of African territory, which would reflect their general standing in world affairs as much as their already established interests on the ground.

During the decade following the Berlin conference, therefore, the partition of Africa proceeded first by the enlargement of coastal enclaves until their boundaries touched, and secondly by the projection inland of spheres of interest based upon the extended coastal enclaves. In the event there proved to be some 33 such coast-based spheres, of which 18 faced the Atlantic Ocean, six the Indian Ocean, four the Red Sea and five the Mediterranean. Considering the size of the continent, this was not a wholly irrational division. It certainly did not reflect a mad scramble in which predators were rushing to take advantage of every gap. The inland projection of these spheres developed likewise in a mainly logical manner, through a series of bilateral agreements between neighbouring European claimants. If Bismarck had been the presiding genius of the first stage of partition, the British prime minister Lord Salisbury was certainly the key figure in the second. His command of the swiftly developing field of African geography was unrivalled, and as a statesman he recognized that a peaceful partition depended upon there being roughly equal gains by France and Britain, a generous satisfaction of German claims even though they had no historical basis, a place in the sun for the recently unified kingdom of Italy, and some respect for what he termed the 'archaeological' claims of Portugal. By 1891 he had achieved a series of bilateral agreements with Germany, France, Portugal and Italy, in which the broad outlines of the ultimate partition were clearly visible. In the western bulge of Africa, France would be predominant. Down the eastern side it would be Britain, although Madagascar was recognized as a French sphere, and no 'Cape-to-Cairo' dogma was allowed to prevent the largest possible settlement of German claims in eastern and south-western Africa. Italy would have a wide sphere in the north-east, and Portugal, while retaining an extensive coastline, would have to submit to a disjunction between its territorial claims in western and eastern Central Africa. The only act of force used by Salisbury against another European power during this period was the sending of a naval squadron to blockade the Tagus, in order to secure the ratification of the Anglo-Portuguese agreement of 1891.[7]

During the 1880s real occupation, as distinct from paper claims, was still so slight that it gave rise to little violence. Only the French were fighting a war of conquest, in the region between the Senegal and the upper Niger. Elsewhere, most activity on the ground was in the form of treaty-making or concession-hunting expeditions, which to the Africans were probably indistinguishable from the caravans of explorers and missionaries which had been criss-crossing their territories since the middle of the century. In general, such expeditions paid for food and protection with the usual trade goods, and for their treaties with small gifts of arms and flags, and then passed on their way. It might be many years before the next white man appeared in the area in the exercise of a claim to stay and rule. There were, to be sure, some cases where treaty-making gave rise to hostilities, as, for example, in Buganda, where emissaries of both the British and the German chartered companies tried to make treaties. The Anglican missionaries at the capital advised their followers to sign the British treaty, while the French White Fathers favoured the German one. In the event, the issue was settled in Europe by the Anglo-German agreement of 1890, but not before the representative of the British company, Frederick Lugard, had used his Swahili soldiers and his single Maxim gun to support the Protestant party against the Catholic one.[8]

A more frequent cause of violence during the early stages of partition was the kind of resistance which emanated from existing élites who saw their positions being undermined. All over eastern and central Africa relations between the Europeans and the Swahili Arabs were especially delicate. Already in 1888 there occurred a rising among the Swahili Arabs of the eastern coastal belt against the German occupiers, which was serious enough to provoke an Anglo-German blockade of Zanzibar and the take-over of the chartered company by the German government. King Leopold was astute enough to appoint the leading Swahili Arab merchant prince of the eastern Congo basin to be his governor in the eastern province of his state, thereby postponing the inevitable confrontation until the following decade, when his river fleet was large enough to open up the country from the west.[9] The most problematic situation in the whole of tropical Africa during the first decade of partition was that in the Sudanese hinterland of British-occupied Egypt, where an Islamic leader, Muhammad Ahmad, known to the outside world as the 'Mahdi', in 1881 organized a succcessful rebellion against the Egyptian colonial government and instituted an independent state. Following their occupation of Egypt in 1882, the British advised the Khedive to withdraw the Egyptian garrisons from the Sudan and eventually sent Charles Gordon to supervize an evacuation. Gordon disobeyed his instructions and tried to defend Khartoum, where he was annihilated by the Mahdi's forces in March 1884, leaving the future possession of the Sudan undecided until 1897.[10]

As partition moved into its second decade, the competition between the participants became keener, and forceful encounters with the African peoples more numerous. It was partly that the boundaries still to be decided were those in the far interior, where simple projection inland from the coastal spheres no longer produced unambiguous solutions. To the French, for example, it seemed increasingly important that, having gained access from the Senegal to the upper Niger, they should extend their control along the whole length of uninterrupted waterway between Bamako and the Bussa rapids, which were to become the river frontier with British Nigeria. And having thus set their sights on the upper and middle Niger, it was natural that they should seek to open alternative lines of access from the river valley to the Atlantic coast by joining it to their coastal spheres in Guinea (Conakry), the Ivory Coast and Dahomey. This involved large-scale campaigning against Samory, who was finally defeated only in 1898. From control of the upper and middle Niger, however, it was an equally natural progression of thought that the Niger valley should be linked northwards with Algeria and Tunis, and also eastwards with Lake Chad, which in turn could be regarded as the hinterland of Gabon. It was an unforgivable (and uncharacteristic) jibe of Lord Salisbury's that much of the territory in question consisted of 'rather light soil'. To the French, still recovering from the trauma of the loss of Alsace and Lorraine in the Franco-Prussian war, it meant much to be establishing 'a second India in Africa'. Even deserts have significance on political maps, and the 'Chad plan' embraced much more than a desert. Its back door on the eastern side faced across Wadai and Darfur towards the domain of the Mahdi, where the withdrawal of the Egyptian garrisons constituted an invitation to take over the Egyptian Sudan from the south.[11]

Again, to King Leopold, as his agents spread out along the 4,000 miles of navigable waterways ramifying eastwards from Lake Malebo, it became increasingly clear that the chief wealth of his river basin lay around its rim – particularly in the copperbelt of Katanga, but also in the rumoured gold and copper of the western Rift Valley around Lake Albert. From here it was but a short step to looking for alternative trade exits, especially down the upper Nile. Leopold, no less than the French, had studied the political implications of the Mahdi's successful rebellion. Next, there was Cecil Rhodes, the multi-millionaire proprietor of Kimberley diamonds and Witwatersrand gold, who from 1881 till 1895 was prime minister of the internally self-governing Cape Colony. He was also the founder of the British South Africa Company, which in 1889 received a royal Charter to occupy and develop the region north of the upper Limpopo. Rhodes was well informed about the mineral resources of the Zimbabwe plateau and also about the copper of Katanga. To gain possession of the first, he organized in 1890 an expedition of well-armed white volunteers, 'the pioneer column', each of whom was to be rewarded with a farm and a number of mining claims in the land which they would seize by force from its Shona and Ndebele inhabitants. The copperbelt lay far beyond the Zambezi, a thousand miles north of Rhodes' business capital at Kimberley and nearly twice as far from his political capital at Cape Town. Nevertheless, he sent out his concession-hunters, and they met those of King Leopold more or less on the line of the Congo-Zambezi watershed in 1891. Such were the origins of Southern and Northern Rhodesia. Nyasaland (later Malawi) was a shaving from the north-eastern corner of Rhodes' empire, which Lord Salisbury took under direct imperial control, because British missionaries were already established there (above, p. 166), who had made plain their antipathy to Chartered Company rule.[12]

North of Nyasaland, and of the German sphere on which it abutted, lay the territory of the Imperial British East Africa Company, which was the creation of the Scottish shipowner, Sir William Mackinnon. Lacking the mineral lustre of its British South African counterpart, the East African chartered company remained undersubscribed. By 1893 it was visibly sinking, and during the two following years it was redeemed by the British government, which established the two protectorates of British East Africa (later Kenya) and Uganda in its former sphere. Northwards again, lay the Mahdi's state, in what was still in theory the Egyptian Sudan. On this, the British position since the disasters of 1883–4 was that it would be reconquered as and when the Egyptian treasury was in a state to bear the cost. By 1896, however, wider considerations had supervened. The Italians had invaded Ethiopia from their coastal enclave at Massawa with 17,000 European troops, and had been resoundingly defeated by the Ethiopians at the battle of Adowa. Italy and her allies in the Triple Alliance pressed Britain to act in the Sudan in the interests of European prestige in the region as a whole. There was also the known interest of King Leopold in the upper Nile, and the challenge posed by the despatch of a French expedition under Colonel Marchand from Gabon. The British at last sent Kitchener with 20,000 imperial troops to Port Sudan. The forces of the Mahdiyya were defeated at the Atbara confluence with the Nile, and again at Omdurman, where 11,000 Mahdists perished. The French from Gabon had already reached Fashoda, some 200 miles further up the river, but they had no option but to withdraw in the face of Kitchener's greatly superior force. Thus, the former Egyptian Sudan became in name an Anglo-Egyptian condominium, but in practice a British protectorate, like Egypt itself.[13]

At the other end of the continent, the thorniest problem of the partition period was posed by the independence of the Transvaal, which was no longer merely the ranching terrain of 30,000 to 40,000 errant Afrikaner farmers, but the centre of the gold-mining industry and the main magnet of investment, immigration, migrant labour and railway development in the whole subcontinent. Naturally, Cecil Rhodes, as the leading capitalist of the Witwatersrand, was the chief advocate of intervention, and in 1895, with the collusion of the imperial authorities, he tried to change the government of the Transvaal by coup d'état. Recruiting 500 strong men, ostensibly for the police force of his chartered company, he set them riding to Johannesburg, where it was assumed that the non-Afrikaner majority of the white population would rise in their support. But they failed to do so, and the raiders were ignominiously surrounded, arrested and put on trial. It was the end of Rhodes' political career. For the British government, however, the problem of the Transvaal persisted in a greatly exacerbated form. The Transvaalers flirted with Germany for possible protection, and made practical arrangements to build a railway through southern Mozambique to avoid dependence on the Cape system. It seemed not merely that the great economic prize might fall into actively hostile hands,

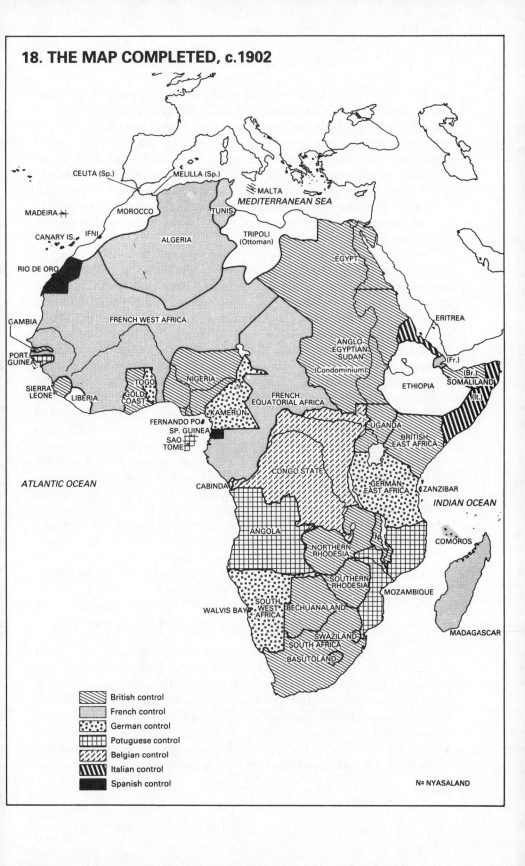

18. THE MAP COMPLETED, c.1902

CEUTA (Sp.)

MELILLA (Sp.)

MALTA

MEDITERRANEAN SEA

MADEIRA

MOROCCO

TUNIS

CANARY IS.

IFNI

ALGERIA

TRIPOLI
(Ottoman)

EGYPT

RIO DE ORO

ERITREA

GAMBIA

FRENCH WEST AFRICA

ANGLO-
EGYPTIAN
SUDAN

(Condominium)

(Fr.)

PORT.
GUINEA

(Br.)

SOMALILAND

SIERRA
LEONE

LIBERIA

TOGO

GOLD
COAST

NIGERIA

ETHIOPIA

(It.)

FRENCH
EQUATORIAL AFRICA

KAMERUN

FERNANDO PO

SP. GUINEA

UGANDA

SAO
TOME

BRITISH
EAST AFRICA

ATLANTIC OCEAN

CONGO STATE

GERMAN
EAST AFRICA

CABINDA

ZANZIBAR

INDIAN OCEAN

ANGOLA

COMOROS

NORTHERN
RHODESIA

SOUTHERN
RHODESIA

MOZAMBIQUE

WALVIS BAY

SOUTH
WEST
AFRICA

BECHUANALAND

MADAGASCAR

SWAZILAND

SOUTH AFRICA

BASUTOLAND

N= NYASALAND

but that the Transvaal government might rally the Dutch of the Cape Colony and the Orange Free State to their side. It was in these circumstances that the British deliberately provoked hostilities. At the start of the South African war, the British garrisons in the Cape and Natal numbered little more than 15,000 men. By its end half a million men and a similar number of animals had had to be brought in from the other side of the world. It was a war that, once started, could not be lost without risking the British imperial position world-wide. The unforeseen price of victory, however, was the forging of an Afrikaner nation strong enough and united enough to win the peace.[14]

The South African war may justly be considered the concluding act in the European partition of Africa. Many frontiers still remained obscure, but the problems were mostly of a detailed nature, and would be settled by a series of bilateral boundary commissions, which would continue their work right through the first decade of the twentieth century. But in essentials by 1901 the political map of Africa had been drawn. The Italians would seize Libya from the Turks in 1911, and the French would declare a protectorate over Morocco in 1912, but the approximate shape of both these countries was already known. Further changes of sovereignty would occur after the First World War, when the German colonies were shared out among the Allies. In this second scramble Togo and Cameroon would be divided, and attached as Mandated Territories of the League of Nations to neighbouring British and French colonies. German East Africa, henceforward known as Tanganyika Territory, would lose the kingdoms of Rwanda and Burundi to Belgian rule. South-West Africa would be mandated to South Africa. But, taking the continent as a whole, these were not large changes. In the main, modern Africa owes its internal frontiers to the juggling of European statesmen and diplomats during the 1880s and 1890s, whose main concern was to get as much as they could for their own countries without endangering the peace of Europe. It may seem bizarre that future nations should have taken their origins from such a hastily improvised framework, but world history shows many examples of nations which came into existence from military and diplomatic action rather than from ethnic and cultural propinquity.

Above all, it has to be remembered that the 'partition of Africa' is a phrase that has meaning only in relation to the actions of outsiders in respect of other outsiders. Seen from the inside, in the deeper perspective of African history, the so-called 'partition' was on the contrary a ruthless act of political amalgamation, whereby something of the order of ten thousand units was reduced to a mere forty. It has become a commonplace of political polemic that the diplomats of Europe, equipped with pencils and rulers, drew straight lines across the largely blank interior regions shown on African maps, bisecting and sometimes trisecting the territories of African peoples. The accusation is true so far as it goes, but by constant repetition it has obscured the larger truth that African polities were mostly very small, and that nearly all of the new European colonies comprised within their frontiers many times more indigenous groups than they divided. It was quite normal for a single one of the newly defined colonies to comprise two or three hundred earlier political groupings, even after discounting those societies which recognized no authority wider than that of the extended family. Often, as we have seen (above, pp. 147–8), the smaller precolonial states formed clusters which spoke mutually intelligible dialects and observed similar social customs. In colonial parlance such clusters would be known as 'tribes', and some effort would normally be made to align the local government units of colonial administration with existing 'tribal' ones. In course of time, this greatly strengthened the sense of unity existing within the clusters, which was further complemented by the linguistic work of Christian missionaries in standardizing groups of related spoken dialects into much smaller numbers of written languages. Thus, by the end of the colonial period, the 'tribal' concept had come to assume a significance far greater than that which existed at the time of the colonial partition. The tribal concept was in fact an expression of the first stage of amalgamation resulting from colonial rule. The reality, at the start of the process, was one of much greater diversity at the grass roots of society, but equally one of less sharp distinctions between ethnic and linguistic groupings.

The drawing of the map, therefore, had very little immediate effect on the peoples whose nationality was ultimately to be determined by it. Colonial rule normally began at the sea coast and ramified gradually up-country, using and developing the precolonial caravan routes. Frontier districts were nearly everywhere the last to be brought under regular administration, and meanwhile their inhabitants came and went much as they had done in pre-colonial times. Local trade and labour migration flowed easily enough across colonial frontiers. When colonial taxation was introduced, frontiers of course determined to whom it should be paid; but it was only much later, as colonial or missionary education reached the frontier districts, that important differences, such as the European language to be taught, began to affect any large number of people. Where the few larger traditional African states were divided by colonial frontiers, as for example in western Asante, there was a loosening of relations with those subjects who lived on the opposite side of the colonial frontier to the traditional ruler. But mostly it was the ethnic and linguistic clusters, rather than the actual political units which were divided by colonial frontiers, and the significance of the separation was therefore not so great. In general, during colonial times the colonial frontiers affected mostly the foreign elements present in the new colonial governments. It was only with the approach of post-colonial independence that African populations as a whole really had to face the full implications of national boundaries.

CHAPTER 15

THE NEW TASKMASTERS

The first truth about colonialism in Africa is that it was cumulative. The European powers had not partitioned the continent with a view to securing early gains through its rapid development. They had done so as an insurance against a future of growing protectionism, and their main concern was that the annual premiums should be kept low. The ideal colony, therefore, should be financially self-supporting; but obviously this could not be achieved until the population recognized the fiscal authority of the new rulers, and until there was the means of transporting local produce to the outside markets where it could be sold for cash. Meantime, most costs of government had to come from imperial exchequers in the form of grants-in-aid, the amounts of which could be seen and criticized by parliamentary oppositions in Europe. In these circumstances the initial level of colonial occupation was grotesquely insufficient for the task. The colonial government of Nyasaland (Malawi) started its existence in 1891 on a grant of £10,000 a year, enough in those days to employ ten European civilians and two military officers, 70 Sikhs from a Punjab regiment and 85 armed porters from the Zanzibar coast – this for a territory measuring some 500 miles from north to south and with a population of between one and two millions.[1] In 1894 the Uganda government was allotted £50,000 a year, which enabled it to recruit some 200 Sudanese troops, survivors of the former Egyptian garrison of Equatoria, in order to police a territory twice as large as Nyasaland with a population of between three and four millions. In 1900 Northern Nigeria received £100,000, which paid for six civilian administrators and a force of 2,000 'Hausa' soldiery, mostly ex-slaves from Lagos and the Gold Coast, led by 120 British officers and NCOs, for a population of about ten millions, mostly organized in large and seemingly powerful Muslim states.[2] Despite all the superiority of European weapons and military discipline, not much real government could be attempted with forces as slender as these, when a single little riot or a small scale ambush could wipe out half of a colony's entire garrison. It was only as a series of such incidents brought one colonial government after another close to the point of disgraceful evacuation that imperial grants were gradually raised to about ten times their original levels, and unpopular functions of government, such as the levying of taxation, could be begun. Even then, colonial governments in tropical Africa remained essentially *weak* governments – so weak that they could not undertake any serious military action without the help of African allies, so weak that they could only mobilize the labour needed for the porterage of supplies and the construction of roads, railways and other public works by respecting and bolstering the privilege of traditional élites who could draft slaves, ex-slaves and other subject elements to do the hated tasks.[3]

Given the feeble resources at the disposal of the new rulers, any attempt to characterize the early colonial period in terms of conquest and resistance-to-conquest must be seriously misleading. Conquest there was, at least in some parts of nearly every African colony, but it was mostly carried out in small actions, spread over twenty or even thirty years. Conquest was, in fact, but one aspect of a slow process of infiltration, much of which was completely bloodless.[4] In most colonies there was a coastal region which made an obvious starting-point. Here, some of the inhabitants would have been dealing with foreigners in a commercial way since long before partition. It is remarkable how seldom coastal peoples came into conflict with the new rulers. Mostly, they saw the opportunity for an extension of their role as middlemen between outsiders and the peoples of the interior. Usually, they became the favourite subjects of the colonial governments, supplying the clerks and interpreters who accompanied the colonial officials in their penetration of the hinterland. The early soldiers and caravan porters were often their slaves and dependents.[5] The first duty of the military was not conquest, but the protection of caravans and installations from simple pilfering.

In most cases the lines of colonial infiltration were determined by perceptions of the future of mechanical transport, in which the role of waterways, wherever they existed, tended to be greatly over-emphasized. Africa was partitioned during the heyday of the ocean steamship and the river steamer, and railways were at first seen mainly as a way of connecting one kind of waterway with another. Thus, the French developed their occupation of West Africa along a series of routes intended to link the Atlantic coast with the great waterway of the upper and middle Niger (above, pp. 180–1). The penetration of the Nigerian hinterland by the Royal Niger Company prior to the takeover by the British government in 1899 was mainly concerned with the development and monopolization of river ports on the lower Niger and the Benue. Both French Equatorial Africa and King Leopold's Congo were essentially fluvial in conception, using short stretches of rail to gain access to the great waterways of the Congo basin: early government stations were placed on riverside sites near confluences, rapids or other ports of trans-shipment. Inland Angola was

19. MECHANICAL TRANSPORT IN EARLY COLONIAL AFRICA: RAIL AND WATERWAYS

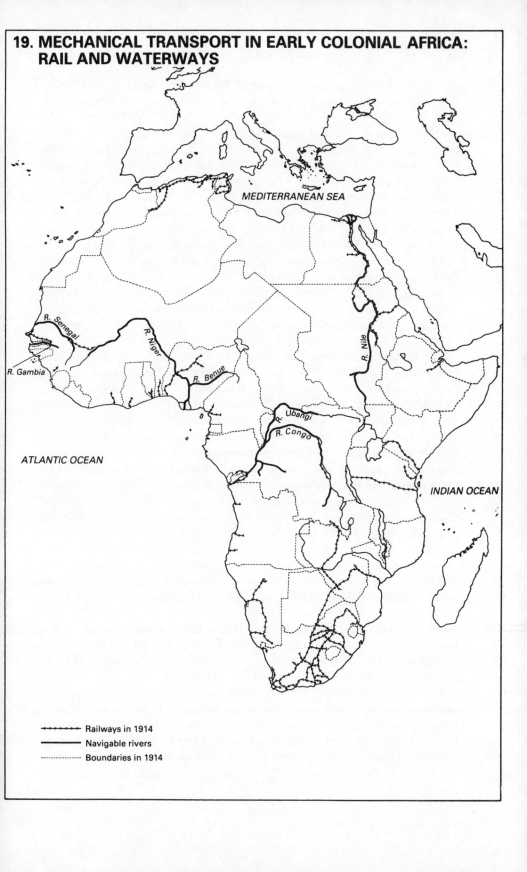

MEDITERRANEAN SEA

R. Senegal

R. Niger

R. Gambia

R. Benue

R. Nile

R. Ubangi

R. Congo

ATLANTIC OCEAN

INDIAN OCEAN

++++++ Railways in 1914
———— Navigable rivers
-------- Boundaries in 1914

dominated by the navigable course of the Cuanza, and inland Mozambique by that of the Zambezi. Though less obvious today, it is remarkable how much the colonial penetration of East Africa was determined by considerations of access to inland waterways. Nyasaland depended for its access to the sea on the Zambezi and the lower Shire, and for its internal cohesion upon the upper Shire and Lake Malawi, while early access to both north-eastern Rhodesia and the south-western part of German East Africa was by the same route. The so-called Uganda Railway from Mombasa to Kisumu not only provided the central line of communication through British East Africa (Kenya), but also access to the British and German ports on Lake Victoria, as well as commanding the 'back door to Egypt' by the White Nile waterway leading through northern Uganda and the Sudan. It was only in southern Africa that long stretches of railway were projected independently of connecting water routes. Here, it was the indispensable need to carry in mining machinery and the high profits associated with mineral extraction that justified exceptions to the general rule.

The initial establishment of colonial government stations did not as a rule lead to resistance by the local people. Save at the colonial capitals, there was seldom more than a single European officer to be seen at them, and the earliest buildings were not different from those erected by traders and missionaries, who were likewise accompanied by retinues of servants, porters and armed retainers. Where the earliest government officials were also the representatives of chartered companies, whose main occupation was with the trade in ivory or palm-kernels, or with the prospection and extraction of minerals, it was inevitable that they should be identified as merchants rather than rulers.[6] Even when they arrived in river steamers, these were seldom the first such vessels to have been seen. Trading steamers had long been familiar on the Senegal, the Gambia, the lower Niger, the Cuanza and the Zambezi, while even on the Congo and the Ubangi, and on the great lakes of eastern Africa, the earliest steamers to be assembled and launched were those of missionaries and traders. To people who saw only the local manifestations of early colonial government, these often did not seem very important.[7] Even when the new arrivals began to show that they had power behind them, the normal reaction of the traditional rulers was to try to make use of that power for their own ends, by enlisting the newcomers as allies in their local rivalries, and by providing the help which they asked for in exchange.

The first requirement of every colonial government was a supply of biddable labour, which in societies as yet ignorant of wages meant *forced* labour. Almost from the birth of a colony, there was an immense amount to be carried into the interior from the outside – building materials, military stores, tools and machinery, steamers in sections, trade goods, fuel, rails, telegraph wire, medical supplies, and all the domestic requirements of European frontiersmen from wines and spirits to hip baths and camp beds. Thus, although ultimately they rendered them unnecessary, colonial governments initially added greatly to the swelling caravans of precolonial times. There were road gangs, rail gangs, dockers and porters, and those who supplied their physical needs. And there were the soldiers and policemen, upon whose training and discipline everything else depended. The usual source of most of this labour was found, directly or indirectly, in the servile class of precolonial Africa, usually known in colonial parlance as 'freed slaves'.[8] Where, as in the French advance to the upper Niger, colonial occupation followed behind a military spearhead attacking African 'conquest states' like those of Samory and Ahmadu (above, pp. 174–5), there developed a flow of refugees, who were mostly first generation captives trying to return to their homelands. These the French tried to intercept, settling them in so-called *villages de liberté*, sited at intervals along the lines of colonial communications, where they received protection from recapture in exchange for providing *corvée* labour as porters and roadmen.[9] On the Gold Coast it was refugee slaves from Asante, mostly of northern origin, and in southern Nigeria (Lagos) it was the refugee captives from the wars of expansion of the Fulani emirates who, under the name of 'Hausas' formed the main pool of recruitment for the colonial police and garrison troops of British and German colonies all the way from Sierra Leone to Cameroon. From the interior of French Equatorial Africa came the lapidary instruction from a senior administrator to his junior: 'As you need them, get yourself men by liberating slaves. The price of liberation will be deducted from the wages you deem appropriate.'[10]

In King Leopold's Congo, the population living between the estuary and Lake Malebo were impressed by military means into labour for porterage and road-building, while the army, the *force publique*, was built up by purchases of 'freed slaves' from the Swahili Arab traders of the Ituri forest and the Lomami. These recruits were taken a thousand miles from their homes for their training, and then engaged for seven to nine years under the rules of martial law for desertion. By 1900 their numbers had grown to nearly 20,000, and it was these men, later posted as *gendarmes* in almost every village of the forested areas, who were used to compel the unfortunate inhabitants to go out and tap the wild *landolphia* rubber vines, often to the neglect of their own food plantations.[11] 'The more gendarmes, the more rubber', as the saying went.[12] All that can be said is that the period of outrageous exploitation was a short one, lasting from about 1898 till about 1905. While it endured, the boom in 'red rubber' saved King Leopold from otherwise certain bankruptcy. No private fortune could possibly sustain the twenty to thirty years of steady deficits involved in establishing an African colony.[13] And once the rubber market collapsed, there was no alternative to a takeover by the Belgian state. Similar conditions prevailed in the forested regions of French Equatorial Africa, where the beneficiaries were some forty concessionary companies, most of which followed King Leopold's example. In Angola it was the Ovimbundu kingdoms of the southern plateau, rather than any extraneous elements, which continued to raid for slaves among their neighbours right through the 1880s and 1890s, bringing the captives in large caravans to Benguela and other southern ports, whence many of them were shipped as 'contract labourers' to the plantations of the northern coastal region and the islands of São Thomé and Principé.[14]

While eastern and southern Africa could show nothing so overtly scandalous as the system of production at gunpoint prevalent in much of western central Africa, there is ample evidence of the part played by forced labour in the gradual transition from slavery to wage employment. It is clear that in Uganda, for example, early colonial government was dependent for at least the first twenty years of its existence on an alliance with the ruling élite of the kingdom of Buganda, which had been, and for a time continued to be, the foremost slave-owning and slave-catching society of the region. In the interests of the alliance, Ganda chiefs detailed thousands of their slaves to work for the protectorate government in road building, porterage, brick-making and other public works. In the interests of the alliance, the British set about the conquest of the neighbouring state of Bunyoro, using Ganda levies, and rewarding them with the cattle taken as booty, and turning a nearly blind eye to the Nyoro captives taken as slaves. This kind of warfare apart, there were still during the 1890s, all round the frontiers of Buganda, regular markets where the neighbouring peoples came to exchange their slaves for Ganda hoes, and for the imported textiles of India and Europe. It was their wealth in these newly acquired captives, who could be ordered to all tasks, which enabled the Ganda chiefs to be so co-operative with their foreign friends. Churches and schools, as well as government offices, were built in this way. When the Anglican missionary bishop, Alfred Tucker, approached the first Commissioner of the territory, Sir Gerald Portal, with a proposal by some of the Christian chiefs for a general liberation of slaves, Portal quickly smelt a rat. 'It would make it at once impossible to get any work done by anyone, and it is perhaps only a pretext to avoid work on roads, etc., by pleading as excuse no slaves.'[15]

It is clear that no colonial government could establish effective occupation of its territory, let alone prepare the way for a better economic future, without extensive use of forced labour. The peculiar hardship caused by the use of slaves and 'freed slaves' was that the largest burden fell upon a minority of the poorest people. As colonial governments grew a little stronger, they were able to spread the load by imposing a system of taxation payable by all, either in cash or by labouring for a specific period on public works. But this stage could seldom be reached before there had been some kind of a trial of strength with the ruling elements of the stronger societies within a colonial territory. For the most part, these confrontations took place during the second decade of colonial rule rather than the first. The initiative might come from either side. It could happen when the colonial government felt strong enough to tackle its mightiest group of subjects. Or it could come at the moment when the mightiest subjects realized that the colonial government was posing a serious, long-term threat to their autonomy. In the Gold Coast, for example, it was the British who, after spending twenty years establishing their ascendancy in the southern provinces, took the initiative in 1895 by sending an ultimatum to the Asantehene Prempeh that he must accept a British Resident at Kumasi. When he refused, his kingdom was invaded, he himself was deported to the Seychelles and his office left in abeyance. Similarly, the French waited until 1892 to conquer the traditional kingdom of Dahomey, and challenged the Fulbe rulers of the Futa Jallon highlands in central Guinea only in 1896.[16] In south-western Nigeria, the colonial government at Lagos took forcible issue as early as 1891 with the Yoruba town of Ijebu for closing the main trade route into the interior, and two years later bombarded the metropolitan city of Oyo into overt subjection. But further east, the decisive moves were those against Benin in 1897 and the Aro in 1901. In the north Lugard's decisive confrontations with Kano and Sokoto took place in 1903.

In King Leopold's Congo, the Swahili Arabs and their Manyema followers drove the state's garrison from its only foothold in the eastern half of the country, at Stanley Falls (Kisangani) in 1887, but it was not until 1892 that the state dared to deliver its counter-offensive in a series of campaigns, using many ill-controlled native allies, which lasted two years and is thought to have involved tens of thousands of casualties.[17] In Uganda the critical moment came when Kabaka Mwanga of Buganda in 1897 reacted to growing British interference by defecting to join the already dissident monarch of neighbouring Bunyoro. The resulting campaign drove both rulers from their kingdoms and ended with their deportation and replacement by their young children.[18] In German East Africa it was the expedition of 1898, which put an end to the long resistance of the Hehe chief, Mkwawa, and put the colonial government in a position to interfere decisively in the ethnic politics of the south-western part of the country. In Nyasaland it was only in 1896 that Johnston felt strong enough to tackle the Swahili Arab hegemony to the north of the lake, which had been a standing challenge to the advance of British influence since 1889. In Southern Rhodesia, thanks to the unusually large force of 500 European mercenaries employed to protect the pioneer settlers, war with the

Ndebele was deliberately provoked as early as 1893, so that, when it was over the expensive garrison could be reduced. On the other hand, the great Shona rising of 1896–7, occurring when nearly all of Rhodes' mercenaries had been withdrawn to take part in Jameson's abortive raid on Johannesburg (above, p. 182), was a purely African initiative, which necessitated the intervention of imperial troops from the Cape Colony before it could be brought under control.[19]

If such is a representative selection of the military episodes which marked the transition from infiltration to something more like the practical recognition of the authority of the new rulers, then it scarcely merits G.N. Uzoigwe's characterization of the early colonial period as 'a generation of continuous war'.[20] Most of the larger scale fighting occurred in the West African region, of which John Hargreaves has written, 'Military operations meant a period of violence, but it was rarely protracted, and in any case violence was usually no new experience.'[21] Only in Southern Rhodesia and German South-West Africa, as earlier in Algeria and southern Africa, did military confrontation result in large numbers of African people being driven off their land, to begin life anew in 'native reserves' selected for their poorer soils and greater distance from the railways than the land allotted to whites. Only in King Leopold's Congo and French Equatorial Africa did it result temporarily in the rule of armed police in African villages where there was natural produce at hand to be gathered. In general, military confrontation paradoxically marked a transition from military to civilian rule, of which the economic hallmark was the collection of taxes and the definition of labour obligations, while its political counterpart was the confidence to replace uncooperative office-holders by others more compliant. In the case of hereditary rulers, this often meant the appointment of minors. In the case of administrative chiefs, it began to mean the promotion of those who had previously worked for the colonial power as clerks and interpreters, soldiers and policemen, and thereby acquired some idea of what the new rulers expected of them. The significance of the new interventionism can perhaps be best appreciated from the exceptions. In southern Africa four ethnic groups – the southern Sotho, the northern Tswana, the Swazi and the Lozi – managed to obtain British protection on special terms. Because of their early connection with powerful missionary societies, and also because of their geographical isolation from the main centres of settler-colonial interests, all four were able to maintain their internal autonomy very nearly intact until the 1930s. In the case of Bechuanaland (Botswana), the British Commissioner actually resided in the nearby Cape province. There were resident magistrates who lived in the tribal capitals and regulated affairs involving African and European relations. For the rest, power remained in the hands of the Tswana élite – to the extent that, as late as 1926, it was possible for a member of the Ngwato ruling house to give evidence in a court of law that his relations with the Sarwa hunters and gatherers of his country were as follows:

The Masarwa are slaves. They can be killed. It is no crime. They are like cattle. If they run away, their masters can bring them back and do what they like in the way of punishment. They are never paid. If the Masarwa live in the veld, and I want any to work for me, I go out and take any I want.[22]

Such sentiments might have been heard with approval by the Trekboers of the 1830s, or the Ganda élite of the 1890s. By the 1920s they were decidedly anachronistic, and could probably have been matched only among the Amhara rulers of southern Ethiopia or the Tuareg nobility of the central Sahara.

The period of greatest military activity between colonial governments and their mightier subjects, which lasted from about 1895 till about 1905, was also that when imperial grants-in-aid reached their highest levels in most colonies. During the decade which followed, most colonial budgets came gradually into balance, and this signified not only that somewhat less was being spent on arms and garrisons, but also that the arts of peace were being more extensively cultivated, especially by young African manhood. 'In economic terms,' Christopher Wrigley has written, 'conquest meant . . . that the function of protection was specialized, taken away from the general body of adult males and assigned to very small numbers of soldiers and policemen, whose organization and weapons gave them an unchallengeable monopoly of force. For the others, there was a loss of autonomy, even of the sense of manhood . . . but the economy of human effort was very great.'[23] Another such economy which began to occur during the same decade was the gradual elimination of long-distance porterage. The railways planned during the first decade of colonial rule, and mostly still under construction during the second decade, reached their main destinations during the third. And it was reckoned that every goods train, even those drawn by light, wood-burning engines, did the work of at least 15,000 human porters. Henceforward, head-loading began at the railway stations, or at the ports on the connected waterways. With the advent of the motor lorry during the fourth decade of colonial rule, porterage began at roadhead and necessitated no long absences from home. One of the longest surviving forms of porterage was the accompaniment of colonial officials on tour through the remoter parts of their districts. It took forty men to carry the normal camping gear of a European officer, and no one volunteered for such work at the rates of pay offered. It was always performed under duress.

The time and effort saved from old style military responsibilities did not usually flow of its own accord straight into production for the world market. It came closer to doing so in West Africa than anywhere else, because in large areas of West Africa there already existed from precolonial times a demand for European manufactures, and an infrastructure of cash-cropping farmers, produce buyers and transport agents, which only needed to be extended to include wider areas and some new crops. West Africa had its forests, yielding timber and palm kernels, to which wild rubber became an important addition during the 1890s, to be followed in the 1900s by cocoa. North of the forest, the savanna had its areas suited to ground-nuts, especially in the Senegambia and, given rail transport, northern Nigeria. All these opportunities could be exploited by local people, with no more external stimulus than the necessity to earn some money to pay tax. Nevertheless, the productive areas and the means of access to them were unequally distributed across the map, and in West Africa as in other parts of the continent higher production in order to produce an exportable surplus could only be achieved by a great deal of labour migration from remoter or less fertile areas, such as the northern Ivory Coast and Upper Volta, the northern territories of the Gold Coast and the Nigerian 'middle belt'. Many of the migrants moved of their own free will, on the basis of information brought back by a few brave pioneers. But, even in West Africa, chiefly 'encouragement' played some part in labour recruitment, notably for the gold mines operated by British companies in the western Gold Coast, where chiefs in the northern territories were paid five shillings a head for labour migrants sent southwards for employment underground. In western central Africa, including German Cameroon as well as French Equatorial Africa, the Belgian Congo and Angola, the allocation of land for plantations to European companies and individual settlers necessitated a much greater degree of 'encouragement' in labour recruitment, in which the hand of the encouraging chief was often strengthened by those of soldiers and armed police. More broadly, tax collection, especially during the early years of its institution, was almost everywhere accompanied by some degree of police violence, in which villages were burned, crops destroyed, cattle confiscated, and individuals subjected to beating and assault.[24]

In eastern Africa, by contrast, there was hardly any precolonial experience of agricultural production for the world market on which economic development and therefore colonial revenues could be built. There was only the clove industry of Zanzibar and Pemba, and some grain and mangrove production for export from the northern Swahili coast. Both were traditionally based on slave labour, and began to wither as soon as the supply of new slaves was cut off. Otherwise, from the Sudan to Natal, the only significant article of export at the start of the colonial period was ivory, of which the sources were rapidly dwindling, as the elephant was hunted out in one region after another. Much more stimulus was therefore required than the mere provision of mechanical transport. In the Anglo-

Egyptian Sudan everything turned upon the introduction of the long staple Egyptian cotton as a cash crop grown in irrigated land, and therefore upon the building of dams and the cutting of canals in the very restricted riverine areas, such as the Gezira triangle above the confluence of the Blue and White Niles, where fresh irrigation was feasible. By 1914 the condominium government had solved its revenue problem by concentrating its efforts on a minute fraction of its vast territory. But the fortunate proprietors and tenant farmers of the new irrigated lands recruited their labour force from migrant workers, many of whom were in fact West African pilgrims working their way to and from Mecca by the savanna routes to the south of the desert.[25] The southern Sudanese were left to stagnate in their precolonial and largely pastoral way of life under the genial guidance of a special type of district administrative officer known in the service as the 'bog barons', who liked to live as far as possible from conventional civilization.

In Uganda it was first coffee and then cotton which brought the colonial budget into balance. It could not have been done without the railway and the lake steamers. And certainly it could not have been done without the Indian traders, large and small, who came up the railway and spread out into the villages of Buganda and Busoga with their imported cotton goods, their steel hoe-blades and cutlasses, their pots and pans and their sewing machines, to stimulate the desires of the African producers. But, even so, it could not have been done without a great deal of chiefly pressure upon the ordinary peasant farmers, who in addition to all their other obligations, were now required to cultivate experimental plots of the new cash crops.[26] In British East Africa (Kenya) economic development inevitably centred upon the line of rail which, as luck would have it, passed through some four hundred miles of sparsely occupied, pastoral country before descending into the densely populated Lake Victoria basin. This raised the question whether the land on either side of the route might not yield more under European management, and between 1900 and 1914 some 4,000 square miles were alienated in land grants to European and Indian settlers. The main losers were the pastoral Maasai, whose grazing grounds were bisected by the railway and who in the end were required to move all their cattle to the south of the line. Curiously, the Maasai never rebelled. Most of the early opposition came from the Nandi of the western highlands, who lost more than 1,000 killed in various punitive expeditions. In the longer run, more ill will was inspired among the Kikuyu, of whom it is reckoned that some 1,600 families suffered expropriation with grossly inadequate compensation from 125 square miles at the southern margin of the tribal territory.[27] This was where the cultivation of high grade *arabica* coffee was set in hand on European-managed estates. At lower altitudes, between Nairobi and Mombasa, sisal was established as a railside plantation crop.

Sisal was likewise the main plantation crop of German East Africa, where the estates followed the two main lines of rail, from Tanga to Moshi and from Dar es Salaam to Morogoro.

On the whole, not many African farmers were dispossessed by the establishment of plantations, while their immediate neighbours often found their way into the market economy by supplying the plantation workers with food. Their widest significance for the African population lay in the migrant labourers they employed. Many of these came from far away, and their participation was secured by tax collection and chiefly 'encouragement' in the less developed interior regions. Strangely enough, the worst human disaster to occur through the introduction of cash crops happened in the southern province of German East Africa, where peasant production was the aim. Here, a whole group of neighbouring peoples rose together in 1905 to resist a programme for compulsory cotton-growing by village communities. As an exercise in inter-ethnic collaboration, the Maji Maji rebellion was initially so successful that it provoked the Germans to use terror tactics. The whole region was laid waste by colonial soldiery, who burned villages, destroyed standing crops and confiscated livestock. In the resulting famine more than 200,000 people are thought to have died.[28] It was one of two horrid episodes of German imperialism in Africa. The other, though somewhat less costly in life, was the repression of the Herero people of South-West Africa between 1905 and 1907, when some three-quarters of an entire population was exterminated by direct military action.[29]

South of the great lakes, although there were still roads and railways to be built and loads to be carried, the transition from unpaid to paid labour turned essentially upon the needs of the mining industry. Large-scale mining had begun with the diamonds of Kimberley in the 1870s and continued with Witwatersrand gold in the 1880s. By 1895 Johannesburg had attracted a European population of 100,000, and needed about 250,000 African workers to provide the unskilled labour of the mines and to service the town. This large urban population had to be kept supplied with food and other necessities on a scale which transformed the white farming industry of the whole surrounding region from a system of extensive pastoralism to one of intensive agricultural food production wherever climatic conditions and the developing rail network permitted. All this added up to a very formidable demand for African labour, and according to the presently prevailing school of South African historiography, it was the labour needs of the Rand and its suppliers which dictated the timing of the conquest of the last remaining independent African societies of the subcontinent and the character of the labour relations that resulted. This was a system which confined African communities within territorial limits far too narrow for their survival on a self-supporting basis. Taxation was imposed at a level which forced all but a very few families to send out their young men as labour migrants, or else as 'squatters', or labour tenants, on the white farms. It was this system that was carried north to Rhodesia following the conquest of the Ndebele and the Shona in the 1890s, and which later formed the basic premise of European settlement in Northern Rhodesia and Nyasaland also. The British South Africa Company took to itself enormous areas of land on the pretext that it was 'unoccupied', that is to say, land that was not currently under actual cultivation by African communities, which thus found themselves forced onto European-owned land as tenants as soon as the fertility of their current farms was exhausted. From then on, they had to find rent as well as tax, and labour migrancy, mostly to the Rand, imposed itself here also.[30]

All in all, it would seem that the early colonial period was not mainly about conquest, although conquest was certainly involved. Usually, however, conquest was preceded by infiltration. The earliest military campaigns were undertaken in conjunction with African allies, often following the lines of precolonial rivalries. The more severe military encounters occurred later, in the context of repression rather than conquest, when African communities rebelled against actual interference in their daily lives, in the shape of demands for labour, taxes, compulsory cultivation of cash crops or collection of natural products. Such protests, however, were sporadic and for the most part fairly localized. Meanwhile the relations between colonial governments and most traditional societies remained outwardly peaceful. Many of the traditional rulers and their advisers had come to power in the precolonial period, and were treated with more respect by the colonial authorities than their successors of a later date. Where there were no traditional rulers, as among the Kikuyu, strong men emerged and built up paramilitary retinues to enforce their control, while the colonial rulers were only too happy to recognize their chiefly status in exchange for co-operation in the matters that concerned them.[31] The most imperative requirement of the colonial administrations in every part of the continent was in the direction of young men to various kinds of labour. This did not affect the whole of any society. Women and children and men of mature age remained in the villages, and schemed to relieve the returning migrants of as much as possible of their hard-earned wealth. Not all forms of migrant labour were entirely miserable, and in retrospect many found in their experiences the same kind of prestige as that earned by the long-distance traders and caravan porters of earlier times. These men had explored a wider world. They had seen the city lights and lived close to fellow Africans speaking many different tongues. They had seen trains and steamers and mining shafts, and the machinery used to gin cotton and decorticate sisal. They had seen white and brown people, if only at a distance. Some of them had been attracted enough to the new world to return for a second or a third time. It was perhaps the drudgery performed nearer home on roads and local porterage and compulsory crop-planting that seemed less tolerable, especially to those who were most accessible to the authorities who exerted the pressure on behalf of the foreign taskmasters.

CHAPTER 16

THE THINGS OF GOD

For Christianity and Islam alike, the coming of colonial rule created a wholly new situation, which in the event proved highly favourable to both religions. In the case of Islam, this result was scarcely to be foreseen. To any Muslim, the partition of Africa meant a great extension of rule by infidels, which could not be anything but a cause of profound dislike and dismay. Through the practice of pilgrimage and the news spread by those who returned from it, educated Muslims were informed about the broadest aspects of geopolitics. Senegalese and Moroccan Muslims knew about developments in Egypt and the Nilotic Sudan. The Muslims of northern Nigeria, no less than those of the Indian Ocean coast, knew that former Islamic states in South and South-East Asia had long since passed into the hands of the British and the Dutch, and that the Christian Russians were colonizing the Muslim lands of Central Asia. African Muslims knew that the only great Islamic society still gathered around a significant political core was the Ottoman empire, but they also knew how far it, too, had declined since the eighteenth century. It had lost the Crimea and the Balkans, Cyprus and Crete. It had lost Algeria and Tunis, Egypt and the Sudan. In 1912 it was to lose Libya, the last of its African possessions, to Christian Italy. The alignment of Turkey with the Central Powers in the Great War of 1914–18 was finally to destroy any fading hopes of a revived pan-Islamism based on Istanbul.[1]

And yet in the new African colonies Islam mostly flourished. At the start of the colonial period it was, of course, by far the most widely spread and deeply rooted of the world religions. It had been predominant in Egypt and North Africa since the eighth century, in the Sahara since the eleventh century, in the Sudanic belt since about the fourteenth century. The jihadic movements of the eighteenth and nineteenth centuries had carried it almost to the southern Atlantic coast of West Africa. Throughout the northern third of the continent, to be connected with either the ruling or the trading élite, or even to be a plain city-dweller, was almost inevitably to be a Muslim. North of about the tenth degree of northern latitude, virtually every substantial settlement had its mosque and its Koranic school presided over by a literate holy man who lived on the gifts and services of his people. By the late nineteenth century a very large proportion of such clerics, and a goodly number of less literate co-religionists, were members of one or other of the great *sufi* brotherhoods – Qadiriyya, Tijaniyya or Sanusiyya – which provided a spirit of élitism in religious observance and also a loose, hierarchical organization under *shaykhs* and *muqaddams*, capable of inspiring a sense of unity and purpose over wide areas. Typically a shaykh presided over a religious settlement, or *zawiya*, which provided more advanced religious education than that of the ordinary Koranic schools, and which accommodated pilgrims, travellers and merchants, some of whom might stay for a time to practise a kind of religious retreat. In Morocco and Algeria on the one hand, and in the Nilotic Sudan on the other, such places were almost invariably built around the tombs of saints, and were the centres of mystical devotion as well as religious training.[2]

At least within its longer-held territories, therefore, Islam was rather well set up to endure a period of infidel rule, and the infidel rulers for their part had no desire to disturb it. Both the British and the French prided themselves on their tolerance of Islam as a religion which produced dignified and well-mannered followers with high ethical standards, very different from the brash and unreliable behaviour associated with the first generation of Christian converts. They also reckoned with its potential for resistance if frustrated. What primarily concerned them as rulers was the competence of local bureaucracies in collecting and accounting for tax revenues, and the standards of justice applied in the administration of Islamic law. To these ends, they were prepared to support the system of Koranic and Zawiya schooling by providing some élite education for the training of civil servants and teachers. The French had pioneered such a system in Algeria, and applied it south of the Sahara in the so-called *madrasas* established at Timbuktu and St Louis. The British, too, developed a thin network of intermediate schools, teaching Arabic and Islamic law as well as western subjects, of which the show-piece was the Gordon Memorial College opened in 1902 in Khartoum. Similar establishments were instituted in northern Nigeria, at Kano, Katsina and Sokoto. Colonial rule thus actively encouraged Muslim education, and did its best to keep Christian missionary competition away from predominantly Muslim areas. Colonial rule likewise favoured regional uniformity. In situations where Muslim towns supplied the local government services for a countryside that was still in practice pagan, colonial support for the Islamic authorities helped greatly to consolidate Muslim observance among the country people.[3]

The testing-ground for Islam during this period, however, was not in the northern third but in the middle third of the continent, where its widespread presence was only a little older than that of its Christian rival. The middle third comprised most of the territory between the tenth degree north of the equator and the fifteenth degree to its south. It included the forest belt of West Africa, and all the land from the northern rim of the Congo basin to the Zambezi valley. The advance of Islam through the western forest region began in earnest only in the middle of the nineteenth century, as Muslim teachers from the Sudanic belt turned their attention southwards to meet the opportunities opened to them by the diversification of the Atlantic trade made possible by the advent of the steamship. Mandinka merchants to the west, and Hausa to the east of them, extended their commercial networks by local migration, planting Muslim trading quarters in every significant market town. The migrants learned the local languages, married the local girls and employed the local people. Wherever they settled in any numbers, a Muslim teacher would follow them to open a Koranic school. But for Christian competition, the Islamization of West Africa would have been complete, and in time it would have rolled on round the Bight of Benin to the lower Congo.

The main line of Islamic access to the middle third of Africa, however, lay through the ports on the Indian Ocean coast. Here, the towns had been Muslim for many centuries, but the penetration of Islam into the interior began only in the mid-nineteenth century, when Swahili Arab merchants started to participate in the long-distance caravan trade on a scale which required the establishment of permanent relay stations at key-points inland. As in West Africa, the initial conversions were due to intermarriage and economic dependence, and until the eve of the colonial period they do not seem to have been very numerous. There is no doubt, however, that in Kabaka Mutesa I of Buganda a series of devout Swahili Arab traders found a genuine convert to Islam, who during the last years of his life studied the Koran assiduously, discussed it intelligently, held public prayers on Fridays, kept the fast of Ramadhan and did his utmost to see that his subjects followed his example – to the extent of sending out inspectors to ensure that mosques were constructed at the capitals of his county chiefs and to enforce the observance of Ramadhan.[4] Given a few more years without Christian competition, Buganda might have become a solidly Muslim society. But the king's conversion did not take place until about 1867 – just ten years before the arrival of the Christian missions. In eastern Zaire, the Manyema followers of the Swahili Arabs began to adopt Islam during the years of attempted resistance to the forces of King Leopold, when Christian missionaries were already pushing up the Congo from the west. Around Lake Malawi, where Yao chiefs had been in close commercial contact with the Swahili Arabs since the late eighteenth century, the first reports of active Islamic proselytism refer to the early years of the colonial period.[5] To the British and German colonial governments, however, as they began their operations in the long converted coastal belt, Islam appeared as a force to be treated with as much respect as in northern Nigeria or the Anglo-Egyptian Sudan. The earliest government schools, designed for the training of teachers and junior civil servants, were established in the coastal towns. Kiswahili, already the lingua franca of the caravan trade, became the general medium of colonial government communications. Swahili-speaking Muslims spread into the interior as clerks and interpreters, foremen and skilled artisans, so that to Christian missionaries of the first colonial decade it seemed that Christianity was facing very serious adverse discrimination, when in fact it was very soon to take the lead.

The great expansion of Christianity in the southern two-thirds of Africa was on the one hand very closely linked with the process of colonial expansion and, on the other hand, very distinct from it. It was linked in that, wherever an act of colonization took place, there Christian missionaries would inevitably seek to enter or, alternatively, to reinforce their precolonial presence. Missionaries, though initially prepared to operate beyond colonial frontiers, nearly all came to value the security and protection offered both to themselves and to their humbler adherents by the existence of the colonial state. On the other hand, missionaries were mostly very far from being merely the spiritual arm of colonialism. Many of them came from countries which had no involvement in colonial expansion, and very many more went to work in the colonies of other nations than their own. However much they valued colonial protection, missionaries usually brought a critical spirit to bear upon the actions of colonial governments, acting as the advocates of their adherents in times of unrest, and even, as in King Leopold's Congo, reporting scandalous situations to the outside world. Moreover, the doctrines and the sacred scriptures of which missionaries had of necessity to be the purveyors, were in themselves revolutionary and egalitarian influences within the colonial context. They denounced oppressive rulers and praised those who cared for the widow and the orphan. Above all, they presented a divine figure, who had been unjustly judged and crucified by the cynical representative of a colonial power. It was a simple message, with a unique radiance, which only needed to be introduced here and there in order to become self-propagating. The main lesson of African ecclesiastical history is that the core message tended to run far ahead of its expatriate preachers. Most African societies first received the gospel from fellow Africans. The main contribution of the missionaries was in building the Church.

Leaving aside the Portuguese missions of the sixteenth and seventeenth centuries, which were too intermittently supported to achieve long-term results, Christian missions re-entered the southern two-thirds of Africa through two main doorways – first, through the colony for freed slaves planted by the British at Freetown, Sierra Leone, and secondly through the colony of European settlement which grew out of the Dutch revictualling station at Cape Town and was conquered by the British during the Napoleonic wars. The Sierra Leone venture led on, through the migration of Christian freedmen back to their home areas in other parts of West Africa, especially the Yoruba country of southern Nigeria, to a widespread dispersion of Anglican, Methodist, Baptist and Presbyterian missionaries along the whole length of the coastal belt. By the time of the colonial partition there were already in existence churches with a second generation membership, with some primary and secondary schooling of the western kind, and a sprinkling of ordained African clergy. Roman Catholic missions to West Africa had taken about forty years longer to get organized, but by the 1880s they, too, were well established, especially in the eastern part of the area, from the Niger delta to Gabon. The effect of partition was to open doors from the coastal towns to the hinterland.

In southern Africa the beginnings of missionary work were due to German Lutherans and to a mixed bag of evangelical Calvinists in the employ of the congregationalist London Missionary Society. They worked among the Khoi (Hottentots) both within and beyond the Cape frontier, and so became the first to carry the gospel to the Tswana people north of the Orange river. The Scottish gardener, Robert Moffat, 'cradled in Presbyterianism . . . and warmed by Methodist experience', established his pioneer settlement in the 1820s at Kuruman, from where his son-in-law David Livingstone travelled northwards to the Zambezi on the first of his three great missionary journeys of exploration in 1853.[6] With the eastward expansion of the Cape Colony and the annexation of Natal during the middle years of the century, missionaries from all the main denominations and drawn from many countries – Britain, Holland, France, Germany, Norway, Sweden and the United States – moved into southern Africa, establishing their first bases under the protection of the colonial authority, and, as they gained in confidence, pushing outwards into the lands still under Sotho and Nguni rule between the Cape and Natal. The Boer republics did not provide an ideal seed-ground for missionary work, but their African residents and neighbours – Sotho, Pedi and Venda – began to travel southwards in search of employment as early as the 1850s and 1860s, with the result so well described by Bengt Sundkler:

The theme in all these cases is the same: groups of young men looking for a job in order to buy the best that money could give, a musket of one's own or a new rifle, and in the process finding a new religion. And then the triumphant return home, the people of the village congregated to welcome their intrepid young men. They lift their guns to shoot, and thus to punctuate their travel story. But in the evening they will gather their contemporaries, and show them their greatest treasure: a book, a Gospel of St Matthew, or perhaps even a New Testament, and they can read from it.[7]

In the Cape Colony as in West Africa, there were by the 1880s Christian churches with a second generation African membership, with some access to western schooling and at least a handful of African clergy. The situation in the vast region between the Zambezi and the Bight of Benin was very different. Here, Christianity was by the 1880s widely present in the shape of scattered missionary outposts, nearly all of them of very recent establishment. Their expatriate occupants had braved the unstable political conditions of the 1870s and early 1880s, but at the cost of devoting most of their energies to mundane matters, dancing attendance at the courts of kings, and providing for the slaves and refugees who were their first adherents. Because of the insecurity and the harsh conditions of life, their numbers had remained small. Nevertheless, they were to be found not just at the Indian Ocean and South Atlantic coasts, but right along the caravan routes of the interior, plying their little steamers on the rivers and lakes, ransoming slaves and putting them to work on brick-making, building and plantations, which would be the scene of the schools and seminaries of the future. It was in this intermediate region, as yet only partly broached by Islam, that the missionary reinforcements made possible by colonial rule would have the most significant effects.

Although missionaries did not think of themselves as the running dogs of imperialism, there were few among them who had worked in precolonial conditions who did not welcome the change to colonial rule, even if this meant government by a nation not their own, speaking a different European language, following different legal procedures and favouring different Christian denominations. One of the least enthusiastic about the change was Charles Smythies, the Anglican Bishop of Zanzibar, who in 1886 found most of his vast diocese assigned to the Germans. Nevertheless, he went at the next opportunity to Berlin, to assure the Kaiser of the loyalty of his missionaries working in German territory. A majority of the Roman Catholic missionaries in Africa at the time of the partition were French, of whom most subsequently found themselves working under non-French governments. Given time, some adaptations were possible by opening 'provinces' for recruitment and training in English- and German-speaking countries. The role of the Irish and the French Canadians was significant in this respect. But throughout the colonial period large numbers of French missionaries continued to work in British, German and Portuguese colonies, and by the same token many Protestant missionaries of British, American, German and Scandinavian origin worked in French, Belgian and Portuguese Africa. One of the most striking cases of the last kind was that of the English and West Indian agents of the Baptist Missionary Society who, in the Congo, were some of the most reluctant critics of King Leopold. Their pioneer leader, George Grenfell, whose wife was a black West Indian, wrote:

I claim to know better than a great many what is meant by native rule. After ten years of it, I knew enough to make me grateful beyond measure when I learned that King Leopold of Belgium was taking on his shoulders the burdens involved by the administration of the Congo territory. A marvellous change, during the second decade of my African life, came over the distracted country I had previously known under the chaotic sway of hundreds of independent chiefs.[8]

The scale of missionary reinforcements which followed upon the advent of colonial rule was such that, in most of the southern two-thirds of Africa, missionaries were thicker upon the ground than colonial officials – including, in southern Africa, the officials appointed to administer 'native affairs'. This was a remarkable manifestation of the religious faith and charitable giving of the ordinary church-going people of Europe and North America, and also of the organizational power of the great 'societies' and 'congregations' which recruited and trained missionaries and supported them while they were at work. On the ground in Africa, it meant the ability to spread out across the land, so that soon there were few ethnic and linguistic communities without at least one set of missionaries living in their midst, learning the local language, reducing it to writing, standardiz- ing the dialects, producing translations of the scriptures and educational and catechetical materials for the schools. A 'mission station', of whatever Christian denomination, had something of the character of a medieval Benedictine abbey. Catholic priests, supported by lay brothers and sisters, lived in residential quarters around a church, boarding schools, work- shops, printing press, medical dispensary, farm buildings, with orchards and plantations sufficient for the community's needs. Protestant stations had a collection of family houses and private gardens grouped in an otherwise similar pattern. The school of a mission station was the activity which kept it most closely in touch with the people of the surrounding area. Nearly always in the early days, it was a school for catechists and evangelists, who, when qualified by a year or two of reading, writing and bible study, went out themselves to teach school and lead prayers in the villages around. These, rather than the foreign missionaries, were those who lived in direct contact with people observing earlier systems of belief and custom, and who brought them, mostly through their school work, into some kind of relationship with one or other of the Christian churches. For, although churches might disagree on matters of doctrine, for the rural consumer his denomination depended purely on the accident of which mission lay closest to his home.

At its exceptional best, the process of Christianization was a genuinely religious phenomenon, which produced scenes reminiscent of the Acts of the Apostles. In Uganda, the first Anglican and Roman Catholic converts had been gathered among the royal servants at the court of Kabaka Mutesa I, who died in 1884. His successor, Kabaka Mwanga, put more

THE THINGS OF GOD

than thirty of them to death in 1885 and 1886 for resisting his unnatural desires. There was a series of persecutions at the capital, during which Christians fled to the countryside and began to convert their rustic neighbours. During the civil wars of 1888–9 Christians emerged as the political leaders, and their rank and file supporters were labelled as Catholic or Protestant. But the real Christian expansion in both denominations began in 1894 and coincided with the opening years of the British protectorate. Up until this time, there was but one Anglican and one Roman Catholic mission, both sited in the Buganda capital. By 1914 there were 41 Catholic stations spread out over the protectorate as a whole, served by 149 missionary priests and 40 nuns, while the Anglicans, harder to locate in fixed stations, had 37 clergy, 11 laymen, 32 wives and 33 single women at work in the same area. More impressive still was the growth in the number of African catechists and evangelists. Unfortunately, we do not have the Catholic figures, but in 1896 the Anglican church was employing 200 such people, with 500 more working voluntarily for a part of their time. By 1902, there were 2,000 men and 400 women evangelists, many of whom were working as 'missionaries' outside their own linguistic areas.[9]

The mass movement to Christianity in Uganda was such that it required some form of control by which to test the sincerity of so many applicants for baptism. By and large, it was literacy which served this purpose. Catechumens were known as 'readers'. Normally, a neighbourhood would ask for a teacher and build a school by voluntary labour. The mission would send a teacher to live in the village. His classes would be attended by people of all ages. Baptism would follow after a catechumenate of three or four years. In most parts of Africa, however, the 'bush school' was more the attraction than the discipline, and the motives for attending it were frankly secular. The village would ask for the school as a means of coming to terms with the colonial situation, and often following a brush with the colonial state. Parents sent their children, or some of them, in order to learn the new ways. The pupils, in the course of a year or two of sporadic attendance, learned to read and write a little, using scriptural or catechetical texts, which nevertheless taught them more about the wider world than they could acquire from the initiation procedures of traditional society. To turn such beginnings into Christian conversion was an uphill struggle, and, according to the best statistics we have, it achieved something less than a doubling of the Christian population of the continent as a whole, from about four million to about seven million, between 1900 and 1914.[10] During the same period Islam might have increased its constituency from about 60 to about 70 millions.

One aspect of the missionary reinforcement of the early colonial period was a change in the attitude of many missionaries, especially in relation to the emergence of African leadership in the Church. This was particularly visible in West Africa, where some highly educated Africans had risen to positions of authority. The Anglican church had in 1864 consecrated an African freedman, Samuel Crowther, as a missionary bishop on the Niger, and by the 1880s there were several other senior African clergy, who had every right to assume that within a comparatively short time the management of the local church would be in their hands. But reinforcements meant more expatriates, more money and greater responsibilities, and in the 1880s there appeared a new generation of British missionaries who regarded themselves as employers rather than helpers. As Jacob Ajayi has written, 'From fellow men and brothers, they were becoming part of a ruling caste . . . . The group of missionaries who came to darken Crowther's last years were able, young, zealous, uncharitable and opinionated.'[11] All these adjectives are just. The new missionaries hounded the aging Bishop Crowther from the financial control of his own diocese and some of his younger colleagues into open schism. This caused one of the first manifestations of 'independency', by which some African Christians broke away from the ecclesiastical organizations introduced by western missionaries, in order to gain control of their own church life.

Significantly, the other region where the new missionary authoritarianism led to independency was in southern Africa. Here again, there were senior African clergy and lay workers who could see that the progress of white immigration, and the consolidation of the mainline western denominations under white clerical leadership, was threatening to place an indefinite delay upon their own prospects of autonomy. Southern African independency began with the advocacy of 'tribal churches' on the model of the national churches of Protestant Europe. But it assumed a new dimension when African church workers of various denominations migrated from the rural areas to Johannesburg, and there faced a colour bar in the use of church buildings and parish organization. Their response was to turn to the black churches of the United States, and in particular to the American Methodist Episcopal Church, which in 1898 despatched one of its bishops on a visit to South Africa, in the course of which he ordained some 65 African ministers. These formed the nucleus of an 'Ethiopian' church movement (so-called in honour of the Emperor Menelik's victory over the Italians in 1896), which although infinitely fragmented, came to form collectively a large minority element in the Christian life of southern Africa.[12]

The general significance of independent churches should not be exaggerated. In point of fact, the majority of African Christians seem always to have preferred the mainline denominations planted by the expatriate missions. But the very possibility of independence was a salutary warning to the authoritarian tendency rife among early twentieth century missionaries. It compelled them to look to their preparations for training an indigenous clergy and for creating ecclesiastical institutions within which their voices could be heard. Meanwhile, through the 1910s and the 1920s, it was the catechists and evangelists, operating in their 'bush schools' which served also as chapels, who were mainly responsible for the enlargement of the Christian frontier. The numbers of Christians are thought to have more than doubled during these twenty years, reaching a total of some 16 millions by 1930.[13] Moreover, there began to be erected a thin superstructure of schools for the Christian élite – junior and senior seminaries for the training of Catholic clergy; prestigious boarding schools for the children of the African middle class, like Mfantsepim and Achimota in the Gold Coast, King's College in Lagos, Budo and Kisubi in Uganda, the Alliance High Schools in Kenya, Livingstonia in Nyasaland, Lovedale in the eastern Cape; and everywhere some higher schooling for the training of primary school teachers. In the southern two-thirds of Africa, until the middle of the 1920s Christian missions did all these things on their own initiative and at their own expense. They set up, as Richard Gray has put it, 'a narrow and precarious ladder, up which a few persistent and fortunate individuals could climb towards a position from which they could claim to challenge the whites' claim to superiority'.[14] Few they may have been, but seldom in history has a numerically insignificant minority been of greater ideological importance. Until their emergence, Europe in particular and the wider world in general was prepared to believe in the potentialities of those Africans whose forebears had long been Muslim, but it was far more cautious in its attitude to those of animist ancestry. Only when a sample few had shown themselves capable of travelling through the whole process of western education, and emerging from it as individuals who could mix in any company and measure up to international standards, could either colonial powers or their critics argue that here were people not destined to be ruled for ever by others, but capable, one day, of governing themselves.

In British colonial Africa at least, the 1920s witnessed the crucial debate between those who believed that much of Africa was destined to be a white man's country, in which the African population would gradually diminish in the face of much more extensive European immigration, and those who were confident enough of the innate equality of African people with others to foresee a period of imperial tutelage, conducted in the spirit of the Mandates system of the League of Nations, leading eventually to the emergence of self-governing African nations. Most white settlers, from South Africa northwards to Kenya, including the Belgian settlers of Katanga and Kivu, were in the first camp, with Jan Smuts as their foremost advocate on the world stage. Most colonial officials recruited in Europe for service in West, East and Central Africa were in the second, and they had the solid support of all Christian missionaries, whatever their country of origin. The missionaries could defend their cause in argument from the scriptures and doctrines they were pledged to preach. In their schools, however, they possessed a weapon more potent than any dogma. Every African trained by education to function in the modern sector of the colonial economy presented a warning-sign to every would-be immigrant who might otherwise be tempted to occupy that niche. The emphasis here was no longer on the mass literacy offered by the 'bush school', though even that had its importance, but increasingly upon the more professional education which could be offered only to a few. The opportunity came at a time when colonial governments had generated revenues sufficient for a little expenditure to be made on education, and that little could go much further if used to subsidize and professionalize the best of the existing mission schools than in building up a separate government education system. The price which the missions had to pay for their participation was to divert some more of their resources away from direct evangelism into education of a standard that could be recognized by government inspectors. In the Protestant missionary world it was a remarkable backroom figure, J.H. Oldham, Secretary of the International Missionary Council, who alerted the missionary societies of Europe and North America to the opportunity offered to the Christian Church to take a leading role in the educational movement that was about to transform colonial Africa. The Catholic Church was not slow to follow his example. In 1927 Pope Pius XI appointed Apostolic Visitors to co-ordinate mission policy in British Tropical Africa, the Belgian Congo and Southern Africa. The first among them was Francis Hinsley, later Cardinal Archbishop of Westminster. At a conference of the missionary hierarchy in Dar es Salaam in 1928 he gave his orders: 'Collaborate with all your power; and when it is impossible for you to carry on both the immediate task of evangelism and your educational work, neglect your churches in order to perfect your schools.'[15]

Perfection might seem a large word for a system which, even twenty years later, was capable of delivering only four years of primary education to the more fortunate children born during the 1920s and 1930s, of which minority only a handful would proceed to a further four or five years of full primary and junior secondary education. Nevertheless, this modest achievement, made possible by the recruitment of a new generation of missionary educationists, carried the Christian schools of Africa far ahead of their Muslim counterparts, with the result that, by the 1940s and 1950s, employment in the modern sector of the developing colonial economies was becoming very much a monopoly of those Africans who had enjoyed a Christian education. While the total numbers of Christians somewhat more than doubled during these two decades, from some sixteen to some thirty-four millions, the prestige of Christianity advanced much more sharply. Between 1950 and 1970 the number of Christians trebled, reaching some ninety-seven millions by the end of the period, and so perhaps approaching the number of Muslims in the continent as a whole. No less significantly, the Christian effort in education ensured that, as the inevitable opposition to foreign rule developed among Africans, this opposition would be inspired by western Christian models of the nation state rather than by those of oriental and Islamic theocracy. Finally, and above all, Christian missionaries, under constant pressure from their headquarters organizations, proved much more adept than colonial governments at transferring power to African leaders. There were African priests and ministers long before there were African district commissioners or *commandants de cercles*. There were diocesan synods with African participation long before there was anything similar in colonial legislatures. So long as there were colonial states, it was expedient that the highest positions in the Christian churches should likewise be filled by expatriates with easy access to the colonial authorities. But at the moment of political independence their African successors were much readier in the wings than their counterparts in secular government, and this meant that western constitutional forms had a correspondingly better chance of survival. Richard Gray tells the story that Pius XI, when one of his cardinals criticized the lavish redecoration of the Collegio Urbano as a training place for higher clergy from Africa, replied that from these 'late developers' would come the salvation of the Church.[16]

CHAPTER *17*

THE FULLNESS OF TIME

Right up until 1914, the colonial powers had been too busy completing the occupation of their African territories to spare any thought for the question of how long that occupation might be destined to last. It was, in fact the First World War which forced the issue on their attention. For the war was fought partly in Africa, and partly for the redistribution of African territories. At the peace conference at Versailles in 1919, Germany was stripped of all its colonies (above, Chapter 14). However, in deference to the United States and other non-colonial powers involved in the peace settlement, these transfers were characterized as Mandates, and made accountable to the newly instituted League of Nations. The inhabitants of the mandated territories were described as peoples 'not yet able to stand by themselves in the strenuous conditions of the modern world', whose well-being and development constituted 'a sacred trust of civilization'. Implicit in the trusteeship metaphor was the notion that one day, in the fullness of time, the wards would come of age, and take over the management of the property. And what was to be accorded to the mandated territories could hardly be denied to the other colonies which had not changed rulers.

Still, no one in 1919 was concerned to propose a period within which the purposes of trusteeship might be accomplished. Lugard, the architect of Indirect Rule, now in his retirement the first British representative on the Permanent Mandates Commission of the League, expressed the view that the era of complete independence was 'not yet visible on the horizon of time'. His vision of the future, propounded in 1922 in his book, *The Dual Mandate in British Tropical Africa*, presupposed a very long period during which tribes would be taught to govern themselves in an efficient way at the local level, before being introduced into regional federations, which in turn might eventually come together as nations. Meantime, it would be the duty of the colonial powers to exercise a double mandate, first in protecting the indigenous people, and secondly in promoting the economic development of the continent in the interests of the world as a whole.[1] A contemporary French minister of colonies, Albert Sarraut, popularized

20. COLONIAL AFRICA BETWEEN THE TWO WORLD WARS

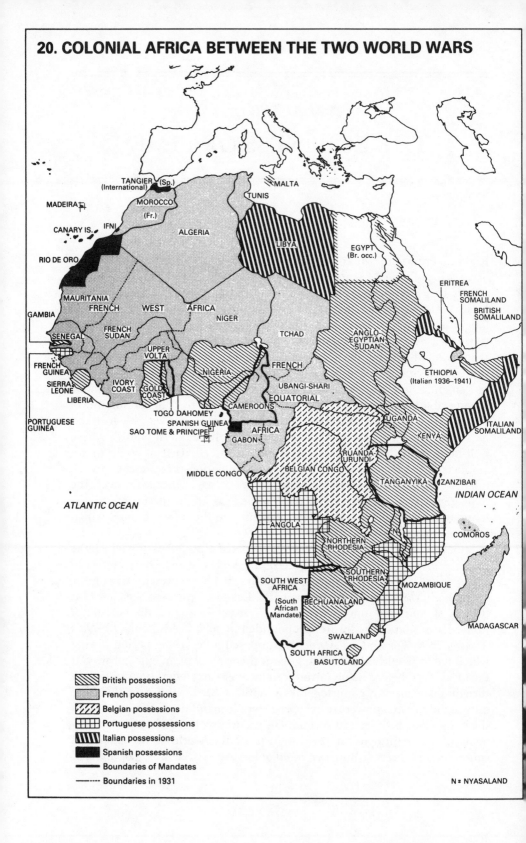

MADEIRA

CANARY IS.

RIO DE ORO

TANGIER (Sp.)
(International)

MOROCCO
(Fr.)

IFNI

ALGERIA

MALTA

TUNIS

LIBYA

EGYPT
(Br. occ.)

ERITREA

FRENCH
SOMALILAND

BRITISH
SOMALILAND

GAMBIA

MAURITANIA

FRENCH   WEST   AFRICA

NIGER

TCHAD

ANGLO-
EGYPTIAN
SUDAN

SENEGAL

FRENCH
SUDAN

UPPER
VOLTA

FRENCH
GUINEA

SIERRA
LEONE

IVORY
COAST

GOLD
COAST

NIGERIA

FRENCH

UBANGI-SHARI

EQUATORIAL

ETHIOPIA
(Italian 1936–1941)

ITALIAN
SOMALILAND

LIBERIA

PORTUGUESE
GUINEA

TOGO DAHOMEY
SPANISH GUINEA
SAO TOME & PRINCIPE

CAMEROONS

AFRICA

GABON

UGANDA

KENYA

MIDDLE CONGO

BELGIAN CONGO

RUANDA-
URUNDI

TANGANYIKA

ZANZIBAR

INDIAN OCEAN

ATLANTIC OCEAN

ANGOLA

NORTHERN
RHODESIA

N

COMOROS

SOUTH WEST
AFRICA

(South
African
Mandate)

BECHUANALAND

SOUTHERN
RHODESIA

MOZAMBIQUE

MADAGASCAR

SWAZILAND

SOUTH AFRICA

BASUTOLAND

British possessions

French possessions

Belgian possessions

Portuguese possessions

Italian possessions

Spanish possessions

Boundaries of Mandates

Boundaries in 1931

N = NYASALAND

the expression *mise en valeur*, which was accepted in both France and Belgium as possessing the same kind of positive ambiguity as Lugard's 'dual mandate'. Although the accent was placed on economic management, this was held to include the protection and development of the colonial peoples, who provided the essential manpower. It implied some recognition of the fact that in many territories population had fallen drastically since the beginning of the colonial period, both through epidemic diseases like small-pox, sleeping sickness and influenza, and through excessive demands for labour, not least during the recent war. Health and education services were thus at the heart of a successful *mise en valeur* of the colonies.[2]

But it was a programme conceived in terms of centuries rather than decades, and in this respect the expatriate rulers of tropical Africa did not differ significantly from the leaders of the white settler communities established in the north and the south of the continent. Algeria, though legally a part of France, was in practice a nearly autonomous entity, in which political power over four million Muslims had, since 1905, been handed over to the local white community of some 600,000.[3] The only way in which Muslims could gain the rights of citizenship was by the path of assimilation, which involved the renunciation of Islamic law. Only a few thousand individuals desired or dared to choose this option. Again, in South Africa internal autonomy had been granted to 1,276,000 whites by the Act of Union in 1910 – in effect, the right to rule over four and a half million non-whites.[4] A small non-European electorate, based on a high property qualification, survived from colonial days in the Cape Colony, but even this would be removed in 1936. 'It will be a slow, gradual schooling of peoples who have slumbered and stagnated since the dawn of time,' wrote Jan Smuts in 1930, 'and only an ever-present, settled permanent European order can achieve that high end.'[5] Yet a nearly similar degree of autonomy was conferred upon the small white population of Southern Rhodesia in 1923, and it remained on the cards that other territories northwards to Kenya might go the same way. Colonial officialdom in Britain, France and Belgium felt that it could exercise a more disinterested trusteeship than that of settler regimes; but the controlling politicians knew that where white settler communities had grown too numerous to be controlled from Europe, the transfer of power must be conceded, and the future of indigenous peoples committed into the hands of local white minorities. The choice was seen, not as one between opposing poles of political philosophy, but rather as two slightly different ways of governing Africans, in both of which it was envisaged that whites would remain in charge of central government institutions for a very long time.

In retrospect, the self-confidence of the colonial powers during the 1920s and 1930s may seem excessive. It assumed that they, and only they, would remain the leaders in world politics, able to shoulder the military responsibilities of empire and to brush off all attempts at interference from outside. It failed to take into account the extent to which colonial power in Africa was a confidence trick based upon past imperial success in Asia, of which the end was already beginning to be in sight. Already in 1917, the Montagu–Chelmsford reforms had committed Britain to 'the increasing association of Indians in every branch of the administration, and the gradual development of self-governing institutions, with a view to the progressive realization of responsible government'.[6] It was surely unrealistic to imagine that Africans, as they gained education, would not seek to follow in the path of Indian nationalism. And, nearer home than India, there was the situation in Egypt where, faced with an educated élite organized in political parties, Britain was forced in 1922 to relinquish the protectorate it had assumed in 1914, and to grant internal autonomy in exchange for control of foreign affairs and continued military occupation. Egypt was a partner in the Sudanese condominium, and educated Sudanese Muslims looked to Egypt as much as to Britain. It was inconceivable that the Sudan would fail to share in the political ambitions of its northern neighbour. In the Maghrib there was even more reason to expect resistance than in Egypt. In Libya, during the 1920s, the Arab tribes under the leadership of the Sanusi order were only kept from driving the Italian settlers into the Mediterranean by the use of aeroplanes and armoured cars, and their retreat into the desert was not to be construed as acceptance of Italian rule.[7] In Morocco, the first French Resident, Marshal Lyautey (1913–25) had achieved a mainly peaceful occupation of the country by his tactful treatment of the Sharifian dynasty; but when the Spaniards in 1921 tried to consolidate their coastal footholds by occupying the mountainous hinterland of the Rif, they sparked off a resistance movement by the northern Arabs and Berbers which it required all the mechanised weaponry of the French as well as the Spaniards, deployed over five years, to repress.[8] Although white settlement increased in all three French possessions in the Maghrib, it should have been clear that Arab nationalism was only pausing to regroup.

Nevertheless, however faulty the long-term vision of the colonial powers, for a quarter of a century in practice it almost sufficed. Between the two world wars there reigned in much of Africa an outward tranquillity very different from the period of colonial occupation on the one hand, and from the period of decolonization on the other. Except in North Africa, the primary resistance to colonial rule – the resistance which merely aimed to restore the *status quo ante* – was over. The secondary type of resistance, led by people with a modern view of the future, who aimed to replace colonies by nation states, had scarcely yet emerged. On the economic side, most colonies were at least precariously self-supporting. Revenues were sufficient to cover the costs of administration, policing and defence, and small surpluses were beginning to be available for health, education, agricultural and veterinary services and forestry. Forced labour had not quite disappeared, but it was confined to recruitment for the most unpleasant tasks of all, such as the completion of the railway from Katanga to Port Francqui through sparsely occupied forest country, when, around 1925, labourers detailed by chiefs on the instructions of the Belgian administration, had to be marched to the building-sites roped together by the neck like any slave-coffle of bygone days.[9] For most of the migrant labour required on farms and plantations, in mines and docks and domestic service, the wages offered were a sufficient incentive, and not only because of the need to earn money for taxes. With motor transport now radiating outwards from every railway station and steamer port, the production of economic crops had become a real alternative to wage labour as a source of cash. As Andrew Roberts has written, this was the period when 'large numbers of Africans became purchasers of imported hoes, bicycles, saucepans, boots and shoes, paraffin, salt, tinned food, tea, sugar and cigarettes'.[10] It was also the period which saw the end of lethal famine, which had been a perennial anxiety in most African societies since precolonial times. Agricultural services spread the use of storeable food crops like maize and cassava. Motor roads and the motor lorry made possible the rapid movement of relief supplies.[11]

All this did not mean that African colonial subjects, during the 1920s and 1930s, were content with their lot, but it did mean that they were not being left to stagnate. The small cadre of British colonial administrators, encouraged by the theorists of indirect rule, might be devoting a certain amount of their time to identifying the correct traditional authorities through whom a 'truly African' form of local government should be brought into existence. Their French and Belgian opposite numbers might be searching out the most logical divisions of *cantons* and *cercles* which might grow into the communes and departments of the future. But the reality was that more and more Africans were spending more and more of their time outside the ethnic compartments within which theorists were trying to categorize them. Some of them were migrating long distances, and crossing colonial frontiers, to reach mines and plantations where wages were, comparatively speaking, high, although the conditions of work might be appalling. Others were on the move within one colonial territory, as soldiers or policemen or clerks or teachers or employees of any of the burgeoning civil service departments. These were the people who first began to think of themselves as Ivoiriens or Tanganyikans or Congolese.[12] Their work often took them into towns, where systems of administration and justice designed for the countryside had little application. During the First World War, some 300,000 Africans, mostly from French territories, had seen service in other continents. Many more than that number had been involved as soldiers or carriers in the African campaigns, and had been exposed to modern technology, large organizations and ethnic mixing.

These were the new experiences on which the future would be built. The further south in Africa, the larger the proportion of those who spent at least a part of their time in wage employment of some kind in towns, where neither 'assimilation' nor 'indirect rule' had much application. In South Africa, since the Land Act of 1913, 87% of the land was in white ownership, and the remaining 13% could not support even half of the African population.[13] Here, therefore, both the pressures and the opportunities led towards the towns, although nearly every family still kept a foothold in the countryside. Town life for the most skilled and best paid, meant the segregated life of the mining compound, where a wholly male population lived in closed dormitories, lest they abscond after a Saturday night out. For the majority, however, it meant the life of the shanty-town built of corrugated iron and old petrol cans, from which tens of thousands set out daily, walking or clinging to the sides of overcrowded trains and buses, to earn small wages as servants and factory hands, washerwomen and street cleaners. Such people might seem poor, but they were usually not so poor as those who lived as 'squatters' on the farms of white land-owners, giving a statutory ninety days labour in lieu of rent, for tiny holdings on which they scratched a bare living during the time that remained. In Southern Rhodesia, from 1930 on, half of the land was allocated to the African population, but it was the worse half, with the lowest rainfall and the poorest access to the roads and railways by which produce reached the market. Here again, therefore, there was pressure to work for wages in mining, factories and plantations, and because of the competition wages could be kept low.[14] Further north, in central and eastern Africa, there was a freer choice between home production and wage labour away from home. Where white enterprise faced unpredictable labour shortages, administrative pressure was applied through chiefs, but on the whole sparingly. Very many Africans seem willingly to have chosen the option of migrant labour, and one of the incentives to do so was precisely to escape the constraints of traditional society, which colonial governments were trying so hard to shore up.

The most dirigiste country in Africa between the wars was not South Africa but the Belgian Congo. Here the Belgian state, having taken over responsibility from King Leopold in 1908, gradually developed the most centralized, the most closely administered and the most heavily policed of all the colonial systems. In one sense, it took the protection of the Congolese very seriously. Although it encouraged Belgians to settle in the country, it never gave them the vote, nor held out to them any hope of exerting political influence. Again, although it worked hand in glove with the great mining corporations which produced two-thirds of the colony's revenue, it nevertheless made strong efforts to limit migrant labour by forcing the companies to recruit a privileged class of industrial workers, who would bring their families and settle around the workplaces living in company housing built to prescribed standards. The other side of the coin was that the government had to take strong measures to keep the rest of the population in the countryside. To this end, it imposed restrictions on internal travel, compelled rural communities to concentrate by the roads and rivers and, increasingly, prescribed what crops they should grow, both for subsistence and for the market. Back-sliders, to the tune of ten thousand and sometimes even twenty thousand a year, were prosecuted, imprisoned and often flogged. Though well enough motivated, the system bred massive discontent, and it was not a good way to introduce the Congolese to 'the strenuous conditions of the modern world'.

The case of the Belgian Congo merits special consideration in connection with the question that is often asked, whether the colonial powers, had they known that their time would be short, could not have accelerated the pace of development between 1920 and 1940, as a preparation for early independence. In a sense, the Belgian Congo provides the example of a colonial economy driven at full throttle in the conditions of the 1920s and 1930s. 'The model colony', as it was often described, had proportionately larger revenues than those of most colonies, but most of them went to pay the high salaries of a massive European administration. Most Congolese enjoyed far less exposure to the modern world than those of more loosely governed territories. 'What,' asked the sociologist Georges Malengreau in 1949, 'is the sum of the riches of a large bush village developed by our colonising effort? At most a few houses built in permanent materials, a few huts with doors and window-frames, some cooking-pots, some metres of cotton cloth, perhaps a bicycle or an old sewing-machine.' The Belgian monopoly system did not yield good prices for the cash crops compulsorily grown. And it placed the greatest obstacles in the way of human circulation, so necessary to the broadening of experience.[15]

The colonies in Africa where things moved most swiftly towards the possibility of an early political autonomy were those situated on the west coast. Here, right along the seaboard from the Senegal to the Congo, there was a commercial class, accustomed to organizing transport and to buying and selling in small or large quantities at narrow margins of profit. Here, in the immediate hinterland, were farmers who had been among the first to cultivate cash crops – ground-nuts, palm-oil, cocoa and coffee – and who had the experience and enterprise to open up fresh farming land, often at a distance from their earlier holdings, by the use of paid, migrant labourers from further inland, where the rainfall was less and communications worse. It was the advent of the motor lorry and the so-called 'mammy-wagon' – a light, pick-up vehicle, adapted with a box body to carry twelve to sixteen people and their luggage – which made the expansion of economic farming possible, and most of the vehicles were, from the start, in African ownership. In these circumstances some individuals and families could become wealthy, and educate their children at the best mission schools, and even send some of them abroad for professional training as doctors and lawyers, journalists and newspaper proprietors. By the 1920s colonial administration was having to function under the scrutiny of a critical press, and in the knowledge that any journalist arrested for sedition would be ably defended in the courts. Of course, as the administrators were quick to point out, these articulate West Africans were an infinitesimal minority of the population as a whole. But the colonial administrators were an even smaller minority. In Nigeria in 1930, they numbered less than five hundred for a population thought to number twenty millions, and they were supported by some four thousand soldiers and the same number of police, each force commanded by around one hundred British officers.[16] The proportions were similar in all the British colonies in West Africa, and those in French colonies, though somewhat larger, were less than double those of the British. It was unrealistic to think that such tiny minorities of outsiders could continue for any long period to control the rival minorities of educated and articulate insiders. South Africa, too, had a class of educated Africans, but in that country the white settler minority which held the reins of power was perhaps one hundred times as numerous as the black and coloured élites, and most of its adult men were potential reservists.

It is often suggested that the first cracks in the colonial system appeared in the aftermath of the world slump of 1929–30.[17] The effects of the slump in Africa were indeed dramatic. In a continent dependent for its revenues on its sales of primary products, colonial governments found themselves obliged to cut their expenditure by as much as one-third, abandoning most projected investment and drastically pruning their civil service establishments. At a time when governments were expanding their attempts to set up social services, especially in health and education, they had suddenly to retract. The African producers of cash crops suffered even more severely, as did the merchant communities which served them. In a crisis the weakest go to the wall. Small farmers left their land to try their fortunes in town. Small traders were caught with unsaleable stocks and went bankrupt. In West Africa particularly, the big European trading firms moved into their places, and African initiatives in business were seriously inhibited. Yet, when all is said, the slump did not shake the fundamental expectations of colonialism. It caused shudders, but no important changes of policy.

Much more disturbing to European complacency on the one hand and to African tolerance on the other was the Italian conquest of Ethiopia in 1935–6. Here was an African state of venerable age, Christian and in some degree literate since the fourth century, which had defeated the Italians in 1896 and so made itself the cynosure of every movement for Christian independency and long-term political aspiration in black Africa. Here was an African country that had done much to modernize itself, which had built a railway to the Red Sea, and motor roads to connect the capital with the provinces, which had introduced an elective legislature and a written constitution, and which had been since 1923 a member of the League of Nations, a much more select body than its modern successor. And here was the Italy of Benito Mussolini using every weapon of modern warfare, including aerial bombardment and poison gas, to crush it and divide it into a set of colonial provinces complementary to Eritrea and Somalia. The European nations failed to deter Mussolini. They allowed him to move his troops through the Suez Canal. They sold him oil for his weapons. But they also knew that he had devalued colonialism by the naked conquest of a civilized people, who were making an honest effort to stand by themselves in the modern world. For Africans all over Africa, as well as for the black population of the United States, Haile Selassie in his exile in England was the symbol of a great wrong done, and one done in some measure to themselves also.[18]

It was fitting, therefore, that, just five years later, during some of the earliest campaigns of the Second World War, Ethiopia should have become the first country in Africa to be liberated from colonial rule, and this with the assistance of African soldiers from both East and West Africa. The whole of the Italian empire in north-eastern Africa was in fact overrun during the early months of 1941 by British colonial contingents operating from Kenya and the Sudan; but whereas Somalia and Eritrea were placed under British military administration for the duration of the war, it had been agreed that in Ethiopia the emperor should be restored to his throne, and he personally accompanied the expeditionary force which recaptured Addis Ababa.[19] Probably very few people were aware at the time of the continent-wide significance of this event, which was that Ethiopia was no longer merely the symbol of a respectable past, but the standard of what was acceptable for recognition as an independent nation state in the post-war world. It was an example to which every aspiring African politician of post-colonial Africa could point. And what was true of Ethiopia was to prove even more dramatically true of Somalia, where a post-war settlement by the United Nations in 1948 awarded a ten-year trusteeship to Italy, with independence guaranteed in 1958. If such were the prospects for a small nation composed mostly of transhumant pastoralists, it became difficult for any colonial paternalist to argue that the people of other, more developed African colonies were unready for independence. Had there been no other consequences of the Second World War for Africa, the decolonization of the Italian empire would have drastically affected the pre-war concept of the fullness of time.

Other lessons of the same kind became apparent as the war proceeded. The next one of major importance followed from the Japanese entry into the war in December 1941, and their lightning success in taking over all the European empires in South-East Asia during the early months of 1942. For those who had ears to hear, the message was clear, that colonial quiescence was not to be interpreted as loyalty, or even as contentment with the system. Colonial peoples acquiesced in the way they were governed primarily because they could see no alternative. To outside powers offering liberation in any credible form, colonial peoples would respond, and the more readily if the self-styled liberator was non-white. As the Japanese example showed, the appeal would be most effective in colonies composed of different racial communities, of which some were privileged over others. In South-East Asia, the order of privilege ran from Europeans to Chinese, and then to Indians and South-East Asians. The nearest African parallels were in eastern and southern Africa, where white rulers and settlers depended in varying measure on Indian clerks, craftsmen and traders, both immigrant communities enjoying a visibly privileged status over the native African majority. One particularly sensitive listener, who made her views known to the British public within weeks of the main events, was Margery Perham, the Reader in Colonial Studies at the University of Oxford. Miss Perham had been since 1930 an ardent disciple of Lugard, and the outstanding public advocate of the theory of indirect rule. She, more than anyone else in public life, had hitherto represented the social-engineering view of colonial policy, according to which everything depended on studying and then harnessing the latent energy of the 'tribe', with results which would show themselves in perhaps fifty years. Suddenly, in March 1942, she wrote in a letter to *The Times*:

The Malayan disaster has shocked us into sudden attention to the structure of our colonial empire . . . . Dutch colonial experts have classified the strange, composite communities which have emerged under western imperialism as 'plural societies'. Of these, Malaya and Kenya are striking examples . . . . Let us imagine that Japanese transports and aircraft carriers appear outside Mombasa harbour. How would the plural society of Kenya respond? Even to imagine Kenya in the throes of desperate war is to set us wondering whether it is wisdom to encourage separate communities to develop their own lives upon parallels that will never meet. Can we afford the assumptions that a common citizenship is impossible, and that the steel frame will be there to hold the groups in their uneasy suspension for all time? A revision of the time factor is necessary for all aspects of our colonial policy . . . . [20]

As the war proceeded, it became clear that the world balance of power was changing, that America and Russia were emerging as the super-powers of the future, and that both wished to distance themselves from the colonialism of their western European allies. At the summit meetings of the heads of government, President Roosevelt was not above getting into anti-colonial huddles with that other great liberal, Joseph Stalin, and even claiming that the so-called Atlantic Charter, which he had signed with Churchill in 1941, was intended to apply not only to the peoples under German domination, but to all the colonial peoples as well. As Roger Louis's important researches have made clear, however, the Americans, once they had thought their position through, did not press for the immediate decolonization of Africa in the way that they had done for the end of the Dutch empire in South-East Asia.[21] Rather, they set themselves the target of procuring it within about fifty years, by encouraging the initiatives of the United Nations Trusteeship Council, by insisting on free access to African markets and, as soon as the development of colonial education allowed it, by a generous programme of scholarships tenable at American universities. The Russians were not yet close to the African scene, but they too offered scholarships, along with financial and military aid to likely supporters. However much they might dislike the idea of a time-table, the British and French, if not yet the Belgians or the Portuguese, became accustomed to the view that their post-war colonial policies must be set within the framework of a programme of decolonization within about half a century, at least for the 'more advanced' colonies, such as those in West Africa. Where British officialdom hesitated was in relation to eastern and central Africa, where European minorities had established themselves in privileged positions, which they would not lightly abandon. Southern Africa was already autonomous under white minority rule, and there the encouragement given to black majority aspirations by the Atlantic Charter and that of the United Nations was the main cause of the white counter-revolution which gave the Nationalist Party its sweeping victory of 1948, and so allowed the establishment of the Apartheid legislative system.[22]

The colonial powers thus entered the post-war period with a sense that their rule was in a terminal phase, but with a set of diverse and divergent time-tables for its winding-down. They fondly imagined that it would be possible to leave West Africa within thirty years and to remain in western and eastern equatorial Africa for fifty, while allowing the strongest pockets of European settlement, in Algeria and South Africa, to work out their own salvation with the majority peoples over whom they ruled. Meanwhile, however, the economic conditions of the post-war world left the colonial powers in no doubt that, for the first time in their brief histories, the tropical colonies were becoming a source of real profit to their European overlords. Before entering the war in December 1941, the United States had all but bankrupted its future allies by the sale of vital food and arms. The post-war world was one in which the dollar was the only strong currency. Europe could not repay its debts to America, because there was little produced in Europe that America wished to buy. But the primary products of tropical Africa – minerals, coffee, cocoa, tea and sisal – could readily be sold for dollars, and the proceeds credited to the franc and sterling areas, to be shared out as the metropoles dictated. There was thus, as never before, an incentive for the colonial powers to invest in the development of their tropical colonies, and to try and hold onto them until the investment had paid off.

Colonial Development and Welfare, as it was known in Britain, and the *Fonds d'Investissement pour le Développement Economique et Social* (FIDES) in France, provided metropolitan funds for infrastructure in the shape of main roads with tarred surfaces, harbours, hydro-electric dams, agricultural and social research, and many other things. Some of it was also directed into hospitals and clinics, schools, universities and adult technical training. The results were almost entirely beneficial to the colonies. Their towns got paved streets, piped water, lighting and drainage. Their remoter rural areas were opened up to market agriculture. The skills of the local workforce were greatly increased. A political price was, however, paid for this economic hustling. It could not be done without a huge increase in the expatriate personnel of colonial government, with all the expensive financial privileges and inducements necessary to recruit it. Hitherto, most Europeans in tropical Africa had lived in houses of wattle-and-daub or sun-dried brick, with roofs of thatch or corrugated iron. Now there appeared around every district headquarters whole suburbs of brick and tile villas, with garages, running water and inside drainage. To the politically conscious among the Africans, it looked like a second layer of colonial occupation, and it whetted their sense of urgency to gain control before the process went too far. It also raised their expectations of the just rewards of a ruling class, when their turn came.[23] Meanwhile, South Africa and Rhodesia, Angola and Mozambique were deliberately stimulating their last great wave of European immigrants, consisting mainly of blue-collar workers, whose presence would both delay the necessity to train skilled Africans and at the same time strengthen the white stake in continued political control. In these circumstances it was hardly surprising that the most politically active sections of African society should have drawn the conclusion that the tide would not be turned by peaceful means alone.

In the event, programmes of development and welfare were scarcely launched before the British decided to take the vital steps towards decolonization in West Africa. In 1947 Kwame Nkrumah returned to the Gold Coast after completing his education at a black university in the United States, and after pausing to make contact with a wide circle of aspiring African politicians in self-chosen exile in France and Britain. Within about a year, he had turned a small, élitist, gradualist political

party of professional men into the first serious mass-party in colonial
Africa. The British tried to outmanoeuvre him by instituting an all-
African legislative council under a constitution designed to put power into
the hands of the older moderates. Nkrumah responded with a call for
'Self-government Now' and a programme of disruption for which he was
duly convicted of sedition, but nevertheless managed to win the ensuing
election from his prison-cell. He was released in February 1951 in
order to take office as leader of government business and later as prime
minister. He was prepared to serve a six years' apprenticeship under a
British governor before officially gaining his country's independence as the
state of Ghana in March 1957. But from 1951 on, it had been clear that the
die had been cast. The whole world knew that, not only the Gold Coast but
all the rest of British West Africa, was in the fast lane to independent
nationhood.[24]

In 1952, the second year of the Gold Coast 'experiment', there broke out
in the Central Province of Kenya the rebellion known as Mau Mau. Small
bands of freedom fighters, seldom more than a few hundred at a time, took
to the nearly impenetrable bamboo forests high on Mount Kenya, and
from there systematically disrupted the teeming agricultural life of the
fertile foothills. A handful of white farmers were killed, but at least a
hundred times as many Kikuyu, Meru and Embu people from settlements
which failed to support the activists. The disturbances lasted five years,
and necessitated the committal of more than 50,000 British troops – a
worrying proportion of the British strategic reserve. The lesson was
learned that, if more than one such episode were to occur simultaneously,
imperial forces might be stretched beyond endurance. There was, in fact,
no possibility of defending small minorities of white settlers in a position of
political and economic privilege for more than a brief transitional period.
In East Africa no less than in the West, accelerated independence must be
the rule. In 1958, one year after the independence of Ghana, the British
governor of Tanganyika agreed with Julius Nyerere a date for independence in 1961. Kenya and Uganda, Nyasaland and Northern Rhodesia
were all to follow within three years of Tanganyika.

The decisive event for the French African empire was the Algerian war
of independence, fought with the utmost vigour and bitterness between
1954 and 1962. Algeria was constitutionally a part of France, and the
nearly one million French people who lived there had relations all over the
mother country, who mostly supported their cause. It could not be
abandoned without a struggle to the end, with the French army fully
committed. At all costs, therefore, it was necessary to avoid wars of
repression elsewhere.[25] Independence was conceded to Tunisia and
Morocco by peaceful negotiation in 1956, and in the same year the French
parliament passed the *loi cadre*, an outline law applicable to all the

component colonies of French West and Equatorial Africa, and also to Madagascar, granting full internal autonomy, save in foreign policy, defence and overall economic policy affecting the franc zone. The *loi cadre* had been amicably drafted with the assistance of West Africans, including Houphouët-Boigny and Senghor, who were active in French politics. It was rather dramatically put into effect by de Gaulle, following his resumption of the presidency in 1958, by a referendum, in which its terms were formally accepted by all the colonies except Guinea, which thus became the first French African colony to receive full independence. For the rest, it followed, for the asking, in 1960. Thus the end of colonialism in French and British Africa was, near enough, contemporaneous. And, greatly to the surprise of all observers, the Belgian Congo caught up with the race at the very last moment. Congolese nationalism only showed itself after the independence of Ghana and the promulgation of the *loi cadre*. There were riots in Leopoldville in 1959. By June 1960 Belgium had granted full independence. By 1965, only Portuguese Africa, Southern Rhodesia and South Africa were left representing the old order of things. Thus, it may be said that the colonial period in Africa had lasted in general for about seventy years, from about 1890 till about 1960, and also that the expectation of its duration by the colonial powers had fallen – from infinity in 1920 to zero in 1960. It is the second of these conclusions that is mainly relevant to what came after.

CHAPTER 18

THE BIRTH OF NATIONS

With only a handful of exceptions, the nations of modern Africa were the direct successors of the European colonies which preceded them. Their frontiers were the colonial frontiers, agreed in the 1880s and 1890s. Their capitals were the colonial capitals, from which radiated the colonial infrastructures of roads and railways, posts and telecommunications. All retained, in some measure, the languages of the colonizers as languages of wider communication. All followed basically western systems of education. Administration continued along colonial grooves, with district officials reporting to provincial officials, and so to the departments of the central bureaucracies, which inherited the procedures and the archives of the former colonial secretariats. The police and the armed services, initially at least, used the same methods of recruitment, the same training manuals, the same uniforms and the same weapons as their colonial predecessors. Some new functions of government had to be undertaken at independence, notably in the field of foreign affairs. But the largest difference was in the education and experience of those who held the commanding positions. For 97% of the population, independence as such made little practical difference.

For the most part, the actual birth of the new nations took place peacefully. However unwilling colonial governments had been to contemplate their own demise from a distance, there had usually been a moment of truth at the end, when for a brief year or two expatriate officials worked hand in hand with their likely African successors. In most colonies political parties were by this time in existence and at least one general election had been held, so that the future legislators were identifiable, and the leaders of the largest parties could be invited to form provisional ministries with some element of participation by nominated expatriates. Such collaboration often led to mutual respect and even warm friendship. Henri Brunschwig, the leading historian of French decolonization, remarks with some Gallic scorn that 'the French did not surrender to victorious enemies, such as Nkrumah and Kenyatta. They stood aside before friends of long standing'.[1] Yet Kwame Nkrumah describes in his

THE BIRTH OF NATIONS

autobiography the meeting in September 1956 at which the colonial governor, Sir Charles Arden Clarke, told him of the British government's agreement to set a firm date for independence in the following year. He reports Arden Clarke as saying, 'Prime Minister, this is a great day for you. It is the end of what you have struggled for.' And he says that he replied, 'It is the end of what *we* have been struggling for, Sir Charles,' and he adds, 'Perhaps we were both looking back over the seven years of our association, beginning with doubts, suspicions and misunderstandings, then acknowledging the growth of trust, sincerity and friendship, and now finally this moment of victory for us both, a moment beyond description, and a moment that could never be entirely recaptured.'[2]

In circumstances like these, which were replicated in many French-speaking as well as English-speaking countries, independence ceremonies were mostly pleasant, even nostalgic, occasions, when one flag was lowered and another raised in its place, to the accompaniment of feasting, music and dance. It is said that at Kenya's independence celebrations Prince Philip was heard jesting with Jomo Kenyatta as they walked together to the flagpole, to the effect that it was still not too late to put matters into reverse if he so wished. Even after six years of bitter fighting in Rhodesia, Robert Mugabe, fresh from his own imprisonment, established relations of close personal friendship with the transitional British governor, Lord Soames, and in his first speech as prime minister assured the local European community, as Kenyatta had done in Kenya, that they had nothing to fear from an African government. Only in the Belgian Congo did the newly appointed prime minister, Patrice Lumumba, lose his temper at a particularly patronizing speech by King Baudouin and reply with a vitriolic denunciation of all the humiliations inflicted by Belgium upon the Congolese during the colonial period.[3]

No amount of last minute good will, however, could overcome the sheer lack of educated and trained manpower with which African countries entered upon their independent nationhood. There was a very small class of professional people, largely confined to North and West Africa, who had studied abroad to become lawyers, doctors and clergy. For the rest, the colonial universities, dating from the late 1940s and 1950s, had been founded to train the rulers of nations expected to emerge at earliest in the 1990s.[4] By the early 1960s they had produced only small numbers of young and inexperienced graduates, who were just beginning to enter the administrative grade of the civil service, and to teach at the higher levels of the few full secondary schools. Graduates apart, the wider élite of African countries consisted of those who had received some secondary education, even if only for three or four years. These comprised most of those who were fully literate in English, French or Arabic, and they filled the executive, technical and clerical grades of the civil service, the noncommissioned officer ranks of the police and the army, the junior posts in the expatriate commercial firms and the teachers in the primary and junior secondary schools. It has been suggested by the late Billy Dudley that in most countries this wider élite may have constituted about 3 per cent of the population of working age.[5] Whatever the talk of democracy by universal franchise, these were the people on whom the future of Africa was now to depend.

From this small and not very highly qualified élite there had to be found replacements for all the higher posts vacated by the former colonial officials, as well as whole new cadres of legislators and party workers, directors of public utilities, diplomats and international civil servants. The problem had been foreseen by the independence leaders no less than by the former colonial authorities, and it had been hoped that a high proportion of expatriate officers would be retained in the service of the new states, perhaps for many years, until suitably experienced nationals were available. In the event, even so partial a solution proved to be short-lived. The new governments soon needed their scapegoats, and pressure from below to seize the best rewarded positions came sooner and more insistently than had been anticipated. Moreover, there were shop-window posts and other exposed positions for which nationals were essential. And so, for example, a young lecturer at the University of Nairobi found himself at twenty-four hours' notice Kenya's first High Commissioner in London, while a Congolese student just graduated from the College of Europe in Bruges was appointed ambassador in London and soon in Washington. Within every African country comparable promotions occurred – from headmaster to permanent secretary, from serjeant-major to general. The sharpest upward mobility of all was naturally to be found in the political field. Although the first generation of top leaders – the heads of state and a few of their ministers – often came from the professional class which had been educated abroad, the great majority of party henchmen came from the wider élite, and these demanded their share of the rewards, and their right to bring friends and relations onto the public payroll. Moreover, when it came to appointments involving state security, ethnic relationship to the leading figures became an important consideration. People do not easily share their secrets with those with whom they do not share a mother tongue.

The first great test for independent Africa concerned the stability of the national frontiers, and the aspect of this which soon became clear was that there was no future either for the pan-African conception of a United States of Africa, or for the federations and quasi-federations created by the colonial powers. It is often said that the French deliberately balkanized their African empire, by granting independence not to the two great federations of French West and French Equatorial Africa, but to the twelve colonies of which they were composed. But the reality was that these colonies had very different economic resources, and the federations had been created mainly in order that the richer ones might be made to share their wealth with the poorer. This presupposed the presence of an overlord with compulsive power. With the retreat of that power, it was inevitable that the richer members would contract out. Felix Houphouët-Boigny, as a minister of the French metropolitan government which drew up the *loi cadre* (above, pp. 225–6), had made it clear that such would be the view of an independent Ivory Coast, with its rich plantations of cocoa and coffee and its easy access to the sea routes and the world markets. In Equatorial Africa, the political leaders of Gabon, which was rich in oil and minerals, took a similar stance. It mattered not that figures as considerable as Léopold Senghor of Senegal and Modibo Keita of Mali were in favour of maintaining the larger units. The fact was that such a policy was no longer enforceable upon those who wished to keep their natural advantages to themselves.[6]

With the Central African Federation, created by the British in 1953 and comprising the colonies of Southern Rhodesia (Zimbabwe), Northern Rhodesia (Zambia) and Nyasaland (Malawi), the problem was that Southern Rhodesia with its white settler population of 250,000 and its common frontier with South Africa, was clearly capable of resisting African majority rule for longer than the two northern territories. These, therefore, had to be allowed to secede from the federation, in order that they might gain their independence at the same time as the countries to the north of them. In East Africa, where the British had long been trying to promote closer union between Kenya, Uganda, Tanganyika and Zanzibar, the historical impediment had been the same. European communities of unequal size had created different expectations of the future, so that nothing more than a customs union and certain common services had been attempted. Nevertheless, with the approach of independence, even this measure of regional co-operation began to wither. Julius Nyerere, like Senghor, was a federalist at heart, but his socialist philosophy held no attraction for the Kenyans, and before long he was closing his frontiers against their economic penetration. The pre-emptive merger of Tanganyika with Zanzibar as the new state of Tanzania was one of very few cases where colonial frontiers were modified by mutual agreement for the sake of forming a larger unit. The other case was the unification of the former British and Italian colonies in Somalia: here the strength of a common ethnic identity was decisive. Some other unions were declared from time to time on the impulse of individual leaders, such as those between Ghana and Guinea; Senegal and Mali; and that between Egypt, Libya and Syria; but none of them stuck any more effectively than the momentary union between France and Britain declared amid the military disasters of 1940.

The failure of attempts to create or consolidate larger political groupings during the early years of African independence was, however,
balanced by a remarkable degree of success in preventing the disintegration of the basic territorial units set up during the colonial period. For
these, the most serious challenges came very soon, and had they succeeded, the unity of almost every country in Africa might have come into
question. As, one by one, they were defeated, so the general danger
gradually receded. Although the causes of attempted secession were
nearly always internal, the practical expression always involved the
intervention of outside powers as suppliers of arms and technical help.
Yet, however obscene the spectacle of the developed countries unloading
their outdated weaponry into Africa, it was perhaps the world-wide
balance of power between East and West during these years which
ensured that intervention from one side was always countered by intervention from the other before major changes of sovereignty could be
effected. The 'cold war' was fought partly in Africa, but the very threat
which it presented helped to ensure the ultimate stability of African
frontiers.

The first challenge came in the ex-Belgian Congo, where, four days after
independence, the troops responsible for the security of the capital
mutinied against their Belgian officers. Lumumba, still in his first week as
prime minister, responded by dismissing all the European officers of the
force publique and promoting African NCOs to fill all the commissioned
ranks up to commander-in-chief. Panic spread through the entire Belgian
community, and within a week or two most fled under cover of a Belgian
force sent by air to protect their evacuation. Only in Katanga, where the
copper-mining companies had so much to defend, did a nucleus of
Europeans stay on and encourage a local leader, Moïse Tshombe, to
declare Katanga's secession from the rest of the country. Tshombe's
motive was the same as Houphouët-Boigny's, but he applied it within a
country rather than a federation, asserting the right of a rich province to
keep its riches to itself. Nevertheless, as Crawford Young, the leading
political scientist to have studied these events, has written, 'Although the
African dimensions of the secession should not be overlooked, it could
never have been undertaken without large-scale public and private
Belgian support.'[7] In Katanga the mutinous soldiers of the *force publique*
were disarmed by Belgian paratroopers, and a new *gendarmerie* was
recruited with a stiffening of white mercenaries, while Belgian administrators remained at their posts. Four weeks later, the diamond-rich province
of South Kasai followed Katanga's example.

Faced with the loss of two provinces and more than half its revenue, the
government in Kinshasa appealed to the United Nations to send an
international force to help it to restore order, while also, under the impulse

of Lumumba, inviting the Soviet Union to exercise a watching brief. The Americans began covert action to remove Lumumba, while the Russians sent him arms, which he channelled to his own home district of Kisangani (Stanleyville). In November 1961 he himself was captured by his political opponents while attempting to join his supporters there and later murdered. The secession of the two southern provinces apart, the stage now seemed to be set for a division of superpower patronage between the Americans in the lower Congo and the Russians in the eastern provinces. It was the United Nations, working with the African governments which had supplied its peace-keeping force, which saved the unity of the Congo, by mediating between Kinshasa and Kisangani on the one hand, while not hesitating to use its miliary force against the secessionists in the south. By January 1963 the Katangan rebellion was over, and although a series of Lumumbist revolts continued for some time to disturb the eastern provinces, there was no longer any doubt that international opinion was consolidating around the central government in Kinshasa, no matter what the configuration of political influences dominant there at any given moment.[8] When former Serjeant-Major, now General, Mobutu was installed as President by the army in November 1965, it was the beginning of a new chapter in the history of the country, known henceforward as Zaïre, in which the basic unity of the state was taken for granted by insiders and outsiders alike.

There were other countries besides Zaïre where the departure of the colonial rulers encouraged minorities to seek their independence from the successor states. The Sudan, for example, was divided in religion and social customs between the Muslim north and the Christian or animist south. The difference was in part an ancient one, going back at least to the Arab invasions of the fourteenth and fifteenth centuries. But it had been compounded during the period of Turko-Egyptian rule, when the south had been a hunting-ground for slaves and ivory (above, pp. 160–3, 196–7), and again during the Anglo-Egyptian condominium, when the government chose to administer the north and the south in separate compartments, and to place the thrust of economic development in the riverine areas of the north, where modern communications with the outside world were easiest. As the Sudan prepared for independence in 1955, the politically conscious among the southerners began to feel that they were about to be handed over to a government which still thought of them as slaves and unbelievers, to be ruled by coercion. Distrustful southern troops mutinied when posted to the north so that northerners could take their places in the south, and this was the signal for the outbreak of guerilla warfare, which continued actively until 1972, and sporadically thereafter. Israel helped the southern guerillas as a way of distracting the attention of the Arab world, while the surrounding African countries,

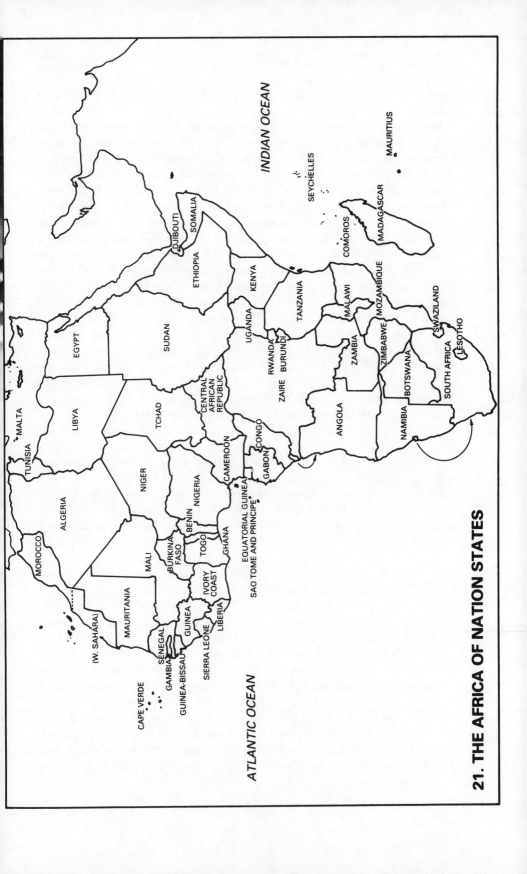

21. THE AFRICA OF NATION STATES

INDIAN OCEAN

MAURITIUS

SEYCHELLES

MADAGASCAR

COMOROS

DJIBOUTI

SOMALIA

ETHIOPIA

KENYA

UGANDA

TANZANIA

MALAWI

MOZAMBIQUE

SWAZILAND

LESOTHO

EGYPT

SUDAN

RWANDA

BURUNDI

ZAIRE

ZAMBIA

ZIMBABWE

BOTSWANA

SOUTH AFRICA

LIBYA

TCHAD

CENTRAL
AFRICAN
REPUBLIC

CONGO

ANGOLA

NAMIBIA

TUNISIA

MALTA

CAMEROON

GABON

NIGER

NIGERIA

ALGERIA

BENIN

EQUATORIAL GUINEA

SAO TOME AND PRINCIPE

MOROCCO

MALI

BURKINA
FASO

TOGO

GHANA

MAURITANIA

(W. SAHARA)

SENEGAL

GUINEA

IVORY
COAST

LIBERIA

SIERRA LEONE

GAMBIA

GUINEA-BISSAU

CAPE VERDE

ATLANTIC OCEAN

especially Ethiopia, took in refugees and facilitated their acquisition of arms and other supplies.[9]

Here, then, was one festering sore in the map of independent Africa, which threatened the integrity of the inherited frontiers. Another soon emerged in northern Ethiopia, where the province of Eritrea, though undoubtedly an integral part of the historic kingdom, had developed a sense of separate identity during half a century of Italian colonial rule, followed by a decade of British military administration during and after the Second World War. In particular, the Tigrinya-speaking population of the north was fearful of domination by the Amhara who formed the ruling element in the central government. When, in 1962, the imperial government of Haile Selassie revoked the federal constitution left behind by the British, Eritrean and Tigrean patriots left for training in the USSR and eastern Europe, and in due course returned to organize guerilla operations inspired by Marxist anti-imperialist doctrines. While Addis Ababa was helping the southern Sudanese, the northern Ethiopians were supplied and supported by Khartoum. At first, the imperial government was strongly supported by the United States, but when in 1974 the empire was overthrown by a military revolution inspired from eastern Europe, the Americans withdrew, the Russians changed sides and the Eritrean and Tigrean patriots had to find new allies. But the guerilla war went on, adding greatly to the problems of famine which beset the region during the 1970s and 1980s. The lovely highlands of northern Ethiopia became a disaster area, in which, while the soldiers fought, the old and the poor died of hunger and the young migrated to Djibouti or the Sudan.

Despite the human suffering which they provoked, however, neither the southern Sudanese nor the northern Ethiopian situation rivalled in danger that which exploded in 1967 in Nigeria. Here, in the largest and most populous country of sub-Saharan Africa, the constitution devised for the country's independence had provided for three regional governments, of the north, the west and the east, to operate under a federal government at Lagos. The system had not worked well, and in 1966 it was replaced by a military regime, established by coup d'état, which gave the impression of being dominated by officers of the Ibo ethnic group from the eastern region. The imbalance was corrected following a second coup, which brought to the head of the federal government a northern Christian, Colonel Gowan, who attempted to solve the constitutional problem by breaking up the three regions into twelve states. At this point the military governor of the eastern region, Colonel Ojukwu, took the disastrous decision to resist the division of his region into three states, by leading it into secession as an independent country named Biafra. Ojukwu was not just an Ibo nationalist, for he aimed to control an area much wider than Iboland. Rather, his calculation resembled that of Tshombe in Katanga, in that most of the exportable wealth of Nigeria came from the off-shore oil of the eastern region, and Ojukwu meant to seize all of it for Biafra. By forcing the oil companies to pay their royalties directly to him, he could both impoverish the federal government and finance the military operations necessary to maintain his secession. Ojukwu's international propaganda was handled by a multinational public relations company, and it was superbly successful in presenting the image of a brave little Christian people fighting for its freedom against a tyrannical and mainly Muslim federal government, intent upon draining it of its natural wealth. When he declared the independence of Biafra in May 1967, four significant African countries – the Ivory Coast and Gabon, Tanzania and Zambia – none of them averse to the diminution of the Nigerian colossus, soon gave him their diplomatic recognition. In the outside world he gained the tacit support and the supply of arms from France, Portugal and South Africa, all of them for different reasons eager to promote the break-up of independent Africa's most powerful state.[10]

The Nigerian civil war, which lasted for two and a half years, was thus in military terms a struggle between two sections of the best trained and equipped national army in independent Africa. It began with a swift and deeply penetrating invasion by the Biafrans of the central and western regions of the country, which captured Benin and was halted by federal forces only about one hundred miles short of Lagos. As time went on, however, the federal government recovered its poise and attracted more outside help than Biafra. Though British opinion was deeply divided, the British government was quietly steady in supporting the federal side, while the Soviet Union was led by its current involvements with Egypt and Algeria into the federal camp, which included the main centres of Nigerian Islam. Within a matter of months, the Biafrans had been driven back across the Niger, and from then on federal efforts were concentrated in stripping away the areas of Biafra inhabited by non-Ibo people. Districts around the northern periphery of Iboland were the first to fall, and by May 1968 the main centre of the oil industry around Port Harcourt was in federal hands. During the next eighteen months the Ibo heartland was constricted within a tightening noose of federal armies, and the casualties from famine among the civilian population brought the estimated death toll to more than a million. Yet the Nigerian civil war was more than just an unmitigated disaster. It gave rise to efforts at mediation which made it the dominant subject of inter-African diplomacy, and greatly reinforced the lessons of the Congo troubles, that the inherited colonial frontiers must be respected at almost all costs. Outside Africa, sympathy for Biafra was sublimated into a great building up of the international aid charities, which tried to heal the sick and feed the hungry. These organizations were to play an increasing part in the Africa of the 1970s and 1980s. Above all, within Nigeria itself, the civil war proved to be a nation-building event, which greatly increased the sense of unity in the country as a whole. Though many political trials lay ahead, Nigeria by 1970 had achieved a political maturity which contributed much to the stability of the whole continent.

The Nigerian civil war highlighted one trend which became common to almost every African country within about five years of independence, namely the increasing size and influence of the military forces. Whereas colonial military establishments had been modest, since imperial reinforcements could be moved rapidly to the scene of any emergency, independent countries had to be self-sufficient in the means of defence and internal security, and most began at once to expand their military forces. In Nigeria, for example, the army grew from about 10,000 to about 50,000 men during the five years before the civil war, and to nearly 250,000 before the end of hostilities.[11] Although numbers were then gradually reduced, nothing could prevent the army from being a major interest-group in the allocation of public revenue, or its commanders from enjoying a prestige which spilled over from the military into the political sphere. The tendency became stronger as the political leaders began to lose their initial popularity and yet were for the most part unwilling to allow any organized opposition to contest their record in free elections. In these circumstances, the military commanders saw themselves, and were often seen by others, as the only means of forming an alternative government. The precedents were established first in Egypt, where as early as 1952, King Farouk was deposed and exiled by a military junta, and then in the Sudan where, only two years after independence, power was seized by the army commanders. The real spate of military coups, however, occurred in 1965 and 1966, when not only Nigeria, but Algeria, Zaïre, Ghana, the Central African Republic, Upper Volta and Burundi all passed under military rule, while in Uganda the army was used by Milton Obote to upset the independence constitution in a move that would lead, five years later, to his own displacement by the egregious General Idi Amin.

By 1967, therefore, most of the new nations of Africa were in the hands no longer of elected legislators, but of self-appointed soldier-administrators. Political parties had been dissolved. Parliaments had ceased to meet. Civil servants took their orders from senior military officers acting the parts of ministers and provincial governors. This did not necessarily mean, however, that military rule was more tyrannical than that of the civilian governments which survived elsewhere. Most of these, while piously protesting that their countries could not afford the luxury of confrontational politics in the western style, turned themselves into single party states, in which the voters retained at best the right to choose between rival candidates nominated by the party machine. Civilian governments no less than military ones used forceful methods against opponents and critics. Under civilian governments no less than under military ones, the press survived only by daily sycophancy. Even the courts failed to provide adequate defence for the most basic civil liberties. Initially, at least, military governments tended to have hands cleaner of corruption, and this alone accounted for much of their early popularity. Moreover, at the end of the day many military governments proved more willing to surrender power than their civilian counterparts, so that many countries experienced an alternation between civilian and military rule. For all these reasons, the conclusion must be that African armies served an important purpose in helping to preserve the integrity of African nations during the dangerous period of their early independence. Democracy during those years could have little real meaning. Whether civilians ruled or soldiers, they could do so only through and on behalf of the small and slowly expanding élite of relatively educated and upwardly mobile people who thought of themselves as citizens rather than as tribesmen. But at least it could be said that with every year that passed, the danger of disintegration was receding, and the shapes of the new nations were becoming firmer.

* * *

While most African countries were thus drifting towards nationhood within a framework of independence obtained without violence, for some others the years between 1960 and 1975 were those of armed struggle against colonial and settler-dominated regimes which still believed that they had the capacity to resist political change. In these cases, the sense of nationhood had to be built up around liberation movements operating as alternative, outlaw governments alongside the surviving colonial structures, supported by groups of exiles dispersed in other countries. The prototype for this kind of nation-building was Algeria, where in the long guerilla war of 1954–62 emergent Algerian nationalism had to contend with a million French settlers, defended by 400,000 metropolitan soldiers. The bureaucratic capital of the Front de la Libération Nationale (FLN) was in Tunis, where it could maintain links with the other Arab countries, while the military training-grounds were established in the natural fastnesses of the Aures mountains astride the Algerian-Tunisian frontier. From here guerilla forces, numbering only some 40,000, were deployed among the six provincial commands (*wilaya*) operating within Algeria itself.[12] Like all guerilla armies, that of the FLN depended on the covert assistance of the civilian population, and therefore upon a mixture of ruthless terror practised against internal dissidents and the appeal of an ideological offensive which accompanied the military one. It was in the 'free Koranic schools' of the FLN that the idea of an independent Algeria, embracing both Arabs and Berbers within the framework of an Arabic-speaking, Islamic state, was mainly inculcated. When the revolutionary forces triumphed in 1962, Algeria at once assumed a high profile in inter-African affairs. It was a leading member of the Organisation of African Unity founded in 1963, and especially of the Liberation Sub-Committee set up to assist the development of armed resistance in the Portuguese colonies, Rhodesia and South Africa. While the operational bases of these liberation movements were situated in the 'front-line states', much of the political inspiration and guerilla training was provided in Algeria.[13]

Guerilla warfare in the Portuguese colonies lasted from 1961 until 1974, and continued in the form of civil war between rival liberation movements long after the Portuguese withdrew. The classic case was that of Guinea Bissau, which has been brilliantly described by the historian Basil Davidson from his own participant observation.[14] Here, a liberation movement headed by Amilcar Cabral began its operations in neighbour-ing ex-French Guinea. Starting from a heavily forested stretch of the frontier, Cabral's guerillas infiltrated district after district, setting up their own schools, clinics, courts, administrative and trade networks, until after ten years the Portuguese were left ruling only a small enclave around the capital. In Mozambique the same tactics were tried from bases in southern Tanzania, and in Angola from bases in Zaïre, Zambia and the Congo Republic. The difficulty in both cases was that rival movements sought aid from rival patrons. Russians, Americans, Chinese, Cubans and South Africans were all involved, with the neighbouring African states also backing different sides. The combined guerilla effort was eventually effective in overstretching the Portuguese defence forces of some 220,000 men, and costing 40 per cent of the Portuguese national budget.[15] They led directly to the military revolution of 1974, which put an end to the Portuguese empire, but did not assist the rapid growth of nations. Although in each former colony one of the contending factions achieved international recognition, large-scale fighting continued, and the neigh-bouring states were flooded with refugees.

The retreat of the Portuguese from Mozambique undoubtedly hastened the end of the white settler regime in Rhodesia, which in 1965 had shaken off the last vestiges of British control by a unilateral declaration of independence. The two main liberation movements, hitherto confined to the Zambezi valley frontier with Zambia, were now able to extend their operations right down the eastern frontier with Mozambique, where the terrain was better suited to guerilla warfare. By 1978 the government of Ian Smith was so far beleaguered that it at last tried to pre-empt a guerilla victory by promoting a political coalition with non-combatant African 'moderates', but at the first free election, held under temporary British supervision early in 1980, Robert Mugabe's militant followers in the Zimbabwe African National Union won an overwhelming victory, and were eventually successful in absorbing the rival militants of Joshua Nkomo. The growth of nationhood in Zimbabwe was thus essentially the result of seven years of armed struggle.

South of the Limpopo, the concentration of wealth and power in the hands of the white community made for a very different course of development, yet here too the 1960s and 1970s were significant for the birth of national consciousness. Three areas of southern Africa, where European settlement and economic interest were weakest, had escaped incorporation into the Union of South Africa in 1910, and had survived as the British protectorates of Basutoland, Bechuanaland and Swaziland. To these Britain gave independence in the years from 1966 to 1968, under the names of Lesotho, Botswana and Swaziland, but it was an independence different from most of the new states of Africa, in that in each case only a single ethnic group was involved, while all three were completely dependent for their economic survival on the employment of most of their citizens of working age in the Union. With populations of less than one million apiece, the three states were little more than autonomous labour reserves for their powerful neighbour. The same could be said even more sharply of the attempts by the South African government to devolve political powers upon certain ethnically defined rural areas known as Bantustans. These areas were all carved out of the 13 per cent of the land which had been left in African ownershp following the land Act of 1913. Many of them consisted merely of fragments separated from each other within a patchwork of black and white owned territory. None of them possessed anything like enough land to support themselves by agriculture, and they contained neither mines nor industries to give them any direct share of the country's wealth. They were simply rural reserves from which the adults of working age travelled out as migrant labourers to earn money in the white areas. Even so, most of the African population of South Africa now lived without any base in the countryside, in overcrowded satellite townships ringing the white cities. The Apartheid dream of ethnic nations developing separately alongside one another, and alongside the white and coloured communities, was a mirage.

Given the degree of demographic and economic integration which had taken place by the 1960s, a single South African nationality, embracing all the people of the subcontinent had become the only practical possibility, and it is a matter of great interest that such a sense of unity could grow up among the voteless majority of South Africans, while being blindly repudiated by the minority in power. In 1960, when so much of Africa to the north was in the process of gaining independence under African governments, the British Prime Minister Harold Macmillan made a famous speech to the all-white parliament at Cape Town, in which he warned that South Africa, too, would have to face the 'winds of change'. A few weeks later, an over-nervous unit of police fired into a peaceful demonstration at Sharpeville, killing 69 people. The outside world reacted in anger, and for a day or two it looked as though the South African authorities might embark on fundamental changes. Instead, they banned the African National Congress and took further emergency powers. The spearhead of African resistance thereupon decided that violence could no longer be excluded from its programme, although its leaders proclaimed that action would be directed against installations and property rather than people. They also made it clear that they sought to create a South African society composed of all races. For a brief period it looked as though the campaign of sabotage might gather strength and become the kind of liberation movement which had proved successful further north. But the resources of the South African government, especially its security police, were far greater than those of the Portuguese and the white Rhodesians. The leader of the main militant group, Nelson Mandela, was identified and arrested in November 1962, and the rest of the 'high command' were picked up at Rivonia Farm near Johannesburg the following year. From then onwards, the real focus of South African national consciousness was the prison on Robben Island off Cape Town, where Mandela and his colleagues were to spend the next quarter of a century. A long line of nationalist leaders, including Nkrumah, Kenyatta and Mugabe, had already demonstrated the charismatic power that could be conferred by political imprisonment. But, in an almost unique way, Mandela symbolized both the frustrations and the aspirations of an entire people. The peroration of his statement from the dock at his trial in April 1964 had a quality fit to ring down the centuries:

During my lifetime I have dedicated myself to the struggle of the African people. I have fought against white domination and I have fought against black domination. I have cherished the ideal of a democratic and free society in which all persons live together in harmony and with equal opportunities. It is an ideal which I hope to live for and to achieve. But, if needs be, it is an ideal for which I am prepared to die.[16]

Twenty-seven years later, when repeated verbatim by Mandela on the day of his release from prison, it had lost nothing of its power to move the heart. It is the authentic cry of the last of the African nations still waiting to be born.

CHAPTER 19

THE SLIPPERY SLOPE

Perhaps the greatest misfortune of the modern African nations was that their approach to independence coincided with a period when it was generally believed that the way to a better future lay through more and longer term state planning, with its implementation led by a large and ever-expanding public sector. The decolonizing powers were recuperating from a world war, the waging of which had necessitated a vast enlargement of the role of the state, including the first serious attempts to mobilize the economic resources of the colonies in support of the franc and sterling areas (above p. 223–4). The run-up to independence took place amid a flurry of development planning, which ramified far beyond the mere provision of infrastructure, into grand schemes of industrialization, with the colonial state as chief entrepreneur. Typically, such projects would centre around the construction of a hydro-electric dam, feeding power to manufacturing and processing industries, which would turn the local raw materials into finished products and so reduce the country's dependence on imports. On paper these projects looked very attractive. In practice, they all proved vastly more costly than had been anticipated. When taken over by newly independent governments, they overstretched their technical and administrative resources, and led to borrowing and indebtedness. Above all, because they were government enterprises, economic systems were tilted in their favour, at the expense of farmers who formed the main body of private enterprise producers. These were compelled, at first by colonial governments and later by their independent successors, to sell their crops to official marketing boards at prices much lower than those of the world market. Though first introduced as a means of stabilizing prices, the system quickly became a form of quite heavy taxation of agricultural production, which discouraged the expansion of the most important sector of all tropical African economies.

As to the ruling élites of the new nations, they were mostly far more committed to political centralization and to planned, state-led economies than their predecessors. Of the Africans who had received any kind of secondary education by 1960, virtually all were, in European and

241

American terms, people of the left. They knew that international communism supported colonial freedom. They knew that, within the political spectrum of western Europe and North America, their surest allies were to be found on the left of the left. Although there was little industrialization in Africa, and little of the class structure that accompanied it, they felt that all Africans stood in the role of proletarians in relation to all whites. They responded emotionally to the kind of Marxist rhetoric which urged the oppressed to unite against their oppressors.[1] The significant few who completed their education in Europe, and still more so those who did so in the United States, returned home confirmed in the opinion that western societies were deeply flawed by divisions of race and class, and that in their own countries strong socialist government was necessary to control foreign influence in business and the professions, and to ensure that nationals got the leading positions with the least delay. Moreover, as they contemplated Africa's inheritance from the precolonial past in their search for a rhetoric that would engage the masses, the independence leaders nearly all claimed to discern a kind of indigenous socialism inherent in African tradition – an absence of social stratification, a limited view of property rights which discouraged accumulation of all kinds and excluded the private ownership of land, a tradition of communal co-operation in matters such as warfare and hunting, clearing the land and building, and in promoting the necessary flow of tribute to the chiefs who acted as the redistributors of wealth. As they reflected on traditional chieftainship, no doubt in an idealizing spirit, they thought they saw a system of governance superior to the confrontational democracy practised in Europe and America, in which majorities imposed their will on minorities. African socialism, they said, should act for *all* the people, following as nearly as possible the practice of the ancestors, who had sat under the big tree and talked things through until a common mind had been achieved, after which the chief pronounced the collective decision and all jumped to obey. 'We in Africa,' claimed Julius Nyerere, 'have no more need of being "converted" to socialism than we have of being "taught" democracy. Both are rooted in our past, in the traditional society which produced us.'[2]

On the other hand, despite these nods in the direction of the precolonial past, African socialism was in reality strongly anti-traditional when it came to dealing with the institutions and cultures of particular African societies. One might rename the Gold Coast as Ghana, Sudan as Mali and Rhodesia as Zimbabwe, in honour of medieval 'empires' of unknown constitution and dimensions, but 'tribalism' was a pejorative word, associated with backwardness and threatening the unity of the modern nation, while 'chieftainship' was likewise suspect because of its use by colonial authority. In most African countries hereditary kings and chiefs disappeared from the political scene after independence. Some, particularly in West Africa, were allowed to keep their titles and to perform ritual functions, but most retired into poverty and obscurity. Their places were taken by the district administrators of the central government, and these were essentially people with a modern education, who felt themselves to be the agents of modernization rather than of conservation. They lived and worked in the provincial towns, seldom visiting the villages and looking to the capital city for their promotion. The ambitious among them shunned postings to the peripheral districts, which were staffed by recruits or even by foreigners.

The most characteristic instrument of African socialism was the 'party', seen not as a contender for power at successive elections when its record and programme was presented to the people for approval, but as the animating mind and purpose of the whole nation, established and irreplaceable. This was the engine which was to power the African revolution into modernity. The key word used of it was 'vanguardism', and it did not spring from the African past or from any western democratic model, but rather from the Marxist-Leninist tradition of eastern Europe. The party consisted of the politically committed in every walk of life. Its purpose was to exhort and mobilize, and also to threaten and discipline. Its members staged public meetings and educational activities, but they also listened and reported. They pervaded the teaching profession, the civil and military services, the public corporations, the trades unions and the police. Promotion to all leading positions depended on party approval. Employment in the party organization was the main route into the legislature and central government. The party varied greatly from country to country. In a few, notably in Nigeria and Senegal, the concept of the single party remained untried. There were some countries, like Zaïre and Ethiopia, where a single party was established by coup d'état, as the propaganda machine of a military dictatorship. There were others, like Algeria and Mozambique, where it rode in on the back of a conquering liberation movement. In most cases, however, it was ingrained in the leadership aims of the independence movements which gained power by constitutional means, by winning an election in the western manner prescribed by the departing colonial power, and then slowly attracting enough members of the opposing groups to eliminate any possibility of an electoral challenge. The variations scarcely matter. The result in all of them was to increase the autocracy of governments by frightening away every kind of criticism. Among the earliest victims of African socialism were the trades unions founded on western principles during the later years of the colonial period. These were soon told that their function in a socialist state was not to promote the interests of their members, but to make them more productive.[3] The press, too, quickly learned that the price of survival was daily obeisance, with the front page of every issue respectfully devoted to the doings and sayings of the head of state.

The growing authoritarianism of African governments during the first three decades of independence may have helped the consolidation of nations over the ethnic groupings of which they were composed (above, pp. 236–7), but it was not so favourable to their economic development. Most states quickly hedged themselves about with financial controls designed to prevent the flight of capital, which proved on the whole to be counter-productive in that they tended to deter external investors from coming in. Nationalization of the local operations of foreign companies had the same effect. So did military coups, civil unrest and the harrassment of long-established alien minorities like the Lebanese merchants of West Africa and the Indians of East Africa. Even more serious in the long term was the deterrence of indigenous African enterprise by authoritarian governments pursuing socialist ideals. In West Africa a class of traders already existed which was too strong to be attacked directly, though it could be weakened by import licencing and currency controls. In eastern Africa, while Kenya encouraged the emergence of indigenous capitalism, Tanzania went so far in the opposite direction as to confiscate real property worth more than £5,000, and to confine even retail trading to approved co-operatives. Tanzania also compelled its peasant farmers to abandon their scattered homesteads and rebuild in compact villages, where education and health services could be provided: the result was by no means an unqualified success. All over the continent, governments failed to realize that there was an international market for skilled manpower, and so lost many of their most highly trained and needed citizens, who preferred working abroad to sharing the austerities of a classless society at home. And to the waste of this brain-drain there was added the growing number of refugees from political intolerance, of whom there were by 1989 some four million officially recognized as such, and another 12 million persons displaced within their own countries through civil wars and threatened violence.[4]

According to a long-term survey published by the World Bank in 1989, per capita income in the whole of sub-Saharan Africa, excluding only South Africa, grew by 2.7% per year during the 1960s, levelled off to zero during the 1970s and fell by 1.2% per year during the first half of the 1980s.[5] This meant that, whereas in the 1960s most African countries had per capita incomes similar to those in other developing countries in Asia, the Pacific and Latin America, by the middle of the 1980s most had fallen well behind all but the poorest countries of southern Asia.[6] Obviously, such generalized statements conceal a wide variation in natural resources as well as in economic performance among individual countries. In fact, four states with relatively sparse populations and exceptionally large reserves of oil or other minerals – Libya, Algeria, Gabon and South Africa – enjoyed per capita incomes comparable with those in the poorer of the developed countries. About ten others – Egypt and Tunisia, Morocco and Senegal, Ivory Coast and Cameroon, Congo and Angola, Zimbabwe and Swaziland – formed an intermediate group, with per capita incomes between $500 and $1,000. All the rest – and these included such large and politically significant countries as Nigeria and Ghana, Kenya and the Sudan, Uganda and Zambia – had per capita incomes below $500, while four very large countries – Ethiopia and Zaïre, Tanzania and Mozambique – had per capita incomes below $200.[7]

What really stood out, however, was the relative lack of growth in living standards in African countries, rich and poor alike. It is this fact which demands common explanations, of which the pursuit of socialist policies by autocratic governments supported by inefficient bureaucracies was only one. Another was certainly the demographic explosion which affected the whole continent, and which had its origins in the modernizing changes initiated during the colonial period. Right up until the beginning of the twentieth century, Africa had remained a sparsely populated continent. In 1900 its population is thought to have numbered less than 100 million. By 1960 it had risen to a little over 200 million. In 1990 it was 450 million, and it was expected to reach at least 1,000 million before stabilizing, around the second or third decade of the twenty-first century.[8] The motor force behind this increase was the fertility rate among African women, which is thought to have remained fairly stable at between six and seven live births for each child-bearing woman. According to the Australian demographer, J. C. Caldwell, tropical Africa's high birth rates, which were sustained by culture and religion, were 'undoubtedly a response to high death rates in what had been one of the world's most disease-ridden regions'.[9] It was the increased expectation of life which came with modern medicine and hygiene, and with improvements in food production and distribution, that accounted for the sudden growth of population. The fertility rate changed more slowly. According to one survey conducted in Ghana in 1986, teen-age girls then expected to have five children, whereas their mothers had expected seven. Only among the small minority of girls with ten or more years of education had expectations fallen to three children.[10]

In terms of living standards, therefore, the nations of Africa were, during the first three decades of their existence, climbing a slippery slope, on which any fruits of economic progress were largely nullified because they had to be shared among an ever-increasing number of people. The consequences of this all-important demographic phenomenon stretch widely across the fields of recent economic and social history. The first result of demographic pressure was seen in the countryside, in the division of family holdings into plots too small to sustain the occupants by their own agricultural efforts. This was, of course, an age-old feature of rural life in Africa, particularly in mountainous areas, where the absence of malaria caused population to expand faster than elsewhere. The classic response to such situations was for groups of young adults to migrate to unoccupied land on the periphery of the society and there establish new settlements by clearing bush or forest. During the later twentieth century unoccupied land was harder to find, but the process could still be observed in mountain regions, where farmers constantly encroached upwards into the high-level montane forests previously uninhabited. Surplus populations from the healthy mountain habitats likewise moved downwards into the surrounding grasslands, taking with them practices of cultivation into country previously occupied mainly by pastoralists. The grasslands of western Uganda and eastern Rwanda provide a typical example of an area where land use has changed dramatically within living memory.

Again, the arid lands stretching right across the continent in the zone bordering on the Sahara desert constituted another relatively healthy environment where population was constantly liable to outgrow resources, and from where surplus population tended to seep away southwards to the woodland and forest zones where a more intensive kind of agriculture could be practised, and where export crops such as timber, oil-palm, coffee, cocoa, rubber and kola offered opportunities for an expanding agriculture. Here, migrants could not often establish themselves as independent proprietors, but they settled as labourers on the farms of local people. Ivory Coast, with a population of 11 million in 1987, had absorbed more than two million such migrants during the period since independence, most of them from her northern neighbour, Burkina Faso, which also sent migrants southwards to the gold-mines and cocoa farms of southern Ghana. Niger was another large Sahelian country, the citizens of which tended to move southwards into Nigeria and Bénin. The very dark complexions and the eye-catching dark-blue head bandages of the Saharan Tuareg became a common sight throughout Nigeria during the period following independence, but these were only the most identifiable of the many migrants from north to south in a movement which, though accentuated by the Sahelian droughts of the 1970s and 1980s, can be seen overall as the result of population increase as much as of climatic disaster.

More strikingly obvious than the migration from overpopulated to underpopulated rural areas resulting from the demographic pressures of the late twentieth century, however, was the corresponding migration from the countryside into the towns, and above all into the capital cities. North Africa apart, the growth of large cities was a new feature of the African scene. In 1945, as colonialism entered its last phase, there had been 49 towns in the entire continent with a population exceeding 100,000. Of these no less than 25 were in Egypt and the Maghrib countries, while

South Africa accounted for another 11. Between the Sahara and the Limpopo only 13 towns had reached this size, four of them were in Nigeria.[11] The average late colonial capital was a place of around 50,000 people, housing the bureaucracy, the banks, the commercial houses and a little light industry, besides hospitals, churches, schools, shops and places of entertainment. Probably half of the urban population consisted of domestic servants. During the first thirty years of independence, when overall population rather more than doubled, that of most capital cities multiplied by ten. By the early 1980s, Lagos and Kinshasa each had populations of around three million, while Addis Ababa, Abidjan, Accra, Ibadan, Khartoum and Johannesburg were all over one million, with Dakar, Nairobi, Dar es Salaam, Harare and Luanda not far behind.[12] By 1990 one quarter of all Africans lived in towns, and it was anticipated that by the end of the century the proportion would have risen to one half.

While migration from country to town must be seen as one of the main responses to the surge of population growth, it was so in an indirect rather than a direct way, since it was not the poorest people who normally moved. Famine did not drive people directly to towns, as it did in southern Asia. There were no street dwellers in Africa. On the contrary, much broad-based research has shown that the desire to move townwards was most characteristic of the better educated families in the more prosperous rural areas. Urban migration was not seen as flight, but as a life-enhancing progression. It was undertaken not by whole family units at once, but by siblings who initially went in search of better employment for themselves and better education for their children, and who continued for a long time to maintain close links with their former homes. They returned for holidays, to help with the harvest, to woo their brides and, at last, to retire. They sent money to their rural relatives, and they provided temporary accommodation in town for those seeking to follow their example. Although African cities in the later twentieth century rang with the noise of builders, the result in terms of average living accommodation was still spartan. Few urban households enjoyed more than a single room, with access to communal areas for cooking and sanitation. Most were without either electricity or piped water. Yet the fact remains that most adopted this way of life in order to improve their conditions, and most who tried it believed that they had succeeded in doing so.[13] There can be no more telling comment on the poverty, the hardships and the sheer boredom of rural life in Africa, even during the twentieth century.

While there is no doubt that rapid urbanization was a necessary corollary of rapid population growth, it has been strongly argued by the World Bank and other donor agencies that, in the event, urbanization took place under economic, and especially under fiscal conditions which unduly favoured the city-dweller, and failed to maintain a proper balance between the interests of town and country. On the one hand, local farmers were forced to sell much of their produce at controlled prices, and therefore actually produced less in the 1980s than they had done in the 1960s. On the other hand, city dwellers in most African countries were able to buy relatively cheap imported food – rice, maize and wheat – from the surplus production of the developed world, where farmers were supported by state subsidies. Again, city dwellers mostly paid direct taxes only if they were in full-time, registered employment, and only about 20% were so. The rest lived on casual earnings, and yet had access to the lion's share of the social services available in the country as a whole. Granted the harshness of urban conditions in all but the leafiest of the suburbs, it was nevertheless arguable that most African countries were being governed increasingly in the interests of their urban, and above all of their metropolitan populations.[14] Around the capital cities, the inner provinces usually flourished, both by supplying the city dwellers with their vegetable foods, and by enjoying relatively easy access to the urban facilities. The outer provinces, by contrast, received the lowest priority for every kind of infrastructural development, while even that which they had received during colonial times was frequently allowed to decay. Roads fell into hopeless disrepair, schools were left without books or writing materials and clinics without medical supplies, while government services of every kind ran down. John Iliffe's study of the African poor has shown conclusively that the most wretched poverty of post-colonial Africa was concentrated in the peripheral areas of nearly every country, which were also those where the majority of refugees from group violence in neighbouring countries were likely to be found. Thus, civil war in the southern Sudan sent refugees fleeing to Ethiopia, Uganda and the Central African Republic, while recurrent trouble in Uganda scattered refugees into all the countries around its frontiers. In these circumstances mass famine, unknown since the advent of the motor lorry in the 1920s, reappeared in one country after another during the 1970s and 1980s, and nearly always in frontier regions.[15]

Many oscillations in the recent economic history of Africa were the result of successive discoveries of oil in some countries, and from fluctuations in its price world-wide. During the 1960s oil was cheap, selling for less than $2 a barrel. This was already enough to boost significantly the revenues of the more fortunate producer countries. For example, Libya until the middle of the 1960s was one of the poorest countries in the world, but oil began to flow from its newly discovered wells in 1965, and by 1969, the year in which the monarchy of King Idris was overthrown by Colonel Gaddafi, its export revenues had risen to £900 million a year. Again, the Nigerian civil war of 1967–70 was largely concerned with the control of oil revenues, at a time when the price was around $2. In 1973, following the Yom Kippur war between Israel and Egypt, the OPEC countries cut their production and forced up the price to $12. Between 1979 and 1981, as a result of events in Iran and Iraq, the price of oil reached $34 a barrel.[16] For Nigeria this meant a rise in export revenues from $4 billion to $26 billion, and a temporary rise in per capita income from $360 to more than $1,000.[17] Algeria, Gabon, the Ivory Coast, Angola and Congo also shared handsomely in the oil bonanza. However, for the majority of African countries which lacked significant oil reserves the period of high prices, which lasted through the early 1980s, was a disaster, for their economies were largely dependent on imported oil. During these years most of them borrowed themselves into insolvency. Within less than a decade, however, their plight came to be shared by the producer countries also, which had over-committed themselves during the boom and in the following slump were unable to sustain what they had begun. The acute scarcity of foreign exchange in countries still so largely dependent on essential imports meant hospitals and clinics without medicines, universities and schools without books and vital machinery without spare parts. In Nigeria during this period per capita income fell back to little more than one third of what it had reached at the height of the boom.

By the later 1980s the indebtedness of most African countries had reached a level at which it was impossible for them either to service existing loans or to obtain further credit. In 1988 the debt service obligations of tropical African countries averaged 47% of their export revenues, while the amount actually paid averaged 27%.[18] Many debts in both the public and the private sectors were written off by the lenders, but in the circumstances almost the only source of further loans was the World Bank operating through the International Monetary Fund, which was able to use its near monopoly of credit to impose strict conditions of what was euphemistically known as 'structural adjustment'. Essentially, this meant the adoption by all fresh borrowers of an effective policy for maximizing exports and minimizing imports. It meant redressing the balance of economic advantage in favour of the rural producers of food and export crops as against the urban bureaucrats, soldiers and industrial wage earners who were the main consumers of cheap imported food and also of luxury goods from abroad. The World Bank did not confine its prescriptions to purely economic matters. Increasingly, it advocated an underlying political philosophy for encouraging private enterprise and decentralizing the decision-making process. It blamed political authoritarianism for economic inefficiency.

Although for different reasons, South Africa too was a country in which economic progress was seriously impeded by the increasingly authoritarian system of government made necessary by the forlorn attempt to bring about separate development of the black, white and coloured sections of the population. Throughout the twentieth century, the peoples of southern Africa had increased their numbers very much in line with those of the rest of the continent, with the exception only of the white minority, which grew only half as fast as the rest. Between 1950 and 1990 the black population of South Africa almost quadrupled, from about 7.5 to around 27 millions, and this at the very time when Apartheid policies were redesignating the former 'native reserves' as 'tribal homelands' and insisting that, outside them, Africans were to be treated as foreigners, admissible only as temporary workers, without even the right to bring their families to the scene of their labour. The crucial legislative measure was the Native Laws Amendment Act of 1952, which restricted the right of urban residence to around two million Africans who had been born in a particular town or lived there continuously for fifteen years. All other Africans became subject to deportation to their supposed ethnic home-lands as soon as their presence was deemed surplus to labour requirements in the town. To implement this legislation the police relied on the hated 'Pass', which recorded the identity and employment record of each individual, and which had to be carried by every African and produced on demand. During the twenty years from 1950 to 1970 prosecutions under the Pass Law increased from 280,000 to 631,000 cases a year.[19]

While the Africans of South Africa, supported by most of the outside world, focused their attention on the undeniable oppression and injustice of the Apartheid legislation, its alternative aspect, which was more apparent to the enlightened self-interest of thinking white South Africans, was that of a gigantic set of constrictions placed upon the natural development of the economy. From very early in the century it had been obvious that the reservation of certain not very skilled jobs for white workers was an uneconomic practice, which made building, mining and transport services, to name only a few examples, much more expensive than necessary. With the growth of manufacturing industry between the 1920s and the 1940s, there came the demand for a more skilled and more stable African labour force than could be supplied by the migratory system. During this period the black urban population grew from around 600,000 to nearly 2.5 million. From the 1950s onwards, when government was actively trying to restrain urban growth, the expansion of industry was working in a directly contrary sense. With the growth of population pressure in the 'homelands', the number of Africans who defied the Pass Laws and settled in the towns doubled and then redoubled during the forty years to 1990. Official attempts to keep the situation under control were both costly and unavailing. The main cities were ringed with satellite townships, built to replace the shack settlements of the earlier migrants. The process of compulsory rehousing caused social and political unrest on an unprecedented scale, and new shack settlements grew up faster than they could be replaced. The continuing drift to the cities by a populace increasingly conscious of its real political grievances required, by the 1980s, policing on a scale which only the military could supply, and even so, taxes were difficult to collect and much of the initiative in local government passed into the hands of street committees. It was in the black townships of South Africa that the defence of Apartheid was in practice abandoned as hopeless.[20]

For the time being, until much more archival evidence becomes available, it is impossible to be sure by what mixture of motives the white government of South Africa was inspired when, on 2 February 1990, it announced to an astonished world that the time for 'reconciliation and reconstruction' had arrived, and that it was accordingly rescinding the prohibition of the African National Congress, the Pan-African Congress and the South African Communist Party, and would shortly be releasing Nelson Mandela unconditionally from his long imprisonment. The statement referred to the collapse of the Marxist economic system in eastern Europe, and to the reduced danger of Soviet intervention in South African affairs. More positively, it suggested that one objective of reconciliation should be the adoption by all the countries of southern Africa of a common development programme sufficiently attractive to ensure that the whole region would be able to obtain adequate investment and loan capital from the industrial countries of the world.[21] This was perhaps an oblique recognition of the embarrassment caused by the partial sanctions imposed by some western countries on trade with and investment in South Africa. But it was probably even more of a reflection upon the unsatisfactory performance of the South African economy under the internal conditions created by Apartheid. The statement was arguing between the lines that in southern Africa, as in eastern Europe, command economies needed to be restructured so as to allow market forces to operate. In southern Africa, no less than in the rest of the continent, economic development had been overtaken by population increase. The successful ascent of the slippery slope required that all the people should be free.

CHAPTER 20

THE PAST AND THE PRESENT

As Africa approaches the threshold of the third millennium, it seems right to conclude with some attempt to discern which strands in the African experience show most signs of continuing relevance to the present. In this context, the long and distant period of man's evolution as a scavenger, hunter and gatherer may seem at first sight to be of marginal significance. Yet the primacy of Africa in human evolution is a recent discovery, which has so far had time to achieve only a fraction of its potential impact. Already men of science are learning to see Africa not as a quaint backwater, but as the scene of man's acquisition of his deepest genetic characteristics. It seems likely that, as this knowledge spreads and is pondered by the next generation of scientists across the whole spectrum of intellectual disciplines, the outside world will learn to think of Africa with more respect and that Africans themselves will face their fellows with a new confidence. If the recent findings of molecular biology find acceptance, to the effect that the planet was not merely first colonized from Africa, but also largely recolonized by the first fully sapient men spreading out, again from Africa, within the last 250,000 years, the general impact should be even stronger (above, pp. 25–6).

Shorter-term by these standards, but still extending backwards at least ten thousand years to the early stages of food production, and still full of significance, is the small-scale pattern of Africa's linguistic and cultural ethnicity (above, pp. 147–8). Mainly, this seems to have been the result of small units of food-producing population forming in the most favourable pockets of a generally hostile environment. These pockets became the areas within which a large measure of endogamy was practised over a long period, thereby giving rise to divergent streams of language and culture. The resulting ethnic groups had no necessary pattern of social and political organization. Some remained entirely stateless. Most eventually gave rise to clusters of very small states sharing a common language and culture. Some became incorporated temporarily into larger states by conquest. With the coming of colonialism, the whole continent was reorganized into larger states, but even then the ties of language and culture proved extremely tenacious. Indeed, during the first half of the colonial period they were actually consolidated, since they tended to be chosen as the natural units of Christian evangelism and also of local administration. Only as western education reached the stage of using a European language as the medium of instruction did the bonds of the vernacular begin to weaken, and then slowly. Towns were places where many different languages were spoken, but only with the large-scale urbanization of family groups during the postcolonial period did a generation of urban children grow up speaking a European language, and perhaps also an African lingua franca like Hausa or Kiswahili, better than their mother tongue.

The logic of the situation would seem to indicate that, within another generation or two, African ethnicity will be greatly modified by the displacements caused by rapid and uneven population increase (above, pp. 246–7). Even if the migrants from one rural area to another tend simply to lose their own language and culture and adopt those of the host society, as has usually happened in the past, migrants from country to town will be placed under much more promiscuous pressures of neighbourhood, work and school, of which the long-term outcome must lead more towards national and less towards ethnic consciousness. Meantime, however, the persisting strength of ethnicity, even in an urban situation, was well illustrated when, during the early months of 1988, the newspaper-reading élite of Kenya was riveted by the daily reports of an action fought in the appeal court concerning the body of S.M. Otieno, who had been a leading criminal lawyer in Nairobi. Otieno, himself a Luo from the Lake province, had been married to a Kikuyu lady, a sister of the then foreign minister of Kenya, who claimed that Otieno had expressed the wish to be buried on his farm at Ngong, on the outskirts of Nairobi. Both Otienos were highly educated people, whose marriage and whole way of life seemed to have been lived as far as possible independently of the ethnic norms. Yet the husband's family claimed the body, on the grounds that it was unthinkable for a Luo to be buried elsewhere than in the land of his ancestors, and after 155 days of sophisticated argument in the highest court, they won. Essentially, the case tested the balance between indigenous, ethnic, customary law as against the statutory and common law imported into Kenya during the colonial period, and it showed that, over a wide field of family and inheritance law, considerations that were not merely broadly African but narrowly ethnic were still paramount.[1]

Again, the pattern of rural settlement and subsistence production established in most of Africa early in the Iron Age have mostly proved very durable, with West and Western Central Africans living compactly in their small towns and Eastern and Southern Africans in their dispersed homesteads (above, Chapters Eight and Nine). Even where whole areas were seized for European farms and plantations, the dispossessed Africans usually tried to establish a similar pattern of settlement elsewhere. Rural housing and domestic equipment have as yet changed little from those of precolonial times. Nor has the division of labour between the sexes, whereby men were responsible for clearing, building, herding, hunting and defence, whereas women hoed, planted, harvested, cooked, carried water and went to market, while maintaining an average of live births, which is thought to have remained fairly stable for a long period, of about seven for each child-bearing woman.[2] What has perhaps changed most in the pattern of rural settlement during the twentieth century has been the progressive decline of polygamy and, above all, of the very large polygynous families that used to exist in the households of chiefs and other rich men. In some measure this may have been the result of Christian teaching, but the main reason was undoubtedly economic. It was that in small, isolated societies with limited foreign trade and few facilities for storage, differences in wealth and social status were expressed primarily in the capacity to exercise hospitality. To be rich and respected, one needed a larger vegetable garden, a larger field and a larger herd than other men, and therefore one needed a larger family circle, with more women and children to provide the labour. Colonial rule and economic development opened other avenues of advancement, but the traditional conception of wealth and influence survived in the sense of obligation felt by those who succeeded in any walk of life to help a wide circle of client kin.

All through history, new crops were being added to those domesticated in Africa, and strategies of food production were changing, little by little, in consequence. Among food-plants, the bananas and yams of south-eastern Asia and the maize and cassava of the New World were especially important, while the colonial period saw the introduction or wider diffusion of many tropical crops grown for export, and therefore of significance for the economic survival of African countries in the modern world. Of the latter, a few such as tea, sugar, sisal and tobacco, were essentially plantation crops requiring expensive processing machinery close to the scene of production, but most, including cotton, coffee, cocoa, ground-nuts and palm-oil, could be grown on small plots by peasant farmers, using simple hand-tools for digging and weeding, harvesting and decortication. African systems of land tenure, often described as 'communal' but in fact closer to usufruct, changed very slowly, and small family holdings remained the norm. Tractors, and even ox-ploughs, were few and far between, even towards the end of the twentieth century. In fact, by far the greatest outside contribution to African agriculture during the colonial period was the introduction of mechanical transport for getting produce to distant markets and providing the means for relieving local shortages.

In 1990, more than 300 million out of a total of some 450 million

Africans still lived on the land, and of these the majority, and among women the *large* majority, still followed a pattern of life not very different from that of their precolonial ancestors. The largest change was perhaps that by the late twentieth century most land holdings no longer sufficed for a livelihood unless supplemented by some kind of wage-earning by some members of the family. At first, the need was met by the temporary migration of individuals to employment in towns, or else on mines or plantations, but from about 1960 there began the wholesale drift of family groups into the towns. This process is expected to escalate until, by about the year 2010, half the population of most African countries will be town dwellers. However, due to population increase, this will still leave some 500 million people – more than the entire population of Africa in 1990 – living in the countryside.[3] As with ethnicity, therefore, great changes in the methods of agriculture and in the character of rural life must be expected. The simple process of mechanization by the expropriation of small holdings and the elimination of surplus labour through still more rapid urbanization will scarcely be possible. The first requirement of African agriculture will be that it should remain labour intensive, and the relevant models are more likely to be found in southern Asia than in Europe or North America.

The role of Islam in Africa continues to be of great significance, and it is a role which is to a very large extent defined by past achievement. While reliable statistics are lacking, it is likely that there are still more Muslims in Africa than Christians. At the same time, because of its history, Islam is still, more so than Christianity, a regional religion, heavily concentrated in the northern half of the continent, and with its main outside links in the adjacent countries of the Near and Middle East. Indeed, looked at from the traditional standpoint of both European and Middle Eastern history, the part of Africa to the north of the central Sahara is not really African at all. Egypt and the Maghrib, conquered in the seventh and eighth centuries and fully Islamized by the tenth, belong almost to the Islamic heartland. They are the Muslim West. Seen from the African end, however, Mauritania, Senegal, Gambia, Guinea, Mali, Niger, Nigeria, Chad, the Sudan and Somalia are all countries where Islam has been established for six to eight centuries, and where the main direction of trade, travel, forced migration and cultural influence has been northwards across the desert. It is the Islamic factor in all its historical depth that makes the North African countries inescapably a part of Africa, whatever other affiliations may be claimed for them.[4]

During the colonial period the connections between Islam north and south of the Sahara were temporarily muted. Long distance trade was diverted to the sea routes, and the desert trails fell into disrepair. The pilgrimage diminished, along with the rest of the caravan traffic, to revive only with the coming of cheap air travel. Above all, the political reins were in European hands, and while the practice of Islam as a religion was tolerated and even supported, its ecumenical and political aspects were discouraged. With decolonization, however, the connections reappeared. Egyptian independence hastened that of the Sudan. The Algerian revolution quickened the whole of French colonial Africa. Muslims north and south of the Sahara not only engaged in a common struggle for political independence but felt a common dismay with that of Middle Eastern Muslims at the implantation, with western aid, of a Jewish state in what had been for thirteen centuries an Arab, Muslim land. Last, but not least, there were the curious accidents arising from the distribution and the price of oil. Nigeria, with the largest Muslim population of any country to the south of the Sahara, became, along with Libya and Algeria, a member of OPEC and so was involved in close diplomatic as well as economic relations with the oil producers of south-western Asia. Again, as a result of rising oil prices, several Muslim countries, including Libya, Saudi Arabia and Kuwait, suddenly found themselves with revenues larger than they could easily spend in their own sparsely populated lands, and thus in a position to fund aid and missionary activities, and sometimes even political adventures, in less well endowed Muslim countries. Egyptians and Sudanese flocked to Saudi Arabia to earn big money. General Amin armed his Muslim-oriented tyranny in Uganda with Libyan help. Villages in southern Malawi suddenly boasted glistening new mosques built with Kuwaiti funds. While the overwhelming strength of Islam remained concentrated in the north and the east, and there was no reason to expect any sudden expansion of its numbers in the areas of Christian growth in the centre and the south, it was clear that everywhere the spirit of unity among Muslims was strengthening and their presence becoming more confident and assertive.

Although the first in the field by six centuries, Christianity had soon lost the initiative to Islam, which by its successes in North Africa and the Saharan region had effectively blocked any Christian advance until the opening of the Atlantic seaways. Even then, the first Christian footsteps in sub-Saharan Africa had been hesitating, and it was not until the eve of the colonial period that any deep penetration had been made. However, once launched in tandem with the colonial state, Christianity had built itself an effective role as the main educator of colonial subjects in the western style, and as the principal interpreter of the modern world to the Africans living to the south of the Sudanic belt. White missionary leaders had been more perceptive than their secular contemporaries in the colonial administrative services about the likely duration of colonialism, and the rapid advent of political independence found the Christian churches with an indigenous leadership ready to take over. Nevertheless, the great growth of Christian numbers has occurred quite recently. In 1950 they stood at around 25 million. By 1975 they had reached a staggering 100 million, and by 1990 this figure may have nearly doubled. In part this was a reflection of the general demographic trend, and in part it was the continuation of an exponential increase which had occurred from one generation to the next throughout the colonial period. However, in its later stages this increase had moved twice as fast among Roman Catholics, who in 1950 were less than half of all Christians, but by 1975 formed three quarters of the whole.[5] The success of the Catholic church was important, in that it left the majority of African Christians affiliated to a strong international structure which was comparatively untainted by colonial associations. In this way, Christianity overcame the crisis of African independence, and indeed found itself in the new situation to be almost the only institution which was capable of facing up to the increasingly authoritarian states of the new era. In Zaïre, between 1971 and 1974, General Mobutu made a serious attempt to humble the Catholic Church by his campaign for 'authenticity', but under the leadership of Cardinal Malula it emerged successful in what Adrian Hastings has described as a *Kulturkampf* between church and state.[6] In Uganda, the Anglican Archbishop Janini Luwum was bold in his criticisms of General Amin, and paid for it with his life, but the Church went from strength to strength during the years of tyranny. In Ethiopia the Stalinist revolution of General Mengistu overthrew the devoutly Christian emperor, but the Orthodox church of the country retained the allegiance of the vast majority of Christian Ethiopians. Above all, in South Africa, apart from one section of the Dutch Reformed church, the Christian churches stood out for their opposition to Apartheid. The Anglican church in South Africa, despite its large white membership, elected Desmond Tutu first as Dean of Johannesburg and then as Archbishop of Cape Town, and so gave him an unassailable position from which to speak for the unrepresented majority of the population. It was a fitting tribute that in February 1990 Nelson Mandela spent his first night of freedom under the Archbishop's roof.

Although slavery, after a long history in almost every region of Africa, had virtually ceased to exist by the middle of the colonial period, the diaspora resulting from the trans-Atlantic slave trade continued to exert a kind of gravitational pull upon the continent of its origin. No comparable influence was generated in that part of the diaspora which had flowed towards the Ottoman empire and the countries further east, where visible African identity had been submerged by miscegenation from the first generation on. Even within the New World, most of Latin America saw enough miscegenation even in the days of slavery to blur the perception of racial difference into a broad spectrum of class distinction based upon degrees of colour. It was in the Caribbean, and above all, in North

America that the sense of African identity remained sharp enough to survive long after the emancipation of the slaves. The United States developed in the nineteenth century into a unique melting-pot of nationalities, but for a long time afterwards it failed to assimilate the descendants of those whom, as slaves, it had oppressed. The black Americans kept their sense of African-ness, married their own kind, nurtured their own folklore and music, organized their own Christian churches and schools, and dreamt of a possible return to Africa one day. A very few actually went as missionaries and settlers, and of these some founded the Liberian settlements and managed to expand them into an internationally recognized state which survived through the colonial period. More significant for Africa, however, was the community of African Americans who stayed in the land of their forced adoption and came to form one-seventh of the most powerful nation of the twentieth century. It was among them that the Pan-African idea developed, and in their midst that Nkrumah, Azikiwe and other leaders of the independence period grew up with the vision of a United States of Africa, which, though premature in the 1960s, found some permanent expression in the Organization of African Unity. It is an idea which may in the fullness of time recur. Meanwhile, during the period of Africa's post-independence troubles, the existence of the forty million African Americans has made the United States the natural gathering point for Africa's best educated refugees. By the 1990s it was American universities, rather than those of Africa or Europe, which led the world in African studies. It may well be, as Andrew Young has predicted, that with the ex-colonial powers increasingly preoccupied with European interests and problems, the Africa of the twenty-first century will find its complementary continent in North America.[7]

To a very large extent, the central theme of African history during recent centuries has been the opening-up of the continent to itself and to the outside world. And neither part of the process is as yet complete. The camel men opened the desert routes in early medieval times, at about the same period as Muslim seafarers pioneered the monsoon traffic of the Indian ocean coast. Five centuries later, the Portuguese completed the circuit of coastwise communication from southern Morocco to the Limpopo. But everywhere to the south of the Sahel the difficulties of movement inland still limited long-distance trade to items of value like gold, ivory and slaves, textiles, hardware and guns. Until the eighteenth century, with insignificant exceptions, foreigners came only to the coast. It was the Africans who developed the inland routes and used them for their own local purposes as well as for the export trade. By the same token, south of the Sahel, Africans seldom left the shores of Africa, except as slaves, never to return. The nineteenth century is traditionally regarded as that which saw the opening up of Africa, and indeed much was learned and set on record by travellers from the outside world, whose writings constitute the earliest documentary evidence concerning many parts of the continent. But the exploration of Africa by outsiders was not in itself important in African history. The second half of the nineteenth century witnessed a growing level of disturbance in the African interior, as ivory and slave-hunters from the Sahel and the coastal regions used improved fire-arms to assert new patterns of political and economic dominance. At the end of the century came the beginnings of systematic colonial occupation. Yet during the whole of the nineteenth century not much was learned by Africans about the outside world. African rulers interrogated explorers and missionaries about their home countries, and other questions were prompted by Muslim and Christian teaching. But still not many Africans travelled further afield than the coastal ports, or participated in any kind of production in the interests of world trade.

The partition of Africa placed each of some forty colonial territories squarely within the political ambit of a single European power, and under this new dispensation contact with the outside world continued to develop slowly. For the first generation of colonial Africans there was perhaps even a diminution of foreign links, while the new masters were establishing their authority and building their new lines of communication. By the second colonial generation, however, Africans were becoming increasingly invol-ved with the world market as producers of economic crops, as wage-earners and as consumers of foreign imports, which were by this time being carried into the interior in unprecedented quantities by the new mechan-ical transport. By this generation also, Christian missionary education was beginning to create a literate élite with greatly widened horizons, causing awareness of the outside world among Africans in the southern half of the continent to rival that already existing in the Muslim north. The third colonial generation saw two world wars, which involved millions of Africans as soldiers and carriers in journeys far from their own countries. All these, however, were still the more or less passive experiences of individuals in subordinate positions. They were the twentieth-century equivalent of service in the long-distance caravans of earlier times. A very different level of contact was reached during the final decade of the colonial period, when the fortunate few who had achieved secondary education in the African colonies suddenly found themselves with the opportunity of studying abroad, and not merely in the institutions of the colonial metropole, but in the United States and Canada, India and China, the Soviet Union and the countries of the eastern bloc. These Africans became the masters of their own destinies. The qualifications which they gained were internationally viable, and nothing compelled them to return to their own countries. In 1989, there were believed to be 70,000 African graduates who had elected to remain in Europe after completing their studies, while in the United States there were reported to be more than 10,000 in highly skilled employment from Nigeria alone.[8] Nevertheless, the majority of students did in the end return to their own countries, bringing back with them a wide variety of experience about conditions in the developed countries.

With the coming of independence, the opening up of Africa to itself and to the outside world gathered pace. Up until this point, movement between African countries had been limited to labour migrants, and official contacts had been minimal. If, for example, a simple border problem occurred between neighbouring districts of Uganda and the Belgian Congo, it could only be handled through Entebbe, London, Brussels and Leopoldville. Independent countries had very quickly to establish their own diplomatic links, and most urgently of all with their African neighbours. Differences in the languages of wider communication were at first a grave obstacle. While smugglers in the frontier districts were often happily polyglot, few Francophone African officials knew any English, or vice versa. At meetings between African governments, the interpreters were usually from Europe or Asia. Yet the early years of independence were active ones in inter-African relations. From the very beginning, those countries which had gained their independence conspired to promote the liberation of the rest. In 1958, the year after Ghana's independence, Kwame Nkrumah hosted an important conference for the leaders of liberation movements elsewhere, which greatly hastened the pace of events in the Belgian Congo and East Africa. Five years later, most of tropical Africa was free, and was united with Egypt, Ethiopia and the Maghrib countries in the Organisation of African Unity, of which the main unifying objective was the liberation of the Portuguese colonies and the settler-ruled states of the south. The prosecution of these aims demanded constant activity at the United Nations and regular co-operation with the recently emancipated states of southern Asia.

If the issues which caused African countries to get to know each other were mainly political, those which governed their relations with the developed countries, including the former colonial powers, were mainly economic and social, and concerned trade and aid. These, too, helped the opening up of Africa. It was a commonplace of the early years of independence that the presence of foreigners was much more conspicuous in most African countries than it had been in colonial times, and likewise that nearly all the high buildings that sprang up in the capital cities during these years were attributable to foreign firms and property developers. Despite the fact that most African governments professed to be of the political left, foreign capitalists from all over the developed world were at first more prepared to risk certain kinds of investment than they had been in colonial times. Banks, insurance companies, building contractors, civil engineers, oil men, motor dealers, plantation managers and many others proliferated and competed, many of them helped on by concealed subsidies from their home governments in the shape of tied loans for the purchase of their products or export guarantees to assist with their losses. It was the presence of these foreigners which created the demand for the international hotels and other amenities which distinguished African city centres from the countries in which they were set, and also created the lucrative market for rented housing for foreign residents, which became the main target for private investment by the African professional class.

And then, widely spread through the rural hinterland, there were the foreign 'aid personnel', familiar in some form in every independent African country. A few of these were the highly skilled consultants employed by the international agencies. The big battalions consisted of young volunteers, whose earliest contribution was in helping to expand the education systems of newly independent countries to the stage at which primary education was available to most children. The French and Belgian governments made such service an alternative to military conscription, and tens of thousands of young people responded. The United States recruited the Peace Corps, and Britain saw the establishment of several charitable organizations such as Voluntary Service Overseas, which did the same tasks. As time went on, all these organizations became more professional, employing fewer, older and more skilled volunteers, and developing away from formal education into a wide variety of projects for economic and social development, health work and famine relief, and they were joined by aid agencies in Scandinavia, Canada, Israel, Switzerland and countries of the European Community. What was achieved by all these activities cannot easily be quantified, but one very significant factor was the mere presence of outside witnesses across wide expanses of the African scene at a period when inexperienced and unrepresentative governments were prone to the abuse of power. Where volunteers were excluded, the worst could usually be expected.

Other types of relationship there were which went under the name of aid, but which usually included a large measure of national self-interest on the part of the donor. Most developed countries, for example, had armaments industries anxious to export their products and especially to dispose of outdated weapons. While such arms might be sold on a commercial basis, the sales were usually promoted by training and 'advice' provided from aid budgets. Again, several of the developed countries maintained military, air or naval bases in Africa, renting the facilities from their African hosts, but also retaining their long-term good will by favoured treatment in aid allocations for other purposes. Again, a great deal of food aid, whether given free for famine relief or sold year in year out at knock-down prices, was strategically motivated. It provided governments in the developed countries with the opportunity to subsidize their own farmers by buying up the agricultural surplus at artificially high prices and then disposing of it in the third world at artificially low ones. Such operations had the real if unintended effect on the economic policies of African countries of encouraging them to rely on cheap food from abroad and therefore of discouraging their own farmers by monopoly buying at heavily controlled prices.

Consciously or unconsciously, a great deal of the outside influence that played upon Africa between 1960 and 1990 was motivated by the global rivalry between the western and eastern blocs. It was the 'Great Game' of the later twentieth century, and in it the western countries held most of the trump cards. They had the great advantage of the languages of wider communication spread by the former colonial powers, which were also those of the United States and Canada. An African student in any country of the eastern bloc had to spend two years in language study before beginning his course of instruction, and also to encounter a way of life even more unfamiliar and forbidding than in any western country. Again, it was the western countries, and above all the United States, which had the agricultural surplus for disposal on favourable terms. It was indeed one of the most bizarre features of the cold war that the Soviet Union remained throughout it dependent on grain imports from North America. Finally, it did not take the Africans long to discover that the eastern countries made poor trading partners. Arms apart, their industrial products were manifestly inferior to those of the west, and supplies of spare parts were quite unreliable. Nevertheless, the mere presence of the Soviet Union and its allies was of great importance to the Africans in their relations with the western world. When Guinea voted itself out of the French 'Community' in 1958, it was the Russians who came to the rescue. When the United States quarrelled with Egypt at a critical moment in the construction of the Aswan high dam, the Russians moved in to finish the job. The eastern bloc countries played a vital part in planning the revolution which overthrew the Ethiopian government of Haile Selassie, and the Soviet Union supplied arms and training to its successor. Above all, when in 1975 the South Africans, with covert American help, invaded Angola on the eve of the Portuguese withdrawal, the Russians promptly flew in and paid for 30,000 Cuban troops and kept them supplied throughout a fifteen-year war between the MPLA government in Luanda and the South African-supported UNITA insurgents of Jonas Savimbi.[9] By 1987 Soviet expenditure in Angola was estimated to have reached 1.5 billion annually, and MiG. 23s, flown by Angolan pilots, were capable of seeing off the French *Mirages* of the South African airforce.[10]

Moreover, until about 1988, it was not only what the Soviet Union and its allies were actually doing in Africa which counted, but also what they might do in the future. Southern Africa, in particular, from the copperbelt of Zaïre and Zambia southwards to the gold, diamonds, cobalt and uranium of South Africa and Namibia, was full of strategic minerals which the United States and its allies would have been most unwilling to have denied to them in war. So long as there was a chance that the Soviet Union might at some time seek to increase its influence in the region by championing a forceful overthrow of the white minority government of South Africa, so long would the United States feel obliged to go on shoring up the corrupt dictatorship of Mobutu in Zaïre and supporting Savimbi's civil war in Angola, which meant turning a blind eye to South Africa's military operations in Namibia as the lifeline for Savimbi's supplies.[11] Only as it became apparent that the Soviet Union was genuinely anxious to reduce its African commitments, and in particular to withdraw the Cubans from Angola, did it become practical politics to encourage a corresponding withdrawal of South Africa from Namibia, leading to Namibian independence in 1990. The most drastic effect of the Soviet withdrawal from the African scene, however, was that which came about in South Africa itself. Apartheid, we have seen (above, p. 250), carried the seeds of its own demise in the limitations which it placed on the free growth of the South African economy. But its internal defenders were difficult to dislodge so long as they could claim that the only alternative was a Soviet-dominated system of black majority rule. Now, shorn of their main talking-point, and with socialist egalitarianism discredited worldwide, it suddenly became clear to the Pretoria government that the time for discussions with the black majority of the population had arrived.

While it is still too early even to guess at the outcome of such discussions, the repeal in June 1991 of the Population Registration Act of 1950 was taken by the United States and most other western governments as a sufficient indication that the legislative basis of Apartheid was being so irreversibly dismantled that trade sanctions could safely be lifted. A much more widespread reflection of political changes in the eastern bloc countries became evident in 1989 and 1990 with the decision by a whole series of African countries to review the operation of their single-party systems.[12] While it is too early for any convincing analysis of their motives, the significant fact would appear to be that African states were here responding to events not in the Soviet Union itself, but in Poland, East Germany, Czechoslovakia, Hungary and Romania. What was moving them was the sight of people demonstrating in the streets, in the full view of police and soldiers who mostly did not shoot, because they were in so great sympathy with the crowds that the normal chains of command failed to operate. What the Africans must have seen also was that populist movements, once successful, quickly turned to accusations of corruption and to the destruction of every kind of privilege practised by the party bosses. They may to some extent have been influenced by the fact that, coincidentally, the World Bank and other major donors had been pointing to authoritarianism as a major cause of economic immobility. They knew, therefore, that a change of course would bring them credit in that part of the outside world which henceforward would most concern them. But mainly their antennae must have sensed that the élites of two and three per cent, which had sufficed to dethrone and replace colonialism in the 1960s, now needed the support of a much wider following. There were many more people, and more of them had some kind of secondary education to make them politically conscious. Above all, a quarter of all the people now lived in towns, where they would be far less easily controlled than their parents in the countryside. The era of mass participation in the political process was about to begin.

NOTES

CHAPTER 1

1 Robert Ardrey, *African Genesis* (London, 1955), p. 23.
2 Mary Leakey, *Disclosing the Past* (London, 1984), p. 51.
3 Sonia Cole, *Leakey's Luck* (London, 1975), p. 89.
4 To the author, in July 1961.
5 *Punch* 10.vi.1964, cited in Cole, *op.cit.*, p. 260.
6 F. Clark Howell, in *Cambridge of Africa* (henceforward *CHA*), vol. 1 (1982), p. 106.
7 D.W. Phillipson, *African Archaeology* (Cambridge, 1975), p. 22.
8 Glynn Isaac, in *CHA*, vol. 1 (1982), p. 245.
9 L.R. Binford, *In Pursuit of the Past* (London, 1983), pp. 57, 68.
10 Glynn Isaac, in J. Clutton-Brock and C. Grigson (eds), *Animals and Archaeology* (Oxford, 1983), pp. 3–19.
11 Howell, *loc.cit.*, p. 125.
12 K.W. Butzer, in *CHA*, vol. 1 (1982), pp. 455–6.
13 C. Loring Brace, *The Stages of Human Evolution* (Englewood Cliffs, 1967), p. 74.
14 K.W. Butzer and Glynn Isaac (eds), *After the Australo-pithecines* (The Hague, 1975), pp. 828–30; O. Bar-Yusef, 'Pleisto-cene connections between Africa and south-west Asia', in *African*

Archaeological Review, 5 (1987), pp. 29–39.
15 P. Teilhard de Chardin, *Le Phé-nomène humain* (Paris, 1955), p. 205.

CHAPTER 2

1 K.W. Butzer, *Environment and Archae-ology* (Chicago, 1971), pp. 149–50.
2 Glynn Isaac, in *CHA* vol. 1 (1982), pp. 221–2; O. Davies, *West Africa before the Europeans* (London, 1967), pp. 98–104.
3 D.R. Pilbeam, in K.W. Butzer and Glynn Isaac, *After the Australopithe-cines* (The Hague, 1975), pp. 829–30; D.W. Phillipson, *African Archaeology* (Cambridge, 1985), pp. 52–3.
4 Glynn Isaac, *Olorgesaile* (Chicago, 1977), pp. 80–7.
5 Glynn Isaac, in *CHA*, vol. 1 (1982), pp. 211–12; J.D. Clark, *The Pre-history of Southern Africa* (Harmonds-worth, 1959), pp. 105, 129.
6 K.W. Butzer in *CHA*, vol. 1 (1982), p. 67.
7 R.J. Singer and J. Wymer, *The Middle Stone Age at Klasies River Mouth* (Chicago, 1982), pp. 148–9; D.W. Phillipson, *op.cit.*, p. 61.
8 R.L. Cann, M. Stoneking and A.C. Wilson, 'Mitochondrial DNA and human evolution', in *Nature*, vol. 20 (1979), pp. 1–29.

CHAPTER 3

1 R.J. Singer and J. Wymer, *The Middle Stone Age at Klasies River Mouth* (Chicago, 1982), pp. 87–106, 112–4.

2 D.W. Phillipson, *The Prehistory of Eastern Zambia* (Nairobi, 1976), pp. 119–69.

3 C.B.M. McBurney, *The Haua Fteah* (Cambridge, 1967).

4 A.E. Close, ' . . . radiocarbon dates from Northern Africa', in *Journal of African History* (henceforward *JAH*), vol. 21 (1980), pp. 145–67.

5 D.W. Phillipson, in *CHA*, vol. 1 (1982), pp. 420–1, 428–9.

6 A.E. Close, *op.cit.*, pp. 146–7.

7 Ann Stemler, in J.D. Clark and S.A. Brandt, *From Hunters to Farmers* (Berkeley, 1984), p. 129.

8 c.f. N. Howell, in Clark and Brandt, *op.cit.*, p. 352.

9 J.E.G. Sutton, 'The Aquatic Civilisation of Middle Africa, in *JAH*, vol. 15 (1974), pp. 527–46.

10 A.J. Arkell, *Early Khartoum* (Oxford, 1949).

11 *Ibid.*, p. 112.

12 D.W. Phillipson, in *CHA*, vol. 1 (1982), p. 570.

13 P.E.L. Smith, *ibid.*, pp. 371–2.

14 G. Camps, *Les civilisations préhistoriques de l'Afrique du Nord et du Sahara* (Paris, 1974), pp. 22, 225–6.

15 G. Camps, in *CHA*, vol. 1 (1982), p. 570.

16 J.G.D. Clark, *World Prehistory* (3rd edn, Cambridge, 1977), pp. 45–54.

17 G. Camps, in *CHA*, vol. 1 (1982), p. 575.

CHAPTER 4

1 Jean Hiernaux, *The People of Africa* (London, 1974), p. 50.

2 Colin Renfrew, *Archaeology and Language* (London, 1987), pp. 124–6.

3 J.E.G. Sutton, 'The Aquatic civilisation of Middle Africa', in *JAH* vol. 15 (1974), pp. 536–7.

4 S.K. and R.J. McIntosh, 'Recent archaeological research and dates from West Africa' in *JAH*, vol. 27 (1986), pp. 417–22.

5 C.G. Seligman, *Races of Africa* (revised edn, London, 1939), pp. 18–19.

6 J.H. Greenberg, *The Languages of Africa* (3rd edn, The Hague, 1970), p. 51.

7 D.W. Phillipson, in *CHA* vol. 1 (1982), pp. 796–803.

8 *Ibid.*, pp. 806–7.

9 J.H. Greenberg, *op.cit.*, p. 149.

10 D.G. Coursey, in J.R. Harlan, J.M.J. de Wet and A.B.M. Stemler, *Origins of African Plant Domestication* (The Hague, 1976), pp. 390–4.

11 P.J. Munson, *ibid.*, pp. 204–5.

12 S.K. and R.J. McIntosh, *op.cit.*, pp. 421–3.

13 J.R. Harlan, in *CHA* vol. 1 (1982), pp. 645–7.

14 J. Vansina, 'Western Bantu Expansion', in *JAH* vol. 25 (1984), pp. 129–45.

15 D. Dalby (ed.), *Language and History in Africa* (London, 1970), pp. viii–ix.

16 M. Guthrie, *Comparative Bantu* (4 vols., Farnborough, 1967–70).

17 A. Henrici, 'Numerical Classification of Bantu Languages', in *African Language Studies*, vol. XIV (1973), pp. 82–104.

18 Colin Turnbull, *Wayward Servants* (London, 1965), pp. 34–43.

CHAPTER 5

1 Cyril Aldred, *The Egyptians* (London, 1961), pp. 51–3.

2 B.G. Trigger, in *CHA* vol. 1 (1982), pp. 484–6, 528.

3 *Ibid.*, pp. 509–17.

4 C.f. V.G. Childe, *New Light on the Most Ancient East* (revised edn, London, 1954), pp. 82–8.

5 Aldred, *op.cit.*, pp. 159–61.

6 *Ibid.*, p. 161.

7 D. O'Connor, in *CHA* vol. 1 (1982), p. 842.

8 *Ibid.*, p. 896.

9 G. Camps, in *CHA* vol. 1 (1982), pp. 620–2.

10 Herodotus, *History*, Book IV, Chapters 168–85.

11 S.K. and R.J. McIntosh, in *JAH* vol. 27 (1986), pp. 424–6.

12 W.Y. Adams, *Nubia – Corridor to Africa* (London, 1977), p. 203; B.G. Trigger, *Nubia* (London, 1976), pp. 89–96.

13 Barry Kemp, in *CHA* vol. 1 (1982), p. 754.

14 Adams, *op.cit.*, p. 292.

15 *Ibid.*, p. 294.

CHAPTER 6

1 R.F. Tylecote, in T.A. Wertime and J.D. Muhly (eds), *The Coming of the Age of Iron* (New Haven, 1980), p. 209.

2 R. Haaland, in R. Haaland and P. Shinnie (eds), *African Iron Working* (Oslo, 1985), pp. 51–61; P. de Maret, *ibid.*, pp. 66–71.

3 T.A. Wertime, in Wertime and Muhly, *op.cit.*, p. 13.

4 N.J. Van der Merwe, *ibid.*, p. 486.

5 F.J. Kense, in Haaland and Shinnie, *op.cit.*, pp. 21–5.

6 W.Y. Adams, *Nubia – Corridor to Africa* (London, 1977), pp. 317–18, 365–6.

7 R.C.C. Law, in *CHA* vol. 2 (1978), p. 145.

8 D. Calvocoressi and N. David, in *JAH* vol. 20 (1979), p. 9.

9 Thurstan Shaw, *Nigeria – its archaeology and early history* (London, 1978), pp. 70–82.

10 S.K. and R.J. McIntosh, in *JAH* vol. 27 (1986), p. 426.

11 *Ibid.*, pp. 427–30 and *JAH* vol. 22 (1981), pp. 1–22.

12 S.K. and R.J. McIntosh, *op.cit.* (1986), pp. 429–30.

13 R. Haaland, in Haaland and Shinnie, *op.cit.*, p. 69.

14 D.A. Livingstone, in J.D. Clark and S.A. Brandt, *From Hunters to Farmers* (Berkeley, 1984), p. 23.

15 R. Oliver and B.M. Fagan, in *CHA* vol. 2 (1978), pp. 366–7.

16 D.W. Phillipson, *The Later Prehistory of Eastern and Southern Africa* (London, 1977), p. 108.

17 B.M. Fagan, *Southern Africa* (London, 1965), pp. 52–3, and in *JAH* vol. 4 (1963), p. 163.

18 D.W. Phillipson, *African Archaeology* (Cambridge, 1985), pp. 173–5.

20 F. Van Noten, *The Archaeology of Central Africa* (Graz, 1982), pp. 80, 85.

21 R. Mauny, in *CHA* vol. 2 (1978), p. 288.

CHAPTER 7

1 D. Kessler, *The Falashas* (London, 1982), p. 42.

2 W.H.C. Frend, in *CHA* vol. 2 (1978), p. 412.

3 *Acts of the Apostles*, Chapter 8, vv. 23–39.

4 Kessler, *op.cit.*, pp. 42–3.

5 W.H.C. Frend, *loc.cit.*, p. 451.

6 H.Z. Hirschberg, 'The problem of the Judaized Berbers', *JAH* vol. 4 (1963), pp. 317–339.

7 W.H.C. Frend, *loc.cit.*, pp. 414–25.

8 Eusebius of Caesarea, *History of the Church from Christ to Constantine* (Harmondsworth, 1965), pp. 337–8.

9 W.H.C. Frend, *The Rise of the Mon-ophysite Movement* (Cambridge, 1972), pp.x, 141, 213, 137.

10 *Ibid.*, pp. 285–7.

11 *Ibid.*, pp. 298–303, and in *CHA* vol. 2 (1978), pp. 447–8; D.A. Welsby, 'Recent work at Soba East', *Azania* vol. XVII (1983), pp. 165–80.

12 W.H.C. Frend, *The Donatist Church* (2nd edn, Oxford, 1971), pp. 315–23.

13 W.H.C. Frend, in *CHA* vol. 2 (1978), pp. 468–78.

14 *Ibid.*, pp. 475–89.

15 M. Brett, in *CHA* vol. 2 (1978), pp. 514–37.

16 N. Levtzion, in *CHA* vol. 2 (1978), pp. 641–5.

17 *Ibid.*, pp. 656–7.

18 M. Horton, 'Asiatic colonisation of the East African Coast: the Manda evidence', *Journal of the Royal Asiatic Society*, (1986, Part 2), pp. 201–13.

CHAPTER 8

1 C.F. Beckingham and G.W.B. Huntingford, *The Prester John of the Indies*, vol. II (Cambridge, 1961), p. 509.

2 Frank Willett, *Ife* (London, 1967), p. 18.

3 Yves Person, *Samori* (3 vols., Dakar, 1968–75), pp. 945–8.

4 Thurstan Shaw, in J.F.A. Ajayi and M. Crowder, *History of West Africa*, vol. 1 (3rd edn, London, 1985), p. 78.

5 R. Mauny, in *CHA* vol. 2 (1978), pp. 304–5; Person, *op.cit.*, p. 944.

6 S.K. and R.J. McIntosh, 'The Inland Niger Delta before the Empire of Mali', *JAH*, vol. 22 (1981), pp. 18–20.

7 F. Willett, in *JAH*, vol. 12 (1971), p. 357.

8 A.M.D. Lebeuf, *Les principautés Kotoko* (Paris, 1969), pp. 53, 103.

9 Person, *op.cit.*, pp. 943–4.

10 *Ibid.*, pp. 64–73.

11 Ivor Wilks, in Ajayi and Crowder, *op.cit.*, vol. 1, p. 487.

12 Graham Connah, *African Civilisations* (Cambridge, 1987), pp. 134–6.

12 A.M. Obayemi, in Ajayi and Crowder, *op.cit.*, vol. 1, pp. 260–74.

14 e.g., N. Levtzion, *ibid.*, (1st edn, 1971), pp. 121–4.

15 Murray Last, *ibid.* (3rd edn, 1985), pp. 192–209.

16 H.J. Fisher, in *JAH*, vol. 13 (1972), pp. 368–9; R.C.C. Law, *The Horse in West African History* (Oxford, 1980), pp. 24–8.

17 B. Barkindo, in Ajayi and Crowder, *op.cit.*, (3rd edn, 1985), p. 237.

18 R. Mauny, *Tableau géographique de l'ouest africain au moyen âge* (Dakar, 1961), pp. 481–2.

19 N. Levtzion and J.F.P. Hopkins, *Corpus of early Arabic sources for West African History* (Cambridge, 1981), pp. 79–84.

CHAPTER 9

1 D.W. Phillipson, in *CHA* vol. 1 (1982), pp. 803–8, and *African Archaeology* (Cambridge, 1985), pp. 144–5; Peter Robertshaw, *Early Pastoralists of South-western Kenya* (Nairobi, 1990), pp. 1–3.

2 Phillipson, *African Archaeology*, pp. 183–6.

3 R. Oliver, 'The Nilotic Contribution to Bantu Africa', *JAH*, vol. 23 (1982), pp. 434–5; P. de Maret, 'The Smith's Myth and the origins of leadership in Central Africa' in R. Haaland and P. Shinnie, *African Iron Working* (Oslo, 1985), p. 6.

4 L.P. Kirwan, 'An Ethiopian-Sudanese frontier zone in

Ancient History', *Geographical Journal*, vol. 138 (1972), pp. 457–65.

5 C. Ehret, *Southern Nilotic History* (Evanston, 1971), pp. 48–9.

6 M. Hassen, 'The Oromo of Ethiopia, 1500–1800'. (unpublished PhD thesis, University of London, 1983), pp. 81–9.

7 J.E.G. Sutton, *The Archaeology of the Western Highlands of Kenya* (Nairobi, 1973), pp. 5–33.

8 R. Oliver, *op.cit.*, p. 438.

9 D.W. Phillipson, 'Iron Age history and archaeology in Zambia', *JAH* vol. 15 (1974), pp. 1–25.

10 D. Birmingham and S. Marks, in *CHA* vol. 3 (1977), p. 606.

11 T. Huffman, 'The origins of Leopard's Kopje', *Arnoldia* 8, No. 23 (1978), p. 20; D.N. Beach, *The Shona and Zimbabwe* (London, 1980), pp. 19–20.

12 P.S. Garlake, *Great Zimbabwe* (London, 1973), pp. 155–6.

13 *Ibid.*, pp. 153–60.

14 E.W. Herbert, *Red Gold of Africa* (Madison, 1984), p. 108.

15 P.S. Garlake, 'Pastoralism and Zimbabwe', *JAH* vol. 19 (1978), p. 479.

16 D.N. Beach, *op.cit*, pp. 82–5, 245.

17 E.E. Evans-Pritchard, *The Nuer* (Oxford, 1940).

18 E. Mworoha, *Peuples et rois de l'Afrique des Lacs* (Dakar-Abidjan, 1977), pp. 200–1.

19 R. Oliver in *CHA* vol. 3 (1977), pp. 630–45.

20 Monica Wilson and L.M. Thompson (eds), *Oxford History of South Africa*, vol. 1 (Oxford, 1969), p. 125.

21 *Ibid.*, p. 130.

CHAPTER 10

1 C.H. Perrot, *Les Anyi-Ndenye* (Paris, 1982), pp. 143, 162.

2 V.G. Childe, *New Light on the Most*

Ancient East (revised edn, London, 1954), p. 53.

3 Jean Bazin, in C. Meillassoux (ed.), *L'esclavage en Afrique pré-coloniale* (Paris, 1975), p. 143.

4 B. Trigger, *Nubia* (London, 1976), pp. 47, 93–5.

5 L. Casson, *Ancient Egypt* (New York, 1965), p. 102.

6 J.R. Willis, *Slaves and Slavery in Muslim Africa* (London, 1985), vol. 1, pp. viii–ix.

7 M. Brett, in *CHA* vol. 2 (1978), pp. 528–9; D. Piper, *Slave Soldiers and Islam* (New Haven, 1981), pp. 46–50.

8 H. Barth, *Travels and Discoveries in North and Central Africa* (Centenary edn, 3 vols., London, 1965), vol. II, pp. 369, 418.

9 Willis, *op.cit.*, vol. II, p. 83.

10 Kings Phiri, 'Chewa History in Central Malawi', unpublished PhD thesis, University of Wisconsin, 1975, p. 127.

11 E. and S. Bernus, in Meillassoux, *op.cit.*, p. 22; Perrot, *op.cit.*, p. 165.

12 S. Miers and I. Kopytoff (eds), *Slavery in Africa* (Madison, 1977), p. 29; Marc Augé in Meillassoux, *op.cit.*, pp. 438–40.

13 Claude Meillassoux, in Meillassoux, *op.cit.*, pp. 17, 229.

14 *Ibid.*, pp. 127, 152, 203.

15 N. Levtzion, in *CHA* vol. 3 (1977), p. 447.

16 Meillassoux, *op.cit.*, p. 200; Miers and Kopytoff, *op.cit.*, pp. 32–3.

17 Meillassoux, *op.cit.*, pp. 17, 29.

18 *Ibid.*, pp. 499–500.

19 Willis, *op.cit.*, vol. II, pp. 123–36.

20 H.N. Chittick, in *CHA* vol. 3 (1977), pp. 209, 215–16.

21 *Ibid.*, p. 223.

22 G. Balandier, *Daily Life in the*

Kingdom of the Kongo (London, 1968), p. 191.

23 John Roscoe, *The Baganda* (London, 1911), pp. 14–15.

24 M. Twaddle, in S. Miers and R. Roberts (eds), *The End of Slavery in Africa* (Madison, 1988), pp. 122–6.

25 P. Lovejoy, *Transformations in Slavery* (Cambridge, 1983), pp. 24–5, 36, 46, 51.

26 P. Lovejoy, 'The Volume of the Atlantic Slave Trade', *JAH*, vol. 23 (1982), pp. 473–501, and 'The Impact of the Atlantic Slave Trade on Africa', *JAH* vol. 30 (1989), pp. 391–3.

27 M. Klein, in Miers and Kopytoff, *op.cit.* (1977), pp. 335–42; P. Lovejoy, *op.cit.* (1983), pp. 36–7.

28 M. Klein, *loc.cit.*, pp. 339–42.

29 Walter Rodney, *A History of the Upper Guinea Coast 1545–1840*, (Oxford, 1970), pp. 46–7, 56–61, 223–9.

30 Alan Ryder, *Benin and the Europeans 1485–1897* (London, 1969), pp. 11–14, 30–6.

31 R.C.C. Law, *The Oyo Empire c.1600–1836* (Oxford, 1977), pp. 150–69.

32 K.Y. Daaku, *Trade and Politics on the Gold Coast 1600–1720* (Oxford, 1970), p. 31.

33 Joseph Miller, *Kings and Kinsmen* (Oxford, 1976), pp. 151–221.

34 J.E. Inikori, *Forced Migration* (London, 1982), p. 22.

CHAPTER 11

1 H.J. Fisher, in *CHA* vol. 3 (1977), p. 267.

2 A.C.P. Gamitto, *King Kazembe* (tr. I. Cunnison, Lisbon, 1960), p. 132.

3 R. Bulliet, *The Camel and the Wheel* (Harvard, 1975), p. 23.

4 W.Y. Adams, *Nubia – Corridor to Africa* (London, 1977), pp. 302–4.

5 Bulliet, *op.cit.*, p. 116 sq.

6 N. Levtzion and J.F.P. Hopkins (eds), *Corpus of early Arabic Sources for West African History* (Cambridge, 1981), p. 128.

7 E.W. Bovill, *Caravans of the old Sahara* (Oxford, 1933), p. 156.

8 *Ibid.*, p. 251.

9 A.G. Hopkins, *An Economic History of West Africa* (London, 1973), p. 48.

10 N. Levtzion and J.F.P. Hopkins, *op.cit.*, p. 106.

11 A.G. Hopkins, *op.cit.*, p. 82.

12 H.J. Fisher, in *CHA* vol. 4 (1975), p. 86.

13 H. Barth, *Travels and Discoveries in North and Central Africa 1849–1855* (Centenary edn, London, 1965), vol. 1, p. 511.

14 Ivan Hrbek, in *CHA* vol. 3 (1977), p. 88.

15 Y.F. Hasan, *The Arabs and the Sudan* (Khartoum, 1973), pp. 66–87.

16 G. Nachtigal, *Sahara and Sudan* (tr. A.G.B. and H.J. Fisher, 4 vols., London, 1974–87), vol. III, p. 132.

17 *Ibid.*, vol. IV, p. 454.

18 *Ibid.*, vol. IV, p. 200.

19 Yves Person, *Samori* (3 vols., Dakar, 1968–75), pp. 101–22.

20 N. Levtzion, *Muslims and Chiefs in West Africa* (Oxford, 1968), pp. 15–20; *cf.* P. Lovejoy, *Caravans of Kola* (Zaria, 1980), pp. 14–20.

21 H. Clapperton, *Journal of a Second Expedition* (London, 1966), p. 68.

22 R.C.C. Law, *The Oyo Empire* (Oxford, 1977), pp. 212–14.

23 R.W. Harms, *River of Wealth, River of Sorrow* (New Haven, 1981), pp. 48–9.

24 T. Hodgkin, *Nigerian Perspectives* (2nd edn, Oxford, 1975), p. 232.

25 Harms, *op.cit.*, pp. 51, 93–4.
26 P.M. Martin, *The External Trade of the Loango Coast 1576–1870* (Oxford, 1972), pp. 117–19, 131–2.
27 Monica Wilson and L.M. Thompson, *Oxford History of South Africa* (vol. 1, Oxford, 1969), pp. 176–7.
28 E.A. Alpers, *Ivory and Slaves in East Central Africa* (London, 1975), p. 43; D.B. Birmingham, in *CHA* vol. 3 (1977), p. 529.
29 H.N. Chittick, in *CHA* vol. 3 (1977), p. 216.
30 J. Lamphear, in J.R. Gray and D.B. Birmingham (eds), *Precolonial African Trade* (Oxford, 1970), pp. 78–80.
31 Alpers, *op.cit.*, pp. 61–3.
32 Gamitto, *op.cit.*, p. 204.
33 R.F. Burton, *The Lake regions of Central Africa* (new edn, London, 1961, vol. 1), p. 337.
34 *Ibid.*, p. 341.
35 D.B. Birmingham, in *CHA* vol. 5 (1976), pp. 246–7.

CHAPTER 12

1 D.W. Cohen, *Womunafu's Bunafu* (Princeton, 1977), pp. 144–5.
2 A.W. Southall, *Alur Society* (Cambridge, 1956), p. 82.
3 G.M. Theal (ed), *Records of South-Eastern Africa* (9 vols, Cape Town, 1898–1903), vol. 7, p. 190 sqq.
4 R. Oliver and A.G. Mathew (eds), *History of East Africa*, vol. 1 (Oxford, 1963), pp. 181–91; R. Oliver, in *CHA* vol. 3 (1977), pp. 630–45.
5 J. Vansina, *The Children of Woot* (Madison, 1978), pp. 104–5, 131–2, 137–40.
6 T.Q. Reefe, *The Rainbow and the Kings* (Berkeley, 1981), pp. 78, 153–4; J. Vansina, *Kingdoms of the Savanna* (Madison, 1966), pp. 78–84; Joseph Miller, *Kings and Kinsmen* (Oxford, 1976), pp. 128–9, 137–8, 176.

7 S. Marks and J.R. Gray, in *CHA* vol. 4 (1975), pp. 394–404.
8 S. Marks and A. Atmore (eds), *Economy and Society in Pre-Industrial South Africa* (London, 1980), pp. 14–15, 88–9, 115–17.
9 Monica Wilson and L.M. Thompson (eds), *Oxford History of South Africa* (vol. 1, Oxford, 1969), pp. 391–4, 398–9, 404.
10 J.D. Omer-Cooper, *The Zulu Aftermath* (London, 1966).
11 Ivor Wilks, *Asante in the Nineteenth Century* (Cambridge, 1975), pp. 110, 80, 88.
12 *Ibid.*, pp. 380–1, 392.
13 *Ibid.*, pp. 692–3.
14 *Ibid.*, pp. 163–4.
15 C.H. Perrot, *Les Anyi-Ndenye* (Paris, 1982), pp. 92–4.
16 R.C.C. Law, *The Oyo Empire c.1600–1836* (Oxford, 1977), p. 229.
17 Murray Last, *The Sokoto Caliphate* (London, 1967), p. 63.
18 *Ibid.*, pp. 72–3.

CHAPTER 13

1 A. Sheriff, *Slaves, Spices and Ivory in Zanzibar* (London, 1987), pp. 87–8.
2 Gavin White, 'Fire-arms in Africa', *JAH* vol. 12 (1971), pp. 174–6, 181–2.
3 *Ibid.*, pp. 177–8.
4 P.M. Holt, in *CHA* vol. 5 (1976), pp. 19–27.
5 J.R. Gray, *A History of the Southern Sudan 1839–1889* (Oxford, 1961), pp. 21–3, 33–5, 48–52.
6 Holt, *op.cit.*, pp. 42–3; Gray, *op.cit.*, pp. 103–4.
7 Sheriff, *op.cit.*, p. 43.
8 O. Kalinga, *A History of the Ngonde Kingdom of Malawi* (Berlin, 1985), p. 74.

9 Sheriff, *op.cit.*, pp. 48–9.
10 A.C. Unomah and J.B. Webster, in *CHA* vol. 5 (1976), pp. 276–7; D. Birmingham, *ibid.*, pp. 272–3.
11 R. Oliver, *Sir Harry Johnston and the Scramble for Africa* (London, 1957), pp. 161–2.
12 D.K. Bimanyu, 'Waungwana resistance to the establishment of the Congo Free State 1887–1901' (unpublished PhD thesis, University of London, 1976).
13 R. Oliver, *The Missionary Factor in East Africa* (London, 1952), pp. 134–40.
14 S. Marks and J.R. Gray, in *CHA* vol. 4 (1977), pp. 437–55.
15 Monica Wilson and L.M. Thompson, *Oxford History of South Africa* (vol. 1, Oxford, 1969), pp. 235–42.
16 *Ibid.*, pp. 249–52.
17 C. Bundy, *The Rise and Fall of the South African Peasantry* (London, 1979), pp. 33–40, 58–9.
18 Wilson and Thompson, *op.cit.*, vol. 1, pp. 406–12, 355–60.
19 P. Delius, *The Land belongs to us* (London, 1984), p. 62.
20 M. Hiskett, in *CHA* vol. 5 (1976), pp. 125–60.
21 J.F.A. Ajayi and B.O. Olorun-timehin, *ibid.*, pp. 202–5.
22 A.G. Hopkins, *An Economic History of West Africa* (London, 1973), pp. 141–3.
23 C. Fyfe, in *CHA* vol. 5 (1976), pp. 181–8.
24 J.D. Fage, *A History of West Africa* (3rd edn, London, 1969), pp. 142–5.
25 Ch-A. Julien, *Histoire de l'Algérie contemporaine* (Paris, 1964).
26 A.A. Boahen, *Britain, the Sahara and the Western Sudan 1788–1861* (Oxford, 1964), pp. 160–80, 219–21.
27 Douglas Johnson, in *CHA* vol. 5 (1976), pp. 122–3.

CHAPTER 14

1 S. Marks, in *CHA* vol. 6 (1985), pp. 382–99.
2 A.S. Kanya Forstner, *The Conquest of the Western Sudan* (Cambridge, 1969), pp. 84–94, 98–102.
3 J.E. Flint, *Sir George Goldie and the Making of Nigeria* (Oxford, 1960), pp. 25–33.
4 J.D. Hargreaves, *Prelude to the Partition of West Africa* (London, 1963), pp. 126–9, 133–4.
5 E. Axelson, *Portugal and the Scramble for Africa* (Johannesburg, 1967), pp. 2–12, 39–40; A.K. Smith and W.G. Clarence Smith, in *CHA* vol. 6 (1985), pp. 493–7, 498–9.
6 R. Oliver, 'The Partition of Africa: the European and the African Interpretations', in *Le Centenaire de l'Etat Indépendant du Congo* (Brussels, 1988), p. 42.
7 R. Oliver, *Sir Harry Johnston and the Scramble for Africa* (London, 1957), pp. 137–43.
8 R. Oliver, *The Missionary Factor in East Africa* (London, 1952), pp. 138–48.
9 J. Vansina, in *CHA* vol. 6 (1985), pp. 327–36.
10 G.N. Sanderson, *ibid.*, pp. 610–16.
11 Kanya Forstner, *op.cit.*, pp. 87–92, 98–103, 154–60.
12 J.E. Flint, *Cecil Rhodes* (London, 1976), pp. 128–36.
13 Sanderson, *op.cit.*, pp. 149–51.
14 W.K. Hancock, *Smuts* vol. 1 (Cambridge, 1962), pp. 104–6.

CHAPTER 15

1 R. Oliver, in *Le Centenaire de l'Etat Indépendant du Congo* (Brussels, 1988), p. 44.
2 R. Oliver and J.D. Fage, *A Short*

History of Africa (6th edn, London, 1988), p. 173.

3 S. Miers and R. Roberts, *The End of Slavery in Africa* (Madison, 1988), p. 17.

4 J. Lonsdale, in *CHA* vol. 6 (1985), p. 722.

5 R. Dumett and M. Johnson, in Miers and Roberts, *op.cit.*, pp. 90–92.

6 J. Vansina, *ibid.*, p. 330.

7 J.D. Hargreaves, *ibid.*, p. 258.

8 Miers and Roberts, *op.cit.*, pp. 42–3.

9 R. Roberts, *ibid.*, pp. 284–5.

10 D.D. Cordell, *ibid.*, p. 156.

11 J. Vansina, in *CHA* vol. 6 (1985), pp. 331, 340.

12 C. Coquery-Vidrovitch, *ibid.*, p. 312.

13 J. Stengers, *ibid.*, pp. 318–19.

14 L.M. Heywood, in Miers and Roberts, *op.cit.*, pp. 417–20.

15 M. Twaddle, *ibid.*, pp. 129–32.

16 J.D. Hargreaves in *CHA* vol. 6, pp. 262–5, 271–3.

17 J. Vansina, *ibid.*, pp. 330–1.

18 M. Twaddle, in Miers and Roberts, *op.cit.*, pp. 135–7.

19 T.O. Ranger, *Revolt in Southern Rhodesia* (London, 1967), pp. 46–8.

20 G.N. Uzoigwe, in *UNESCO General History of Africa*, vol. 7 (1985), p. 19.

21 J.D. Hargreaves, in *CHA* vol. 6 (1985), p. 289.

22 S. Miers and M. Crowder, in Miers and Roberts, *op.cit.*, p. 172.

23 C. Wrigley, in *CHA* vol. 7 (1986), p. 78.

24 D. Dorward, *ibid.*, pp. 402–4; C. Coquery-Vidrovitch, *ibid.*, pp. 330–44.

25 P.M. Holt, *A Modern History of the Sudan* (London, 1961), pp. 120–2.

26 M. Twaddle, in Miers and Roberts, *op.cit.*, p.141.

27 R. Tignor, *The Colonial Transformation of Kenya* (Princeton, 1976), pp. 25–7.

28 A.D. Roberts, in *CHA* vol. 7 (1986), p. 654.

29 A.P. Walshe, *ibid.*, p. 558.

30 J. McCracken, *ibid.*, p.612.

31 R. Tignor, *op.cit.*, p. 48.

CHAPTER 16

1 Cf. D.A. Rostow, in *Cambridge History of Islam*, vol. 1 (1970), pp. 93–7.

2 J.S. Trimingham, *Islam in West Africa* (Oxford, 1959), pp. 92–3.

3 C.C. Stewart, in *CHA*, vol. 7 (1986), pp. 204–7.

4 A. Oded, *Islam in Uganda* (Jerusalem, 1974), pp. 66–83.

5 C.C. Stewart, *op.cit.*, p. 213.

6 C. Northcote, *Robert Moffat* (London, 1961), p. 25.

7 B.G.M. Sundkler, *Church History in Africa*, in press.

8 H.H. Johnston, *George Grenfell and the Congo* (London, 1909), vol. 1, pp. 375–8.

9 R. Oliver, *The Missionary Factor in East Africa* (London, 1952), pp. 184–6.

10 J.R. Gray, in *CHA* vol. 7 (1986), p. 141.

11 J.F.A. Ajayi, *Christian Missions in Nigeria 1841–1891* (London, 1965), pp. 234–5, 250–7.

12 B.G.M. Sundkler, *Bantu Prophets in South Africa* (London, 1948), pp. 38–40.

13 J.R. Gray, *op.cit.*, p. 141.

14 *Ibid.*, p. 189.

15 R. Oliver, *op.cit.*, p. 275.

16 J.R. Gray, *op.cit.*, p. 164.

CHAPTER 17

1 F.D. Lugard, *The Dual Mandate in British Tropical Africa* 6th edn, (London, 1965), pp. 198, 217.

2 J. Stengers, *Congo: Mythes et réalités* (Paris, 1989), pp. 205–6.
3 M. Brett, in *CHA* vol. 7 (1986), p. 269.
4 A.P. Walshe, *ibid.*, p. 545.
5 J.C. Smuts, *Africa and some World Problems* (London, 1931).
6 Cited in W.H. Moreland and A.C. Chatterjee, *A Short History of India* 2nd edn, (London, 1944), p. 455.
7 M. Brett, in *CHA* vol. 7 (1986), p. 297.
8 *Ibid.*, pp. 300–2.
9 J. Stengers, *op.cit.*, pp. 210–12.
10 A.D. Roberts, in *CHA* vol. 7 (1986), p. 671.
11 John Iliffe, *The African Poor* (Cambridge, 1987), p. 158.
12 A.D. Roberts, in *CHA* vol. 7 (1986), p. 223.
13 A.P. Walshe, *ibid.*, pp. 547–51.
14 J. McCracken, *ibid.*, p. 628.
15 J. Stengers, *op.cit.*, pp. 189, 208–9.
16 A.D. Roberts, in *CHA* vol. 7 (1986), p. 49.
17 E.g. J.D. Hargreaves, *Decolonisation in Africa* (London, 1988), pp. 30–4.
18 Cf. S.K.B. Asante, 'The Italian-Ethiopian conflict', *JAH* vol. 15 (1974), pp. 291–302.
19 M. Crowder, in *CHA* vol. 8 (1984), p. 17.
20 M. Perham, *Colonial Sequence* vol. 1 (London, 1967), pp. 225–7.
21 W.R. Louis, *Imperialism at Bay 1941–1945* (Oxford, 1977), p. 47.
22 Leo Kuper, in Monica Wilson and L.M. Thompson (eds), *Oxford History of South Africa* vol. II, (Oxford, 1971), pp. 454–9.
23 J.D. Hargreaves, *op.cit.*, pp. 95–101, 107–8.
24 J.D. Hargreaves, in P. Gifford and W.R. Louis (eds), *The Transfer of Power in Africa* (New Haven, 1982), pp. 135–40.
25 Yves Person, *ibid.*, p. 159.

CHAPTER 18

1 P. Gifford and W.R. Louis (eds), *The Transfer of Power in Africa* (New Haven, 1982), p. 222.
2 Kwame Nkrumah, *Ghana* (London, 1959), p. 233.
3 J. Stengers, *Congo: Mythes et réalités* (Paris, 1989), pp. 268–70.
4 Gifford and Louis, *op.cit.*, p. 125.
5 B. Dudley, in *CHA* vol. 8 (1984), p. 75.
6 R.S. Morgenthau and L.C. Behrman, *ibid.*, pp. 626-8.
7 Crawford Young, *ibid.*, p. 719.
8 *Ibid.*, pp. 722–3, 729–31.
9 H.H. Kopietz and P.A. Smith, *ibid.*, pp. 526–8.
10 I. Duffield, *ibid.*, p. 125; D. Williams, *ibid.*, pp. 364–5.
11 B. Dudley, *op.cit.*, pp. 88–9.
12 C.H. Moore, *ibid.*, pp. 579–81.
13 B. Davidson, *ibid.*, p. 785.
14 B. Davidson, *The Liberation of Guiné* (London, 1969).
15 B. Davidson, in *CHA* vol. 8, p. 782.
16 Mary Benson, *A Far Cry* (London, 1988), p. 157.

CHAPTER 19

1 W.H. Friedland and C.G. Rosberg (eds), *African Socialism* (Stanford, 1964), p. 82.
2 *Ibid.*, p. 246.
3 *Ibid.*, pp. 89–93.
4 The World Bank, *Sub-Saharan Africa: From Crisis to Sustainable Growth*, (Washington, 1989), p. 22.
5 *Ibid.*, p. 2.
6 *Ibid.*, pp. 17–18.
7 *Ibid.*, p. 221.
8 *Ibid.*, pp. 4, 40, 70.
9 J.C. Caldwell, in *UNESCO General History of Africa* vol. VII (1985), p. 463.

10 World Bank, *op.cit.*, p. 71.
11 R. Oliver and J.D. Fage, *A Short History of Africa* 6th edn (London, 1988), p. 243.
12 Anthony O'Connor, *The African City* (London, 1983), p. 43.
13 *Ibid.*, pp. 74–8, 168–9, 271–93.
14 World Bank, *op.cit.*, p. 43.
15 John Iliffe, *The African Poor* (Cambridge, 1987), pp. 230–3, 250–5.
16 Oliver and Fage, *op.cit.*, p. 241.
17 World Bank, *op.cit.*, p. 48.
18 *Ibid.*, p. 21.
19 P. Maylam, 'The Rise and Decline of Urban Apartheid in South Africa', *African Affairs*, vol. 89 (1990), p. 69.
20 *Ibid.*, pp. 81–2.
21 *The Times*, 3.ii.90.

CHAPTER 20

1 D.W. Cohen, 'Wish not a man from England', (Unpublished paper, Johns Hopkins University, 24.x.89).
2 J.C. Caldwell, in *UNESCO General History of Africa* vol. VII (1985), p. 463.
3 World Bank, *Sub-Saharan Africa: From Crisis to Sustainable Growth*, (Washington, 1989), pp. 43–4.
4 C.C. Stewart, in *CHA* vol. 7 (1986), pp. 208–9.
5 Adrian Hastings, *A History of African Christianity 1950–1975* (Cambridge, 1979), p. 258.
6 *Ibid.*, p. 191.
7 Andrew Young, Speech to the African Studies Association, Atlanta, 1.xi.89.
8 World Bank, *op.cit.*, pp. 43, 81.
9 W. Minter, *King Solomon's Mines Revisited* (New York, 1986), pp. 265–9.
10 *The Economist*, 7.iv.90.
11 W. Minter, *op.cit.*, pp. 339–40.
12 *The Times*, 28.iv.90.

INDEX

Abbasid dynasty, 85–6
Abd Allah b. Yasin, reformer, 87
Abd el-Kader, resistance leader, 172
Acheulian industry, 12–13, 16–25
Afar people (Ethiopia), 88, 135
Afrikaner people (South Africa), 152, 166–9, 174, 182–4
Afroasiatic language family, 38, 40–4, 49, 57–8
Aghlabid dynasty, of Ifriqiya, 86
Ahmad bin Muhammad of Masina, 169
Aja people (Bénin, Togo), 126
Ajayi, Jacob, historian, 209
Akan peoples (Ghana, Ivory Coast), 95, 125–7, 130, 170
Akjoujt, Bronze Age site (Mauritania), 69
Aksum, kingdom of (Ethiopia), 66, 81–3
al-Bakri of Cordoba, geographer, 99
al-Hajj 'Umar, jihad leader, 169–70, 175
Alfonso I, of Kongo, 122
Algeria (French), 171–2, 174, 215, 225–6, 236; republic, 236–8, 245, 249
Algiers, Ottoman regency, 154
Almoravid dynasty (Morocco), 87–8
Alwa kingdom (Sudan), 82–3
Amekni, Neolithic site (Algeria), 35
Amin, Idi, 236, 257
Ancient Egyptian language, 38, 40
Angola (Portuguese), 128, 141, 151, 175–6, 188, 192, 196, 226, 238, 262–3; republic, 245, 249
Apartheid, 223, 239, 250–1, 257, 263
Arabs, 84–6
Arden Clarke, Charles, 228
Arkell, Anthony, archaeologist, 33–4
Asante kingdom (Ghana), 95, 126–7, 155–7, 171, 175, 185
Askiya dynasty of Songhay, 100–1

Aterian industry, 24
Athanasius, Patriarch of Alexandria, 81
Atlantic Charter, 223
Australopithecine, 1–6

Baker, Samuel, explorer, 163
Bambandyanalo, Iron Age site (South Africa), 109
Bantu languages, 46–9, 71, 109
Bari people (Sudan), 161–3
Barth, Heinrich, explorer, 118, 170
Baudouin, King of the Belgians, 228
Beach, David, historian, 112
Bechuanaland (British), later Botswana, 194–5
Beja people (Sudan), 133, 135
Belgian (Congo), 191–2, 196, 217–19, 226, 231
Bénin, city and kingdom (Nigeria), 70, 96–7, 112, 125–6, 193
Bénin republic (formerly Dahomey), 246
Berber languages, 38, 40, 42, 59
Berber peoples of N. Africa, 84–6, 97, 118, 171
Berlin West Africa conference (1884–5), 176–8
Biafra, 234–5
Biberson, P., archaeologist, 19
Bilma salt mines (Niger), 131
Binford, Lewis, archaeologist, 9, 22
Bisa people (Zambia), 130, 143, 164
Bismarck, Otto von, 176
Bobangi people (Congo, Zaire), 140–1
Boer war, 182–4
Borana people (Ethiopia, Kenya), 131
Border Cave, MSA site (South Africa), 25
Borgu kingdom (Nigeria), 96

277